THE FOUNDING
OF THE JESUITS

IGNATIUS LOYOLA

TURNING POINTS IN HISTORY

General Editor: SIR DENIS BROGAN

THE FOUNDING OF THE JESUITS

1540

BY

MICHAEL FOSS

WEYBRIGHT AND TALLEY

NEW YORK

Published in the United States by
WEYBRIGHT AND TALLEY, INC.
3 East 54th Street, New York, N.Y. 10022

Library of Congress Catalog Card No. 69–17199

Printed in Great Britain

CONTENTS

CONTENTS

ILLUSTRATIONS

vii

PART ONE

EUROPE IN TROUBLE

Chapter I

IDEALS AND DISASTERS

WHEN THE city of Constantinople fell to the Turks in 1453, Islam finally accomplished what it had threatened since the time of the Prophet. The wise eye of Mohammed had noted the importance of the New Rome; he had declared that 'the best leader is he who shall capture Constantinople, and his the best army'. And to spur his followers on to a work which promised to be so beneficial to Islam, he built his exhortations on the ultimate Authority: Allah himself, in the Sacred Traditions, had told Mohammed that the Great Day of Judgment would not come before the sons of Isaac had taken the city. The orthodox and strongly believing Moslem considered the city doomed. The ambition of princes and the avarice of soldiers could be safely relied on to fulfil the holy work. In 672, after the death of the Prophet, a mighty force had spread itself before the walls. This Arab army, so strong and so fanatical, seemed irresistible, for the Arab generals had with them Eyoub, now an old man, but in his youth the favourite and the standard-bearer of Mohammed. For seven years this army lived beneath the magnificent defences of the city walls, sowing the fields and collecting their harvest from the surrounding countryside quite diligently. Finally the Arabs left, and other besieging armies— both Arab and Turkish—came and went. At the beginning of the fifteenth century, seven hundred years later, the doomed city waited to be taken.

In spite of diminishing authority, loss of population and revenue, and the pains of religious discord, the Eastern Empire had presented a weak but continuous resistance to the advance of Islam. Even when, at the start of the fifteenth century, the rising power of the Ottoman Turks had reduced the Empire almost to Constantinople itself, surrounded on all sides by land possessed by, or paying tribute to, the Turks, the city and its inhabitants had acted with a certain disdain for the realities of political life. Living under the axe, the Greeks still thought that their last days might be elegant and ordered.

3

They were the inheritors of a great tradition; the Emperor was the successor to Caesar, and Byzantium was, in Greek eyes, the seat of orthodox Christianity. The Burgundian traveller la Brocquière, who visited Constantinople in January 1433, saw the gridiron on which St. Laurence was broiled and 'a large stone, in the shape of a wash-stand, on which, they say, Abraham gave the angels to eat when they were come to destroy Sodom and Gomorrah'. Such relics were important to a nation which had little more than its sense of tradition to support it against the intimidation of the Turks and the enmity of the Christian West; and la Brocquière, who recognized gridirons and angels' tables as valuable ammunition in wars of religion, was impressed. But he noted too the emptiness of the great city and the dilapidation of the great buildings. He watched the Empress come from church and thought her young and fair, but added, signifi-cantly, 'I should not have had a fault to find with her had she not been painted.' The man of the West thought he perceived a civiliza-tion in decay, and responded with censoriousness instead of sym-pathy.

Centuries of mutual disgust and suspicion had ensured that Byzantium and the West could never understand each other. Since each side claimed, with equal idealism, to be the representative of orthodox Christianity, the quarrel was irreconcilable. And the ambi-tion and greed of Western traders and adventurers had kept the theological wound raw in the declining years of Byzantium. Indeed, the West itself, and not Islam, had broken the power of the Eastern Empire. In 1204, the Fourth Crusade had abandoned the hard march to the Holy Land and fallen on Constantinople. The city had been taken, amid much Greek suffering. Though this disaster hap-pened through the ambition of the crusading leaders and the greedy connivance of Venice, jealous of the rich Byzantine trade, the Cru-saders explained their conduct as an attack against schismatics and therefore justified. And it is quite possible that this explanation satisfied the minds of the West. To men governed by the forms of religion only, without religious feeling or sympathy, the distinction between schismatic and infidel is not important. The illicit jump can be made with a clear conscience and the weaker can be attacked for the greater profit. In the middle of the thirteenth century, Michael Palaeologus did recapture Constantinople, and put an end to the Latin Empire which the Crusaders had established, but the old power of Byzantium was broken and the frontiers of the Empire contracted before the feet of the advancing Turks. The Fourth

Crusade was not the only body of Westerners to damage Byzantium. In 1305 the Emperor Andronicus II hired a mercenary band of Spaniards, called the Catalan Company, to fight against the Turks. The Catalans duly defeated the Turks, but then revolted and pushed the Empire into ten years of civil war. The Turks prospered in the interval.

Hatred leads to exploitation and violence. When la Brocquière complained that the Greeks tried to cheat him, and said that he had found more probity in the Turks, we are not surprised. But the Turks continued to profit from the dissensions of Christendom. The Eastern Emperor knew that the price of Western help was submission to Rome, yet the pressure of the Turks forced him to attempt something. In 1438, he crossed to Italy with his theologians and helpers. After some untidy bickering about whether the Pope's chair should be trimmed with fur and the Patriarch's not, and whether the Patriarch should kiss the Pope's foot or not, in 1439 the Council settled down in Florence to discuss the union of the churches. The meetings ended in July with the Greek church apparently joined to the Latin. But this was no triumph for Rome. The Emperor was sincere, and honourably tried to implement the agreement reached at Florence; but the mass of his subjects would have none of it. Their mood was expressed quite clearly by Lukas Notaras, the highest ranking noble in Constantinople, who is said to have exclaimed, 'Better the Sultan's turban to a Cardinal's hat.' And la Brocquière caught the temper of the city quite accurately when he wrote, 'These people do not love the Christians of the Roman persuasion, and the submission which they have since made to this church was more through self-interest than sincerity.' But who can blame the Greeks? In 1400, the sad, dignified figure of the Emperor Manuel II had been seen travelling through the royal courts of Europe in search of arms and money. Charles VI of France had given him distinguished entertainment and little else; Henry IV of England had thought a banquet at Eltham Palace sufficient. 'How grievous it was,' wrote Adam of Usk, 'that this great Christian prince should be driven by the Saracens from the furthest east to these furthest western islands to seek aid.' And not to receive it. Since the West would give no assistance—or more correctly would only give a token help on debasing conditions of submission to Rome—the Greeks would fight alone, trusting only in God, a God conceived according to their own theological notions. Turk versus Greek: this conflict which for seven hundred years had been muddled by the ordinary human passions of greed, ambition and violence in its last moments found itself raised to a severe and elevated plane. It became truly Islam against Christendom. Allah had foretold the fall of Constantinople; God would protect his own. Any Christian prince, wrote la Brocquière, who had ambitions against the Turk 'ought at first to propose to himself for his object, not glory and renown, but God, religion, and the salvation of so many souls that are in the road to perdition'. The moment appealed to the chivalrous mind. The work of saving Constantinople, which the rulers of the West had abandoned through indifference, jealousy or political caution, was taken up with a high sense of virtue by many private Western gentlemen. These men demonstrated an aspect of Western conduct which had been quite common in the early Middle Ages—the disposition of an individual to be possessed by an ideal which transcended political expediency, and perhaps even common sense. The same ideal had fashioned the First Crusade; for that brave undertaking had been a movement of individuals who recognized the formal claim that Christianity had upon them, a movement of the people independent of the policies of rulers and nations. The men who defended Constantinople—the Venetian sea-captains Diedo and Trevisano, the Genoese soldiers Cattaneo, the brothers Bocchiardo and, greatest of all, Giustiniani, the general and strategist in charge of the defences—reconciling among themselves the bitter hostility between Venice and Genoa, each one echoed to some degree the proud claim of Trevisano to act '*per honor de Dio et per honor di tuta la Christianitade*'.

By May 24, 1453, the 8,000 defenders in the city had withstood for six weeks the 150,000-strong army of Mahomet II. The great cannons, cast by the Hungarian gun-smith Urban especially for Mahomet, the largest of which threw a stone ball reputed to weigh 1,200 pounds, had battered the walls terribly. Each night old men, priests, women and girls carried up earth, stones, planks to mend the breaches. The defenders, with fourteen miles of walls to guard, were over-extended and without sleep. The huge Turkish gun boomed seven times a day, and when its shot hit the wall a tremor, the Venetian doctor Barbaro noted in his diary, passed through the city even to the ships anchored in the Golden Horn. Since the defence of the city had been so firmly placed in God's hands, the inhabitants watched for the heavenly omens. On the night of the 24th, the full moon was eclipsed for three hours. The next day, when the icon of the Virgin was being carried in a solemn procession, it slipped and fell to the ground. There it lay so unnaturally heavy that the priests were at first unable to lift it. Then the procession was engulfed and swept away by a torrential thunderstorm. On the 26th a fog covered the city, which cleared at evening and displayed flames encircling the dome of Hagia Sophia. God, concluded the citizens, had abandoned the city, leaving under the cover of the fog. The Turks, who had their share of qualified augurers, interpreted the flames on Hagia Sophia to mean that the true faith of Islam would soon light up that great church. And both sides were right—a rare triumph for interpretation.

Shortly after dawn on Tuesday, May 29, the city fell. The general, Giustiniani, seriously wounded, had retired from the walls. The weary, demoralized defenders had wavered in the breaches and the Turks had rushed through. The Emperor Constantine had been overborne by that powerful tide and died fighting. His body was found later, only recognizable by the Imperial insignia on the clothes. Mahomet the Conqueror, a young man of twenty-one, entered after his marauding soldiers and took possession of the city. Standing before Hagia Sophia, he realized most clearly what he had done. He was heard to murmur the lines of the Persian poet Firdawsi, 'The spider weaves the curtains in the palace of the Caesars; the owl calls the watches in Afrasiab's towers.' The poet, as is fitting, has the last word on Byzantium. The city survived. The Turks had raped and plundered for three days, in accordance with Moslem tradition, but Mahomet had reserved the churches and public buildings as his own share of the spoils. After the fall, men could still see why the first crusaders had thought it the equal of Rome, why the Slavic nations had considered it the capital of the world, why the Icelandic saga of *Skalholt* had called Hagia Sophia the most magnificent temple in the world, and why the Spaniard Benjamin of Tudela had called it the most beautiful. The architecture and the town-planning remained; but the spirit of the city responsible for those achievements did not survive the change of masters. This strange, unpractical, slightly demented spirit had persuaded a handful of people in an elegantly decaying city, with little political influence, no army to speak of, and few territories, that their sad little Empire was the *oikoumene*, the Christian world. It was a grand and artistic concept. It gave their lives a formal and harmonious structure, and from this they could look with calmness, and even indifference, on the world of horror, ambition, perfidy and greed which boiled around them. The unclouded mind with a clear eye on the evidence of experience—and

there had always been a few of these men in the Eastern Empire—
could see well enough that the dangerous world threatened to destroy
Byzantium. But there was nothing to be done. The mass of the
people would not abandon their conception, so there could be no
real help from the West, and no mercy from Islam. Since the claims
of Byzantium were absolute, the destruction of the Eastern Empire
was complete.

The defence of Constantinople was an affair of desperation, well
and bravely conducted by the Emperor Constantine and his subjects. One has sympathy and admiration for that small band, and one
tends to condemn the nations of the West for the self-interest and
jealousy which prevented them from coming to the help of the
beleaguered Byzantines. But that is not quite fair. Pope Nicholas,
ensnared as he was in Italian troubles, exerted his influence and
spent his money. His influence achieved little: Frederick III, visiting
Rome in 1452 to be crowned German Emperor by the Pope, was
prevailed upon to send a stern, but empty, warning to the Sultan.
The Pope's money did slightly better: it paid for a Neapolitan fleet,
which the King of Naples then stopped from going beyond the
Aegean, and it paid for a body of archers recruited by Cardinal
Isidore, the Papal Legate to the Eastern Empire. France and England were both suffering from the effects of the Hundred Years'
War; and in England the barons were still killing each other with
much treachery and dishonour in the Wars of the Roses. Among the
European powers, only the great Duchy of Burgundy was sufficiently
settled and prosperous to attend to the needs of Christendom. The
reaction of Duke Philip the Good to the conquest of Constantinople
is instructive, and should help one to see more clearly both Byzantium and the West.

On February 17, 1454, intending to start a crusade against the
Turks, Duke Philip arranged at Lille a feast and entertainment of
grotesque and gigantic ingenuity, in which men, animals and
machinery competed in a lively but confused symbolism. In the
banqueting hall three massive tables were set, each one loaded with
strange representations. On the first table, among other objects
hardly less notable, was the statue of a naked child who, according to
Olivier de la Marche's description of the scene, '*pissoit eaue rose
continuellement*'. The second table, more crowded than the first,
supported nine ornaments. There was a sort of pie enclosing twenty-
eight musicians who, in the intervals of the feast, performed hollowly
from the depths of the pastry: a tiger fought with a serpent in the

desert: a savage on a camel seemed about to set out on a long journey: a knight and his mistress caught and ate small birds which had been driven from a bush by a man with a long pole: a fool was mounted on a bear among mountains and rocks covered with icicles. The third table had three decorations, including an Indian forest full of clockwork animals walking about, and a lion fastened to a tree beside a man beating a dog. On two pillars next to the tables appeared the statue of a half naked lady, and a lion. From the waist down the lady wore a cloth embroidered with Greek letters; the lion was a live animal. The woman, of course, represented Constantinople, and the lion stood for the Duke of Burgundy.

The feast consisted of numerous dishes lowered by machinery and accompanied by outriders, knights, musicians, automata and actors performing allegorical pantomimes. But all this was mere preparation. The real business of the evening began with the entrance of a giant, turbaned in the Moorish fashion:

> He held in his left hand a guisarme of the antique mode, and with his right led an elephant. This animal bore on its back a tower in which was a female to represent the church [Olivier de la Marche himself played this role]: she had on her head a white veil, after the manner of nuns: her robe was of white satin, but her mantle was black, to mark her grief. When she was come near to where the duke sate, she sang a triolet to have the giant stopped—

> > Giant, I wish to stop here,
> > For I see noble company
> > To whom I must speak. etc.

She then made a long complaint in verse, setting out the wrongs that the Church had received at the hands of the infidel, and imploring the duke and the knights of the Golden Fleece to help her.

> Different officers now entered with the king at arms, of the order of the golden fleece, followed by two knights of the order, each leading a damsel, one of whom was natural daughter to the duke. The king at arms bore a live pheasant, decorated with a collar of gold and precious stones: approaching the duke, he made a profound obeisance, and said, that it being the custom at grand festivals to offer to the princes and gentlemen a peacock, or some noble bird, for them to make a vow upon, he was come with two ladies to offer to his valour a pheasant.

The duke then made his vow:

> to God pre-eminent, then to the glorious Virgin, His mother, and afterwards to the ladies, and to the pheasant, that if the king of France,

his lord paramount, or any other princes, would undertake a croisade against the Turks, he would accompany or follow them; and that he himself would combat the sultan body to body, if he would accept his challenge.

And the rest of the great company made their vows, some extravagant and some preposterous. One vowed that if he did not possess his mistress before he left he would marry the first lady he should meet who had 20,000 crowns.

Was the Oath of the Pheasant a silly charade? and the Duke of Burgundy an eminent practical joker who found in the Oath an easy way to escape from the responsibilities of his position and power? Duke Philip's real intentions cannot be known. Certainly his oath was carefully phrased so as to allow him an escape; and certainly neither the duke nor any other Christian prince came forward to oppose the Turks. The Popes pleaded and issued Bulls in vain. Nicholas V died in 1455. Calixtus III, his successor, made a brave show, fitted out his own small fleet and captured Lemnos, Naxos and Samothrace. But Calixtus was old and ill, and he died in 1458. He was followed by Pius II, the brilliant, cynical Aeneas Sylvius who, before his pontificate, had shown that he thoroughly understood the wiles of the world. Yet knowledgeable realist that he was, and though he worked with devotion and energy, he could not rouse the princes of Europe. He died in 1464, on the road to Ancona, intending to bless the crusade which never met. Only John Hunyadi, the Hungarian leader, seemed capable of containing the Turks, and he died after saving Belgrade in 1456. From that time the Turks steadily advanced. Trebizond, on the southern shore of the Black Sea and the last Greek capital, fell in 1461. The kings of the West were busy elsewhere when Louis II of Hungary fought and died at Mohacz in 1526. By 1529 the Turks were at the gates of Vienna which they were prevented from taking more by sickness and bad weather than by the efforts of the Habsburgs. Even the islands of Naxos, Lemnos and Samothrace reverted to the Turks, for the Pope could find no Christian prince to accept them.

But there is no need to reflect too severely on Philip of Burgundy. The proceedings of the Oath of the Pheasant were according to a well marked European tradition, and illustrate very clearly the workings of the mediaeval mind. For example, the practice of trying to solve international quarrels by hand-to-hand combat was well established. Louis of Orleans challenged Henry IV of England. Henry V challenged the French dauphin before Agincourt. And

Philip the Good, like a heavyweight boxer of our own age, thought it necessary to take on all-comers. Before his offer to the Grand Turk in 1454, he had on two occasions challenged first Humphrey, Duke of Gloucester, and then the Duke of Saxony. The custom continued. Francesco Gonzaga sought by a duel to save Italy from Cesare Borgia, and in the sixteenth century the Emperor Charles V twice offered to fight the King of France. The ideal behind these offers was chivalric and generous; the prince, as he sat at the top of the hierarchic order in his country, elected to champion his country, and thus prevent much waste and bloodshed. The ideal motive, as Philip the Good expressed it, was 'to prevent Christian bloodshed and destruction of the people, on whom my heart has compassion . . . this quarrel may be settled by my own body, without proceeding by means of war, which would mean that many noblemen and others, in your army and mine, would end their days pitifully'. The mediaeval prince was often bound tight by chivalric ideals. The French book *Le livre des faicts du mareschal Boucicaut* had set down as a common opinion:

> Two things have, by the will of God, been established in the world, like two pillars to sustain the order of divine and human laws. . . . These two flawless pillars are Chivalry and Learning, which go very well together.

And the strict observance of the chivalric code sometimes presented the knight with an obstinate problem. In 1415, during the English march towards Agincourt, Henry V had overshot the village marked by his vanguard for that night's rest. Since he was dressed in full armour, his honour did not allow him to go back, for the chivalric code ordained that a knight once dressed for battle could not retreat from the enemy. The king thus spent a dangerous and uneasy night stranded between the two armies.

The chivalric knight had also been a great swearer of oaths and maker of vows, and the oaths taken by the princes at the feast of the Pheasant showed them to be true followers of their knightly forbears. An Englishman, in the Hundred Years' War, had vowed to use only one eye until he had performed some brave deed, and so went into battle with a bandage over an eye. A Pole was well thought of for his vow, which he kept for nine years, only to eat and drink when standing. Pope Benedict XIII swore not to shave his beard until he was released from captivity at Avignon. And the famous French soldier du Guesclin usually seemed to have some difficult and unnatural promise on his conscience, as if the task of driving the English out of France during the Hundred Years' War were not hard enough.

One sees immediately, however, that there was a great difference between the vows of the early knights and the vows taken at the Oath of the Pheasant. The vows of the early knights were sincerely meant and, in general, performed in full; while in the conditional vows of the Pheasant, each prince or knight built a cunning loophole in among the crenellations and turrets of his gaudy promises. Chivalry in international relations did not work. The code was really an agreement among individuals which allowed each person to preserve intact an artificial commodity known as his honour. So long as a man was concerned with his own conduct and his own affairs only, chivalry worked. Jennet de Rebreviettes, the knight who had cynically sworn, at the Oath of the Pheasant, to marry the first rich girl he could find, later quite honourably went as a poor squire to fight against the Moors in Spain; and the desire of Trevisano, at the siege of Constantinople, to fight 'for the honour of God and the honour of Christianity', was real and admirable.

But to try to govern the conduct of armies and nations by a set of rules devised for individuals was disastrous. A prince or general did not fight for himself alone; the success of his country and the safety of his subjects depended on his abilities. 'Honour' had its place at jousts and tournaments, but cunning and careful strategy were the qualities to take into the field. At the battle of Najera, in 1367, Henry of Trastamara, anxious that it should be a fair contest, came down from his advantageous position and lost the battle. The French, according to the fourteenth-century *Debate of the Heralds of the French and English Armies*, suffered the disadvatange of having no fleet because at sea 'there is danger and loss of life, and God knows how awful it is when a storm rages and sea-sickness prevails, which many people find hard to bear'. Sea-sickness was undignified and did not 'beseem the nobility'. These, however, are isolated examples. In spite of chivalry, armies soon found that a reckless adherence to this code of honour did not pay. In 1333, the Scots declined the English invitation to come down from their strong position, and on the whole the armies of Europe followed the wise example of the Scots. Europe was preparing itself for the prudent and unscrupulous principles of Machiavelli long before the Italian wrote down his ideas.

If chivalry did not work in the campaigns of the West, it was not likely to help in the struggle against the Turks. Islam had its own standard of honourable conduct—for example, a town that capitulates was never sacked—but it did not agree to abide by the rules of the West. Yet the one business which never failed to appeal to the chivalric mind was the recovery of the Holy Places. Prince after prince felt bound to undertake the good work. But if they set out, and most did not, each one went as an individual, satisfying his own honour and reputation. The idea of taking concerted action, so necessary when facing such a well-drilled, numerous and powerful body as the Turkish army, hardly occurred to anyone. With the least preparation and the most gaiety and splendour, the army of King Sigismund of Hungary, supported by the aristocracy of France, Spain, Italy and Germany, met the Turks of Bayazid II at Nicopolis in 1396. The Turks destroyed the Christian army. Debonair courage could make no headway against the strength of the Janissaries. The Western knights cut the toes off their long and pointed shoes, so that they could flee from the battle more quickly.

Any effective defence of the West against Islam was prevented not only by hatred and distrust among the Western nations but also by strange rules of conduct, outmoded principles and puzzled consciences. After John Hunyadi had twice defeated the Turks in 1442, Sultan Murad had thought it wise to conclude a ten years' peace treaty with the Hungarian King Vladyslav. Almost at once the Hungarians took up arms again, absolved from their oath by Cardinal Cesarini, the Papal Legate, who claimed that a promise to the infidel did not count. Within a year, Hunyadi and the Hungarians suffered a disastrous defeat at Varna; four years later Hunyadi was again defeated at Kossovo. Although the Eastern Empire benefited from any Hungarian action against the Turks, the Orthodox in Constantinople were shocked that the Hungarians should break their oath. Varna and Kossovo seemed to be fit retribution for perjury. Hunyadi learnt the lesson too well. In 1451, he signed a three years' truce with Sultan Mahomet, and in 1453, when Mahomet laid siege to Constantinople, Hunyadi consequently refrained from coming to help the Byzantines. Hunyadi preserved his honour, but Constantinople fell.

What, then, was happening in the West to allow the Turks such easy success? The spirit of the old mediaeval formula was dead. The Oath of the Pheasant indicates that. European life, for some centuries, had been becoming increasingly complicated and increasingly puzzling. New knowledge was accumulating, new experiments were being attempted. Men perceived that their everyday experience seemed more and more removed from the old ideals and the old principles. But there was not as yet any clear light towards which men could stumble, though many small lamps illumined the gloom. Men still clustered round the hems of the old traditions. Though the spirit was dead, the practice continued. The Oath of the Pheasant indicates that also. And to keep some animation in the shell from which the spirit had departed, men invested the old forms with the life-giving breath of art.

Duke Philip was not a great artist, and the Oath of the Pheasant was not a great artistic occasion. It was messy, vulgar and over-played. And similar late mediaeval feasts, such as that given at Bruges in 1468 at the marriage of Charles the Bold and Margaret of York, were equally cluttered and distasteful. But they were care-fully constructed according to certain patterns, and were held to be successful if they fulfilled the form. From the artistic point of view, the vows and promises at the end of Duke Philip's feast provided the climax to the entertainment: from the practical point of view, they should have been the incentive for a great campaign against the Turks. But so much did the artificial life predominate over the practical life that the feast was a success and Christendom went undefended.

It seems that, in the Middle Ages, men generally had before their eyes some kind of pattern, fashioned according to authority and antiquity. And they attempted to make their conduct conform to the pattern, even though the real state of affairs urgently demanded some other approach. This tendency—this striving towards a model—can be seen most clearly in the arts; for the mediaeval approach was imaginative and synthetic, rather than practical and analytic. Some-times the pattern and its effects can be easily seen. The popularity of the dream allegory continued undimmed for several hundred years, from the *Romance of the Rose* through Chaucer even to such a late author as John Skelton whose *Garlande of Laurell* was written shortly before 1529. Again, the Nine Worthies—three Pagan, three Jewish and three Christian—were forever appearing in mediaeval works. The same respect for models can be seen in the habit of using old stories over and over again. Chaucer borrows from Boccaccio, Malory borrows from the French romances and Shakespeare bor-rows from everyone. The results of all this imitative artistic activity were not necessarily bad; for the good writer infused his model with his own daring imagination and produced something original.

Chaucer's *Troilus and Creseide* is a quite different work to Boccaccio's *Filostrato*. But often the influence of the pattern could not be anything but bad. Round about the year 1200 a certain Geoffrey of Vinsauf, in his *New Poetics*, had worked out some highly artificial rules for rhetoric. These rules had been based on Latin practice, and may well have been appropriate for the composition of Latin prose. But the odd thing is that writers in the vernacular still felt bound to follow the old master. Chaucer himself was infected by 'Gaufred, dere mayster souverain', and the translation of Boethius shows the results of misplaced respect. The following of this most inappropriate model finally led to this extravagant example. Skelton, setting out to translate eight words of Poggio's Latin—*Semelem Iuppiter ob pulchritudinem in forma hominis cognovit*—in accordance with Geoffrey's principles, begins:

> Jupiter, so as he was much amorous, surprised inwardly with the passing beauty of Dame Semeles, whose goodly eye, as a smaragdine stone radiant, enpierced through the starry heaven the inward aspect of Jupiter's heartly mind or thought,

etc., etc., and so on for nearly two hundred words. Whatever that jumble may be, it certainly is not English; and the men of the time, if they could have freed themselves from their allegiance to the pattern, must have known this. But the saddest, and perhaps most instructive, tale about the force of the old authorities concerns the Italian poet Tasso. Having written one successful and popular epic poem, he was bitterly attacked by critics who claimed that his poem did not follow correctly the epic conventions. Tasso was upset and determined to write another, scrupulously exact epic. He failed in the attempt, and went mad.

Faced with the authority of the patterns, men seemed to lose their critical faculties. The authority was absolute. To the Middle Ages, the imaginative conjectures of a poet about the nature of the universe carried equal weight with the sober findings of those who attempted to investigate the world in a scientific spirit. So Dante, in the *Convivio*, discussing the Antipodes, quotes Albert the Great—an eminent scientist of the period—as an authority for their existence. But he also supports his case with a quotation from Lucan's *Pharsalia*: as much value is given to the poet as to the scientist. Similarly, at a much later date, Burton, in the *Anatomy of Melancholy*, cites the Orpheus myth as evidence that beasts can appreciate music; and in his discussion of sexual perversion in the same work he mentions

Pygmalion and Pasiphae together with many historical cases. This uncritical—and it seems to us inexplicable—application of old authorities led to many strange instances, not only in the arts, but also in practical life. Among the models which appealed most to the Middle Ages was, quite naturally, the Bible, and men went to extraordinary lengths to explain or justify events in accordance with the Scriptures. After John the Fearless had shamefully murdered Louis of Orleans in 1407, Bishop Jean Germain did not hesitate to compare the victim to the Lamb. Molinet compares the Emperor Frederick III to God the Father; he also exclaims, on seeing the Emperor, his son Maximilian and Philip the Good together, 'Behold the image of the Trinity.' The great and austere Jean Gerson, chancellor of the University of Paris, claimed in a sermon that the guardian angels of royalty were higher in the celestial hierarchy than the guardian angels of ordinary men. John the Fearless, attempting to justify the murder of the Duke of Orleans, compared himself to Joab and Orleans to Absalom, but he considered himself less guilty than Joab because he had not disobeyed a royal order. Arguments and expositions were quite frequently founded on biblical texts. *Radix malorum est cupiditas* formed the starting point for both Jean Petit's defence of John the Fearless' crime, and Chaucer's Pardoner's sales-talk to promote his dubious relics and indulgences. Mediaeval musicians composed masses to the melody of love songs; and the words of the mass found their way into many a secular poem. The learned mediaevalist Johan Huizinga, who mentions many of the above cases, sees in these examples a depreciation of religious things through over-familiarity and over-use. Men had lost sight of the distinction between the temporal and the spiritual. If the laity was lost it is not surprising, for the papacy itself could not reconcile its spiritual responsibilities with its temporal ambitions. The Christian model seemed to demand that ordinary life should mirror as closely as possible biblical life. And although this was an impossible task—the world had drifted a long way in the last 1,500 years—with great effort, and some art, men tried to fit their actions into the obstinate pattern.

But the Bible was not the only model. The contemplation of the Pagan past—the great ages of Greece and Rome—stirred the mind almost as much as the Scriptures. Plato's *Timaeus*, the works of Aristotle and Cicero, and Boethius' *De Consolatione Philosophiae* had enduring popularity and force. The moral and philosophical preoccupations of these pre-Christian thinkers are, of course, reflected in the Christian synthesis of Thomas Aquinas. The ideal of Roman republicanism, so eloquently expressed by Cicero, found an energetic supporter in the unstable figure of Cola di Rienzo who, in 1347, in his few hectic, bombastic months as tribune, tried to restore the old Roman civic liberties. Again, as imperial Rome had developed out of republican Rome, men still hoped some great political revival might spring from Christian Rome. The idea of *renasci*, 'rebirth', was present in the European mind long before the age we now call the Renaissance. And here the pagan model and the Christian model became entangled, for the notion of rebirth lies at the heart of the New Testament. In the twelfth century Joachim of Floris confidently expected a transformed Christian world, a world rich in grace spoken of in St. John's Gospel. The Franciscan Spirituals continued to preach the idea of a 'renewal of life', and the same idea lies behind Dante's *Vita nuova* and *De Monarchia*. The idea was further reinforced by yet another pagan authority. Virgil's Fourth Eclogue had generally been understood by Christians as a prophecy of Christ's birth. But now the words:

The great sequence of the Ages starts again.
The virgin, Justice, comes back, the rule of Saturn returns;
Now the First-born of the New Age descends from heaven.

are taken by Dante to refer to the political renewal which he awaited so eagerly.

The political events of Europe stubbornly refused to fall into the pattern created for them by the idealists; yet men in the late Middle Ages continued to deceive themselves by relying on the old authorities, both Christian and pagan. Virgil himself helped to prevent the West from avenging the fall of Constantinople. The educated West remembered too well Virgil's account of the sack of Troy by the Greeks, and they looked upon the destruction of the Greek Empire as retribution for that act. This unintelligent delusion was encouraged by a confusion of classical terms. Even such a knowledgeable man as Cardinal Isidore was inclined to call the Turks 'Teucri', and thus to see them as the descendants of the Trojans. In a spurious letter, supposedly written by Mahomet II to Pope Nicholas V, the Turk claims kinship with the Italians, both peoples coming from Trojan stock. And Pius II, attempting to stir up a Crusade, found it necessary to point out that the Teucri and the Turcae were quite different people.

To act as if life corresponded to a great pattern—Christian

or pagan—gave to the men of the late Middle Ages a certainty of a kind. To the inhabitants of the Greek Empire in 1453, life was dangerous and insecure. Between the West and the Turks, they had little to hope for in the future. All this could be borne more easily when they recalled the greatness of the past and saw in themselves the heirs to the Roman imperial splendour. But as their high concept was unreal, so their political action was often foolish. On the accession of Mahomet II, shortly before the siege of Constantinople began, the Emperor Constantine had sent an embassy to Brusa, demanding more money for the maintenance of the Turkish prince Orkhan, then residing in Constantinople, and even hinting veiled threats against the Sultan. The Sultan's adviser, Halil Pasha, who was well disposed towards the Christians, burst out in anger at this inept diplomacy, for he knew the temper of his master. And Constantine had enough evidence to know this, too. Only an exalted and erroneous view of the power of the Eastern Empire could have pushed him into such an infantile step. The experience of the time, so complicated, so contradictory, so threatening, was transformed and refined so as to fit a past order. Naturally, this was unrealistic. But the great image of Rome still shone, symbol alike of political stability and security and of Christian unity, and men still tried to read their future by the light of that powerful but fading beacon. For both Dante and Petrarch unhappy Rome wept at the chaos in the world, and clearly cried out for that *renovatio vitae* that the age demanded.

The ideal which the Middle Ages sought behind the model was a kind of perfection—a perfection which combined Christian unity and faith with Roman civilisation, uprightness and political justice. This ideal was expressed by Erasmus, in 1517, in a letter to Pope Leo X:

This our age,—which bids fair to be an age of gold, if ever such there was,—wherein I see, under your happy auspices and by your holy counsels, three of the chief blessings of humanity are about to be restored to her. I mean, first that truly Christian piety, which has in many ways fallen into decay, secondly, learning of the best sort, hitherto partly neglected and partly corrupted, and thirdly, the public and lasting concord of Christendom, the source and parent of Piety and Erudition.

But this ideal, which seems so large and generous, was inevitably narrowed by the twin sources of its inspiration. As it looked back to classical Rome, and beyond her to Greece, so it maintained the distinction between the civilized and the barbarians. And as it was Christian, it tended to discount all peoples not of the Christian faith. To the Middle Ages human development was equal to Western Christian development; and the line between the civilized and the barbarian was variously placed, sometimes to include all the Western Christian peoples, and sometimes just to include the Italians. Certainly the line never extended beyond the borders of Christendom.

For many centuries there had, perhaps, been some historical justification for this attitude. At the fall of the Roman Empire in the West, such civilization as remained had been in the hands of the Christian communities concentrated and then spreading out from Italy. The ferocious energy of the pagan hordes that swept around and threatened Christendom only became disciplined and amenable when tempered by Christianity. Then the old barbarians newly Christianized—whether Orthodox like the Russian slavs or supporters of Rome like the Hungarians—became the indispensable guardians of the borders of the Christian world against the new waves of invasion. But the older parts of Christendom far from the front line, and in particular Italy, never quite lost their fear of the barbarian. Ramusio, introducing an account of the travels of the fifteenth-century Italian Angiolello, saw only discord following the barbarians:

> So it happens that nowadays there are many races whose origin is not known, of which miserable Italy is an example, as, after the ruin of the Roman Empire, a multitude of strange and barbarous nations entered from the North, ousted the inhabitants, changed the vulgar tongue, the names of the provinces, rivers and mountains, moved the towns from their proper sites, and built them up afterwards at a distance from the spots where they first stood.

And the fear of the barbarians was kept alive in the Middle Ages by the two horrifying Mongol incursions into Europe, the first sparked off by Chingiz Khan in the thirteenth century, and the second under Timur (Tamerlane) in the late fourteenth. In 1238, Matthew Paris, writing his chronicle at St. Albans, noted that the fear of the Mongols prevented the Gothland fishermen from crossing to Yarmouth for the herring fishing, and consequently abundant herrings were sold that year in England for as little as one piece of silver for forty or fifty. Three years later, on April 9, 1241, the Mongol army completely destroyed 30,000 Austrians, Germans, Hungarians and Poles at Liegnitz. These Mongols were especially terrible because no plan could be devised against them. They could not be subdued by force of arms; they could not be reached by any appeal (as yet no Westerner spoke their language); they were not touched by civilization or notions of mercy. The effect of this elemental force on Western society is graphically recorded by Matthew Paris in his chronicle for the year 1240:

> That the joys of mortal man be not enduring, nor worldly happiness long lasting without lamentations, in this same year a detestable nation of Satan, to wit the countless army of Tartars, broke loose from its mountain-environed home, and piercing the solid rocks poured forth like devils from the Tartarus, so that they are rightly called Tartars. Swarming like locusts over the face of the earth, they have brought terrible devastation to the eastern parts, laying them waste with fire and carnage. . . . They have razed cities, cut down forests, overthrown fortresses, pulled up vines, destroyed gardens, killed townspeoples and peasants. . . . For they are inhuman and beastly, rather monsters than men, thirsting for and drinking blood, tearing and devouring the flesh of dogs and men, dressed in ox-hides, armed with plates of iron, short and stout, thickset, strong, invincible, indefatigable, their backs unprotected, their breasts covered with armour.

Two things may be noted in Matthew's account. First, the incorrigible beastliness of the Mongols—for which there was good evidence; and secondly the idea, suggested in the opening sentence, that this invasion was permitted by God to chastise an erring people.

These two notions fitted in well with the Western nations' self-centred pre-occupation with themselves, and, applied indiscriminately to all peoples beyond Christendom, increased the distance between Christians and all others. If a nation of infidels was peaceful it became an object of curiosity, a place for merchants to exploit for the most profit, or for wandering friars to take on rather hopeless missions. The people of such fabulous lands were hardly taken seriously. The most popular accounts of the travellers, such as that of Marco Polo, were full of knick-knacks and wonders, about witches and cobblers who move mountains. The atmosphere is exotic, as in Mandeville's *Voiage and Travaile*. The figures moving in those shadowy realms, at the court of the Great Khan and elsewhere, are not sentient beings but the simplified representations of a peep-show. Yet had the Western nations wished to know what really happened beyond Christendom, they could have found out easily enough; for the men of the Middle Ages were great travellers. The Franciscan John Pian de Carpine bore a letter of the Pope to the Mongol Kuyuk Khan in 1246, and another friar, William of Rubruck, spent eight months of 1254 in Mangu Khan's capital at Karakorum. Friar Odoric travelled widely in Persia in 1318, and Venetian representatives were at Tabriz between 1305 and 1332. Peaceful Mongols even came west. In 1307, two envoys, Mamlakh and Tuman, presented their outlandish selves to Edward II at Northampton, and took back a letter in Latin. The Pope and the King of France also received visits from this deputation.

But the errors bred in peacetime were compounded by the problems of war. Christian ignorance did not distinguish between the enemies in the East. Mongol and Moslem were considered equally dangerous. When, in 1238, a Moslem Isma'ili (Assassin) from Alamut came to France and England seeking help against the Mongol invasion, he received this characteristic reply from the Bishop of Winchester: 'Let these dogs devour each other and be utterly wiped out, and then we shall see founded on their ruins the universal Catholic Church, and then shall truly be one shepherd and one flock.' Yet Islam was quite as terrified by the Mongol invasions as was the West. The Persian historian Juwayni's account of Mongol atrocities agrees with Matthew Paris: 'Wherever there was a king, or local ruler, or city warden who ventured to oppose, him they annihilated, together with his family and his clan, kinsmen and strangers alike, to such a degree that, without exaggeration, not a hundred persons were left where there had been a hundred thousand.' A mutually suspicious alliance of Christians and Moslems might not have stopped the Mongols; perhaps nothing could have stopped them. But the presence of a great, common danger might have drawn the Western mind a little out of its narrow groove and inclined it slightly towards a better understanding of the world beyond Christendom. Instead, the West retired into a tighter isolation, while Islam suffered a great upheaval. For just as the conversion to Christianity of the barbarian Germanic tribes in the West had invigorated and extended Christendom, so the acceptance of Mohammedanism by the Il-Khans, the Ottomans and the Timurids rejuvenated and strengthened Islam. That great moment in the West, when in 496 Clovis and his Franks professed their Christianity en masse, was mirrored in the East on June 19, 1295, when Ghazan and 10,000 of his heathen Mongols became true followers of Islam. Christendom felt the consequences. The Ottoman Turks, covered by the shield of Islam, marched more strongly towards Constantinople.

The West could not resist the temptation to interpret the events

in the East in accordance with the Christian model. And the unlovely monster Timur is transformed into a 'Minister of God' fulfilling the prophecy of Isaiah. According to Fortescue's *The Forest*,
'all such cruel and incarnate devils, are instruments wherwith God
chastiseth sin, as also with the same approoveth and tryeth the just.'
As the West was moral or immoral, so God permitted it to advance
or to suffer setbacks. Tyrants and oppressors of Christians were
'scourges of God', the agents whereby God expressed his displeasure.
Corruption in the communal body was punished by events. Thus
Sir Walter Raleigh, writing his *History of the World* at the beginning
of the seventeenth century, regarded the Christian defeat at Varna
in 1444 as inevitable punishment for oath-breaking:

> It was Eugenius the Pope, that perswaded, or rather commanded the
> King of Hungarie after his great victorie ouer Amurath the Turke,
> and when the said King had compelled him to peace, the most aduan-
> tagious that euer was made for the Christians, to breake his faith, and
> to prouoke the Turke to renew the warre. And though the said King
> was farre stronger in the field than euer; yet he lost the battaile with
> 30,000 Christians, and his owne life. But I will stay my hand: For this
> first volume will not hold the repetition of Gods iudgements vpon
> faith-breakers;

Olivier de la Marche, almost two centuries before, had shown this
same simplicity of mind when he concluded, from a single case of
impartial English justice, that England was more virtuous than
France and therefore rightly the victor at the beginning of the
Hundred Years' War.

The attempt to preserve the ideal qualities of the classical and the
Christian world was a noble work. Possessed by 'the blessed rage for
order', the men of the Middle Ages devoted to the task their intelligence and imagination. Their best achievements reflect the strong
influence of their models. St. Francis, the Cluniac reformers, the
Popes Gregory VII, Innocent III and IV, and Boniface VIII discovered their paths by the light of the great past. The minds of
antiquity nourished the work of Albert the Great and Thomas
Aquinas. 'What says our Arbiter?' wrote John of Salisbury every
few pages, his mind perpetually straying to the Rome of Augustus
though he lived in the England of Henry II. The business of life was,
quite literally, to 'live up to' the pattern of the past. The business of
art was to praise and perpetuate the great exemplars. In Chaucer's
House of Fame, as C. S. Lewis points out, the members are not
present in the House because of their own fame, but because they

pass on the fame of their subjects. The stories of Troy and Aeneas mattered more than the prestige of Homer and Virgil. Josephus, in Chaucer's words, 'bar upon his shuldres hye' the fame of the Jewish nation. Poet and historian alike spent a life of service burnishing the well-known contours of the model. Nor did the model shatter when the delightful impetus of Humanism and the Renaissance assaulted Europe. The Middle Ages shared with the new movement the same intellectual grounding. The world that John of Salisbury desired did not differ very much from that which Dante and Petrarch ardently strived to bring about; and Dante would have recognized the features of the country Erasmus created in his mind. The temper of the European mind remained—and remains to this day—classical and Christian. But though so many characteristic men of the Renaissance—Dürer, Ronsard, Machiavelli, Thomas More—looked to Authority, the pressures of everyday European life, the infinite complication of small events, pushed the ideal world further and further away from actuality. The strongest faith could hardly ignore the signs. The wish to believe remained, but certainty gave way to doubts, disillusions, questionings and other agonies. When they contemplated the heavens, people in the high Middle Ages heard only the joyful music of the spheres, but Pascal was terrified by the eternal silence of the celestial spaces.

Any escape towards the air and space of the East from the doubt and ferment of fifteenth- and sixteenth-century Christendom was blocked by the fall of Constantinople in 1453, and by the subsequent strength of the Ottoman empire. At the very moment when Europe needed most both a relief from its pre-occupation with its own past, and a stimulus from foreign societies and cultures, it was cut off from the possibility of both these. This is one of the greatest tragedies in European history. If, before 1453, Christendom thought too exclusively of its own development, when, in the early seventeenth century, Europe emerged from the Reformation and the Counter Reformation fragmented but hardened, it thought *only* of its own development. The great discoveries of the sixteenth century found new lands, but the explorers took with them old attitudes. And since they nowhere found—neither in the New World, nor in Africa, southern India and the East Indies—a society capable of making them change, either by argument of superior culture or by force of arms, they imposed their European pattern with a heavy hand on all alien peoples.

Yet while Europe was boiling in the pot of its ingrown despair, and the Spanish conquistadors set out to show the inhabitants of the Americas the stern morality of the Christian sword, there existed in the Near and Far East well-developed, artistic communities, conducting international relations with dignity and forethought. The descendants of Timur, both in Persia and in India, made up for the ferocity of their terrible forebear by becoming the most generous patrons of learning and the arts. The courts of Shah-rukh, Baysunghur, Ulugh Beg and the Emperor Babur shone with the productions of artists—carpets, figured velvets, miniatures, book decorations and manuscripts. In the enlightened air scientists and poets flourished, such as the poet Jami who died at Herat in 1492, and who was, besides being a poet, an historian, a religious commentator, a grammarian and a musician. The great Mogul Emperor Babur thought Jami 'too exalted for there to be any need for praise', and introduced his name into the *Babur-nama* only 'for luck and for a blessing', noting that 'in exoteric and esoteric learning' there was none equal to Jami. Of Ulugh Beg it is recorded that he was expert in astronomy, geometry and mathematics. Helped by the scientists of his court, he plotted the position of the stars and set down his observations in the tables of the 'Royal Almanac', still in use some centuries after his death in 1450. And the societies of the East, besides fostering so much artistic and scientific effort, carried on at the same time a statesman-like and sensible intercourse between nation and nation. War, of course, was not abolished; but princes also attempted to find common ground on which they could meet reasonably free from prejudice and ill-feeling. Ambassadors travelled freely between China, India, Persia and Turkey. Abdur Razzaq of Samarkand, returning to Hurmuz on the Persian Gulf from an embassy to India, relates the mixed activity of that cosmopolitan port in 1444:

Thither betake themselves merchants from the seven climes; from Egypt, Syria, Asia Minor, Adharbayjan, Arabian and Persian Iraq, the provinces of Fars, Khurasan, Transoxiana, Turkistan, the Kipchaq Plains, the territories of the Calmucks and all the realm of China and Pekin. Thither coast-dwellers from the confines of China, Java, Bengal, Ceylon and the cities of Zirbad, Tanasuri, Shahr-i-Naw, the islands of Diwa-Mahall, as far as Malabar, Abyssinia, and Zanzibar, the ports of Bijanagar, Gulbarga, Gujarat and Kanba'it, the coasts of the Arabian peninsula as far as Aden, Jeddah and Yanbu bring rare and precious things to which the sun and moon and fertilizing virtue of the clouds have given lustre and beauty. To that land come travellers from all parts of the world, and whatever they bring they find in that city without over-much search the equivalent value thereof in whatever form they desire, whether by sale or by exchange. In that city are many adherents of all manner of diverse religions, including heathens; yet they do not deal otherwise than fairly with any creature, for which reason men call the city 'the Abode of Security'.

Perhaps the sensibility of the East, from which the troubled West could have learnt so much, is best summed up in the personality and aspirations of Babur, that most candid and generous of rulers who sought empire that he might advance his friends, and who responded to everything about him with equal sympathy and interest. One does not know what to admire most: the detachment with which he regards his own faults—he related how at Herat in 1507 he was early tempted to drink and how he later formed his great, reckless passion for Baburi; his observations of geography and his descriptions of wild life and vegetation; the grace, accuracy and charity of his historical portraits; or the soundness of his judgment on poets, writers and artists. His life closed with a final act of generosity, for he offered himself as a sacrifice so that his sick son Humayun might live. Walking round the bed three times, he declared, 'I have borne it away.' Then his son, strengthened by the mystical transfer, grew well as the Emperor Babur faded towards death.

But in the West there was no renunciation and little tolerance. Faced with the self-sufficiency and strength, the spiritual and intellectual success of Islam, Christendom refused to moderate its claims one jot. Cut off from the East by the power of the Turks at a crucial point of Western development, Europe lost its ability, never very strong, to understand alien people and alien cultures. The legacy of this sad circumstance lasts to this day in the general misunderstanding between the European nations and the rest of the world. Searching to discover the reasons for the failure of its high classical and Christian destiny, Europe was caught by the muddled web of its past and tore itself with contrary idealisms—Roman orthodoxy against Greek orthodoxy until the Greek empire was destroyed; Church against Holy Roman Empire until the power of the Western emperor was destroyed. Then striving to make the artificial and formal life typified by the Oath of the Pheasant accord more with reality, the Europe of the Reformation nearly destroyed the Papacy and the Catholic Church. A Europe grappling with reality staggered its way through Renaissance and Reformation, and found a new stability (whether good or bad one must judge later) in the world of the Counter-Reformation.

Chapter II

THE BREAKING OF THE PATTERN

IN 1342, Nicholas of Autrecourt, a lecturer at the University of Paris, was summoned by Clement VI to the pleasant city of Avignon where he was invited to explain his curious theological notions. Among other novelties, he held suspect views on the immortality of the soul, and these he attempted to defend before a commission presided over by Cardinal Curti. Seeing that the going was likely to be rough, for Pierre d'Ailly noted jealousy and ill-will in the proceedings, Nicholas spoke cautiously. His views, he explained, were merely probable; but more probable than what had been believed previously. However, he expected his own theories to be superseded in their turn, and, as a consequence of this general uncertainty, he recommended a strict adherence to the dogma of true religion as revealed in the Scriptures. He then displayed his lack of confidence in this line of argument by fleeing to the court of Ludwig of Bavaria, a sturdy champion of all who annoyed the pope. Predictably, Cardinal Curti was unimpressed by Nicholas's *excusatio vulpina*—his 'foxy excuse'—and condemned the writings to be burnt. In 1347, having been expelled from the University of Paris, Nicholas made a conflagration of his words and retired into the obscurity of history.

But Nicholas, though an extreme case, was not alone in wishing to separate the tenets of belief from the speculations of philosophers. Nor was he alone in doubting that reason could throw much light on theological questions. The bold confidence of Aquinas that the rational mind was sufficiently equipped to tackle the problems of the relationship between God and the world was not universally felt by the philosophers of the fourteenth century. The harmonious circle of mediaeval certainty began to show worrying indentations. Formerly, that certainty had seemed to be firmly propped by the thought of Thomas Aquinas, and by the undoubted power and prestige of the papacy after the death of Frederick II, in 1250, had left Innocent IV the clear victor in the contest between Church and

Empire. Then, at the beginning of the fourteenth century, the nominalists began to question the Thomistic synthesis; at the same time Edward I of England and Philip IV of France showed Pope Boniface VIII that the papal power was illusory. The man who, more than any other, led the intellect of Europe under the shadows of doubt was William of Ockham.

Ockham, who died of the Black Death in 1349, would have little to do with the metaphysical systems of his predecessors. He did not think that any philosophical method could prove the existence of God, and he contended that any knowledge of God that we have depended on faith alone; the business of philosophers was with matters other than the divine. Since Ockham himself was a Christian and a priest, he believed firmly in Christian revelation, but his views, no more than those of his follower Nicholas of Autrecourt, did not please the Church. Ockham also ended his life at the court of the accommodating Ludwig of Bavaria. But he had effectively split theology from philosophy, and successors such as Nicholas, Richard Swineshead, Robert Holkot, Richard Billingham and John of Mirecourt—generally known as 'nominalists' and all owing some debt to Ockham—kept the two well separated in the future. The Universities of Paris and Oxford, in the van of intellectual daring, took up the new fashion with enthusiasm. By the fifteenth century, the *via moderna* (so called to distinguish it from the older disciplines of the Thomists and the Scotists) was well set in the universities of Europe, especially in Germany. This 'modern way' was one of the many roads leading to the Reformation.

The consequences of Ockham's thought were many and various, and no doubt most of them were unrealized by Ockham himself. In the Middle Ages, though there had been much scientific inquiry, science had tended to play the modest role of handmaiden to metaphysics. It also showed an undue respect for Aristotelian logic, and was not above relying on *a priori* reasoning. But once theology had been banished to the realm of faith, philosophy and the various sciences set themselves up as independent and dignified disciplines worthy of study in their own right. There was no sudden change in scientific method. The best of the thirteenth-century scientists knew the value of observation and avoided the *a priori*. Peter of Maricourt wrote an *Epistola de magnete* which William Gilbert found very useful three centuries later. Robert Grosseteste developed and extended the Greek and Arabic work on optics; Roger Bacon insisted that mathematics was the key to science. But with the separation of the various branches of knowledge, scientific inquiry, in the fourteenth and fifteenth centuries, was all at once very much more lively. A great number of interesting hypotheses were put forward, some of which appeared to contradict the Bible. But, as Nicholas Oresme pointed out, the Bible spoke according to the common usage, and such statements are not meant to govern our scientific beliefs. In his book *Du ciel et du monde* Oresme stated that a heliocentric theory of heavenly movement would 'save the appearances' quite as well as the geocentric theory. And furthermore he did not think that Aristotle or anyone else had ever managed to show that God could not create a plurality of worlds. Having thus anticipated both Copernicus and modern science, he nonetheless backs the traditional view of a geocentric universe and a single world. But his ideas indicate that, a century before the Renaissance, many scientists were quite free from repressive authority and capable of clear and closely-observed speculation.

Having abandoned Aristotelian physics and irrelevant authority, science tended to become a more severe discipline, pursuing knowledge for its own reward. A passage from Voltaire's amusing *Micromegas* illustrates this development—though Voltaire did not have in mind the contrast between mediaeval and Renaissance science:

'Certainly one must admit that Nature is varied,' said the traveller.
'Indeed, Nature is like a bed of flowers—'
'Oh, forget the bed of flowers!'
'She is,' went on the secretary, 'like a collection of girls, whose hair—'
'Girls, nonsense!'
'Then, she is like a picture gallery, where the features—'
'No. Nature is like Nature; why introduce similes?'

Though the picture is not quite fair, there is a lot of the mediaeval in Voltaire's secretary. For just as an errant imagination often led mediaeval politics astray, as in the Oath of the Pheasant; so, much strange imaginative stuff was mixed in the retorts of the mediaeval scientist. Not having sufficient empirical knowledge to tie it down, the mediaeval imagination winged its way to unknown and rarefied airs. As the sum of knowledge accumulated, more sober and down-to-earth views prevailed; and the Renaissance, perhaps contemptuous of the spritely and absurd tricks of the mediaeval mind, looked askance on that lively fellow, the imagination. Francis Bacon, after discussing the role of the imagination as intermediary between sense and reason, grumbled that it 'usurpeth no small authority in itself'; Milton, in *Paradise Lost*, warns that by 'misjoining shapes' it 'wild work produces oft', and Spenser, in the *Faerie Queene*, saw in imagination's chamber:

Infernal hags, centaurs, feendes, hippodames,
Apes, lyons, aegles, owles, fooles, lovers, children, dames.

As the practical results of applied science became apparent, men rejoiced that the new knowledge had been put to good use. The justification of the theories was in the results; they did not need to be presented in gaudy packets. In the first years of the seventeenth century Francis Bacon, in the *Novum Organum*, pointed out that printing, gunpowder and the magnet 'have changed the face of things and the state of the world; the first in literature; the second in warfare; the third in navigation'. And these, he added, did not come from adhering to the Aristotelian physics, but from experiment based on strict observation. The Italian doctor Cardano, writing a little earlier in the 1570's, had the same admiration for the way in which practical science had extended the world:

It has been my peculiar fortune to live in the century which discovered the whole world—America, Brazil, Patagonia, Peru, Quito, Florida, New France, New Spain, countries to the North and East and South. And what is more marvellous than the human thunderbolt, which in its power far exceeds the heavenly? Nor will I be silent about thee, magnificent Magnet, who dost guide us through vast oceans, and night and storms, into countries we have never known. Then there is our printing press, conceived by man's genius, fashioned by his hands, yet a miracle equal to the divine.

The new ways of thinking and the new stores of knowledge were not kind to the old idealism of the *Respublica Christiana*. The papal claims, very simple and very grand, were quite overborne by the complicated social and economic development of the European states. In the fourteenth and fifteenth centuries Europe was full of revolutions staffed by unwitting revolutionaries. Everyone, from king to peasant, was forced into a hard struggle to try to re-arrange his experience coherently. To the surprise of most people, the re-ordered Europe looked rather different to what they had expected. The Spiritual Power, which in the pontificate of Innocent IV had seemed triumphant, collapsed very suddenly. When, fifty years later, Boniface VIII reasserted the claims of his predecessors, the European princes, who previously had trembled at the pope's anger, now openly revolted. And Philip IV of France was so annoyed by the claims of primacy over the temporal power contained in Boniface's Bull of 1302, *Unam sanctam*, that he sent Guillaume de Nogaret to capture the stubborn pope at Anagni. The shock of this indignity killed the old man; and the popes who followed him were warned to proceed carefully against angry princes. The text from Corinthians, on which the popes relied, 'But the spiritual man judgeth all things; and he himself is judged by no man', did not resound as it used to. 'Lo, I have set thee this day over the nations, and over the king-doms, to root up, and to pull down, and to waste, and to destroy, and to build, and to plant,' wrote Pius V proudly, quoting Jeremiah, in the Bull *Regnans in excelsis* which intended to depose Elizabeth I of England, but by then Europe was hardly listening.

As the ideal of a united Christendom died away, a new ideal, more compact and manageable, rose up to take its place. Nationalism stepped out from the obscurity of the wings to occupy the main light of history, a position it still holds today. In all the late mediaeval turmoil, the European instinct still looked towards some authority; for authority meant direction and order. The lessons taught by Christianity and by the memories of Roman civilization had im-pressed the virtues of a well-ordered society. And the practical example of the barbarian invasions in the Dark Ages—not so very far distant to the people of the fifteenth century—had shown that a society in chaos was a society on its death bed. Both Christendom and nationalism claimed to establish order, and, of course, both had co-existed in the early Christian West. But as the conditions of a national unity were more easily fulfilled than those of Christian unity, nationalism grew as the ideal of Christendom fell away. The times looked fortunately on nationalism. By the beginning of the fourteenth century the restless movements of the European peoples had almost ceased. The frontiers of Europe, subject to small fluctua-tions, were fixed. The population of Europe stopped increasing; with the coming of the plagues of the Black Death in the middle of the fourteenth century, it even declined slightly. The great revival of trade in the previous century, and the consequent rising importance of the cities, had encouraged settled development and stability. In this relatively settled climate the roots of nationalism flourished.

The latent tendencies had always existed, encouraged, as usual, by antiquity. Virgil, whom the Middle Ages admired to distraction, was a keen nationalist—even one might say, in modern terms, a jingoist—and the *Aeneid* was deliberately planned to glorify Roman history, a story, like that of all countries, full of murky episodes and questionable acts. The first major national division in the West (and one which holds its forces to this day) was perhaps between the Germanic and the Romance. The chronicle for the year 887, relating the rupture between the East Franks and the West Franks, says: '*Hic divisio facta est inter Teutonicos et Latinos Francos*'—'Here the division was made between the German and Latin Franks'. And the partisans of both sides, from that day on, spoke with fine ardour and lack of logic. The prologue to the Salic Law saw the Latin Franks as the chosen people:

> Hail Christ, who loves the Franks. May he protect their kingdom, may He fill their leaders with the light of His grace, may He watch over their army, may he strengthen their faith, may He grant them joy and happiness!

And as the foremost temporal dignity of Europe, the crown of the Holy Roman Empire, remained in German hands, much of the early national feeling in the West expressed itself as a dissatisfaction, even a hatred, towards the Germans. John of Salisbury, championing universal Christendom rather than English nationalism, wrote against the Emperor:

> Who has appointed the Germans to be the judges of the nations? Who has given authority to brutal and headstrong men that they should set up a prince of their own choosing over the heads of the sons of men? In truth their madness has often attempted to do this; but by God's will, it has on every occasion been overthrown.

In 1107, Suger of Saint-Denis, a good Frenchman, observed the swaggering antics of a German embassy to the pope, and, borrowing an expression from Lucan's *Pharsalia*, spoke ominously of the *furor teutonicus*. But the national antipathies of the early Middle Ages were inextricably mixed up with the quarrel between Church and Empire. The eleventh-century vision of St. Hildegard of Bingen only gradually became true:

> The rulers of the Roman Empire shall lose the strength with which they had earlier held that empire, grown powerless in their glory. The kings and princes of the many nations that hitherto were obedient to the Roman Empire shall detach themselves from it and no longer be subject thereto. And thus shall the Roman Empire be dispersed by default. For every region and every nation shall place itself under a king, whom it shall obey.

By about 1300 it was clear that St. Hildegard had been right. The

King of France had proved himself to be the most powerful prince in Europe. Building on this piece of political reality, the Norman Pierre Du Bois, in his book *On the Recovery of the Holy Land* (1305), put forward an entirely new plan for Europe. All the lands of the West (and the East, too) must be brought under the sway of the French king, the princes of Europe becoming subordinate vassals to France, and the pope handing over his secular power. This would bring peace, for, Du Bois claimed, 'it is the peculiar merit of the French to have a surer judgment than other nations, not to act without consideration, nor to place themsleves in opposition to right reason.' Moreover, the climate of France is very healthy, and the land is altogether more pleasant than any other. Despite the Gallic exuberance of his attitude, there was much good sense in Du Bois's ideas. He saw the bad results of the pope's temporal policy and, since he hated the Italians, he delighted in showing the papacy its errors:

> Wars therefore are stirred up, numbers of princes are condemned by the Church, together with their adherents, and thus die more men than can be counted, whose souls probably go down to hell and whom nevertheless it is the Pope's duty to save . . . Because of his sanctity the Pope should aspire only to the glory of pardoning, praying, giving judgment in the name of the Church, preserving peace among Christian princes, so as to bring souls safe to God; but he shows himself to be the promoter, author, and exerciser of many wars and homicides, and sets an evil example.

The papacy might end its abuses, says Du Bois, if the pope were to move to that pleasant land of France, relinquish his secular power to the king and receive from the king an adequate pension. And soon after, Pope Clement V, a Frenchman, did move to Avignon where his successors remained until 1378, menaced and intimidated by the French king, heads of a Gallican rather than a universal Catholic Church. For if Du Bois was right in seeing that the pope had ceased to be the leader of a united Christendom, he was wrong in attempting to make him a flunkey in the service of a national government. The ideal of Christendom may not have been possible, but it was a greater notion than the national ideal of France. And the Church as a spiritual power, whatever its temporal misdealings, knew that it must keep itself above national self-interest. The great problem which the Church faced, and which it did not know how to solve, was how to secure its physical well-being so that its spiritual claims could remain unchallenged. Nor could any of the late mediaeval theorists, such as Du Bois or Marsilius of Padua, however acutely they analysed the pope's dilemma, help the papacy. Even in Du Bois's partial, nationalistic account the ideal of internationalism still shines—but, of course, he hoped for a universal order under the rule of France. From the fourteenth century onwards, nationalism and internationalism were in a bewildered conflict. For the most ardent nationalists usually presented their ideas as a step towards internationalism and did not seem to realize that the greatest bar to any universal dominion was the opposition of equally ardent nationalists in other countries. Under the influence of the Christian model, universality was the ideal towards which the imagination strived; under the influence of events, nationalism was the lesser ideal towards which men worked. Few seemed to realize that the two were irreconcilable, certainly not the papacy. Seeing the success of the new national monarchies in England, France and, later in the fifteenth century, Spain, the Renaissance popes attempted to secure their spiritual dominion by strengthening the papal monarchy. Yet the great increase in the papal temporal power, between the years 1471 and 1513, in the pontificates of Sixtus IV, Alexander VI and Julius II, was also the time of the greatest loss of spiritual prestige. The popes were learning the usual lesson that worldly gains must be paid for by loss of spiritual grace.

The spread of nationalism could not be stopped. The tendency to form groups had always been present; slowly the groups joined together to form national conglomerations. This process is seen quite clearly even in the two most international of mediaeval societies—the universities, and, of course, the Church. The turbulent students split up into 'nations' to protect themselves both from other students and from the towns-people. At first, in Paris, there were four 'nations'—the French, the Picards, the Normans and the English—but the definitions were not very exact, for the English 'nation' included Irish, Scots, Germans, Scandinavians and all other northern undesirables. Then, as national consciousness grew, the definition of a nation became more strict. In the middle of the fourteenth century the German 'nation' split off from the English group, and this was quickly sub-divided into a High German 'nation' and a Low German one. In other universities as widely separated as Oxford, Bologna and Prague the same process was at work.

The popes were quick to see the value of the national principle as a political expedient in Church affairs. At the Council of Vienne in 1312 the voting was by nation. The Council which met at Pisa in 1409 to attempt to repair the damage of the Great Schism was organized around the four nations of France, Germany, Italy and England. When that meeting had failed, and when the Council met once more at Constance in 1414, the principle of the nations caused almost as much controversy as the claims of the rival popes. But though the pope may have gained some temporary political success through the rivalries of the various nations, once national attitudes were allowed to play a part in Church business, the establishment of State Churches was not far off. The English nation, which had found its corporate feet first among the principalities of Europe, after Magna Carta in 1215 found it easy to resist papal interference in English Church affairs. In the reign of Edward III, in 1343, Parliament petitioned the king to stop papal provisions. In 1351 the Statute of Provisors prevented the pope from making appointments to English ecclesiastical positions. In 1353, the first Statute of Praemunire went further; it decreed that there should be no appeals beyond the realm. Similar legislation was repeated in 1364 and 1389. In the next century Charles VII of France won like advantages for the Gallican Church. A great assembly of the French Church, in July 1438, passed at Bourges the so-called 'Pragmatic Sanction' which, taking advantage of the problems of Eugenius IV, limited the pope's right to nominate to French benefices and abolished most of the sources of papal revenue within France. In a sense the Anglican Church and the Gallican Church had been established some two hundred years before the Reformation; that one became Protestant and the other remained Catholic was an accident of later history.

A drab time, this age of the rising monarchies. The administration of the realm, becoming ever more efficient, rested in the hands of silent men of no family and little money, whose future prospects depended solely on the king's pleasure. The court of Philip the Fair, in the early fourteenth century, became the pattern for the successful monarchies that followed, both in France and in England. The 'clercs de loi', such as de Marigny, Pierre Flote and de Nogaret, set their ruthless, impassive selves between the king and the populace, and behind this impenetrable screen the king conducted his cold and faithless policies. 'Who is there but knows,' Pope Gregory VII, the great castigator of kings, had cried out, 'that kings took their beginnings from those who, ignorant of God ... spurred by the Devil, who is the prince of this world, in blind passion and intolerable presumption sought to rule over their equals?' Who would have dared speak those words to Henry V and Henry VII of England, or Louis XI of France? Even where, as in England, the monarchy was subject to the law and dependent for its success on the support of Parliament, the monarchal thirst for glory received little check. The megalomaniac dreams of that cruel and bigoted juvenile, Henry V of England, drew from his subjects enthusiastic applause, and pushed England into an unnecessary war with France. The chief cause for that war was the English desire for national prestige. But if the kings in their conduct seem coarse and crude political men, their unadmirable characteristics are too often reflected through the rest of society. The fight for the king's favour was energetically waged by a race of upstart lackeys and time-servers, who then dispensed the political plums in a way which Sir John Fortescue lamented:

> This has caused many men to be such braggers and suitors to the king for to have his offices in their countries to themself and their men that almost no man in some country durst take an office of the king but he first had the good will of the said braggers and engrossers of offices.

The flourishing merchant class grew in wealth and self-satisfaction. In fifteenth-century England, the Cotswold wool merchants, like the Busheys, Boleyns and Wottons, and the ship-owners and traders, like the Canynges of Bristol, were remarkable for both their competence and their greed. The ways of the gentry, as we see them in the Paston Letters, were sour and brutal; their lives were filled with the noise of dynastic squabbles; amid a welter of litigation, they bribed and cajoled and intimidated. Throughout Europe the trade corporations and guilds fought to establish their monopolies, ruthlessly eliminating competition. Advancement from journeyman to master became increasingly difficult as the population and trade declined. Journeymen formed themselves into 'companies' and fought their masters.

The great rage of selfishness was shown in all ranks of society; and on this partiality the nationalism of England and France was built. King and country now claimed that idealism which before had looked towards the vision of a united Christendom. The sovereign State was, no doubt, a poor substitute for the City of God, but kings did their best to set out their claims in fine clothing. 'The Kings of France alone,' the ambassador of Louis XI declared to the pope, 'are anointed with a holy oil sent by the Father of Lights, and carry on their escutcheon the lilies, gifts from Heaven; alone they are resplendent with miracles manifest.' But Sir John Fortescue, in

De laudibus legum Angliae, had a different view of Louis's French government. Louis, he wrote, was a despot, who oppressed and impoverished his subjects; he levied arbitrary taxes, imprisoned without legal form and executed secretly; his standing army destroyed the countryside; and all this he did by virtue of the *jus regale*. Louis XI died in August 1483. If only he had lived two more years, he would have seen Henry VII, the king across the narrow Channel, acting with the same disregard for the niceties of liberty and justice. There is little to choose between these two powerful and successful nationalists: the restless Louis finally stilled at Tours, surrounded by his cloud of king's men, his doctor Coitier and barber le Daim, and his faithful chronicler Commines; the restless Henry prodding the body of England with Morton's fork, watching the greedy hands of Empson and Dudley filling the royal chests.

A great past is a fortunate possession for any aspiring nation, and the strong leader looks to it that his country's history is presented in the correct favourable light. The rising monarchies knew the value of an official historian. For Louis XII, Paulus Aemilius composed in Latin, in 1499, ten large volumes of French history; and in 1507, Polydore Virgil, also writing in Latin, told the English story for Henry VII in twenty-six books. These works, though suffering under official inspiration, are impressive. The historical scholarship of the Renaissance was quite capable of judging between fact and fancy. And though the pious mythologies are repeated, the historian is careful not to fall for them himself. So Paulus, having related the supposed French descent from Troy, dismisses this as a mere assertion. Polydore Virgil, more uncertain under the cold Tudor eye, tells of the arrival of Brutus in England and gives the story of King Arthur; but he also gives a critical account of early English history, and leaves the reader to choose the version he prefers.

One slightly remarkable thing about these two histories is that both the authors were Italians, though one would expect a Frenchman and an Englishman to be the logical choices to gild their respective national images. That such important national work should be given to Italians indicates how well they had established themselves as the intellectual leaders of Europe. The seeds of the Renaissance fell upon Europe as a whole; but in Italy the receptive ground was prepared earlier, and tended more lovingly, than in any other country. Italy, at the centre of Mediterranean trade and travel, was early subject to a maze of complex influences which did not trouble the rest of Europe until later. The very prosperous commercial life of the Italian cities insured that the towns increased in wealth and importance. As the towns grew, the countryside became poorer. Until this time the social organization and the way of life throughout Europe had been based on landholding and agriculture, but now this seemed irrelevant in the Italian urban communities. Consequently, the authority of the old ways was thoroughly questioned. At the same time, these new town Italians, men of some leisure and ability, shared with their predecessors an interest and pride in their ancient history. Gradually the Italians of the fourteenth and fifteenth centuries turned with more and more enthusiasm to their great past, perhaps hoping to find there a pattern which they could suitably apply to the troublesome present. The love and respect for the classical Latin language, which was felt by nearly every humanist, was in part an admiration for what the humanists thought to be the classical Roman virtues. Vivès, speaking of the advantages of the Latin tongue, makes this quite clear:

> It is copious by reason of the great multitude of excellent wits that have laboured in the manuring and augmentation thereof and hath moreover a sweetness in the sound meddled with a certain weight and gravity, not as in some tongues brutish and rustical but lively expressing the image of a right prudent and valiant man born and nurtured in a well ordered commonwealth.

But in spite of their love of learning and their considerable scholarship, the humanists were unable to bring about the 'well ordered commonwealth' they desired. They did, however, help to hasten the end of the old order.

Before the revival of learning in Italy, education had been almost entirely in the hands of the Church. But the new Italian rage to learn overflowed in a desire to teach; education gave a sudden, unexpected jump. The new teachers, such as Vittorino da Feltre who taught at Mantua from 1423, and Guarino of Verona whose methods were published in 1458, were not necessarily churchmen, and they departed from the traditional mediaeval curriculum. Not that these notable teachers were atheists or anti-Christian; in fact, da Feltre worked hard to persuade his brilliant student Cecilia Gonzaga to enter a convent. But the insistence on the importance of classical language shows that education had taken on a definite 'lay' character. The grip of the Church on the European mind, everywhere weakening, was further loosened. The humanists even dared to use their critical intelligence to investigate Church claims. In 1440, Lorenzo

Valla, writing for Naples which was then at war with the pope, proved that the Donation of Constantine, a document on which the papal temporal claims rested, was a forgery. The papal answer to this new learned threat was characteristically shrewd; within a few years Nicholas V had Valla working for him, together with such other humanists as Filelfo, Manetti and Decembrio. But the suspicions raised by such men as Valla were not so easily stilled.

The humanists remained Christians, but puzzled Christians. When such an exciting figure as the Greek Gemistos Plethon came to Florence in 1439, bursting with praise for Plato and supremely contemptuous of Aristotle, the Florentines were amazed and delighted. In his honour, Cosimo de' Medici founded the Platonic Academy; Marsilio Ficino, the first head of the Academy, gave enthusiastic feasts on Plato's birthday, and burnt a lamp before his bust. Among other rhetorical flourishes, Gemistos had promised Florence that the world would soon 'see a new religion, which will be neither of Christ nor of Mahomet', but it was as well for his Italian reputation that Gemistos had not formulated his Greek religion before he left Italy. Ficino, the good Christian, would have been horrified by the chilly classical deities that Gemistos conjured up on his return to Mistrà.

The increasing separation between the religious and the secular, apparent throughout Europe, but most particularly in Italy, forced the men of the age to rely more and more on their individual judgment. The nominalists of the fourteenth century had suggested that a man might believe in one thing as a Christian, yet hold the contrary as a philosopher or scientist. The Church, as in the case of Nicholas of Autrecourt, thought this sort of reasoning particularly dishonest. But what was an intelligent man to do? The new texts and the new theories were coming in so fast—Latin, Greek and Arabic—and so few men had the wonderful ability of Pico della Mirandola to reconcile all points of view. Unfortunately, Pico died young, in 1494 at the age of thirty-one; and in spite of his efforts, Plotinus, Averroes, Aquinas and the Kabbala remained hopelessly confused in most people's minds. But scholars and philosophers were attempting to work things out for themselves, and to this extent the age encouraged individualism. The Middle Ages had certainly not been a time of dull conformity. Various compilations of *Merrie Tales* are full of personalities, such as the parish priest who, when accused by his parishioners of keeping a mistress, confronted them from the pulpit with his new-born child:

'Thou wyfe that hast my childe, be not afraid; bring me hither my childe to me': the whiche was doone. And he, shewynge his childe naked to all the paryshe sayde, 'How saye you neibours all? is not this childe as fayre as is the beste of all yours?'

Nor in the harsh post-Reformation atmosphere is one likely to come across a man like the rector of Whipstock, who, standing on the high altar, flew his hawk at pigeons in the church. The men trained by humanism were not as eccentric; but they did take a new interest in themselves in relation to the world around. As a result, a person's biography, and his psychology, become aspects of him as interesting and important as any other. 'Before my birth', wrote Cardano in his autobiography, 'my mother tried to procure an abortion and failed.' That fact, he implies, may explain something about him and his family. And further hints about his character may be gleaned from the following:

My mother had a bad temper and a good memory. She was short, fat and pious. Indeed, both my parents had bad tempers, and they did not love their son for long at a time. However, they spoilt me; my father insisted that I lay in bed every morning until 8 o'clock, and I think it did me a great deal of good.

The rector of Whipstock will always be a stranger to most of us, but with Cardano we come to a person we recognize.

Neither the study of the ancients, nor the inspection of his interior mind gave the humanist the stability he hoped for in a crumbling world. Man may have become Individual, but he remained uncertain. Round death's corner perhaps there was only oblivion. Cardano longed for even the smallest spot in human remembrance. 'I do not mind whether it is known what kind of a man I was, but I should like it to be known that I existed.' Sir Thomas Browne, who lived when the work of the Reformation was complete, and the world was not so topsy-turvy, knew the futility of Cardano's wish:

To be content that times to come should only know there was such a man, not caring whether they knew more of him, was a frigid ambition in Cardan, disparaging his horoscopal inclination and judgment of himself.

Italy could not find the pattern to make life sweet and smooth-running once more. Nationalism, the new binding of European life which secured so successfully the kingdoms of France, England, and, later, the Spain of the Catholic Kings, could not bring together the warring Italian cities. Their lively independence ensured endless rivalry. The upstart, tyrannical rulers—the Visconti, the Medici, the Sforza and a host of minor figures—strove to recognize no overlord, seizing absolute powers and holding on by force and cunning. Since the social organization had been entirely upset by the flight from the land and the rise of capitalism in the towns, the political organization was new and revolutionary, and varied from city to city. 'In our Italy,' lamented Aeneas Sylvius, later Pius II, 'amorous of change, where nothing endures, and where no ancient lordship exists, varlets may readily aspire to become kings.' It was not that Italians despised nationalism; most of them echoed Dante's sigh for his poor country, *Ahi serva Italia, di dolore ostello*. But, besides the chaos from the continuous political upheavals within the cities, the hope of Italian unity was diminished because the problems of national unity had, historically, become inextricably mixed with the problems of a united Christendom. As the Church lost authority, Italy became evermore unruly and changeable.

The doubtful Italian peace, always a rickety and misshapen structure, collapsed completely when Lorenzo de' Medici died in 1492. As the head of a small commercial state, with no great thirst for military glory, he knew that both the Florentine wool trade and the interests of the Medici Bank required a settled Italy and, if possible, a settled Europe. He gave himself to this work, and his great intelligence and influence did wonders, keeping the King of Naples, Pope Innocent VIII and Ludovico *il Moro* of Milan apart. France had meddled in Italian affairs before (indeed, who in Europe had not?), and the newly powerful French monarchy was prepared to fall for the temptation again. The brute power of France was something Lorenzo could not deal with, and it is as well for his reputation as a peacemaker that he died before the French preparations were complete. Soon after 1492 the round of embassies, deceptions and double-dealings began. In May 1494, the French army crossed the Alps, instituting an age of severe, and quite unchivalrous warfare. The Italian *condottieri*, the professional soldiers among whose ranks had appeared such great names as Gonzaga, Malatesta, Braccio, Colleone, Colonna, Orsini and Sanseverini, and who had shown their military brilliance by avoiding bloodshed where possible, were now surprised to find that the Swiss mercenaries of the French thought a hired soldier's job was to kill and destroy; and this they did with ruthless efficiency. When Spain joined in the scramble for Italian possessions, the famous soldier Gonzalo de Cordoba proved equally merciless. That greatest of glories, the Italian culture of the

fifteenth century, did not survive the pressures which the rest of
Europe put on Italy.

In spite of the chaos in Italian life, in spite of the poisonings and
the treacheries, the nastiness had been limited. The scholar, the
artist, the writer found time to practise their arts, and patrons to
reward them. The tyrant generally managed to combine amorality
with munificence. But the independence and vitality of the city-
states, unable to combine, made them easy prey to the powerful,
united forces of France and Spain. And when France and Spain
plundered Italy, the German Maximilian, the aspiring Emperor,
could not let his traditional interest in Italy lapse. Maximilian (who
died in 1519), Ferdinand of Aragon (who died in 1516) and the
successive French kings Charles VIII, Louis XII and Francis I,
ensured that Italy, and consequently the Catholic Church, were in
the worst state when Luther nailed his theses to the church door in
1517.

The papacy was, quite naturally, as deeply embroiled in Italian
problems as any city-state; for the pope was, in his temporal capacity,
the head of a state. One of the greatest difficulties of the pope was
that he was supposed to finance the organization of the Church out
of the revenue he received from the papal states. That sum was
entirely inadequate, and also ever decreasing as the Italian princes
nibbled away the papal lands. The constant quarrels between popes
and European princes centred most often on money, which the
pope tried to raise by impositions on national churches, and which
kings resisted because they felt the money should come to them. The
problem, made impossible enough by the unreality of Church
economics, was further complicated by the attitude of the Church
towards money. Profit, speculation, financial dealings were condemned; the sentence from St. Jerome was a favourite text—*Homo
mercator vix aut nunquam potest Deo placere*. In the ideal of Christendom the financing of the Church should perhaps have come from
free gifts of the laity, in alms and donations. And so to a certain
extent it did. But the ideal of Christendom was no longer very
strong. The poor are always poor and the rich are usually selfish. A
strong national unity is built on money, too, and the monarchies of
Europe saw to it that what little money was available came to them
and not to the Church.

The strength of the monarchies by the middle of the fifteenth
century made it clear to the papacy that the flow of funds from outside Italy was likely to become thinner and drier. A possible solution

was to secure and even extend the papal holdings within Italy. But the papacy as a temporal power suffered the weakness of being an elected monarchy, that same weakness which prevented Germany from achieving the unity and strength of the other European monarchies. The papacy saw this, and what it could not do by dynastic succession it attempted to do by nepotism. Sixtus IV (1471–1484) first applied this remarkably clear-headed, but remarkably wrong, policy. He established one nephew, Girolamo Riario, in Imola and Forlì; another nephew, Giuliano della Rovere, he made the most important man in the College of Cardinals. This temporal policy was dangerous as the favourites might not be able to hold their advantageous positions. It was therefore necessary to combine nepotism with political bargaining as cunning and unscrupulous as that of any secular prince. Innocent VIII, the successor to Sixtus, made it clear to the Florentine ambassador just how far he would go:

> If none would aid him against the violence of the King of Naples he would betake himself abroad, where he would be received with open arms, and where he would be assisted to recover his own, to the shame and scathe of the disloyal princes and peoples of Italy. He could not remain in Italy if deprived of the dignity befitting a Pope.

The popes let it be known that they had embarked upon the tidal pools of nepotism, aggression and political trickery. And, since they were able men, they navigated these difficult waters as well as any secular prince. Rodrigo Borgia, the most infamous Alexander VI, bought his election in 1492,—soon after Lorenzo de' Medici's death. Alexander's son, Cesare Borgia, undertook a campaign of conquest of quite exceptional brutality and dishonour. Julius II, who followed next but one after Alexander (the twenty-seven-day reign of Pius III intervened), took the field himself at the head of the papal army. Europe had been used to fighting prelates—Cardinals Albornoz and Vitelleschi were two notable examples; but the fierce, stately old Julius advancing towards Perugia showed a novel aspect of papal power. And he was successful. In 1506, Perugia fell without a blow; Bologna, doubly threatened by papal excommunication and papal artillery, collapsed soon after. Heartened by these successes, the fiery old man turned his wrath towards Venice. In 1508 he worked hard to instigate the League of Cambray against Venice; and two years later he received the submission of the proud republic. It was typical of the new thinking in the papacy that the great spiritual threat of excommunication should be used for purely temporal gains. When Bologna was freed from papal rule in 1511, the citizens showed their opinion of their warlike pope by hurling Michelangelo's statue of Julius to the ground. The Duke of Ferrara, whom Julius had excommunicated in a passage which made Peter Martyr's hair stand on end, fittingly recast the broken statue of the pope as a cannon.

This secular progress of the papacy, which the post-Reformation ages have found so extraordinary and condemned so heartily, was accepted with easy minds by some of the most intelligent Italians of the time. Lorenzo de' Medici (perhaps not an ideal witness as he had a daughter married to the pope's son) wrote encouragingly to Innocent VIII:

> Your holiness is now not only excused in the sight of God and man, but men may perhaps even censure this reserved demeanour, and ascribe it to other motives. My zeal and duty render it a matter of conscience with me to remind your holiness that no man is immortal; that a pope is of the importance that he chooses to give himself; he cannot make his dignity hereditary; the honours and the benefits he confers on those belonging to him are all that he can call his own.

And Machiavelli admired the military daring of Julius. 'Formerly,' he wrote, 'no baron was so insignificant as not to despise the papal power; now, a king of France stands in awe of it.' By its nature and its history, the popes' problem could not be easily solved. It was a common opinion that possessions and power meant security and peace, and if this were so any action that led to power became permissible. This at least was accepted logic to both Machiavelli and the Renaissance popes. And as most of their countrymen believed this with them, one can say that they built on the reality of the times. The pictures left us of these times by disapproving hands in later ages are reasonably accurate. Here is Ben Jonson's interpretation of Machiavellian *virtù*:

> There is a Fate, that flies with towering spirits
> Home to the marke, and never checks it conscience.
> Poore plodding Priests, and preaching Friars may make
> Their hollow pulpits, and the empty Iles
> Of Churches ring with that round word: But wee
> That draw the subtle, and more piercing ayre,
> Of that sublimed region of Court,
> Know all is good, we make so, and go on,
> Secured by the prosperity of our Crimes.

Men were immoral, as they usually are in the search of ambition and profit; but, most horrible, they did not even pay lip service to morality. When Alexander VI needed more money he demanded double annates and double, sometimes treble, tithes. Most ecclesiastical offices were for sale. All concessions and favours given by the Dataria had to be paid for according to a fixed scale. These financial arrangements were conducted in the most open way. It is not surprising that such frank policies won Italy a certain reputation among severe northern men who breathed the cleansed moral air after the Reformation. Roger Ascham, who died in 1568, in his *Scholemaster* warned young Englishmen to keep their purity away from Italy:

> Vertue once made that contrie Mistres over all the worlde. Vice now maketh that contrie slave to them, that before, were glad to serve it. All men seeth it: They themselves confesse it . . . For sinne, by lust and vanitie, hath and doth breed up everywhere, common contempt of Gods word, private contention in many families, open factions in every Citie.

Among the moral outrage is the hint of irreligion and even atheism. And atheism became a very popular stick with which to beat the Italians. Philipps' history of atheism, published in 1716, produces a magnificent list of Italian names—Aretino, Bembo, Bruno, Cardano, Campanella, Cesalpino, Cremonini, Ficino, Poggio, Simone Porzio, Pomponazzi, Poliziano and Vanini—though Philipps acquits some of them, and also acquits Machiavelli. But the cases against most of these men are not well-founded. The notable mark of a pre-Reformation Christian was his faith; the mark of a post-Reformation Christian was his morality. The religious emphasis is different.

However immoral Sixtus, Alexander and Julius might have been, there is no evidence that they were either heretical or unbelieving. Their lives were unedifying, but their doctrine was sound. Perhaps even their motives were not unworthy. As practical Machiavellians they had the good end of the Church in view; though at this distance it is hard to separate their own interests from the interests of the Church. The popes seemed to assume that the two coincided. They tried to purge the sick body of the Church according to the prescriptions of the age; it is not entirely fair to blame the papacy because the prescriptions were poisonous, rather than remedial, to religion. The popes of the age are pieces of the age; they do not differ very much in their intentions and practice from the kings who established the much-admired national unities of Europe. But the founders of the monarchies—Louis XI, Henry VII, Ferdinand and Isabella—were heavy people, dangerous and efficient because they believed in their missions and gave them all their energy. The popes were inconsistent and less successful; it was almost as if they felt at heart that their secular ambitions were tainted, and therefore not to be taken too seriously. The age in Italy has usually been called a cynical one, and this quotation from Bandino makes it clear why:

> No one passed for an accomplished man, who did not entertain heretical opinions about Christianity; at the court the ordinances of the catholic church, and passages of holy writ, were spoken of only in a jesting manner; the mysteries of the faith were despised.

Lightness and inconsistency was everywhere. Aeneas Sylvius, on taking holy orders, claimed he 'forsook Venus for Bacchus'; among his many works is the witty but immoral play *Chrisis*, quite unsuitable for a churchman. Cardinal Bibbiena praised God that Giuliano de' Medici was bringing his young wife to Rome, 'the only thing we want is a court with ladies'. Yet Aeneas Sylvius, as Pius II, did everything in his power to try to save Christendom from the Turks.

The intellectual attacks on tradition and authority, and the questionable proceedings of the papal temporal policy, left most in Italy uncertain as to the present or future. In such a climate the consolations of art are felt more keenly. Even the cynical and mannered conduct of the Italian courts was an artifice enabling men to keep their poise in difficult times. And the more difficult the times, the greater was the attraction of the other world of art, contrasting its order and logic to the chaos of everyday life. Thus the rise of the pope's temporal power, under Sixtus IV, marked the beginning of a great age of papal patronage of every kind of artist. Sixtus found Rome squalid and ruined, he left it a planned city of decent thoroughfares and solid, if not very distinguished, buildings. To enrich his new buildings, he called to Rome such artists as Ghirlandaio, Perugino, Domenico, Botticelli, Filippino Lippi and Melozzo da Forlì. According to Vasari, Sixtus's taste was not of the best, and many of his artists strained under his direction. But he gave them work and established a precedent for patronage. Literature, which had suffered a little under the suspicions of Paul II, throve again. Platina had charge of the Vatican library. Argyropoulos lectured in Greek. Filelfo worked for, and quarrelled with, Sixtus. The proud

Julius II, delighting in magnificence, employed the men most capable of realizing his mighty projects. Vasari says that his greatest concern was for his future fame. But he had the genius to entrust his monuments to Michelangelo, Bramante and Raphael; and he deserves his fame, if only as their patron. On April 18, 1506, Julius laid the foundation stone for the new St. Peter's, for which Bramante had drawn up the designs. For both Sixtus and Julius, art had been only a small diversion in their busy political and warlike careers. But for Leo X, befitting the son of Lorenzo de' Medici, art was everything. On the horizon, Luther's clouds gathered; the thunders of theological controversy roared against the Church; but in Rome Leo cultivated gentle and social arts in the papal court. 'His chief object', says the contemporary *Vita Leonis*, 'was to lead a cheerful life, and shut out care and grief of mind by every means.' The garden of the mind produced its fruits—Sannazaro, Bembo, Vida, Raphael; the little world of art asserted itself against the troubled outside.

Beneath the intellectual upheavals of the late mediaeval and Renaissance ages ran the ordinary current of everyday life. And no account of the times can neglect the grimness, and even horror, apparent everywhere. The usual town was neither beautiful nor healthy. To fastidious people, like Erasmus, who had learnt delicacy of mind from the clean Romans and the healthy Greeks, almost every prospect was nauseous. In a letter of 1524, to Wolsey's doctor, he complains about the condition of England:

> Again, almost all the floors are of clay and rushes from the marshes, so carelessly renewed that the foundation sometimes remains for twenty years, harbouring there below spittle and vomit and urine of dogs and men, beer that hath been cast forth and remnants of fishes and other filth unnamable. . . . I feel certain that the island would be far more healthy if they gave up the use of rushes. . . . It would also help if the multitude could be persuaded to a sparer diet and more moderate use of salt meat; and, again, if public opinion required of the officials that the streets should be less defiled with filth and urine, and that the roads in the neighbourhood should be cared for.

Nor is this the evidence of an hostile witness, for he adds, 'I feel favourably towards the land which gave me hospitality for so long time.' There were places in Europe more gracious than the English town, in particular the great trading cities of the Low Countries, southern Germany and northern Italy; but in general the tenor of life, from highest to lowest degree, was coarse and violent. Even the code of chivalry did not restrain the brutality of princes. Concern with pride and honour made men touchy and quick to fight; 'princes are men,' wrote the chronicler Chastellain, 'and their affairs are high and perilous, and their natures are subject to many passions, such as hatred and envy; their hearts are veritable dwelling places of these, because of their pride in reigning.' Froissart, the great historian of chivalric warfare, does not gloss over the many monstrous acts; the English soldiers murdering their prisoners at Aljubarrota, and despoiling and destroying Caen; the Scotch massacre at Durham; Christians mutilating and torturing the Turks at Comette; the rape of the nuns at Origny St. Benoiste. In the inflamed Italian atmosphere, conduct was even more reckless and violent. Giovanni Maria Visconti, who ruled Milan for ten years, fed human flesh to his dogs. His miserable reign ended in assassination in 1412. Most Italian princes acted as if they agreed with Cesare Borgia's remark to Machiavelli: 'It is well to betray those who are masters of treachery.' Cesare himself, able, deceitful and implacable, was the most dangerous of all. His mouth was full of fair words while his hand gave sudden death. In 1503, he inveigled the *condottieri* generals, Oliverotto and Vitellozzo, to Sinigaglia, and had them strangled at night. According to the diary of Sebastiano di Branca, Cesare had his brother killed and thrown into the Tiber. He sent men to waylay and stab his brother-in-law; and when he heard that the murderers had bungled the job, he forced his way into his sister's chamber and ordered an executioner to strangle the wounded man. He killed Peroto, the favourite of his father Alexander VI, while Peroto clung to the pope's robes; Alexander's clothes were sprinkled with his favourite's blood. Egidius of Viterbo found the times terrible:

> The dead of night covered all things. To say nothing of domestic tragedies, never was sedition and bloodshed more rife in the States of the Church; never were bandits more numerous; never was there more wickedness in the city; never did informers and assassins more abound. Not in their houses, in their chambers, or in their towers were men safe. Law of man and God alike was set at naught. Gold, violence and lust bore undisputed sway.

Instructed by the example of their superiors, the ordinary people did not inhibit their brutal instincts. The justice of the day was as hard as the people. Confessions extorted by torture were generally allowed, though Sir John Fortescue denied that this was the case in England. When Philip the Fair of France, with the connivance of the

French pope, Clement V, determined to destroy the Templars, evidence for every absurd proposition was procured by torture. But the king had his way. The people revelled in the inhuman sentences, for executions and tortures were public entertainment. Johan Huizinga gives many instances. The citizens of Mons paid a high price for a brigand so that they could have the pleasure of seeing him quartered. In 1488, at Bruges, magistrates suspected of treason were tortured on a platform in the market-place before the appreciative townsmen. The execution of a gang of robbers pleased greatly— 'people laughed a good deal, because they were all poor men'. In Paris, in 1427, the regent's treasurer taunted a well-born brigand about to be hanged. The treasurer mounted the ladder behind the condemned man, insulting and beating him; he also beat the hangman. The harried executioner made a mess of the job; the rope parted and the condemned fell, breaking a leg and some ribs. In this condition he was forced to mount the scaffold once more.

Very naturally, those who suffered most from the hard life and the brutalities of their fellows were the peasants and (their equivalents in the town) the manual workers drawn into the cities to serve the new industries of capitalism. Their despair at the swiftly changing agrarian and economic conditions of Europe was expressed by a number of revolts and uprisings throughout the late mediaeval period. Rural poverty and oppressive landowners accounted for such insurrections as the Jacquerie of France, in 1357, the English Peasants' Revolt in 1381, and the Hussite rebellions which disrupted Bohemia and Hungary from 1435 until 1514. In Germany especially, where the peasants' lot was perhaps the worst in Europe, owing to the political anarchy of the country and the undiminished feudal power of the petty nobles, the continual struggles of the fifteenth century finally led to the general uprising of 1524 which was put down with the greatest cruelty by the army of the nobles at Frankenhausen, in 1526. The grievances of the industrial workers employed in the important wool trade caused revolts in the Low Countries and in England. The weavers of Ghent, under the successive leadership of James and Philip van Artevelde, made intermittent trouble for some forty years after 1337. They were not properly subdued until young Charles VI of France destroyed the citizen army at the battle of Roosebeke in 1382. In England, the poor of Kent, including many fullers made unemployed by the disruption of the wool trade resulting from the Wars of the Roses, in 1450 marched with Jack Cade to Blackheath. Their complaint was the reasonable one that 'all the common people, what for taxes and tallages and other oppressions, might not live by their handwork and husbandry'. But this rising was as unsuccessful as the rest.

Nearly every rebellion of the lower classes was repressed with unnatural ferocity by their masters; and it is doubtful whether the peasants gained anything by their revolts except a premature death to relieve them from their extreme misery. Behind many of the movements lurked a vague communistic ideal, equally offensive to feudal barons, capitalist merchants and centralizing kings; and this may partly explain the unnecessary degree of force used against the peasants. Also the peasants, brutalized and depressed as they were, found it hard to rise above their element. Their mutual suspicion and lack of organization was foreseen by the great Franciscan preacher, Berthold of Regensburg, who compares them to fishes:

> The fish is a very poor and naked beast; it is ever cold, and liveth ever in the water, and is naked and cold and bare of all graces. . . . Because the fishes are poor and naked, therefore they devour one another in the water; so also do the poor folk; because they are helpless, therefore they have divers wiles and invent many deceits.

Oppressed by landowners, taxed by Church and state, ravaged by the Black Death of 1348 and succeeding plagues, there seemed no end to the peasant's pain. But in one respect the social reorganization caused a small current of amelioration to flow his way. The changes in the pattern of agriculture, away from the feudal strip system, and the new commercial industries of the towns, made the old feudal relationships unworkable. The cry was for free labour, and gradually the peasant was enfranchised. Personal servitude did not disappear; the French Revolution banished it by proclamation, but in Germany and Russia it lasted until the nineteenth century. It was not apparent at once to the peasants that they were much better off. Under the feudal arrangement, the best masters—the more humane monasteries for example—had looked after their peasants with paternal devotion. Now the freed peasant was thrown into the labour market where he suffered from all the vicissitudes inherent in the workings of an incompletely understood capitalism. Those who stayed on the land were often hurt by the agricultural changes. The rage for the quick profits of the wool trade turned England and Spain almost exlusively towards sheep farming, arable soil becoming pasturage and tenants being turned off the land. This policy made Castile the barren desert that it is today. England escaped that fate, but the social injustice caused was great; Thomas More, whose generous heart hated injustice, wrote against the various Enclosure Acts in his *Utopia*. But the loosening of the social bonds, and the freedom of peasant and worker to go from place to place, helped trade to flourish. Population and prosperity rose together, from about the middle of the fifteenth century onwards.

Since there was no part of society or aspect of life in which the Church was not involved, all the changes in the peasants' lot, and all the peasants' attempts at revolt, affected the Church. Indeed, demands for social justice and demands for reformation of the Church usually went together. Wyclif's teachings influenced John Ball and so influenced the Peasants' Revolt, though Wyclif himself showed no sympathy for the rebels of 1381. In Hungary, Hus (himself influenced by Wyclif) was, as the name implies, at the very heart of the Hussite risings. The 'Four Articles of Prague', in which the Hussites set out their principles in 1420, attacked the Church in its double roll of pastor and landowner. The Germans who rebelled in 1524 made both religious and social demands in their 'Twelve Articles of the Peasants'. The poor churchman, secular priest or mendicant friar, was not far removed from his brother the peasant, and the influences, such as the Black Death, which hurt the peasant, hurt the priest, making him poorer, more ignorant and more lax than before. The Church, in attempting to reform itself, faced an enormous difficulty. Since the religious and social implications in the doctrines of men like Wyclif and Hus were very thoroughly mixed, the Church, when fighting the supposed heresy of the doctrine, usually found it necessary to set herself against the just social programme as well. Also men like Wyclif and Hus served the cause of nationalism, demanding local men to be appointed to local offices, instruction of the laity in the vernacular tongue, and less direction from Rome. The Church, as the great champion of internationalism, could not be expected to agree to these nationalistic tendencies. Therefore, though the need for reform was well recognized, the Church insisted on her traditional rights in all their severity. In 1419, Convocation quickly reprimanded an English Franciscan named Russell who dared to preach that the poor people should not pay their tithes. Whatever the value of Wyclif's theological ideas, he assumes a double importance in history. First, wittingly or unwittingly, he connected doctrinal revolution with demands for social justice; secondly, his ideas tended to see a reformed Church as a national Church. These are the roads that lead to Luther. Thomas Fuller, describing the digging up of Wyclif's body, the burning of his remains and the scattering of his ashes—all at the order of the Council of Constance,—saw his doctrines drift out with his ashes:

> To Lutterworth they come, . . . take what was left out of the grave, and burn them to ashes, and cast them into the Swift, a neighbouring brook running hard by. Thus this brook hath conveyed his ashes into Avon, Avon into Severn, Severn into the narrow seas, they into the main ocean. And thus the ashes of Wickcliffe are the emblem of his doctrine, which now is dispersed all the world over.

The cries for reform rose up on all sides, from cardinals to peasants. A sixteenth-century committee of prelates found the state of the Church abominable: 'What a sight for the Christian who traverses the Christian world, is this desolation of the church! The shepherds have all deserted their flocks, and have left them to hirelings.' And another prelate weeps:

> Alas, who are they that make my eyes to be fountains of tears? Even those set apart have fallen away. The vineyard of the Lord is laid waste. If they went alone to destruction, it were an evil, yet one that might be borne: but as they are spread over all Christendom, like veins through the body, their iniquity must bring with it the ruin of the world.

Such poems as Langland's *Piers Plowman* spoke of the distress of the poor man. The voices of condemnation grew louder, some in sadness and some in hatred, from such diverse men as Valla, John Fisher, Ulrich von Hutten and Erasmus. And the Church listened and struggled slightly to reform. Dr. Lea, no friend to the Church, has listed thirty-six occasions before 1538 on which Church Councils complained about abuses in granting indulgences. But the Church faced this predicament; the ways of the Church were also the ways of the age; the one could not be changed without the other. Churchmen and laity, good and bad, were combined in a universal submission to a principle. This is how Langland put it:

> For all we are Christ's creatures, and of his coffers rich,
> And brethren as of one blood, beggars as well as earls.
> For on Calvary of Christ's blood Christendom gan spring
> And blood-brethren we became there, and gentlemen each one.

Religion was so much part of ordinary life that every movement or direction in the life outside religion produced a corresponding disturbance in the Church. Strong monarchs had found it necessary

to increase taxes greatly in order to meet the expenses of their ambitions. The popes, after Sixtus IV, wishing to be as strong as Louis
of France or Henry of England, also increased taxes. So, while the
Church Councils were questioning the abuses of indulgences, popes
like Alexander VI were pushing their sales as hard as they could.
And to make the purchase of indulgences even more attractive,
Alexander was the first to declare that they delivered souls from
purgatory. The mixture of the religious and the temporal was so
profoundly established that the wrongness of promoting temporal
schemes through the abuse of religious practice was not clearly
recognized. It sometimes happened that indulgences were offered
as a prize in a lottery. Two things were possible. Either the complex
society, shot through with religion, could be reformed entirely—
temporal and spiritual alike—so that men remained 'blood-brethren
of Christendom'. Or the secular could be separated from the spiritual,
the latter cleaned and given a different dress while the former continued its independent advance. Calvin tried the first way, and found
it unworkable; the rest of the Reformation took the easier road. The
popes of the Renaissance, those able men, had helped introduce the
Secular Spirit which finally won. After the Reformation, the sense
of the all-permeating ordinariness and naturalness of religion is lost.
Dante's world is, of course, completely shattered. But such figures
as Chaucer's Parson and Langland's Piers disappear from literature
also. After the Reformation, when the spiritual voice is heard, it
comes from the mystical heights of St. Teresa, St. John of the Cross,
Swedenborg or Blake; or it is polemical in Bossuet, and in Pascal and
his Jesuit opponents.

But Europe went towards that great change unsurely, and with no
clear purpose. Perhaps great revolutions, to borrow a phrase of
Hume's, are 'more properly felt than judged of'. Europe waited for
her feelings to tell her that she could go no further in the old ways.
The intellect and declared itself perplexed. Even reason seemed a
fragile tool. Ficino, the Platonic enthusiast, admitted this, but con-
soled himself with the story of Prometheus, who:

Instructed by the divine wisdom of Pallas, he gained possession of the
heavenly fire, that is, reason. Because of this very possession, on the
highest peak of the mountain, that is, at the very height of contemplation, he is rightly judged most miserable of all, for he is made
wretched by the continual gnawing of the most ravenous of vultures,
that is, by the torment of inquiry. This will be the case until he is
carried back to that same place from which he received the fire, so

that, just as he is now urged on to seek the whole by that one beam of celestial light, he will then be entirely filled by the whole light.

But that 'whole light', that perfect and all-combining knowledge, continued to elude. The scientist was abashed by the vastness of his new horizons. 'Seest thou the sun?' says Lipsius,

> He fainteth. The Moone? She laboureth and languisheth. The Starres? They faile and fall. And howsoever the wit of man cloaketh and excuseth these matters, yet there have happened and daily do in that celestiall bodie such things as confound both the rules and wittes of Mathematicians.

The moral philosopher and metaphysician were equally at loss. Jeremy Taylor wrote:

> But besides this, reason is such a box of quicksilver that it abides nowhere; it dwells in no settled mansion; it is like a dove's neck, as a changeable taffeta; it looks to me otherwise than to you, who do not stand in the same light that I do: and if we inquire after the law of nature by the rules of our reason, we shall be uncertain as the discourses of the people or the dreams of disturbed fancies.

Awareness of ignorance displaced the former pride in knowledge. Petrarch, who seems in so many ways to be the first figure of the Renaissance, in 1367 had written a little work entitled *On my own Ignorance and that of many Others*; and this sceptical note had persisted through the next two centuries in such works as Nicholas of Cusa's *De docta ignorantia* (1440), Montaigne's *Essais* (1580), Sanchez's *Quod nihil scitur* (1581), and Charron's *De la sagesse* (1601). The nominalists of the fourteenth century, generally disillusioned about metaphysics, had accepted the need for authority in spiritual matters. The sceptics of the Renaissance, finding man smaller than had once been thought, also looked for authority. The papacy, whose conduct by now was so thoroughly bad, no longer commanded respect. The ideal of a united Christendom seemed more hopelessly far away than ever. It was clear to most that directions for the good life were hardly likely to come from Alexander VI or Julius II; and the Church lost authority in proportion to the papal misconduct. Many now looked to nature for those rules of right conduct which had previously been given by the Church. 'True law', said Cicero, the idol of the humanists, 'is right reason in agreement with nature; it is of universal application, unchanging and everlasting; it summons to duty by its commands, and averts from wrong-doing by its prohibitions.' And those who were impressed with the new wonders of nature, doubly revealed by the discoveries of the Renaissance scientists and by the voyages of Columbus and the Portuguese navigators, were glad to follow the Roman opinion. The community of man under nature became a worthy ideal. But 'nature' took on very different forms in different minds. The philosophies of nature of such men as Giordano Bruno, Campanella, Gassendi and Paracelsus tended towards pantheism, though most of these philosophers considered themselves good Christians. On the other hand, men like Montaigne and Charron saw nature as the regulator of human actions: 'natural' conduct led to wise and moral lives, quite independent of the teachings of religion. 'I desire', wrote Charron, 'that one should be a good man without paradise and hell; these words are, in my view, horrible and abominable, "if I were not a Christian, if I did not fear God and damnation, I should do this or that".'

To those in the fifteenth and early sixteenth centuries who still wished to live the Christian life, appalled by the lurid contemporary history in Church and state alike, simplicity and moral goodness became all important. Gerard Groote, preaching in the Yssel valley between 1380 and 1383, set a simple pattern for the exemplary Christian. His followers, known as the Brethren of the Common Life, establishing two schools at Deventer and Zwolle, by their example and their instruction made the principles of Groote famous through the Christian world. From their little corner in the Low Countries, the Brethren sent out a most profound and wide-spread influence; for among the pupils of Deventer were Thomas à Kempis, Cardinal Nicholas of Cusa and Erasmus. Groote, according to Kempis, 'laboured in the spirit of John the Baptist, laying the axe to the root of the tree'. And the Brethren saw their community as an attempt to return to the fundamentals of Christian piety. Kempis's *Imitation of Christ* is a handbook of the new spirit, which is often called the *devotio moderna*. The Brethren were not all churchmen; the layman had his place in their community. Neither was their education a preparation for the religious life only. The Brethren attempted to break down the mediaeval barriers, often legal and artificial, between the religious and the layman. But in doing so they also raised the secular life to a new dignity. Now devout men saw quite clearly that they could serve God outside religious orders. Thomas More was drawn towards the religious life, but decided that he could serve best in the secular world; and Erasmus, having been forced in his youth (as he later claimed) to take the vows of an Augustinian, spent years trying to escape what was to him a disability.

The secular power of the French and Spanish kings had humiliated the papacy. Now the layman asserted that his life was no less worthy than that of the priest; for morality and good conduct made a man worthy, not the privileges of his position. The Church had never taught that a priestly position would save an immoral man, but many of the clergy acted as if this were so. This pretension became less acceptable, as a witty Dialogue, acted at Paris in 1514, shows. Julius II, in warlike array, arrives at the gate of heaven, and demands entrance; St. Peter is reluctant:

Peter : You must show your merits first; no admission without merit.
Julius : What do you mean by merits?
Peter : Have you taught true doctrine?
Julius : Not I. I've been too busy fighting. There are monks to look after doctrine, if that's of any consequence.
Peter : Have you gained souls to Christ by pious example?
Julius : I've sent a good many to Tartarus.
Peter : Have you worked any miracles?
Julius : What! Miracles are out of date.
Peter : Have you said your prayers diligently?
Julius : You waste your breath.
Peter : These are the qualities that make a good pope.

More and more, the example of men like the Brethren of the Common life seemed to indicate that the organization of the Church was a wicked, unnecessary superstructure, hindering rather than promoting true devotion. The Brethren were truly religious; but in their small community, encouraging simple virtues, they turned away from the great vision of a triumphant Church directing the economic, social and spiritual welfare of Europe. Morality meant more than dominion. In their individualistic way, they encouraged the revolt of the Reformation.

For a while, just before Luther's storm, there were signs that Europe was becoming reconciled to its shaken and uncertain state. The despair caused by the fallen ideal of Christendom grew less sharp. A new ideal of the 'good life' of the citizen, a community of men acting in accordance with 'natural' laws, was replacing the old Christian asceticism. Those who needed authority now looked to the strong monarchies rather than to the papacy or the Church; for the ambitious kings, by their policies, had helped to prepare for the freer social life and the economic prosperity of the early sixteenth century. Though the age was certainly not anti-Christian, the Church lost influence, until even such a traditional Church function as education was now often in the hands of laymen. The Italian humanist school-masters were the greatest teachers of their day; when Colet established his new school at St. Paul's, in 1505, he appointed merchants and city dignitaries, not clergymen, as governors. Men saw that the life of the Church did not correspond with the Christian life, and very many attacked with savage, satiric force corruption in Church organization and practice; hence the violence of Ulrich von Hutten against the monks, and the scurrility of the popular satire against the Church, such as the anonymous *Epistolae obscurorum vivorum* of 1515. Reform was essential, but hardly anyone felt that the Church needed changes in doctrine or structure. Colet, who in a famous sermon of 1511 said the most terrible things about the clergy, also said, 'The waye whereby the churche may be reformed into better facion is not for to make newe lawis For there be lawes many inowe.'

The period just before the Reformation shows an increased perception through the whole of society. The abundance of new information was disordered and puzzling, causing doubt and distrust of reason. But men had so successfully freed themselves from the natural (and primitive) mediaeval desire for wholeness and harmony (the *integritas* and *consonantia* of Aquinas), that they were able to stand a degree of disorder. They were even able to see that some element of disorganization, disorder and uncertainty must rightly exist, and for the good, in all human affairs. This recognition is a sign that the authority of the old patterns which had for so long tied the European mind was losing its hold, and that a new mature culture was emerging. Erasmus, the most characteristic representative of the new culture, describes the spirit of acceptance in *The Praise of Folly*:

> No society, no cohabitation can be pleasant or lasting without folly; so much so, that a people could not stand its prince, nor the master his man, nor the maid her mistress, nor the tutor his pupil, nor the friend his friend, nor the wife her husband for a moment longer, if they did not now and then err together, now flatter each other; now sensibly conniving at things, now smearing themselves with some honey of folly.

'Folly' is tolerance and practical wisdom, two things in which the Middle Ages had been remarkably deficient. The new spirit might have become triumphant. Curiosity, geniality and tolerance spread infectiously. That worldly pope, Leo X, was liberal-minded and generous to a fault. Thomas More, Erasmus's great friend, in his

THE SIEGE OF CONSTANTINOPLE BY THE TURKS

DUKE PHILIP OF BURGUNDY COMBATS WEAKNESS

Utopia wrote a book that was as gay, sparkling and speculative as *The Praise of Folly* itself. Communism, abolishment of money, euthanasia for incurables, natural religion without revelation are all put forward, perhaps not seriously, but as the possibilities from a fertile mind. In the same work More criticizes most seriously the corruption in the Church, and the injustice in the state of his time. More was not afraid of new scholarship, or new thought. He firmly defended the work and learning, often daring, of his friend Erasmus against conservative criticism:

> You charge Erasmus with having said that Jerome, Ambrose, Augustine, and other Fathers made occasional mistakes. Since the Fathers admit it themselves, why do you blame Erasmus? When Augustine translates one way and Jerome another, they cannot both be right.

And again:

> You complain of the study of Greek and Hebrew. You say it leads to the neglect of Latin. Was not the New Testament written in Greek? Did not the early Fathers write in Greek? Is truth only to be found in Gothic Latin?

And on *The Praise of Folly*, he says, '*Folly* contains more wisdom and less folly than many books that I know, including your own'.

The mood did not last. In 1517, Luther burst the doors and diverted the cleansing waters of the Reformation through the Augean stables of Church corruption; but the elegant young bloom of tolerance was swept away too in the rapid current. The religious struggle, once the issue had become clear, was disputed in the old way—full of prejudice, hatred and suspicion. Thomas More, who had so light-heartedly advocated communism in *Utopia*, found it necessary, in the *Confutation* of 1532, to condemn the communism of the Anabaptists as one of their 'horrible heresies'. But More knew that he had been drawn into a harder, narrower and more bitter world; and in the same *Confutation* he added with weary regret:

> Would God, after all my labours done, so that the remembrance of their pestilent errours were araced out of Englishe mennes heartes and their abominable bookes burned up, myne owne were walked with them, and the name of these matters utterly putte in oblivion.

Only Erasmus walked the uneasy balance between the two sides, claimed by both parties though he gave his service to the Muse of learning and knowledge alone. Though his character had defects— he was liable to self-pity and known to use rather too much flattery—

he stands as a reprimand to the age. He was as free from violent national feeling as he was from religious animosity. 'Everyone', he wrote, 'who is initiated in the holy heritage of the Muses which is common to all I consider my countryman.' And, 'Towards all nations I am a blank paper.' He was the last great man who lived as a European, not as the citizen of this or that country. A breed, a way of life, a possibility for the future died with him.

It is often thought that the Catholic Church—or the papacy—is the villain of pre-Reformation history, while nationalism is seen as the dragon-killing hero, releasing the people from foreign domination and spiritual bondage. But corrupt as it was, the Church in its international policy was not without wisdom or conscience. The papal appointments to foreign benefices were very often worthier and more pious men than those the king wished to put in. The actions of the nationalistic kings were often oppressive, arbitrary and tyrannical; and the worst period for the Church was when the Renaissance popes attempted to run the Church and a nationalistic Italian policy at the same time. But the nationalism of countries defeated the internationalism of Christendom, and the papacy, beset by a multitude of historical problems, hastened the process. The ideal of the Church failed because the papacy and the Church ascribed too stringently to theoretical systems which no longer worked (if they ever had). The new ideas which threatened the order of things were not revolutionary in the sense that they had never been thought of before; but they became revolutionary when people saw that they could base their ideas and conduct on them and, in doing so, successfully sweep away the old patterns. One who had been a crank in the thirteenth century would have been a reformer in the late fifteenth century. The late Middle Ages were not overthrown by a violent, irresistible force of new thinking and reform. The men of the late Middle Ages toppled their own structure in surprise. The ideas which, as they thought, had flitted extravagantly but harmlessly round the battlements, had in fact undermined the whole structure. No one realized the gravity of the Church's position until too late. Before the cracks and the rents could be shored up and patched, the building was down, and the foundations of a new kind of European society were being sunk into the ground.

PART TWO

*IGNATIUS LOYOLA AND
THE EMBATTLED CHURCH*

Chapter III

'A GREAT AND VAIN DESIRE
TO GAIN HONOUR'

IGNATIUS LOYOLA was born, most probably in 1491, the thirteenth and last child of the lord of Oñaz and Loyola, in the Basque province of Guipúzcoa. He came into a nation about to enter into its period of characteristic greatness, for the year 1492 in Spain saw such notable events as the surrender of Granada to the Catholic Kings, the expulsion of the Jews, and Columbus's discovery of the New World. And the Spain of the early sixteenth century, unified and powerful but also hard and uncompromising, no doubt helped to direct Ignatius's Basque temperament.

The home of Loyola, something between a manor-house and a castle, stands about a mile from the town. As it was the headquarters for a quarrelsome and energetic clan, the house was perhaps never beautiful. But in 1491 its practical severity was tempered by surrounding trees; now broad avenues display the poor limitations of the house, encrusted and embellished as it is by the unfortunate hand of piety, and the admirers drive in to park their cars where the trees had been. The town of Azpeitia is not beautiful either. An unimpressive little river, the Urola, scratches a rocky course through it, and the buildings jut aggressively over the river banks. In the town are flour- and sawmills, and nearby, jasper, marble and limestone have been quarried for many centuries. The town has always spoken of hard work and the unsettled commerce of a border province. And the family of Loyola had shown the familiar qualities of border chieftains—independence and a touchy pride in their nobility, both the irascibility and the endurance of soldiers. War is the first business of such chiefs, and war determined the fortunes of most of the Loyolas, including Ignatius. Of Ignatius's brothers, two were killed fighting for Spain in the Italian wars and one was killed in the conquest of America. And when the king's wars provided no work, the members of the house proved their manhood in the family feuds of the Basque country. Ignatius's own grandfather, and twenty other troublesome landowners, were banished for four years by the King of Castile.

The profession of arms, which had always been considered a career of great honour among the ill-educated and ambitious aristocracy of Europe, attained a special dignity in Spain. For throughout the mediaeval period Spain attempted to rid the peninsula of the embarrassing presence and alien religion of the Moors. Quite naturally the martial Loyolas were caught up in these campaigns; at the battle of Beotibar, in 1321, no less than seven members took the field. The prolonged crusade, the holy object of driving the Moors from the country, gave to the Christian soldiers a sense of virtue which does not usually attach to the rapine and destruction of armies. The annihilation of a superior civilization and a peaceful, industrious community became a religious duty. And when those forward-looking rulers Ferdinand and Isabella added the ideal of national unity to the existing Christian sentiment the prestige of a Spanish soldier's career stood very high indeed. Perhaps no other soldier in Europe combined religious feeling and national feeling as did the Spaniard. The Crusades and the campaigns against the Turks had been waged in the name of Christ, but these had been ruined by fatal jealousies and antagonisms. Only in the Hungary of Hunyadi and Corvinus had the Christian duty been allied to national hopes; but Hungarian nationalism had not survived the combined enmity of the Turks and the Habsburgs. Spain alone was successful against the infidel; the surrender of Granada in 1492 helped to compensate for the fall of Constantinople nearly forty years earlier. The Spanish soldier felt the pride that comes from success. He had become a forbidding figure, stern and relentless, as the famous Gonsalvo de Cordoba showed himself in Italy and against the Moors, but the more haughty and terrible because his work seemed almost to be an extension of the priestly function. The cruelty and deception that Cardinal Ximenes practised against the defeated Moors between 1499 and 1502 flowed from a man of the sternest rectitude and the very best intentions. The fierceness of his love for Christianity ensured that the Moors could expect nothing but woe from him. When his policy of forcible conversion led to the inevitable revolt, the savage ascetic saw this as the means to another Christian victory. Rebels naturally forfeited life and property, but they might be forgiven if they left the realm or accepted Christianity. In February 1502, Isabella signed an edict to this effect; those who could not leave, and very many could not, became reluctant

Christians and so were brought under the jurisdiction of the Inquisition.

Perhaps Spain gained strength from the nationalistic and religious bigotry which led first to the expulsion of the Jews and then, ten years later, to the expulsion of the Moors. But the proud, fanatical and cruel Christianity of the army, which was the legacy of the successful campaigns against the Moors, hardly made the Spaniards ideal men to bring peace and contentment to the new territories that the great discoveries in the New World had suddenly opened up. The army had converted the Moors; the sword of the conquistador attempted to impress the patient virtues of the New Testament. Ignatius Loyola, later to become a soldier, was born into this military world.

In 1522 Martin Luther, reflecting on the great similarity between his own thought and that of Wessel Gansfort nearly a century before, wondered why his own life was full of pain and persecution while Gansfort, who had gone almost to the same daring limits as Luther, had lived undisturbed in the quiet community of the Brethren of the Common Life. 'Possibly', Luther decided, 'it was because he lived free from blood and war, in which particular alone he differs from me.' The Europe of Gansfort was not in fact that much more peaceful than the later Europe of Luther. But in the fifteenth century much of the warlike energy had been directed in the name of Christendom against Islam. When that business was finished, with complete failure in the East and success in Spain, the princes could expend their irritability, rubbed raw by growing nationalism, only within Europe itself. Besides religious differences, failure, bad temper and the restrictions of Europe brought on the wars of the Reformation. Luther, a fighter if ever there was one, had thrown his challenge at the Church. He wished the Church to admit that its universal pretensions belonged to the past; to maintain them in the present caused only corruption and abuse. In the same way the German princes fought against the impossible claims of the German Emperor. Luther's revolt, whatever the justice and purity of his first intentions, was a German revolt and soon became yet another element in the seemingly endless anarchy of German history. The cause of Protestantism tended to become just another piece of ammunition which the German princes hurled at each other in their complicated manoeuvres after power. In Spain alone the ideal of a universal Christendom had not died. It was kept alive by the piety of Queen Isabella (and after her Charles V and Philip II), by the strength of clergymen such as Ximenes, by the success against the Moors and by the Christian duty to bring the lands of the New World under the rule of Christ. Columbus's second expedition, in 1493, carried Fray Boyl, a Benedictine especially entrusted with the task of converting the Indians. Ignatius Loyola inherited this Spanish confidence in the world-role of Christianity. His compact and well-ordered band was for the service of the Church alone; he was prepared that his Society should be disbanded rather than fall into the hands of an outsider.

Almost nothing is known about Ignatius's early life. He himself found nothing extraordinary and little that was pleasing in his youth. The document known as his Confessions, which he dictated in the severe third person to Gonzales de Camara after 1553, dismisses his early years in one sentence: 'Up to twenty-six years of age he was a man given to the vanities of the world and his chief delight was in martial exercises with a great and vain desire to gain honour.' And such was his lack of interest in the past that even that statement is inaccurate: he was about thirty when he turned aside from his vain ways.

At an early age Ignatius entered the service of Velasquez de Cuellar, Treasurer to Queen Isabella. The way to preferment and military honour lay through such an apprenticeship, and Ignatius's patron was well placed to teach him 'the exercises of a gentleman'. These exercises, while making for an energetic and healthy body, did not tax the intelligence very far. Nor, while Isabella was alive, could the life of a court official have been much fun; the queen's piety was inclined to cast a pall. Perhaps the entertainment became more lively under Germaine de Foix, whom Ferdinand married after Isabella's death, for Cuellar still managed to keep his connections at court. The education which Ignatius received, and the way of life into which he had entered, had a curiously old-fashioned air even at the beginning of the sixteenth century. The new learning, the new science, the social ferments of the Renaissance seemed not to have touched him. In his youth he had always before him the ideals of military chivalry, those conventions which were becoming old and wornout even in the time of Froissart and which appeared so ridiculous at the Oath of the Pheasant. The minor nobility tucked away in the odd Basque corner of Europe might be expected to be conservative. And after his training Ignatius, a Loyola and a potential soldier, seemed typical of his kind. The few glimpses that we have of him in his twenties show a dapper little man elegantly got up, with a sword and dagger at his side, overproud of his rather ruffianly family of whom three brothers were soldiers and one, Pedro, was the unexemplary rector of Azpeitia with four illegitimate children.

A man trained in the artificial modes of chivalry was subject to all the dangers of the system. 'Their natures', as Chastellain had warned, 'are subject to many passions, such as hatred and envy; their hearts are veritable dwelling places of these;' and the young Ignatius had his troubles with authority. In 1515 he and his brother, Pedro, were arrested for some misdemeanour which, in the words of the judge, was 'very enormous because it was committed at night with malice aforethought'. What this act was, we do not know, but the legal argument turned on the status of the defendants. Pedro was obviously subject to ecclesiastical jurisdiction; but Ignatius, too, claimed benefit of clergy on the grounds that he had received the tonsure some time before. His claim was disallowed for his name was not on the list of the vicar-general at Pamplona; moreover he had 'mingled in secular affairs not at all consistent with membership in the clerical order'. The conduct of this young man whose 'long hair covered his ears' was not that of a clergyman. Nor was his dress:

> His mantle was too short and was either blue or green or yellow. He wore coloured hose and a coloured cap and went out in public usually with a leather cuirass or breastplate, with a sword and dagger and carrying a crossbow or some other weapon.

After Ignatius's death, the Bishop of Salamanca recalled that, as a young man, he had seen Ignatius, jostled by a crowd in the street at Pamplona, draw his sword and charge the crowd with such determination that, had he not been held back, someone undoubtedly would have been killed. Obviously a quick-tempered young man, but a gallant and a lover too, as chivalry demanded; Polanco, his secretary for so many years, called the young Ignatius 'free enough in the love of women'.

A rising soldier needed patrons. Cuellar had fallen out with Charles, the new King of Spain, and had paid the usual price of the insubordinate vassal, dying in disgrace and broken, but leaving Ignatius, for his loyal service, two horses and a useful five hundred ducats. With these he went to Pamplona and offered his service to the Duke of Najera, the rich and powerful viceroy of Navarre. A soldier as keen and debonair as Ignatius, and one with two horses and money in his pocket, was not to be turned down. Moreover, the duke faced the greatest difficulties in Navarre, a province poised between Spain and France yet not happy to belong to either. Ignatius, a Basque, was not only a soldier but also a useful diplomatic aide in coming to terms with his fellow Basques. When the town of Najera revolted against the duke, Ignatius was naturally in the van of the attack. And when the town was taken he acted with an elegance and compassion worthy of the highest chivalric ideal: he refused to join in the plunder of the town, for an *hidalgo* served for honour and not riches. How old-fashioned such a gesture was; yet remembering the greed and the barbarism of the French and Spanish armies in Italy, and the dishonour of sixteenth-century warfare generally, how refreshing and humane! He had, said Polanco, a reputation for never bearing malice, and for always fighting like a man of honour. In his few years with the Duke of Najera he had a variety of experience but not much action. When, in 1521, France and Spain once more renewed their argument over Navarre, Ignatius was eager for the honourable rewards that warfare brings.

King Ferdinand had attached great importance to the annexation of Navarre. His anxiety was natural enough as the possession of Navarre extended the territory of the Catholic King right up to the natural barrier of the Pyrenees. Consequently he directed against the Navarrese all the wiles of his political cunning; had them declared heretics and schismatics by the complaisant Pope Julius II, and followed up the bull of excommunication by seizing the crown. His relief at the success of this stroke was so great that, according to Gomara, he wept for what 'he had won with the full authority of the Church . . . in a war for a just cause, as his Holiness had declared'. Between 1512 and 1521 the French made repeated attempts to recapture the province. But with the whole of the peninsula now unified under one crown, Spain was not inclined to let go. In 1521, a revolt in Castile against the foreign, Flemish administration of Charles V gave the French their opportunity, and by the middle of May they were before Pamplona. The Duke of Najera wisely withdrew, seeking reinforcements, leaving only a small garrison in the citadel. Ignatius, in search of reputation, volunteered to stay with this garrison. The other officers, with a sound appreciation of the military position, were all for surrender; but Ignatius had not stayed behind for that. Again, when negotiations were opened with the French, Ignatius was the one who stood out the firmest against the unfavourable terms which the French offered. The Spaniards prepared to fight, Ignatius joyfully, his companions with less enthusiasm. On May

20, in the bombardment before the final assault, a cannon ball smashed his right leg and badly cut his left. The French, finding him shattered and helpless, treated him gently. After some rudimentary surgery, he was placed on a litter and sent the fifty miles back to the family home at Azpeitia.

For a while it looked as if the little man with the painful wounds might end his life in perfect conformity to his favourite chivalric model, the romance *Amadis de Gaul*. He had fashioned his life as 'a gentleman in virtuous and gentle discipline', and now the loyal servitors in the family house waited for his death after heroic action. Three brothers had died in battle, eager aspirants after the virtues which the *Amadis* preached, military virtues which so often led to death that Peter Martyr had wondered whether the whole of the noble blood of Spain would be shed at once so enthusiastic were young Spanish gentlemen for the life of honour. But Ignatius did not add his name to that catalogue of waste. His natural good health, his strength of mind and his physical courage saw him through, hindered though he was by the barbaric efforts of the doctors; for he had, too, the heroic fortitude of the romance. His claim in later life that 'in all those operations which he suffered before and after this, he never spoke a word of showed any sign of pain, except clench-ing his fists hard' showed that he still acted according to a great ideal. Since he was likely to be left a cripple, he thought he could no longer follow the active life of the knight-errant, but the exemplar of his youth still helped him to find patience and self-discipline. This force of the ideal was not surprising. Cervantes himself, the breaker of the dusty statues of chivalry, admitted the greatness of the *Amadis de Gaul*. It was the first book that the barber, the curate and the housekeeper took from Don Quixote's shelves:

> 'There is something mysterious about this matter,' said the curate; 'for, as I have heard, this was the first book of knight-errantry printed in Spain, and all the others have had their origin and source here, so that, as the arch-heretic of so mischievous a sect, I think he should, without a hearing, be condemned to the fire,'
> 'No,' said the barber, 'for I, too, have heard that it is the best of all the books of its kind that have been written, and therefore, for its singularity, it ought to be forgiven.'

At Azpeitia his leg had to be broken and reset again, a process that Ignatius called 'butchery'. The doctors were gloomy and thought that by St. Peter's Day he would be finished. But Ignatius in simple

words recorded his triumph over both medical practice and prog-
nostication: 'the sick man had always been devoted to St. Peter and
it so pleased God that by midnight he was better.' To prevent his
right leg setting rather shorter than his left, he persuaded the doctors
to devise a kind of rack which was as painful as it was effective, and
which kept him in bed for a long time.

Bored, as only a man of action can be when tied to his bed, he
was driven by desperation to the few unappetising volumes that the
castle of Loyola possessed. He found some lives of the Saints and a
Castilian translation of the long, worthy and popular *Life of Christ*
written by a certain Ludolf of Saxony in the fourteenth century.
His Confessions, dictated so long afterwards, recalled the effect of
this simple reading:

> When he laid aside these books, he did not always think of what he
> had read, but, sometimes, of the worldly things about which he used
> to think before. And out of many vain things which offered themselves
> to his mind, one took such possession of his heart that he was buried
> in thought about it two or three and even four hours without noticing
> it; imagining what he had to do in the service of a lady; the means he
> must use to go where she was, his motto, the words he would say to
> her, the deeds of arms he would do in her service.

Stirred by the heroism of the Saints and the calm perfection of
Christ's life, he called to mind the only other ideal world he had
known—the shadow world of service and gallantry of the mediaeval
chivalry which he had followed so eagerly until then. Sanctity and
chivalry are both types of perfection, and both are to be reached
only through sacrifice and training. Both present their challenges.
They are related worlds. Yet of the two sanctity is the more sensible
and practical ideal. There is a fatal silliness at the heart of chivalry,
a sentimentality which hides the true object of the ideal and which
makes the discipline and the ardour of the initiate a lie; the protestations of service were attempts at adultery, and the glorious deeds
were the usual cruelties of warfare. The rest of Europe had found
this out; perhaps Ignatius began to feel that a badly broken leg was
a poor reward for some twenty years of training and service. Lying
in bed, he began to feel the challenge contained in the opening
words of Ludolf's *Life of Christ*: 'A man can have no foundation
other than Jesus Christ. . . . Therefore, whoever wishes to escape
the damnation due his sins and to be corrected in spirit, must not
forsake that foundation, because there he will find remedies for all

his needs.' In his reveries, Ignatius started to wonder whether he might act like St. Thomas or St. Dominic rather than like Amadis or Don Galaor or Lisuarte of the romances. For some time these paladins of the opposing ideals of sanctity and chivalry clambered across the battlefield of his mind until gradually the issues cleared. The Confessions tell of his gradual illumination:

> When he was dwelling on the worldly day dream he found much pleasure, but, when tired out, he ceased to think on that, he found himself arid and discontented: and when he imagined going barefoot to Jerusalem and eating only herbs and doing all the other penances which he saw the saints had done, he was contented and joyful not only in such thoughts but even after he was tired and had ceased to dwell on them. At first, however, he did not really weigh that difference, until one time his eyes were a little opened and he commenced to wonder on that difference and reflect on it, catching hold by experience of the fact that after one sort of thoughts he remained sad and after the others joyful, and so, little by little, coming to know the diversity of the spirits which moved him; the one of God, the other of the devil.

Joy, he makes it quite clear, was the beginning of his conversion, and by all accounts the contained, self-disciplined founder of the Jesuits carried this joy undiminished to his grave.

His leg had healed remarkable well. Even though he walked with a slight limp, he might still have resumed his career as a soldier. Later, he thought nothing of walking across Italy, from Rome to Venice. But he had seen the gleam of new possibilities, and he set himself to find the source of the light with his usual single-minded devotion. At first he felt mainly the uselessness of his past life. The honesty which compelled him to see the foolishness of the chivalric conventions also compelled him to feel disgust at his own conduct in following those conventions. Perhaps the revulsion of a good man at his own past faults always appears a little excessive. And Ignatius was encouraged to loathe his past by the very great force of his visual imagination. His mind was always full of concrete images, almost as if he had never learnt the technique of abstraction. So far as we know, the reading of his youth had included only the old mediaeval literature and the romances; and this reading had no doubt impressed on his mind the concrete vividness of the best mediaeval work and the pictorial effect of the romances. The adroit handling of the abstractions of thought was fostered and spread by the intellectual achievements of the Renaissance; but Ignatius was hardly touched by the Renaissance at all. Reflections on his sinful past

conjured up in his mind a vision: 'lying awake one night, he saw
clearly the image of Our Lady with the Holy Child Jesus; in which
sight he had for a considerable time very great comfort and it left
him with such loathing for all his past life, especially for his carnal
indulgences, that he seemed to be entirely freed from all evil pictures which had before been in his soul.' The 'evil pictures' of the
past were wiped away and his imagination was possessed by the
new, holy images so that 'from that hour [1521] until August 1555,
when this is written, he never again felt the least assenting to any
lustful impulse'. Soon even his brother and the household recognized
that Ignatius was a changed man.

In his enthusiasm for the new life, Ignatius had not thought much
about the practical details of the future. His only plan was to go to
Jerusalem, the typical ambition of the mediaeval Christian, and
after that he would see; perhaps he would enter a Carthusian
monastery, or wander the world as a poor man of God. But whatever
his future, with his customary energy he was eager to set out. So
overcoming the understandable misgivings of his brother, Martin
Garcia, he left Loyola and hastened to Navarette to settle his affairs
with the Duke of Najera:

> And remembering that the duke owed him a few ducats, he presented
> a claim for them to the treasurer and when the treasurer replied that he
> had no money and the duke heard of it, he said that he might fail to
> pay everybody else but not Loyola; to whom the duke wanted to give,
> because of past services, a good lieutenancy if he was willing to accept
> it. And he got the money, sent part to certain persons to whom he was
> under obligation and spent part of it on a picture of Our Lady in a
> shrine which was in bad condition, to restore it and to adorn it very well.
> And so dismissing two servants who had travelled with him, he started
> alone on his mule from Navarette to go to Montserrat.

He had cleared away the clutter of his past, and now set out in pursuit of a new life.

In his retreat from Loyola, abandoning his ambition and his
inheritance, Ignatius acted as a private Christian gentleman. His
only intention was to set his own soul in order, and he thought,
considering the sinfulness of his past life, that this would best be
done by imposing on himself some heavy, even spectacular, pen-
ances. He would strip his wretched body of its carnal affections and,
at the same time, demonstrate his devotion to God. 'All his purpose,'
commented Laynez drily, 'was to do those great outward works
because the saints had done them for the glory of God.' And Laynez,

one of his earliest companions and his successor as general of the
Society, further added:

> It seemed to him then that holiness was entirely measured by exterior
> asperity of life and that he who did the most severe penances would be
> held in the divine regard for the most holy, which idea made him
> determined to lead a very harsh life.

Hence the distribution of his money, and the journey by mule, and
the vow to go to Jerusalem.

Very early in his spiritual advancement he had conceived of the
world as a battleground between God and the devil. His interest at
first was in himself as the field of operations, and, as an ex-soldier, he
expected and prepared for an exacting campaign. The great simplicity of his first conception never altered; but he saw gradually
that the contest for souls takes place not only in the individual, but
also in society generally. He came to see Jerusalem not only as the
happy resting place for the person confirmed in holy virtue, but also
the symbolic ground on which to build the City of God, the perfect
Christian community. In Ignatius's *Spiritual Exercises* the participant hears of the 'two banners: the one of Christ our great Captain,
and the other of Lucifer the mortal enemy of our human nature'.
And the participant must imagine 'a vast plain around Jerusalem
where the supreme Captain General of the good is Christ'. The slow
accumulations of experience between 1521 and 1538 taught Ignatius
that the battle for a Christian society was fought over a terrain
different to the battlefield within the individual. In 1521 he was
hardly likely to have known that society needed some radical surgery
to keep it Christian. His notion was that the Church still enjoyed
universal dominion within Europe, and it would have been surprising for a Spaniard of his birth and education at that time to think
anything other than this. His response to the call of religion was the
typical response of the mediaeval individual who thought that the
Church, even though corrupt, was enduring and sacrosanct, and who
therefore worried only about his own state. In his ambition to go to
Jerusalem he was only following such well known mediaeval figures
as Henry V of England and Philip the Good of Burgundy (but with
a greater sincerity of purpose). Ignatius was still the chevalier of
God, prepared to conduct his own personal skirmishes on behalf of
the forces of the divine.

His holy belligerence was tested almost at once. On the road to
Montserrat he fell in with a Moor and engaged this courteous

Moslem in conversation about Our Lady. The Moor, speaking only with the voice of logic and ordinary human experience, 'said that he believed that the Virgin had conceived superhumanly, but he could not believe that she had remained a virgin after the birth of Christ: which opinion the pilgrim could not shake in spite of many reasons he gave'. The more Ignatius thought about this the more it seemed to him a reflection on the honour of the Virgin, which required revenge. He decided to leave the resolution of this matter to his mule—or rather to fate—allowing the mule to choose at the cross-roads whether he followed the Moor, or took the other road. The mule chose the path of sense, and the Moor was saved from the knife of Christian wrath.

This incident, slightly endearing now though serious enough at the time, helps to indicate the state of Ignatius's imagination. The way to Jerusalem, both practically and in the mind, meant a conflict with Islam. The importance which Ignatius attached to this journey shows the extent to which he looked backwards. He had yet to learn that the great conflict between Christendom and Islam was over. Jerusalem was no longer a challenge to the Christian claim to univer-sality for the very good reason that Christendom was no longer even united, let alone universal. But, of course, it took some time for men to perceive this; and Ignatius, firmly cradled in the literature of romance and in Spanish Catholicism, had a longer road to go towards the reality than most. The Moslem, for obvious reasons, was still very much in the Spanish consciousness, whereas the rest of Europe (except at the frontiers) had very quickly lost its interest in the East after 1453. Moreover, the traditional pre-occupation with Islam still lived in the old-fashioned world of the romances. The action of *Esplandian*, the second most popular (after *Amadis*) of all the Spanish romances, takes place almost entirely in the East, and describes the battles with Turks and Arabs. Though Ignatius had repudiated the ideals of chivalry, he could not shake off its habits. At the start his service of God was very much like his service of the Duke of Najera, except that he had substituted a holy ideal for a worldly ambition. In his Confessions he recalled his dreams on the road to Montserrat:

And as his mind was filled with ideas from Amadis de Gaul and other books of chivalry, things came into his head like them. And so he made up his mind to watch over his arms all one night without sitting or lying down, but now standing and now kneeling before the altar of Our Lady of Montserrat where he decided to leave his garments and clothe himself with the arms of Christ.

The Englishman who covered an eye in the Hundred Years' War and the Pole who for nine years ate standing up would have felt their kinship with the Ignatius of 1522.

> In such thoughts he found all his consolation, not considering anything interior, knowing nothing of humility, or charity, or patience, or discretion in ruling those virtues.

In Montserrat he made a general confession which lasted three days, hung up his sword and dagger by Our Lady's altar, and took a robe of sackcloth. On March 22, 1522, in his prickly garment, with one sandal only for his lame foot, and with a staff, he set out and completed very easily the short distance to Manresa. And there he stayed for nearly a year, detained by the plague in Barcelona and by the difficulty in obtaining a licence for his pilgrimage. At Manresa he began his spiritual education:

> In those days God was treating him like a boy in school, teaching him, and that was because of his rudeness and gross mind.

The history of this schooling is given, clearly and with much simple charm, in Ignatius's Confessions. The record is remarkable for the awareness that Ignatius later showed of the process going on in him during that year. He moved gradually from an extreme to a sensible position, yet he did this without slackening for an instant the force of his love and desire for religion.

He turned first to chasten whatever feelings of niceness and delicacy he retained from his upbringing; and he set about these with gothic exuberance. He let his hair grow long, rough and matted, and he even refused to cut his finger nails. Then he disciplined his body, eating no meat and drinking no wine. He rationed his sleep, spending several hours of the night in prayer: during the day he tramped the streets for alms. He was no doubt an extraordinary sight (he innocently wrote that 'his desire to escape all public notice was very strong'), and a notable addition to the eccentricities of the town. His strong visual sense once more began to draw him visions. Until then he had been invariably joyful 'without, however, having any understanding of inner spiritual things'. But—

> On the days when that vision continued or a little before it began (for it lasted many days) there came a thought which troubled him, bringing before him the difficulty of his life, as if someone had said to him within his soul, 'And how can you endure such a life for the seventy years you have to live?'

Fluctuations of feeling drove him to extreme states:

> Sometimes he was so insipid that he had no taste for prayer, nor in
> hearing mass, nor in any other prayer which he made. And other times
> quite the contrary feelings rose within him, and that so suddenly that
> it seemed as if he were freed from sadness and desolation, as though a
> cloak were lifted from a man's shoulders.

His scruples worried his conscience excessively, and he fought his
fears with even stricter religious observance, saying 'daily seven
hours of prayer on his knees, rising always at midnight, and all other
exercises of the spirit'. But he could find no rest. The horrors of his
mind grew so fast that at last he cried out in despair:

> 'Help me, Lord, for I can find no help in man or in any creature;
> though if I thought I could find help no work would be too great for
> me. Lord, show me where to find help, because, even though I had
> to follow a little dog in order to find a remedy, I would do it.'

Finally, he considered suicide. There is a bottom point to all agony,
and Ignatius reached his there. As soon as he started on the upward
climb he began to see that his spiritual pain had been caused by the
extremes he had driven himself to. He did not find the privations
which he had imposed upon himself unendurable; his self-discipline
had his body well in control. But he found these privations ineffec-
tive in securing him spiritual peace. The way back to well-being
was through a loosening of the bonds. He set aside enough time for
sleep and saw that he kept to his hours. He decided to eat meat, and
felt justified in doing so. As his pre-occupation with himself lessened,
he was able to devote more time to helping others:

> after he began to be consoled by God and saw the fruits of his efforts
> to help souls, he gave up those extremes which he had practised
> before and cut his nails and hair.

He was learning that eccentricity is often a barrier between men.
   The most interesting thing about Ignatius's hard journey back to
peace of spirit is that he moved from extremes of behaviour to
ordinary behaviour, not by applying any theories, but only by
listening to his inner voice. Yet his early life had shown he was by
temperament and training greatly attracted to extremes. He appeared
to be a man well-suited to the mediaeval ideal of individual asceticism; not even the grotesque self-disciplines of a man such as Henry
Suso would have scared him. But he came to understand by experience that the extremes of asceticism can be, in their way, as danger-

ous as the extremes of chivalry, and that to help other people might
be part of the business of saving one's own soul. This was radical
knowledge. With one jump he had altered direction. Turning from
asceticism, he had turned also from much that was typical of mediaeval Christianity, its introspection and idiosyncrasy. And in doing so
he had largely freed himself from the worst part of his mediaeval
heritage, an idealism unconnected with reality. His spiritual experience in the unimportant little city of Manresa taught him exactly
what he would have learnt if his ear had been attuned to the whispers
of contemporary history: the Christian could no longer withdraw
from the complexities of society. Luther had ensured that. Shorn of
its mediaeval excesses, Ignatius's devotion moved more and more
towards helping others. This was the first step towards the foundation of the Society of Jesus, though Ignatius had as yet no idea of his
goal. In the winter he fell very ill, and the kind women who nursed
him insisted that he put on shoes, and cover his head, and they
made him two sensible robes of thick grey cloth. Thus clad, he
marked his full return to society, and looked like any other ordinary
man about to set out on his affairs.

Chapter IV

PILGRIM AND STUDENT

IN FEBRUARY 1523, Ignatius left Manresa and started on his
pilgrimage to Jerusalem. From Barcelona he sailed to Gaeta;
from Gaeta he walked to Rome, arriving in the city on Palm
Sunday. Practically, he was as badly prepared as possible for his
long journey. He had never before been outside northern Spain; he
spoke only Spanish and Basque; he was not sure about the strength
of his right leg, and he had not fully recovered from his winter sickness; he had no money, no friends and no connections. He was alone.
But 'he had great confidence in his soul that God would show him
a way to go to Jerusalem, and that strengthened him so much that
no reasons and fears suggested to him could make him doubt.' The
world of the early sixteenth century was still intimate enough and
interested enough to find such an attitude both laudable and curious,
and so Ignatius was helped over those inevitable administrative
barriers which governments place in the way of travellers. He
entered plague-filled cities without a health certificate; he received
gifts of money (which he then gave to the poor); Pope Adrian VI
blessed him, and the Doge of Venice ordered him a free berth on the
Venetian government ship to Cyprus. He impressed by his determination and sincerity, and he endangered no one but himself.

He himself, for all his enthusiasm, found the going difficult. Rome
was unedifying. Walking the winter road to Venice (some four
hundred miles), he slept in doorways and out of the way places,
avoiding the towns because of the plague. In Venice he fell so ill
that the doctor told him not to embark unless he wanted to be buried
at sea. Embarking immediately (he had learnt at Azpeitia to ignore
the gloomy predictions of doctors), he discovered some moral shocks
in the below-decks of a trading vessel. 'In that ship were committed
openly certain obscene and filthy deeds which he reproved with
severity.' When he was a soldier he must have known well enough
that the ways of ordinary working people are often 'obscene' and
'filthy'. The intoxicating idealism of his search for grace had moved

him some distance from the world of ordinary men. In Manresa he had learnt the simple lesson that he could dress like other men without compromising his principles; now he began the much harder task of attempting to understand the graceless world of ship-men and labourers and shopkeepers.

The journey to Jerusalem was not the success Ignatius had hoped for. In the Confessions he says, 'His firm intention was to stay in Jerusalem and visit the sacred places constantly, and, besides these acts of devotion, he also intended to help souls.' The Franciscans who manned this tiny Christian outpost (by courtesy of the Turks who showed a due respect for the prophet Jesus) knew the futility of his wishes. Christian Jerusalem was dead, and the Turks intended to keep it that way. The faith there had charge of a few relics and all the poignant memories. The pilgrims were allowed nothing but the sentiment and the yearnings of the old associations. The prior of the Franciscans took Ignatius aside, and in the kindest way (backed by the hint of excommunication) advised him to go back to Europe where there were souls who could profit from his devotion. After hazarding one more climb to the Mount of Olives (where he bribed the Turkish guard with his penknife), he left the next day.

When he arrived back in Venice, in January 1524, Ignatius faced a problem. His spiritual programme had included only two simple points—to stay in Jerusalem, and to help souls. The first aim, a straightforward business, he had attempted and failed. The second, more vague and problematic than the first, he had not considered in any detail. He now began to think how he could best help others:

> Since the pilgrim had learnt that it was not the will of God for him to stay in Jerusalem, he was always thinking what he ought to do, and in the end he decided to study for some time in order to be able to help souls, and he decided to go to Barcelona, and so left Venice for Genoa.

This passage is instructive, for it shows once again Ignatius instinct-ively discovering the course best suited to the problems of the age. In an age of faith the example of simple piety is often sufficient. In the high Middle Ages men were edified frequently by holy hermits of the profoundest ignorance. But intellectual attacks on the Church raise questions which cannot be answered by mortification and good works only. A man in doubt is not greatly helped by mere exhorta-tions to believe. Besides, Ignatius had already seen the limitations of uneducated piety. Before his journey to Jerusalem, he had always sought out, with his usual eagerness, 'all spiritual persons, even though they were in hermitages far from the city, in order to talk to them'. He found the results unrewarding: 'Neither in Barcelona nor in Manresa during all the time he was there, could he find people able to help him as much as he desired.' Perhaps he was also encouraged to study by one other circumstance. At Manresa he began the first, tentative work on the *Spiritual Exercises*. The taxing labour of this task must have strained to the limit his meagre education.

For the good, therefore, of both himself and others, he decided to become a student. It was a bold ambition. He was nearly thirty-three years old and did not even know Latin. He had been very badly instructed in a lot of irrelevant nonsense, and then sent out to crack opponents' heads, and get his own cracked, in the pursuit of honour. Moreover, on the evidence that we have, he was no intellectual; book-learning came to him slowly and painfully. On the other hand, he had a single-minded devotion to duty and a native common-sense which became more and more apparent as the dank fogs of chivalry lifted from his mind. He also had a cheerful humility which did not mind the impatience of his teachers or the sneers of his fellow scholars and juniors. With this serviceable, if not brilliant, equipment, he entered the schoolroom.

He studied two years in Barcelona, and made good progress. In 1526, he was considered fit to move on to the University of Alcalá, a recent foundation of Cardinal Ximenes, having at that time a certain reputation for enlightenment and advanced thinking. It was also free. In the Confessions he gives a list of his lectures—'dialectics in Soto, physics in Albertus and theology in the Master of the Sentences'. But there is no evidence here of new subject matter or new methods. If Alcalá was considered advanced it could only have been in comparison to the rest of Spain. Ignatius faced the same tedious instruction that had made scholasticism a word of derision, and which drove Erasmus nearly to distraction at Paris in 1495. 'Those studies,' he had complained,

> can make a man opinionated and contentious; can they make him wise? They exhaust the mind by a certain jejune and barren subtlety, without fertilizing or inspiring it. By their stammering and by the stains of their impure style they disfigure theology which had been enriched and adorned by the eloquence of the ancients. They involve everything whilst trying to resolve everything.

This old, wooden method, a stultified relic left over from the heyday of mediaeval thought, might not have suited such bright sparks as Erasmus and Rabelais (who loosed his contempt at the *Barbouilla- menta Scoti* and the *Sorbonistres*). Its dull vapours damped their fires; as Erasmus said with his usual irony, 'All that you have learnt in the way of *bonae literae* has to be unlearnt first; if you have drunk of Helicon you must first vomit the draught. I do my utmost to say nothing according to the Latin taste, and nothing graceful or witty.' However, the course was well adapted to the needs of Ignatius Loyola. He needed a grounding in theological orthodoxy, and the Master of the Sentences (Peter Lombard) gave him that. He was primarily a moralist, not a theologian or a philosopher, and he needed a solid exposition of Church teaching to back his morality. He did not mind if that had a bad effect on '*bonae literae*', because he had nothing 'graceful and witty' to say in the first place. Indeed, Ignatius was always suspicious of the freedom of thought that men like Erasmus allowed themselves in their treatment of Christianity. Around 1527, having been advised to read Erasmus, he attempted the *Enchiridion Militis Christiani*, but, as he said, a sort of numbness crept into his soul and he was unable to finish it, though he took it up several times.

There is no knowing what was the real cause of Ignatius's aversion to Erasmus. Perhaps he suspected Erasmus of doctrinal error; certainly strict Catholic orthodoxy soon declared against him. When Ignatius came before the Inquisition at Salamanca, the inquisitor asked him: 'Nowadays when there are so many errors of Erasmus and of others in the air, which have led astray the world, are you not willing to declare what you are teaching?' Peter Canisius, an early Jesuit, even went so far as to say '*aut Erasmus lutherizat, aut Lutherus erasmizat*'. But that was later when the world was harder. Perhaps Ignatius suspected him for his equanimity and his reason- ableness, fearing him to be a compromiser. In any case, Ignatius displayed again his remarkable talent for forestalling the judgment of history. Intuitively, he seemed to know that Erasmus was not useful for the Church's work that lay ahead. Erasmus's was a cool voice speaking to unhurried, impartial men; a voice lost in the roarings of the world after Luther. To the unspeculative mind of Ignatius the only alternatives were whether to be arrayed under the banner of the devil, or under the banner of God.

In Barcelona, Ignatius had already begun to attract attention, and within the two years of his stay a small group had formed around him. When he moved to Alcalá, Calisto, Cáceres and Arteaga, three of his companions, went with him. At Alcalá the three Spaniards were joined by Juan Reinalde, a young Frenchman recovering from wounds in the local hospital. They made an odd crew, dressed in shapeless robes of rough grey cloth, and with grey caps. They were busy, serious and contented. Two hundred years before, in the high Middle Ages, when it was acceptable to espouse poverty and to perform good works, they might have passed unnoticed. In the sixteenth century city, given over to Renaissance brilliance and Renaissance selfishness, these dowdy men doing charitable works appeared remarkable. Moreover, a uniform smacked of organization, and the Church wanted to know for whose benefit they were organized. Ministrations to the poor, for the body and the soul, had been the prerogative of the mendicant orders; and since they had generally failed in their mission, and in fact had suffered a great decline and loss of authority, they were naturally jealous of their privileges. The Inquisition, in the hands of the Dominicans, wished to know more of these men who collected alms for the poor, and taught the poor (mainly women) the simple rudiments of religion. Were they priests, and, if not, what had they to do with spiritual things?

Ignatius instructed the poor according to his *Spiritual Exercises*, which he first began to compile in Manresa and which he gradually refined through the succeeding years. His discourse was well tuned to the simple education of his hearers, and he did not have anything very revolutionary to tell them. Anna de Benavente, giving evidence before the inquisitor, testified that Ignatius had 'expounded the articles of faith, the mortal sins, the five senses, the three faculties of the soul, and other good things concerning the service of God, and told her things out of the gospels'. She was seventeen. Leonora, daughter of Anna de Menna, aged sixteen, gave much the same testimony. Ignatius dealt in such simple terms that those eager to penetrate a little more deeply into spiritual mysteries became impatient. Beatriz Ramirez complained that 'while she was there Iñigo said nothing that was new to her, merely all about loving God and your neighbour'. Indeed, Ignatius's troubles stemmed more from his audience than from his matter or method. His words, so plain and orthodox, had an unexpected effect on the susceptible and immature minds of young girls. Both Anna and Leonora were subject to fits of fainting and vomiting. Mencia de Benavente testified:

> She had seen Leonora, daughter of Anna de Menna, after talking with Iñigo, seized by a fainting fit, fall down, be sick, and roll on the ground. And that her own daughter had sweating fits, and she had

seen Anna Dias, wife of Alonso de la Cruz, in swoons, and she had
also seen Maria from Santorcas in a swoon twice, falling on the ground
and putting her hands to her breasts as if she were going to vomit.

Unsurprisingly, the Inquisition was alerted by such hysteria, for the
rumour had spread that Ignatius and his friends were a band of
Alumbrados, religious enthusiasts of a particularly fanatical and
unbalanced kind.

The first investigation by the vicar Figueroa from Toledo cleared
Ignatius of any heresy, and censured his little group only for their
similarity of dress, which was permitted for regular orders alone.
Their clothes were dyed, and Ignatius ceased to go barefoot. A few
months later Ignatius was again under suspicion, and on April
21, 1526, he was put in gaol. For forty-two days he remained in con-
finement while Figueroa looked into the charge that Ignatius had an
unhealthy influence on the minds of two rich widows. But the good
sense of his attitude, even when dealing with emotional women, is
shown by his answer to the inquisitor:

> Then you must know that these two women urged on me many times
> that they wanted to go all over the world to care for the poor, from one
> hospital to another. And I always dissuaded them from this intention
> because the daughter was so young and beautiful, and I said to them
> that if they wanted to visit the poor they could do it in Alcalá, and
> go with the most holy sacrament when it was carried to the sick.

Figueroa was again satisfied as to Ignatius's honesty and orthodoxy;
yet Ignatius and his followers undoubtedly caused some social disturbance, so the inquisitor decided to restrict them severely. They
were to dress like other students, and they were not to speak of
spiritual things for three years as they had not studied, and what
knowledge they had was not well-grounded.

Ignatius's trials at the hands of the Inquisition were not finished
there. Since he thought that Figueroa's investigations had hindered
the work of helping souls in Alcalá, he decided to try his luck in
Salamanca, the foremost of the Spanish university towns. Within
two weeks, he was once more in gaol, chained by his foot to Calisto
in a small room very dirty from age and lack of use. When Ignatius
came before the inquisitors, he was questioned extensively on his
Spiritual Exercises, which he defended fully and boldly. His im-
petuosity was even a little too much for the commission. Ordered
to explain the first commandment, 'He set himself to do it and did it
at such length and said so much that they had no desire to ask him

any more'. They could find no fault in him, and merely thought it presumptuous that one so untrained should undertake to explain these high matters. In other words, they found him poaching on their ground and warned him off. Perceiving the difficulties of a man without formal degrees in a jealous world, Ignatius decided to go to Paris to study.

Ignatius came out of his brush with the Inquisition fortunately. His position was serious, and he knew it. After the first inquiry at Alcalá, Ignatius had asked Figueroa whether he had found any heresy. 'No', replied Figueroa, 'if they had found any they would have burnt you.' The Inquisition was no respecter of persons. At a later date, Bartolome de Carranza, Archbishop of Toledo and the highest churchman in Spain, was attacked and imprisoned. The poet and scholar, Fray Luis de Leon, spent five years in the prison of the Inquisition. Juan of Avila, St. Teresa and St. John of the Cross were all at one time under suspicion. Church politics, as may be expected, played its part in the work of the Inquisition. Carranza, a Dominican, fell foul of two other powerful Dominicans, the Inquisitor General Valdès and the famous theologian Melchior Cano (who later became the confirmed enemy of the Jesuits). The Dominicans were feeling the gradual loss of their old power and prestige, and were holding on to what authority they could. Ignatius, who looked to usurp some of the pastoral function of the mendicants among the poor, might easily have felt the rage of the Dominicans. But he was unimportant, and was let off easily. In one other respect Ignatius was lucky. The reasons for his first examination—the hysterical reaction of the women who heard him—might well have condemned him for witchcraft. Europe had just entered an age of extraordinary savagery against supposed witches. If Ignatius had fallen into the hands of the inquisitors north of the Pyrenees, whose minds were inflamed by the mad lies of the *Malleus Maleficarum*, perhaps he would not have escaped such an accusation. But the Spanish Inquisition, though the resolute scourge of the unorthodox and severe against Jews and *moriscos*, was relatively untouched by the craze for witch hunting.

Ignatius, in all his encounters with the Inquisition, acted as if he were perfectly aware of the justice of his own conduct. He accepted the judgment of the Inquisition, and considered their function to be important. In reply to Figueroa's threat of burning, he had answered, 'Yes, and they would burn you too if they found heresy in you.' He accepted their strictures but did not intend to let them prevent him from going about his holy and proper work. The episode underlined two points: first, the dangerous enthusiasm of pious women. After this time, though he was always attractive to a certain kind of pious woman, he dealt with them circumspectly. He continued to correspond with old friends, particularly Isabel Roser of Barcelona to whom he once wrote, 'I owe you more than any one in this world'; but the rules of the Society are full of prudent safeguards against women. Secondly, he could not but help see that the ancient religious orders, in particular the medicants, had failed to answer the problems of the sixteenth century; for in Barcelona and Alcalá his little group was doing the work of the mendicants. The hints of experience were already suggesting the foundation of his unique society.

From Paris, early in 1528, Ignatius wrote a cheerful letter to Iñes Pascual in Barcelona:

> With favourable weather and in good health, by the grace and goodness of God Our Saviour, I arrived in the city of Paris on February 2. I shall stay here studying until the Lord orders me to do something else.

He had walked from Barcelona driving before him a donkey bearing his books. He brought with him his strong faith, his small stock of Latin, and some experience and success in helping the poor and the devout. It is not evident that he knew very much about what was going on in the contemporary world. In the previous four years he had worked hard to discipline his own soul, and the rest of his valuable time (he had started so late) he gave to helping individuals. About the social system, about the political scene, about the beginnings of the Reformation, he has nothing to say in the Confessions. He appeared to be, as near as possible, a political innocent. Living in Spain, he inhabited the country that led the quietest existence among the disturbances of the Reformation. The Spain of Charles V was of great and growing importance; but the shocks of Spanish policy were felt mainly in Italy, in the Netherlands and in the New World. Neither social unrest, such as the revolt of the Comuneros in 1520–1521, nor Renaissance scholarship, such as the printing of Ximenes's Polyglot Bible in 1514, upset the Spanish homeland. The ideal so firmly supported by the king and the Church—national unity and Catholic orthodoxy—seemed to fit the will of the people. This is seen in the Spanish attitude towards Erasmus. His works arrived in Spain on a wave of enthusiasm, but it was soon seen that among the exciting things he said were many that were critical and some that were revolutionary. The attacks began, and in 1527 Pope Clement VII was forced to issue a Bull to silence the Spanish condemnation. Erasmus was at that time in favour at Rome. Ignatius made the interesting observation that reading Erasmus relaxed his fervour and cooled his devotion. In Spanish eyes—and in Ignatius's too—strong faith and exemplary practice were more important than doctrinal reform or theological scholarship. The rest of Europe had a different point of view, and a Spaniard heading north had to learn to ride the tricky currents of the controversialists.

The journey to Jerusalem had taught Ignatius to look at people and see them, not ideally, but for what they are. The seven years in Paris showed him the European world which the Christian of the immediate future had to live in. His start in Paris was not fortunate. He entered the Collège de Montaigu, an institution that was as unpleasant as it was old-fashioned. Both Erasmus and Calvin had studied at Montaigu, and Erasmus was not complimentary. 'But what with hard beds', he wrote, 'by bad and spare diet, late and hard studies, within one year's space, of many young men full of hope, some are killed, others are blinded, others are driven crazy.' He also spoke of damp chambers, frequent whippings, rotten eggs and sour wine. Ignatius who lodged outside the college, was spared some of this, but poverty and hardship weighed him down. Later, he once told his secretary, Polanco:

> He believed no one had ever studied in spite of such great difficulties and obstacles as he.
>
> He named: his poverty; great ill-health; because he had no hope of power or position, nor any of the ambitions which make effort worthwhile; because he did not like study, but found it always hard work. He studied for twelve years only because he thought it would make him fit for God's service.

He lost his money through entrusting it for safe keeping to a fellow Spaniard, and was forced by this to live in the poorhouse and beg for his food. The distance of the poorhouse from the college caused him to miss lectures (which began at five in the morning), and the need to beg in the streets of Paris, a most ungenerous city, cut down the time he could give to his studies. He offered himself as a servant, but no one would have him. He heard that the Spanish merchants in Flanders gave alms freely, so twice he went to Flanders, and once to England, searching for money. These expeditions were so successful that he was able to set himself up, in Paris, as a sort of relief agency for other poor students. And he arranged all this with the least trouble to himself, showing his usual practicality as well as an unsuspected ability to organize other people. All this took time out of his studies, and he was getting on for forty. In the summer of 1529, Ignatius left Montaigu for the Collège de Sainte-Barbe. In three and a half years he completed the course, and in 1534, graduated, a master of arts.

Ignatius spent only a year at the Collège de Montaigu. He must have left it with relief, for the place was harsh and gloomy. But the Montaigu of the early sixteenth century was the meeting place of many of the men and ideas which between them helped to change the religious condition of Europe. In 1483, John Standonck, a student of the Brethren of the Common Life and trained in the Brethren's school at Gouda, had become head of Montaigu, then in a sad state. As befitted a member of the community who were the foremost schoolmasters in northern Europe, he soon had the college in order. He built the dormitory for poor students in which Erasmus and Calvin suffered, and he stocked the library with the characteristic writings of the Brethren: Gerard Groote and Wessel Gansfort, the *Imitation* of Kempis, the *Spiritual Ascensions* of Zerbolt and the *Rosary of Spiritual Exercises* of Mombaer. Though Standonck was a severe man, educated amidst the mortifications of the impoverished school at Gouda, he was a reformer and a famous preacher who left Montaigu saturated with the ideas and the teaching of the Brethren of the Common Life.

When Ignatius visited the library at Montaigu he moved among old friends. There was Kempis's *Imitation*, the book which Ignatius, from the time of his conversion, had read most and loved best. In the completed Spanish draft of his *Exercises* he gave Kempis a place before the Gospels: 'On the second day of the week and afterwards, it will be very profitable to read a selection from the *Imitation*, the Gospels or the *Lives of the Saints*'—though in the Latin edition of 1545 the order of this sentence was changed. At Monserrat and Manresa, in 1522, Ignatius had read the *Ejercitatorio Espiritual* of Garcia de Cisneros, a work which had helped him plan his own *Exercises*. Now, at Montaigu, he found in Latin Zerbolt and Mombaer, the masters of Garcia; and the finished *Exercises*, completed during the years in Paris, owes more to these two than it does to Garcia. Montaigu confirmed Ignatius as a follower of the *devotio moderna*.

At Montaigu, the Brethren of the Common Life presented their Janus face to the Reformation: one way looking towards Luther and Calvin, the other way towards Loyola. In the large quarries of the Brethren's teachings almost every important man of the Reformation found good material on which to raise his independent fortress. Erasmus had been their scholar in the Netherlands and at Paris. The French reformer Lefèvre of Étaples was so impressed by Mombaer's *Rosary* he induced the other foremost reformer in France, Badius Ascensius, to print it in 1510. In the same year Lefèvre visited the Brethren's house in Cologne. Badius himself attended the Brethren's school at Ghent. Luther was at Magdeburg in 1497 where, he said, he 'went to school with the Brethren of the Common Life'. 'Nowhere have I found,' he once said, 'such a clear explanation of original sin as is in the treatise of Gerard Groote, "Blessed is the man".' In his *Dictata super Psalterium* (1516) he mentions both Zerbolt and Mombaer. Later he found that Gansfort had thought almost exactly as he did. Calvin and Ignatius Loyola were both at Montaigu; and Ignatius thought so highly of the *Imitation* that it was always his first choice to give to his friends and followers.

The Brethren provided something for everyone, and Albert Hyma has shown how each found the spiritual nourishment he needed. Badius Ascensius, in his edition of Thomas à Kempis, gave this picture of the Brethren:

> All were to approach as near as possible the life of the Apostles and of the primitive church of Christ, so that in the whole congregation there should be one heart, and that no one should consider or call anything his own. No one should seek outside the house the cure of souls, ecclesiastical benefices, or worldly occupations for the sake of gain. . . . They were to take care that they themselves, and all whom they taught, should venerate God with the deepest piety. They should love their neighbour with due charity, and should assist the poor with alms, according to their means.

Such a plan, practical, upright and sincerely devout, echoed Ignatius's own ideals. He liked, too, their distrust of asceticism, that unnecessary burden of mediaeval spirituality. 'What is the use of all this needless hardship in trying to attain the impossible?' Gansfort had written:

> There is no necessity for severe fasts, or the wearing of a rough goat-hair garment. The worthy fruit of repentance requires no bodily severity, but only that which is necessary for all, the piety that waits for all things. Be regular in the observance of your duties in your

cloister home, and that will suffice for bodily discipline. In the matter of sleep and food and drink and clothes, follow the common usage and be content.

This was the voice of common-sense which the Ignatius of 1522, the wild man with the long hair and the long nails, had gradually come to hear. The Brethren did not beg, wrote Badius, but they avoided idleness and taught the children, or copied documents. Ignatius, though often forced to beg (he was extremely good at it), disliked the practice as a time-consumer and a distractor from more important work. Though 'holy mendicity' might be good for the individual soul, disciplining pride and encouraging charity, as a practical measure it was useless. In later years Ignatius wrote to Father Araoz:

> It seems to Father Ignatius, generally speaking, that no students of the Society ought anywhere to beg for their bread; because, though mendicity is all right for those who are helping souls, it seems to him that in students, who ought to be devoted to themselves, it is not very edifying, and also it does not help their studies to be distracted by the need for the necessaries of life, or the need of begging for them.

He also felt that if one avoided idleness the necessaries would follow.

Nor was it only the honest, hard-working practicality of the Brethren which attracted Ignatius. He liked their humility before the high mysteries of religion. He thought a strong faith was sufficient and the Brethren did too, for they were all Ockhamists to some degree. In his favourite *Imitation of Christ* he read:

> My son, beware thou dispute not of high matters, nor of the secret judgments of God, why this man is left and that man taken into such favour. ... These things are beyond all reach of man's faculties, neither is it in the power of any reason or disputation to search out the judgments of God.

And Gansfort gloomily adds, 'Shrouded in dense darkness and hidden deep from the sight of all are the judgments of God which are to be revealed in the clear day of the last judgment.' The unspeculative Ignatius agreed with that.

Though there was much for Ignatius to like in the works of the Brethren, there were also some things to worry him. The Brethren were all for reforming the clergy and spoke out boldly against the abuses of the Church. And Ignatius, though he had little to say on these matters, would surely have agreed with them. But the Brethren, writing in the fifteenth century at the time of the worst Roman scandals, looked askance at the papal power and prerogatives. Gansfort wrote:

> How shall he [the pope] judge the faith of a man whose language he does not know? Hence we conclude that the Holy Spirit has kept for himself the task of encouraging, quickening, preserving and increasing the unity of the Church. He has not left it to a Roman pontiff who often pays no attention to it. We ought to acknowledge one Catholic Church yet to acknowledge its unity as the unity of the faith and of the Head, the unity of the corner-stone, not the unity of its director, Peter, or his successor.

Talking of the power of the pope, Gansfort is uncompromising, 'The pope, has no more power in reconciling souls to God than in alienating them from God.' Therefore indulgences and excommunications are equally worthless, unless an excommunication is enforced through an ecclesiastical court. Gansfort spoke as a northerner and so a natural supporter of the conciliar party. He spoke also as a man who hated extremes and human pretensions. He did not see why the pope's position alone should give him authority, for he saw the abusive use the popes made of their authority. To a correspondent who supported the papal authority he replied angrily:

> You admonish me in matters of this sort to regard the authority of the pope, not merely as a substitute for reason, but as superior to it! What, I ask, am I to regard as reason in these matters? Is it not the Holy Scriptures? Do you wish to put the authority of the pope above the Holy Scriptures?

Those are the authentic tones of Luther, and Ignatius, who became the pope's especial servant, if he read those words, must have wondered.

Gansfort was a reformer and a northerner, living in an age of shameless abuse. Ignatius was a southerner more concerned with the reform of individuals than with the reform of the Church. In Spain the internal reform of the Church was well advanced, thanks to the austerity and ferocious energy of such men as Cardinal Ximenes. There, the unity of Catholicism was apparent in a way that had never been apparent to Gansfort, faced with an ignorant clergy and a corrupt church organization. In Spain, the pope was allowed his spiritual pre-eminence, though his actual powers were very firmly limited by the monarchy and the Spanish cardinals. Gansfort, the practical man, questioned the authority of the pope because he did not see how that authority helped the life of the

POPE PAUL III, BY TITIAN

LAYNEZ

Electus in Congrega:	Generali	prima
2 : July	Anno	1558
Obyt 19 Janu: 1565:	ætatis	53

Electus in Congrega:	Generali	4
19 Februar	1581	Obyt
31 Januar	1615	ætatis 72

AQUAVIVA

Church, or aided the individual. 'What could Peter in Italy do', he wrote, 'for those in India endangered by temptation or persecution, except pray for them, even though he had greater power than his successors?' This question Ignatius, in founding the Society of Jesus, set himself to answer. The members of the Society were the pope's men and therefore, as it were, extensions of the pope in foreign lands, aiding the tempted and the persecuted not only in India, but in Japan and China, in north and south America.

There was, then, in the Brethren of the Common Life, despite their piety and good-sense, a gloomy desperation, induced perhaps by northern airs and by the badness of the times, which Ignatius did not share. For all their courage, the Brethren gave the impression that they saw no way out of the impasse. From this they developed an extreme consciousness of their own irredeemable sinfulness; from here another short step led to the theology of justification. Radewijns, from whom Zerbolt, Kempis and Gansfort had borrowed, outlined the effect of original sin:

> For reason, blinded by sin, often accepts falsehood for truth; the warped will takes evil for good; the unstable memory busies itself with those things which cause it to grow restless and vacillating, as it no longer concentrates on the highest good, where it might have everything.

And the gentle Thomas à Kempis prayed for grace:

> that I may overcome my most evil nature which draweth me to sin and to perdition. For I feel in my flesh the law of sin contradicting the law of my mind, and leading me captive to the obeying of sensuality in many things.

Ignatius was well aware of sin. Much of the *Spiritual Exercises* is devoted to ways in which sinful habits may be broken. But he did not feel defeated by sin. He had been very successful in disciplining his own character, turning from the noisy paths of military honour towards the quiet goal of faith, and he thought he could help others to the same end. There was something typically mediaeval in the determinism and pessimism of the Brethren. Having done away with the asceticism of the body—the hair-shirts and the scourgings—they developed a spiritual malaise, based on their consciousness of original sin, which tortured them (and Luther who followed them in this) far more severely than any hair-shirt. Though many of the currents of the Renaissance passed Ignatius by, at least he had the outgoingness and confidence of the early humanists. He felt his strength, with God's help, was sufficient to overcome all trials, physical and spiritual; and to this extent he may be called a Renaissance man.

Like the teeth that Jason sowed, many quarrelsome giants sprang from the ground prepared by the Brethren of the Common Life. The opposing champions took what they wanted, according to their psychological and spiritual needs. The Brethren escaped censure because they lived calm, hidden and useful lives; with a few exceptions, they were schoolmasters not controversialists. They were not, as Luther put it, 'men of blood and war'. But Luther and Loyola, in their different ways, were men of blood and war. Luther took the theology of justification and the sense of sin from Groote and Gansfort: Loyola took the moral concern and simplicity of Kempis, the strong practicality of Zerbolt. Luther went from doubt into despair and revolt, and then into the hands of the princes. Loyola went from morality to authority and unity, and hence to especial service of the pope. Since the papacy was so suspect, Loyola's was in many ways a more visionary and braver road.

Chapter V

THE *SPIRITUAL EXERCISES*

IGNATIUS before 1521—the soldier and the *hidalgo*—was a notable figure. His high pretensions, his quick temper and his elegant set up amused, irritated or endeared. Gradually, in the Paris years, we lose sight of the man and see only the saint. The saint is admirable but not lovable; in acquiring perfection he loses our sympathy. A 'personality 'is a mass of small frailties, and it is the frailties that attract. Some saints are forgiven their perfection because of their eccentricity. Such a one is St. Francis who could not bear to clean his sheepskin for fear of hurting the lice that lived in it; or St. Thomas Aquinas who, it is said, grew so fat that a piece was cut out of the dining table to accommodate his stomach. Ignatius was not redeemed by any fascinating quirks. His conduct was so calm, so sensible and so well thought out. When he was poor and hungry in Paris, he heard that the Spaniard who had robbed him of his money when he first arrived in France lay ill at Rouen. At once, without shoes and without food, he went to Rouen to console the sick man and help him find a passage to Spain. A generous and virtuous act. But Ignatius gives his reason for doing this, 'thinking that under such circumstances he could win him [the sick man] to leave worldliness and devote himself entirely to the service of God'. Ignatius admits that he helped this man for the love of God and not for the love of the man. In doing this, Ignatius was only being honest and following his own logic, but the world will not like him for that. It appears to later generations that there is something both superhuman and too rational about Ignatius. He followed supremely well the discipline expounded by St. John of the Cross, another Spaniard who lived a little after Ignatius:

> First of all, carefully excite in yourself an habitual affectionate will in all things to imitate Jesus Christ. If anything agreeable offers itself to your senses, yet does not at the same time tend purely to the honour and glory of God, renounce it and separate yourself from it for the love of Christ . . . The radical remedy lies in the mortification of the

four great natural passions, joy, hope, fear and grief. You must seek to deprive these of every satisfaction and leave them as it were in darkness and the void.

This is cold advice, and inhuman in the sense that there are hardly any humans capable of doing this.

But Ignatius was no monster. Contemporaries found the religious Ignatius as fascinating as the chivalrous Ignatius. The history of his dealings with popes and cardinals shows his power to attract and persuade. The early history of his Society shows that he called forth great love and devotion from his followers. Although the personal qualities which attracted his contemporaries are obscured by the reticence and self-control of his public figure, the personality that is hidden to history is revealed in the *Spiritual Exercises*.

Ignatius's first group of followers, the companions of Alcalá and Salamanca, had fallen away. When Ignatius left for Paris Calisto, Cáceres and Arteaga stayed, and never rejoined him. It was understandable. Ignatius as yet had no particular plan for the future, and once the spell of his ardent and forceful character was removed his companions felt little urge to follow him: there was holy work to be done in Spain. They had been through an early form of the *Spiritual Exercises*, but this was not enough to hold them. Only in Paris did Ignatius learn to make the *Exercises* both an encouragement towards the spiritual life, and a test of aptitude for the particular kind of religious activity that Ignatius wanted. Even by 1534 Ignatius was not conscious that his small brotherhood was the start of a new religious order. But those who had completed the *Spiritual Exercises* in its final form, and felt the benefits of doing so, were inevitably bound together; only those of similar temperament, and similar thinking, could stand the course.

The little book is not elegant, and not well written. It is a rough, but sturdy structure, showing its joints and its hinges. The material from which it was put together, like so much late mediaeval devotional writing, was not very tractable; the *Exercises* show a bit of Ludolph, a piece of Garcia and Zerbolt, a dash of the *Imitation* and so on: there are asides and afterthoughts. But the book displays very well both the mind and the intentions of Ignatius. The book is a guide for spiritual directors, not a devotional work in the usual sense, and therefore Ignatius did not think it necessary to make it available to the general public. He knew the psychological value of surprise. Those who started the *Exercises* knowing nothing of the technique would have greater profit from the little dramas which Ignatius had in store for them. Ignatius knew that most people, however well intentioned, need a push, especially towards virtue and self discipline. And just how much Ignatius expected may be seen from the 'Principle and Foundation', which is worth quoting in full:

> Man was created to praise, do reverence to and serve God Our Lord, and thereby to save his soul. And the other things on the face of the earth were created for man's sake, and to help him fulfilling the end for which he was created. Hence it follows that man should make use of creatures so far as they do help him towards his end, and should withdraw from them so far as they are a hindrance to him in regard to that end. So it is necessary to make ourselves detached from all created things,—in so far as our free will allows,—so that we on our part should not wish for health rather than sickness, for riches rather than poverty, for honour rather than ignominy, for a long life rather than a short life, and so in all other matters, solely desiring and choosing those things which may lead us to the end for which we were created.

The theory is hard. The practical task of the *Exercises* is to bring a person to the point where, having disciplined his life, he can assent to the theory, and work always with his end in view. He is led forward to make what Ignatius called an 'Election', and having done that he is a marked man of God.

As the theory is hard, so the instruction of the participant must be practical, subtle and understanding. To Ignatius, the individual soul wandered in the no-man's-land between the armies of God and the devil, and that soul must be persuaded to range itself under God's banner. If the soul was inclined towards God, but stuck in the mire of human desires and frailties, then Ignatius is prepared to intimidate and shock it, to blast it, even, into the holy ranks. He said, 'as the devil showed great skill in tempting men into perdition, equal skill ought to be shown in saving them'. The individual psychology must be studied.

> The devil studied the nature of each man, seizing upon the traits of his soul, adjusting himself to them and insinuating himself gradually into the victim's confidence . . . and a master in saving souls ought to act in the same cautious and skilful way.

The general outline of Ignatius's campaign is clear and traditional. The *Exercises* take four weeks. The first week (more or less—time is not important and sections may be curtailed or lengthened at the director's discretion) is for Purgation, driving the soul, through fear, into repentance. In the second week, the chastened and cowed soul is illuminated, and led towards the Election. When the election has

been made, the soul is brought to see the consequences and feel the
spiritual joys of its state. The great interest in the *Exercises* is in the
props and direction that Ignatius provides for each step along the
sticky path to perfection.

The book is a work of contrasts. The great contrast is between
the simple theory and the subtle practice, and underlining this a
number of smaller contrasts: between kindness and harshness, ease
and asceticism, freedom and discipline, joy and fear. No one is to
be forced to take the *Exercises*; the receiver must have a strong will
to do so and 'enter into them with hearty good will and liberality
towards his Creator and Lord'. The giver of the *Exercises* must
remember that the pains of desolation are hard to bear—'let him
not be hard or harsh with the receiver, but bland and suave, giving
him courage and strength for the future'. The receiver need suffer
no unnecessary discomfort. He contemplates, says Ignatius, as he
sees fit, 'now kneeling, now prostrate on the ground, now lying back
with up-lifted face, now sitting, now standing'. Provision must be
made for enough sleep, and enough rest. Yet mortification as a
penance is permitted:

> to chastise the flesh, to wit, by putting it to sensible pain, which is
> inflicted by wearing hair-shirts, or cords or iron chains on the bare flesh,
> by scourging oneself, or wounding oneself, and by other modes of
> austerities.

The timings and duration of the different parts may be altered
according to the state of the receiver, but the actual exercises are not
to be skimped:

> The giver should carefully warn the receiver that as he has to devote
> one hour to each of the five exercises or meditations to be made each day,
> he should always thoroughly satisfy himself that has spent a full hour
> at the exercise, and in fact more rather than less.

The receiver is kept in perpetual balance, considering on the one
hand what his body and soul can bear, and on the other hand the
high standards towards which he must be encouraged.

Much of the book looks backward. The legacy of the Middle Ages
is as heavy upon the *Exercises* as it was upon Ignatius himself. The
mortifications permitted reflect the long tradition of Christian
asceticism; nor are they severe when compared with such tortures
as the holy fourteenth century mystic, Henry Suso, noted in his
autobiography (again written in the third person):

> He secretly caused an undergarment to be made for him; and in the

undergarment he had strips of leather fixed, into which a hundred and fifty brass nails, pointed and filed sharp, were driven and pointed always towards his flesh. He had this garment made very tight and so arranged as to go round him and fasten in the front, in order that it might fit the closer to the body, and the pointed nails might be driven into the flesh; and it was high enough to reach upwards to his navel.

The mediaeval, who did not shrink from self-torture, would recognize too Ignatius's picture of Hell, in the fifth exercise of the first week, with its details of horror and its insistence on pain:

> The first point will be to see with the eye of the imagination those great fires, and those souls as it were in bodies of fire.
> The second to hear with the ears lamentations, howlings, cries, blasphemies against Christ our Lord and against the Saints.
> The third, with the sense of smell, to smell smoke, brimstone, refuse and rottenness.
> The fourth to taste with the taste bitter things, as tears, sadness and the worm of conscience.
> The fifth, to feel with the sense of touch how those fires do touch and burn souls.

Here is the same concreteness and appeal to the sense that had been used in so many mediaeval sermons; and not in sermons only, as this passage by Thomas More on *The Four Last Things* indicates:

> If God would never punish gluttony, yet bringeth it punishment enough with itself: it disfigureth the face, discoloureth the skin, and disfashioneth the body; it maketh the skin tawny, the body fat and fobby, the face drowsy, the nose dripping, the mouth spitting, the eyes bleered, the teeth rotten, the breath stinking, the hands trembling, the head hanging, and the feet tottering.

If More's passage is the more vivid and startling, and Ignatius's slightly flat and tame, it is not because they are of different kinds, but rather because More was the greater writer. They both have the same intention, to shock the hearer or reader out of apathy. This technique, the use of bold concrete detail which strikes the sense, works very well in the first week of the *Exercises*, where the receiver is purged of his sins through fear and disgust. But the joys of union, which Ignatius tries to describe in the last days of the Exercises, are less easy to paint concretely. The compositions of the fourth week, where the senses are applied, are not very successful; they do not capture the imagination. For example: attempting to describe how the resurrected Christ appeared to Mary,

> a composition, seeing the place, which will here be to see the arrangement

of the Holy Sepulchre, and the place or house of our Lady, looking at the parts thereof in particular, likewise the room, the oratory, and the rest.

This is weak. The effect is homely and domestic; the transcendent importance of the event is lost amidst pots, tables and doorknobs. Perhaps Ignatius is not to blame. He was a poor writer, and it took all the genius of Dante to describe the wonder and the majesty of the ascent into Paradise. Ignatius's determination to tie his exercises to the bodily senses led to one other curious result. In the Methods of Prayer, the third method recommends 'that with each breath or respiration one is to pray mentally . . . so that one word only is said between one breath and another'; and again 'when you want to pray, you shall say the Hail Mary by rhythmical beats'. This is novel, though whether it is effective or not is hard to say. The mind seems to play little part in these proceedings.

If much in the *Exercises* reflects older practice, much also is new. Even the bold, uncompromising mediaeval outlines are softened by a new concern for the person. After the passage on scourging, Ignatius adds:

> What seems the more suitable and safer thing in penance is for the pain to be sensible in the flesh, without penetrating to the bones, so as to cause pain and not infirmity. Wherefore it seems more fitting to scourge oneself with minute cords, which cause pain externally, rather than in any other way which might cause serious internal injury.

What is most noticeable in the *Exercises* is the care Ignatius gives to the psychology of each person. The director must treat each case as unique. The Additions to the first week state:

> Be it observed that when the Excercitant still fails to find what he desires, as tears, consolations, etc., it is often useful to make an alteration in diet, in sleep, and in other modes of doing penance . . . because it befits some to do more penance and others less.

And again in the Annotations:

> According to the disposition of the persons wishing to make the Spiritual Exercises, that is to say, according to their age, education or talent, the said Exercises must be adapted, lest to one who is illiterate or of weak constitution there be given subjects which he cannot without inconvenience bear and profit thereby. Thus to each according as he seeks to dispose himself there should be given that whereby he may better help himself and make profit.

In the *Exercises*, Ignatius set the director a most difficult task. To help the participant towards the election, he may encourage, advise, console, castigate; he must be flexible, cunning and tactful, but he must not tell the participant what to do. The participant must see the choices clearly, and choose freely, knowing what he is doing. The director takes him down the narrow path towards choice, governing his dilatory and vagrant spirit. The delightful by-ways of compromise and argument are closed. A thin and ruthless logic hurries him on. The participant's heart is engaged, his emotions are shocked, and then soothed. He feels rather than thinks his way towards a decision. And when the decision is made, when the person elects to follow the banner of Christ and not the devil, he heads, despite the subtlety of the approach, to an end as severely idealistic as the one aimed at by the most fervent mediaeval religious. The religious of the Middle Ages did not need to examine themselves in the manner of the *Exercises*. To choose the religious life was a natural and ordinary thing to do, acceptable to society and surprising no one. In the sixteenth century the secular current had begun to set against religion. The temper of European society was generally against the call of religion. At this vital point, Ignatius provided a test so that men could see whether, contrary to the drift of the age, they really had a secret urge towards the religious life. That such a test was needed is shown by the number who took the *Exercises*, not necessarily to become Jesuits, but as a preparation to the priesthood generally.

Yet without doubt the kind of religious practice put forward in the *Exercises* resulted from Ignatius's own convictions and bears his stamp. There is no great intellectual play, no points of subtle argument, no refinements of theology. Just the very firm conviction that if men are not won for God they will be snapped up by the devil. In keeping with this vigorous concept, Ignatius was all for action. In the mediation on the two banners, he typically has the opposing forces drawn up into armies. He was prepared to fight, and like Napoleon he believed that he who stays behind his barricades is lost. In the Contemplation to Obtain Love, he says shortly, 'love ought to be placed rather in works than in words'. As Ignatius had no great liking for abstraction and theorizing, so he wished to avoid introspection and the pains that it often produces in the spirit. He saw the danger in questions such as Tolstoy asked:

What will be the outcome of what I do to-day? Of what I shall do to-morrow? What will be the outcome of all my life? Why should I live? Why should I do anything? Is there in life any purpose which the inevitable death which awaits me does not undo and destroy?

He feared the conditions which led men to cry, like Luther in his old age, 'I am utterly weary of life. I pray the Lord will come forthwith and carry me hence.' For this reason he wished to externalize—action not introspection, works not thoughts. He understood the intricacies of the individual and how to deal with them; but he saw them more as perils than as advantages. The *Exercises* set out to cure the irregularities of individuality. Ignatius aims at simplicity of character which joyfully offers itself in submission before the authority of God. A man's only purpose is to express through himself God's purpose. God is the one brilliant reality of the world. A man in himself is nothing; he shines only as he reflects God's light. But man does have a positive function; he is a server at the divine feast, and as a server he is called upon to accept orders. A server who attempted to interpret the divine wishes would be scandalously proud and selfish. No, the proper course was to receive direction through the Church, a human agency but divinely inspired. Ignatius thought that the Church held an extraordinarily exalted position, and therefore its authority was limitless and absolute. To make this point quite clear, he added some Rules for Thinking with the Church at the end of the *Exercises*. The first rule is:

laying aside all criticism, we ought to hold our mind ready and prompt to obey in all things the true Spouse of Christ our Lord, which is our holy Mother the hierarchical Church.

The ninth rule is:

to praise in fine all precepts of the Church, holding the mind ready to find reasons in her defence and nowise in her offence.

The tenth says:

we ought to be more ready to approve and praise . . . the personal conduct of our superiors; because, granting that they are not or were not such as to merit praise, to speak against them, whether by preaching in public or in conversation with men of the common sort, would engender rather murmurings and scandal than spiritual profit; and thereby the people would grow indignant against their rulers, whether temporal or spiritual.

And the thirteenth:

To make sure of being right in all things, we ought always to hold by the principle that the white that I see I would believe to be black, if the hierarchical Church were so to rule it, believing that between Christ our Lord the Bridegroom and the Church his bride there is the same spirit that governs and guides us to the salvation or our souls.

To believe so strongly in such an authority presupposes a stable society, saturated with Christianity, and a continuing and immutable Church. Ignatius's visionary eye is fixed so firmly on eternity he tends to discount mere sublunary things. The figures in the foreground are only humans, fidgety, changeable beings whose whims and petty ambitions have no place in the grand scheme. The whole is important, and the parts only important as they contribute to the whole. When Ignatius considered a man, he considered really the end of that man, so that when he hurried to the thief at Rouen he went for God's sake, not for the man's sake; similarly bad superiors are not to be criticized for fear of scandalizing religion, and the Church is to be obeyed because each act of disobedience diminishes the Church. The fervour of Ignatius's love for God ensured that he acted towards his fellow men generally with charity and tenderness, for Christ too had loved man and died on the cross for him. But his view that men must be subject in all particulars to the Church set a cold precedent for the future. The Church, in spite of Ignatius's exalted view of it, was a very human institution, and had never been very good at resisting the temptations of worldly power. Ignatius's techniques, applied without love, were just another means of exploitation.

The whole is all-important and must be actively defended. Man's duty towards God demands that His dominion be recognized. 'Man was created to praise, do reverence to and serve God', says the Principle of the *Exercises*, 'and thereby to save his soul. And the other things on the face of the earth were created for man's sake, and to help him in the following out of the end for which he was created.' Again, without love, this is a cold doctrine. Since Ignatius, man has made a sad work of using the creatures of the earth for his benefit. Ignatius did not see the dangers. He lived in a world expanding beyond the oceans and brimful with new discoveries. Naturally, he wished all this wonderful human activity to redound to the glory of God. He thought also that the glory of God required the dominion of the Church, as the bride of Christ, to extend to wherever there were men, in whatever condition. In the Meditation from the second week, on the Kingdom of Christ, he says:

The first point is to put before my eyes a human king, chosen by God, to whom all Christian princes and all Christian men pay reverence and obedience.
The second, to mark how this king addresses all his people saying: 'My will is to conquer the whole land of the infidels ...'

And touching the first point, if we pay regard to such a call of a temporal king upon his subjects, how much more is it a thing worthy of consideration to see Christ our Lord, the eternal King, and before Him the whole world, to which and to every man in particular He cries and says: 'My will is to conquer the whole world and all mine enemies, and so to enter into the glory of my Father; therefore he who shall wish to come with me must labour with me, that following me in hardship he may likewise follow me in glory.'

In all its force, the mediaeval ideal of Christendom possessed Ignatius. He wished to serve in the holy ranks, helping 'to conquer the whole land of the infidels' and even 'the whole world'. In the *Exercises* he called men to the standard of Christ and trained them severely and hard as soldiers must be trained. He set before them the trinity of Authority, Unity and Universality and drove them on with a discipline of the senses which almost amounted to, in William James's phrase, 'a semi-hallucinatory mono-ideism'. For the first time, Christendom was provided with a spiritual army. But whom were they to fight? The war against the traditional foe, Islam, was finished; the Turks sat very firmly in Asia Minor, and the Moors had been driven from Spain. The Spaniards and the Portuguese in the newly discovered lands advanced in the evangelical stance which Christian and Moslem had made so well known in Europe—with the naked blade prominently displayed behind the holy writ; but they usually found peaceful and curious natives who turned hostile only when their liberties and independence were trampled on. Poised for action and ready to extend Christendom to the ends of the world, Ignatius and his followers suddenly found that Christendom no longer existed. Luther had mined the foundations.

All through his religious life until the founding of his Company in 1538, Ignatius had looked outwards from Europe, to Jerusalem, to the conversion of the infidels in the world beyond. There is no evidence that he thought he had a special part to play in Europe, fighting against Protestantism. But the Reformation attacked the foundation and starting point of his religion; it destroyed the harmonious unity of Christendom. If the Reformation triumphed, Ignatius's system and his work collapsed. Since his base was so narrow, he had to support it at all costs. Inevitably, in order to survive as a spiritual force, Ignatius had to fight the disintegrating influence of the Reformation. Quietly, from the moment of his conversion in 1521, when Luther was hardly known in Spain and the Reformation was little more than a dull, incoherent rumble in

Germany, Ignatius was slowly fashioning the religious mentality and the practical technique which the disorganized Catholic Church needed to stop the spread of Protestantism. He set it all out in the *Spiritual Exercises*. Almost at the same time as Luther, and without reference to the Reformers, Ignatius nonetheless formulated the Church's most effective antidote to the Reformation. It was a strange coincidence.

Chapter VI

THE REFORM OF THE CHURCH
AND THE LIFE OF RENEWAL

THE YEARS Ignatius spent in Paris were inflamed by the passions of religious discord which led, inevitably, to violent deaths. The vacillating mind of Francis I pulled by conscience and policy, was sometimes kind to and sometimes severe against the reformers. In the uncertain atmosphere the scaffold in the Place de Grève was kept busy. The majority of the public, scandalized by such acts as the outrage on the statue of the Virgin of Paris, on May 31, 1528, wished the king to bear down unmercifully on the Lutherans; and in general the king complied. On April 17, 1529, Louis de Berquin, who might have been, said Theodore Beza, 'the Luther of France', was burnt. Synods at Paris, Bourges and Lyons meet to devise ways to fight heresy. In 1533, after Nicholas Cop, the Rector of the University, had delivered an oration entirely favourable to Luther's doctrine of justification, the king angrily demanded action from the Parlement. Within a week fifty suspected Lutherans were in gaol; an edict was passed which said that anyone convicted by two witnesses of being a Lutheran would be burnt. Soon after, the strong arm of orthodoxy relaxed a little while the king entered into a brief political flirtation with the Protestant princes in Germany. Guillaume du Bellay was sent to Melanchthon to try to reconcile the religious differences. Then, shortly before Ignatius left Paris, the reformers once more offended public opinion, and thus ensured that many of them would be burnt. On Sunday morning, October 18, 1534, Paris awoke to find the city well sprinkled with placards condemning the 'atrocious and insupportable abuses' of the Mass. One placard was even fixed to the door of the king's bedroom at Amboise. King and public were equally furious at this blasphemy, and an eager persecution followed. By the end of the year some four hundred heretics were in gaol. By Christmas eight had been burnt. In the next four months a further fifteen died, and many were banished, including the poet Clément Marot. On January 21, 1535, the king returned to Paris for a ceremony of expiation. He went in procession to Notre Dame, heard Mass, and then made a speech at the public banquet promising to destroy heresy; the day ended with the burning of six heretics.

Ignatius mentions none of this. But he lived and worked in the heart of the city and must have seen very painfully the divisions and hatreds of the time. He drew closer to him the friends whom he had won. He had in Paris six companions, men at first primarily interested in setting their own souls in order. Then as the divergent opinions attacked them on all sides they were driven together to defend the faith they had worked so hard to attain. The age had made the orthodox missionaries among their fellow citizens. Encouraged by Ignatius's precept that a strong faith should be an active faith, his little group became less a band of friends and more a brotherhood.

When Ignatius came to the Collège de Sainte-Barbe he shared a room with two men, both nearly at the end of their studies. The first was Pierre Favre, a gentle Savoyard, quiet and kind, who wished to do some good in the world, but lacked confidence and discipline. In the next four years Ignatius gave him both, led him to take the *Exercises* and resolved his perplexities without destroying his natural compassion. Favre felt for everybody and prayed even for Luther, the Turkish sultan and Melanchthon. All men were his friends: 'he crept into their souls', wrote Rodriguez, another of Ingatius's companions in Paris, 'and by his conduct and his slow pleasant words kindled in them all a violent love of God.'

Francis Xavier, the second room-mate, was a very different person. He was twenty-three when Ignatius met him, in 1529, an athlete and a handsome young man who felt that he had the measure of the world. He aimed to settle into a pleasant Church sinecure after leaving the university. Francis came from Navarre, from the same country that had bred the Loyolas, and his family history parallels Ignatius's—the same pride and the same military restlessness. In the wars for Navarre, Xavier had fought on the losing side, being loyal to the old French regime which had employed his father. Consequently, the family castle had been destroyed by the Duke of Najera, Ignatius's old patron, and the family fortunes fell. Not surprisingly, Francis did not immediately take to the worn, balding and slightly lame man who shared his room and attempted to dampen his high spirits with serious and pious talk. For one thing, Ignatius had been on the enemy's side in Navarre; secondly, he was rather old and shabby, without the proper haughty elegance that an *hidalgo* should show; thirdly, Francis was interested in sampling the full variety of Parisian life. Long after, in India, he once admitted to a friend that he was only saved from debauchery by the fear of venereal disease. To begin with, it seems that Francis only put up with Ignatius for the sake of Pierre Favre, to whom they were both devoted. But Ignatius had noted the exceptional qualities of his fellow Basque, and pressed him unremittingly. The issue was not really in doubt. The men were too much alike—their backgrounds, their temperaments, their idealism. Francis gradually succumbed to the sincerity and the serenity of Ignatius. When Ignatius left Paris for Spain, in 1535, he carried a letter from Francis to the family at Xavier, correcting any misconception his brother might have formed about Ignatius:

> I assure you on my honour never in my life will I be able to repay my great debt to him, both for helping me many times with money and with friends, and for having caused me to separate from evil companions whose character in my inexperience I didn't recognize. . . . I also most earnestly entreat you to deal and converse with Señor Iñigo, and to listen to what he may tell you.

It was the start of a remarkable partnership. Within a few years Francis left for the East, from where he never returned. Yet he remained bound to Ignatius by the strongest cords of affection and loyalty which distance seemed to intensify rather than diminish. He was as great a man as Ignatius, and he is perhaps the only Jesuit that posterity has taken unreservedly to heart.

The next two members of Ignatius's small band were both young and both Spaniards. Diego Laynez was twenty-one and Alfonso Salmeron eighteen when they arrived together from Alcalá in 1533. They were both clever, but Laynez was the more brilliant of the two—an intellectual quite unlike any of Ignatius's other early followers. Laynez was partly of Jewish descent and he showed the ability so often found in that talented race. He became the theologian, the theoretician, of the early Jesuits and succeeded Ignatius as the general of the Society. He was quick-tempered and passionate in argument, sometimes lost control of himself, and afterwards was given to extreme remorse. There was something in him which was not quite disciplined by the *Exercises*; his mind, swift and penetrating, felt a touch of the intellectual uncertainty of the age. Without the restraint of Ignatius's training he might have wasted himself in the bitter wrangling of theological controversy. The touch of apprehension in his mind made him impatient and a little ruthless. His generalship left a distinctive mark on the Society.

The last two memebers of Ignatius's original band, the Portuguese Simon Rodriguez and Nicholas Alfonso called Bobadilla after his village in Valencia, both had their faults. Rodriguez, after an exemplary beginning, came to love power and position. He later led a headstrong and independent life in Portugal where he enjoyed the king's favour and, in spite of his conduct, Ignatius's continuing affection. Bobadilla, a simple and hardworking man, had neither judgment or brains. He meddled inadvisably in politics and prided himself on his connections with kings and princes. He was so excitable that on one occasion his listeners thought he must be drunk. Shortly after Ignatius left Paris in 1535, three more joined the company. Claude Le Jay was a preacher and theologian. Paschase Broet undertook a host of jobs from nuncio to college rector and ended his life as provincial in his native France. The third, Jean Codure, died within five years.

This little company of nine men, the companions drawn to Ignatius in France, appeared at first to have few marks of distinction. It did include, in Francis Xavier, one man of genius, but his talents were not revealed until later. It also possessed the powerful mind of Diego Laynez. The rest (with the later exception of Rodriguez) were faithful, hardworking and obedient. The potential of the group, and what gave it strength in the future, lay in its mixed and international composition and its unity of mind and purpose. Among the ten men there were two Basques, three Spaniards (one of Jewish descent), one Portuguese, two Frenchmen, and two Savoyards. In Ignatius's eyes, all men of faith were equal, and all were members of Christendom. He went against the prevalent nationalism of the age, not because he revolted against it, but rather because he had never felt its force. He had a Spanish body, but a Christian soul; in his mind he never doubted which to put first. The *hidalgo* in Ignatius, the man of pure blood, might in the past have objected to Laynez for his Jewish ancestry, but Ignatius, the soldier of Christ, saw the Christianity rather than the Jewishness of the man.

Though the talents of the individuals were not outstanding, there were no failures. Even Rodriguez, an awkward case, had his rewards; for though he annoyed the fathers in Rome by demanding a higher place than was due to him, he delighted the King of Portugal, and the work of the Society in any country depended largely on the attitude of the king. The early followers were consistent and had staying power because they were all informed by the common ideal which Ignatius had impressed upon them. They felt the need to be together and to work together. Even though they were not quite sure what they were to do, they saw from the evidence of the contemporary world around them that they were slightly different. They felt the need of some sort of formal association and, because of their point of view, it had to be a religious association, even though only one of them, Pierre Favre, was a priest. The rest of the original seven, including Ignatius, determined to study for the priesthood. Then they talked about their aims, and Rodriguez, who gives the account of their conversations, says they wished to work 'for any cause whatever for God's greater service and veneration'; they were ready 'to die gladly at need'. Their minds turned, so typically, towards Jerusalem. They agreed that after they became priests they should meet in Jerusalem and decide then by vote whether to stay and convert the Turks, or return. Finally they made up their minds that if they could not arrange a passage to Jerusalem within a year, they would go to Rome and offer themselves to the pope, eager to work in the lands of the Turks, or in the lands of 'other tyrants who hated the Christian religion'.

Early in the morning on August 15, 1534, the companions climbed the hill of Montmartre, to a small and little used chapel about half way up. The priest, Pierre Favre, said Mass, the rest communicated and made their vows. They came out into the August sun and went contented down the hill to the fountain of St. Denis at the foot, where they ate and rested. 'These first Fathers', says Rodriguez,

> gave themselves up to God, and held nothing back. They renounced their own wills so completely, they offered their oblation with so much joy, putting all their hope in the divine mercy, that when I think of it I am all emotion, my piety and my wonderment grows and grows.

With their simple aims and firm intention they formed a small, still point in the midst of a brutally changing world. They tried to recapture a mood of the past, a spiritual life that a thousand years of human problems had twisted and made almost impossible. Ribadeneira, who later tried to relate the essence of this first freshness, describes them like this:

> They were comforted and quickened in their good purpose by the vow of poverty, by familiar intercourse day by day with one another, by sweet peace, by concord, love, and the sharing of what they had and

by the communion of their hearts. They imitated the usage of the ancient Holy Fathers and invited one another to dinner, according to their means, and took advantage of the occasion to talk of the spirit, and urge one another to a contempt of this world and a desire for things divine. These means worked so well that all the time they stayed in Paris to finish their theological studies there was no faintness or lukewarmness in their zeal for perfection, rather it went on growing with marked increase day by day.

They were joined together by their affection and their ideals, and saw each other continually to encourage one another to higher standards, but they were not yet a religious order. 'When we were at Paris', Laynez wrote, 'we did not intend to found an order, but to pass in poverty a life dedicated to helping others by preaching and serving in hospitals and to go to Jerusalem to help ourselves and others, the faithful and the infidel.' Ignatius, in one of his letters, says the same, and Polanco, Ignatius's secretary, wrote of the vow at Montmartre, 'it never entered into their heads to found a new religious order'.

The action of Ignatius and his friends was not unique for the time. There had been for some years a spontaneous movement within the Church towards the reform of the very evident abuses. 'Men must be transformed by religion, not religion by men', said Egidius of Viterbo at the beginning of the Lateran Council in 1512, indicating the way in which a Catholic reformation should be achieved. The evil of man corrupted the Church which would never be cleansed until priests showed Christian virtue and practised Christian charity. And the popes, who had sufficient conscience to see that the reform was necessary, tried to encourage this essential work. The first impetus came from the Lateran Council (1512–17) in the reign of Leo X. Adrian VI, an austere Dutchman and the former tutor of Charles V, attempted to continue the good work, condemning the ostentation of cardinals, the accumulation of benefices and the extortions of the Roman clerks. But he was a humourless and unperceptive old man whom the Romans looked on with great suspicion as a northern barbarian probably in the pay of Charles, his one-time pupil. The people thought of him, said the Venetian ambassador, 'not as the common father of the Christian republic, but as an agent of the German Caesar.' He died after only one year, in 1523, to the relief of Romans, cardinals and clerks. He was the last non-Italian pope. His successor, the Medici Clement VII, in spite of his refinement and intelligence, found the difficulties of

European politics too much for him. He also in typical Medician manner looked after the interests of his family, which were not always for the good of the Church. His reign of eleven years was a curious mixture of good intentions and bad practice. He took the advice of keen reforming churchmen such as Giberti and Sadoleto, yet the cardinals of his appointment were the usual rich and worldly nobles. Antonio Soriano, in a report of 1531, pictures them shrewdly:

> I will not say that the present Cardinals are saints: yet I cannot but speak of them with respect as of men of lordly rank who live in a manner worthy of their noble station.

When Clement died in 1534, the Reformation had done its work of splitting religious Europe.

Partly because the papacy was thoroughly muddled by politics, and partly because the reform that Egidius advocated was such a personal thing, a matter for the individual conscience, the Catholic reform movement owed more to ordinary churchmen—and even lay-men—than it did to the papacy. The desire for reform inevitably led to new religious groups and organizations standing outside the old religious orders. The old monastic orders tried to put themselves straight, under such men as Ximenes, Matteo di Bassi and Battista da Crema. In 1516, Leo X had placed all religious under episcopal control when outside their own houses. But in general the old orders, which had been designed for a previous age and another kind of Christian society, were far gone in lethargy and incompetence. New communities arose to suit the changed conditions. The old orders, born into and ministering to an agricultural and rural society, were helpless before the new culture of the city. Even the mendicants had little place in the cities; they were more often vagrants and beggars than men of God. The new age demanded, not isolation from society, but involvement with it. The shape of the new communities is first seen in the Oratory of Divine Love, a group which started about the time of the Lateran Council, meeting at the little church of SS. Silvestro and Dorothea. The members were of all kinds, from eminent churchmen such as Carafa, Lippomano and Gaetano to the most ordinary layman. The rules were loose; the aims were to regu-late their own lives through prayer, religious exercises and frequent visits to the sacraments, and to help their neighbours through charity and spiritual advice. In other words, their aims coincided almost exactly with those of Ignatius. But there was a difference. In the

Oratory there was not a single, strong, unifying personality. Most of the members led busy lives in the world and so found their lives and purposes divided. And the severe Christian ideal had become a little mixed, under the influence of men like Sadoleto and Manetti, with some of the classical nostalgia of the humanists so well known in Renaissance Italy. There is to this day a memorial of theirs in Rome—a holy water vessel in the shape of a pagan altar, inscribed in very chaste classical Latin. The Roman Oratory was so successful that similar groups were started in Brescia, Vicenza, Verona and Venice.

But the very nature of the Oratories limited the amount of good work they could do. Something more regular and more formal would have more time and more energy to give to the Christian community. Seeing this, Gaetano di Tiene and Gian Pietro Carafa broke away from the Oratory of Divine Love and formed the first of the new orders of 'clerks regular', called the Theatines. The original idea came from Gaetano, a man so quiet and so gentle that Ranke says of him, 'he wished to reform the world without letting the world know he was in it'. His partner, Carafa, was neither quiet nor gentle. He had stormed his way through much of Europe, spending many years in Spain where, as a Neapolitan, he violently objected to the Spanish king's Italian policy. He learnt to distrust the Habsburgs and did not care for the Spaniards. Ignatius later suffered from his displeasure. But he was not a politician. He was a reformer and a scholar, praised by Erasmus for his eloquence, his theology and his knowledge of Greek, Latin and Hebrew. Leo X had called him to Rome to help draft the Bull of condemnation against Luther. His love of what he took to be the true faith was so strong that once in Spain he refused to delay the Mass until the king arrived: 'within these walls,' he said to that absolute monarch, 'I represent the person of Christ, and therefore, vested with such an office, would deem it an indignity to wait the coming of an earthly king.' A Brief of June 24, 1524, established the order, whose members took the three vows, with special emphasis on the vow of poverty. Carafa distributed his property to the poor and resigned both his bishoprics, an extraordinary act for the time which caused astonishment and some laughter among the material men in Rome. Gaetano gave up his benefices, writing to his relations, 'I see Christ in poverty and I am rich.'

The poor, the sick, the plague-ridden, prostitutes, prisoners, beggars suddenly had new friends. And the unfortunates needed friends desperately as incessant wars continued to devastate Italy.

In 1527, the Imperial troops drove Pope Clement into the castle of San Angelo and sacked Rome. Once again the secular forces had shown their power to be greater than the Church's. Erasmus wrote that not only Rome, but the whole world was ruined, and that the barbarian Goths had been less cruel to the city. Sadoleto, in a letter to Colocci, called it the end of the age of the humanists. Perhaps shocked by these horrors and so more aware of the Christian work to be done, many others followed the example of the Theatines. Again, Sadoleto pointed out the work which the Church needed:

> What is God's own, God can take care of; but we have before us a life of renewal that no power of the sword can wrest from us; only let us so direct our acts and thoughts as to seek the true glory of the priesthood and our own true greatness and strength in God.

Girolamo Miani, who in the plague and famine year of 1528 had seen the poor eating dogs and cats and with his own hands had buried the corpses left lying in the streets of his native Venice, started the order which became known as the Somaschi. His special work lay among poor children and orphans, both to look after and to educate them. In Milan, Antonio Zaccaria, a young doctor who had turned to the priesthood, began a mission similar to that of the Theatines. Pope Clement approved the order in 1533, and Zaccaria drew up a constitution similar to that of Gaetano and Carafa. The order, which later became known as the Barnabites, delighted to stir up the public conscience, so much so that they were accused of disturbing the peace, which they certainly did.

Ignatius's aims, in many ways so much like those of the Italian precedents, nonetheless showed some important differences. Ignatius saw that the Italians had found the theoretical solution to the Church's problems; but as he started outside Italy, and independent from Italian influences, he evolved a different practice. Ignatius had a very clear sense of the identity of his group, even before it became an order, and he acknowledged that good ideas taken from other sources might have to be refined and modified to suit his singular purpose. In the five years between leaving Paris and the Bull of 1540 which founded his order, he had plenty of time, particularly in Venice and in Rome, to observe the work of the Oratories and the Theatines and to decide how far to follow them. Ignatius, though a man of the strictest principle, was never bound by theory. If circumstances made him do something which he did not recommend for others, he accepted the inconsistency as an expedient of the moment.

In 1535 he left Paris for Spain, advised by his doctor that a change of air might improve his health (he suffered from gallstones for most of his adult life). Back in his native Azpeitia for the first time in fourteen years, he immediately set to work drafting an Ordinance for the Care of the Poor, appointing officers to receive all alms and distribute them justly, condemning mendicity and sentencing persistent beggars to be whipped. There was nothing original in this: Ignatius was in tune with the social thinking of the time. His Ordinance copied many of the provisions introduced by Luis Vivès at Ypres in 1525, provisions also included in the English acts of 1551 and 1562 which led to the excellent English *Act for the Relief of the Poor* in 1601. Yet shortly after introducing this Ordinance in Azpeitia Ignatius admitted that he begged in Bologna. He did not think it necessary to explain his conduct. His opinions on begging were well known and clearly recorded, but if he had to beg in order to live he did so, and related that too. To some this may appear devious and inconsistent, to others it is merely common-sense. Ignatius, who was not given to reflect on the nice distinctions of conscience, would have been surprised at the first point of view.

Ignatius, who accepted that no man could have an excess of the theological virtues of faith, hope and charity, in practical matters most often steered between extremes of conduct. His experience at Manresa had taught him that extreme attitudes often bedevil ordinary human intercourse; perhaps he felt as well that the relative day to day world was no place for absolutes. In those matters which are, by their nature, morally indifferent, he was guided by pragmatic tests—whether they were useful or not. For this reason he was not keen on the very strict interpretation of the vow of poverty which the Theatines had imposed upon themselves. Of course, Ignatius and his companions had themselves taken the vow of poverty and had no wish to accumulate anything for themselves, especially as material greed was one of the greatest curses of the Church; they scrupulously returned a sum of money which had been subscribed by prominent men in Rome towards their journey to Jerusalem. But Ignatius was sensible about money, knowing its importance. From Venice in 1536, he wrote to Jaime Cazador in Barcelona:

> You say that you will not fail in sending the usual remittance; I should merely advise you when. Isabel Roser has written that by next April she will provide enough so that I can finish my studies. That will be a very good arrangement for me as I shall then be able to provide for the whole year, both as to books and other necessaries.

The mediaeval Church had got itself into financial trouble partly because its ideas on economics were so far removed from the normal economic practices of the secular world. Ignatius ensured that this should not happen to his order. When Laynez was preaching at Piacenza, soon after coming to Italy, Ignatius wrote to him to temper his enthusiastic poverty. Polanco noted:

> At length towards the end of the year he began by the order of Father Ignatius to accept what he needed from alms spontaneously offered. Before this, because of his love of poverty, and in order that he might freely give what he had freely received from God, he had lived by begging from door to door and with his comrade Favre had suffered great need from the bare necessities of life.

After the founding of the order, Ignatius appointed the very competent Codacio, a new recruit, to the full-time job of looking after the finances. Yet in spite of his concern, Ignatius refused to be tied by financial considerations only. 'Even in the days', wrote Ribadeneira, 'of the most extreme narrowness of our resources he would never refuse anyone who seemed fit for the society and called by God to it.' When creditors came to seize the furniture in the house, he said calmly, 'Well, if they take the beds we will sleep on the floor. We are paupers and we can lead the life of paupers.' He knew how to blend sense with faith.

Since it was the task of the Catholic reformation to drive the clergy from their bolt-holes out into the public world, Ignatius, like the Barnabites, knew the value of publicity. In particular he carefully protected himself and his work from the scandalous lies and rumours which grew so luxuriantly in the disordered times. Just before leaving Paris Ignatius once more came under the suspicion of the Inquisition. Nadal, who later became a Jesuit, stayed away from them anxiously in 1534, reasoning to himself, 'I do not want to join these people. Who knows if they will fall into the hands of the inquisitors?' When Ignatius heard the rumours, he went straight to the inquisitor without waiting to be summoned, taking a copy of the *Exercises*, and pressed for a trial. When the inquisitor refused to investigate, saying the matter was not important enough, Ignatius called a notary and prepared a document to say that he had been dismissed without trial. But the whispers did not stop. In Venice, in 1537, it was said that he had been burned in effigy in Spain and in Paris, and had fled to Venice to avoid the death penalty. Immediately he cornered Gaspar de Doctis and demanded an investigation which cleared him entirely, praising him as 'a priest of good and religious life and orthodox belief' who had taught 'religion and morality in Venice up to this day'. Still the suspicions were not silenced. In Rome, in 1538, Ignatius met the inquisitors for the last time. Ignatius and his companions had attacked an Augustinian called Agostino Mainardo in whom they detected Lutheran doctrine. Their fears were correct, for Mainardo later fled to Switzerland and became a Lutheran. But Mainardo had influential friends who were soon at work spreading the now familiar tales about Ignatius's beliefs. Ignatius acted once more with despatch. He tried to bring the detractors before the magistrate, and when the magistrate wished to slide over the matter he went to the pope himself. He recorded what happened in a letter to Isabel Roser:

> Finally I went to the Pope's summer castle and talked alone with his Holiness in his room for an hour. I told him plainly all the times processes had been brought against me in Spain and how I had been arrested in Alcalá and Salamanca. I did this in order that no one could tell him more about it than I did. . . . Pointing out how necessary it was that we should be cleared, not only before God but also before the public, I begged his Holiness to order a full examination. The Pope . . . ordered a formal hearing in our case. . . . Sentence has been given in our favour.

The extent to which Ignatius was attacked shows that men had begun to take note of him. He alone refined the experience of the age for the benefit of his company, and he alone decided what was necessary and what was not necessary for its success. One of the major differences between his company and those already in existence in Italy was the extraordinarily dominating position of Ignatius. Not even Carafa had such a dominance over the Theatines as Ignatius had over his companions. He was anxious that he should not appear to dictate, and all matters of communal interest were discussed and voted upon freely; but he knew (how could he not?) that the others were entirely in his hands, as he indicates in this letter written to his nephew soon after the foundation:

> So since I, although most unworthy, have been able by divine grace to establish foundations approved by the pope for the company of Jesus, I ought to exhort you and very thoroughly to build on these foundations thus laid, so that you may have no less merit in the building than I in the foundation and all by the hand of God.

And to his companions very willingly acknowledged his superiority.

Laynez saw in him great powers of leadership. He possessed, wrote
Laynez:

> Great knowledge of the things of God, and great devotion to them,
> and the more metaphysical these matters were and over our heads, the
> better he knew them; great good sense and prudence in matters of
> business; the divine gift of discretion; great fortitude and magnaminity
> in tribulation; great simplicity in not judging others, and in putting a
> favourable interpretation on all things; and great skill in knowing how
> to set himself and other to work in the service of God.

In the early days, Polanco said:

> Ignatius held the rudder of this little ship, but in the guise of a father
> who had begotten all according to the spirit and won their completest
> confidence by his prudence and charity, not as though he had any
> legitimate power to command.

The *Spiritual Exercises* had triumphantly brought his followers to
this: they could wholeheartedly and lovingly place their futures,
and even their lives, in Ignatius's hands, listening only for his
directions and always ready to serve.

When Ignatius left Paris he had arranged with his companions
for all to meet in Italy by January 1537. After passing through Spain
and across Italy, Ignatius settled in Venice for a year and a half com-
pleting his studies for the priesthood, and seeing at first hand the
Church in its Italian setting. This was important; for though
reforms might begin in the extreme arms of the Church—in the
Netherlands with Erasmus and the Brethren of the Common Life,
in Germany with Nicholas of Cusa, in England with Colet and More,
in France with Lefèvre and Ascensius, in Spain with Ximenes and
Loyola, and so on—the Church could not be put in order until the
Italian heart was changed. When Ignatius arrived in Italy there were
favourable signs of some sort of change. After the timid and accommodating Clement VII died in 1534, a much bolder man, Alessandro
Farnese who took the title of Paul III, ascended the papal throne,
inspired by those ideals which the clerks regular were already putting
into practice. At once he raised Contarini, Sadoleto, Carafa and
Reginald Pole to the cardinal's purple, and in 1536 joined these four
with five other foremost churchmen of the age—Giberti, Fregoso,
Aleander, Cortese and Badia—in a commission to discover what
must be done in the Church. The report *de emendanda ecclesia*,
presented in the next year, was so sensationally shocking that the
Curia did not dare to publish it. It circulated in Rome, and a few

copies of the private printing found their way to Germany. Both Romans and Lutherans were thus confirmed in what they already knew, that the Church was thoroughly infected from papacy to parish priest. But at last the Holy See, and the administration, had taken note of this, and something might be done. Paul never did accomplish what his early years in the pontificate had promised. War prevented the Council he had announced from meeting at Mantua. The policies of the Emperor, the French king and the German princes complicated all his plans, and sapped the waning energies of the old man. But he had shown that the centre of the Church was ready, even eager, for reform, and he had gathered around him in Rome a group of dedicated and able men.

At this fortunate moment Ignatius arrived. The commission of 1537 had found nothing wrong with the laws of the Church; it was the administration of the laws that was corrupt. Ignatius agreed. His beliefs and his instinct had moved him gradually, but inevitably, towards Rome, the centre of the Christian world, and towards the pope, the spiritual father of Christendom. What would have happened if Ignatius had found St. Peter's chair occupied by another Alexander VI, or even another Julius II, is hard to say. A debauched and cynical pope could well have destroyed Ignatius's ideal world, in which the pope had such an exalted role. But Paul III reigned and all was well. Now that Ignatius was approaching the centre he could at last see what he felt called upon to do; the plans which he had never quite formulated in Paris began to come clear. And Venice, that queenly city devoted to many pleasures, was the best place to encourage his zeal, and show him the problems he faced in Italy. For besides the Oratory and the Theatines Venice had a more worldly side. Clément Marot, the banished French poet, described its pagan splendour:

> Their Signors are very wise in worldly matters, prudent to plan and quick to execute; pomp and pleasure are everywhere, but it is hard to discern marks of Christianity. They call themselves by the name of Christ but follow the precepts of Epicurus. Every sense is pampered, and the body seen to as if it harboured man's highest good; and more than elsewhere, among the lesser delights, Venus sits triumphantly enthroned.

Such obvious sinfulness was a challenge to make Ignatius work all the harder. Here too he began to meet important men and to impress them with his subtle diplomacy, such men as Pietro Contarini, a relative of the cardinal, and de Doctis, the vicar to the papal legate. Only Carafa, the most important man of all, failed to respond, and with him Ignatius made a foolish mistake which had serious consequences for the Society in the future, when Carafa became Pope Paul IV.

Ignatius sent him a letter, clumsily written in poor style, which may have been meant for advice, but looked very like criticism. The insignificant clerk with his dusty degree attempted to tell the eminent cardinal how to run the Theatines and, even worse, how to dress and conduct himself:

> For a person like yourself, so advanced in years, so noble and so dignified, to be a little better dressed and to have a room slightly larger and better furnished than others in your company chiefly to receive visitors—so far as this is concerned I see no scandal or lack of edification in it; one may well adjust oneself to the needs of the times, but that which is not perfect ought not to be considered perfect.

This inexplicable action gained Ignatius nothing except the cardinal's hostility.

When, at the beginning of 1537, the companions arrived from Paris, after a long march which took them through the warring armies of the Emperor and the French king, and even included a slight altercation with Protestants, Ignatius was ready to put them to work. For two months they worked in the Venetian hospitals, then all went to Rome to celebrate Holy Week. The pope received them well:

> to those who were not priests he gave letters empowering any bishop to ordain them without benefice. So when they got back here to Venice, we all took the orders, including the priesthood . . . The legate gave us complete authority to preach, interpret the scriptures and teach publicly and privately in all Venetian territory, together with power to confess and absolve all episcopal, archiepiscopal and patriarchal cases.

They still remembered their wish to go to Jerusalem. But passages were hard to find: and now, favoured by Rome and active in Venice, they slowly lost the desire. Ignatius continued to think, perhaps wistfully, of the journey, for Jerusalem was to him an important image. The rest, very busy in Venice, found the work of the present satisfying enough. Now that they were all priests they were caught up in the life of the Church in a way that had not been possible before. The journey to Jerusalem had been a private whim, something they could no longer indulge in. The circumstances of the

Church now dictated their futures, and the work in Venice prepared them to give their energies where the Church needed them. The *Spiritual Exercises* had marked them as men of God; their work as priests in the first two years in Italy confirmed them as servants of the Church. They trained themselves for the service of the Church with the grotesque savagery so well known in the history of Christian self-discipline. They undertook the nastiest jobs in the hospital. Rodriguez gives their duties as 'to tend the patients, make the beds, sweep the floors, scrub the dirt, wash the pots, dig the graves, carry the coffins, read the services and bury the dead'. But this was nothing; their fervent application drove them to strange excesses. A chapel in Venice bears this inscription: '*S. Franciscus Xaverius ulcera lambendo aegrotum sanavit*'—cured a sick man by licking his ulcers. This is the story as Rodriguez told it:

> At the Hospital of the Incurables there was a leper . . . Calling one of the Fathers, he said 'Be good enough to scratch my back.' The Father diligently did so, but began to fear, in a paroxysm of horror and nausea, lest he might catch the contagious disease. However, more anxious to break himself and still the rebellion of nature than to take precautions against contagion, he scraped together the pus with his fingers, and putting them in his mouth, licked and sucked them.

Ignatius, according to his Confessions, did exactly the same in Paris. But Ignatius's account ends with a psychological observation which may help to explain these actions. After he had touched the sores, his hand

> commenced to hurt, so that he thought he had the pest, and that imagination was so strong that he could not conquer it, until, with a strong impulse, he thrust his hand into his mouth saying, 'If you have got the pest in your hand you will have to have it in your mouth'. And when he had done that the imagination left him and also the ache in his hand.

As the psychology of the age was crude, so the remedies were crude; but Ignatius perceived what was happening in his mind and his cure was both effective and heroic, the more so as he was by disposition and training a neat and fastidious man (as was Xavier, his fellow Basque).

After the work in the hospitals, the companions split up, going out into the countryside in small groups to preach and give what help they could. The experiences of the different groups were uniformly uncomfortable. Ignatius wrote from Vicenza, 'They lit upon a house outside the city with neither door nor windows and lived there, sleeping on some straw which they collected.' And Xavier and Salmeron at Monselice 'found a desolated and ruined cottage . . . exposed to rain, wind and weather'. At Bassano, Le Jay and Rodriguez lived with a local hermit in a kind of cave. They fell ill, but persevered. They regarded, says Rodriguez, 'hunger, cold and other hardships as sweetest dainties for their souls, and singular proofs of divine beneficence'. In the autumn of 1537, Ignatius gathered them all together at Vicenza once more to discuss their future. The Turks still prevented the journey to Jerusalem, so they decided that Ignatius, Laynez and Favre should go to Rome and offer the services of the Iñiguistas (as they were popularly called) to the pope. This was the crucial moment. Ignatius, instinctively sorting the evidence of three Italian years in his mind, finally abandoned Jerusalem and offered his services where they were most needed, in the very centre of Christendom. And as usual when he had made an interior decision, he found it confirmed by vision. This happened at Storta, on the road to Rome, as Laynez recounts:

> Then he said to me that it seemed to him that God had impressed on his heart these words: 'I will be propitious to you at Rome', and our Father, not knowing what these words might mean, said: 'I do not know what will become of us at Rome, perhaps we shall be crucified.' Then another time he said that he seemed to see Christ with the cross on his shoulder and the Eternal Father near by, who said: 'I wish you to take this man for your servant' and so Jesus took him and said: 'I will that you should serve me.' And gaining from that vision great devotion to the name of Jesus, he wanted his congregation called *The Company of Jesus*.

Chapter VII

THE COMPANY OF JESUS

ALTHOUGH IGNATIUS walked into Rome confident of divine help, the Romans received him with their usual indifference. Three worn scholars, with only a few words of Italian between them, raised no expectations in a city that had seen more pompous arrivals and more resplendent self-glorifications than it knew how to count: the new-comers looked like beggars or possibly friars, which was even worse. Besides, they were foreigners and ambitious foreigners, from Alaric the Visigoth to the Emperor Charles V, caused Rome much bitterness. The citizens still remembered very well the Sack of Rome, only ten years before.

Pope Paul, who was glad to receive any band of men especially devoted to his interests, made them welcome; and a slight ripple of attention spread among the reforming men gathered around the pontiff. Paul appointed Favre and Laynez to teach at the college of the Sapienza. Ignatius successfully led Cardinal Contarini and Dr. Ortiz through the *Spiritual Exercises*. Ignatius had been lent a little house near the Trinità dei Monti, and there all the companions gathered in the spring of 1538. Authorized to preach, they spread out to all quarters of the city and preached sometimes in Spanish or French, sometimes in Italian, which puzzled their listeners but 'mortified their pride'. The winter of 1538 was one of the severest recorded; 'everywhere,' wrote Rodriguez, 'in the streets and the piazzas, the poor lay huddled, frozen to the bone and dying abandoned in the night from hunger. There was no one to care for them, no one to shelter them, no one to have pity on their misery.' The companions, well used to scenes of misery, energetically gave what help they could. They had moved to a large and rather ruinous house near the Torre del Melangolo, and this they turned into a combined hospital, dormitory and soup-kitchen for the poor. Among the Roman populace their reputation began to improve. Not only was it unusual for clergy to preach and exhort so diligently from the pulpit, but it was nothing short of miraculous for priests to take heed of their own exhortations and practice Christian charity among the poor.

When the worst trials of the winter were over, Ignatius and his company once more faced the unresolved problem—what were they to do in the future? Duty had brought them to Rome when the journey to Jerusalem became impossible. The pope had accepted their offer of allegiance and could find plenty of work for them. According to Bobadilla, Pope Paul wished them to stay, saying to them once at dinner, 'If you wish to have fruit in the Church of God, then Italy is a good and true Jerusalem.' When archbishops and cardinals found reform going sluggish in their territories, they asked for one of Ignatius's men to put a little ginger into the good work. Obviously, they were in Italy to stay; the only questions were under what conditions, and whether they were to remain together. In the spring of 1539 they met to consider the matter. As to whether they were to split up, they quickly answered no; 'as the most merciful and loving Lord had deigned to bring us together and bind us to one another, feeble men of such diverse nationality and character, we ought not to destroy this union of God but rather daily to strengthen and confirm it.' The next decision, which they deliberated for some time, was to choose a leader, add the vow of obedience to those of poverty and chastity which they had already taken, and thereby constitute themselves as a regular religious order (if the pope would permit it). That difficult decision reached, the rest of their intentions followed quite easily and were incorporated in a document addressed boldly to 'Whoever wishes to be a warrior of God under the banner of the cross in our Company, which we call by the name of Jesus'. After such an uncompromising beginning, the document goes on to revolt quietly against the usual practice of religious orders. The general is to decide democratically 'with the advice of the brothers in concilium', but to be obeyed absolutely—'The executive power and the power to give orders belong only to the prepositus (general)', and, 'Every member shall promise obedience to the general in all things concerning the rules'. The Company shall continue its intimate connection with the pope:

All members so long as life lasts shall every day remember the fact that this company and all in it are under the command of our holy master Paul III and his successors, so that we are bound to give him something more than the obedience of ordinary clergymen. We are bound by special oath to do whatever he orders us to do.

As they are active, so they will not have time for the more leisurely
and artistic duties of the monastic orders, and therefore 'shall not
use in divine service either the organ or chanting. For these things
which adorn the divine worship of the other orders, we have found
by experience to be no small hindrance to us; since we devote a
great part of the day and night to the bodily and spiritual care of the
sick'. There were, furthermore, two errors to be avoided. Asceticism
—'fasts, scourgings, going bare-footed or bare-headed, fixed colours
of dress and fixed foods, hair shirts'—was not to be allowed as it
limited activity. And secondly, 'No one can be received into the
Company unless he has been very thoroughly tested for a long time'.

This document, agreed on June 24, was entrusted to Cardinal
Contarini who offered to secure the pope's approval. Having received
a favourable opinion from Badia, the Master of the Sacred Palace,
the pope agreed verbally to the plan. By September, the companions
were happily contemplating a secure future. Ignatius wrote to his
brother Beltran that all was settled; and Salmeron told a Spanish
correspondent that 'the Pope, in spite of accusations, slanders and
law suits, has approved and confirmed our mode of living together
and has given us permission to make our own constitution'. The
rejoicings, however, were premature. The canon lawyers had yet to
give a verdict according to the mysteries of their art. Cardinal
Ghinucci, the papal secretary, found that the rules against asceticism
and the absence of choir duties were without precedent, and
therefore uncanonical, and probably wrong; he could not agree.
With Contarini enthusiastically for the proposal and Ghinucci
firmly against it, the pope then appointed a third cardinal, Bartolo-
meo Guidiccioni, to judge between them. Guidiccioni took a novel
position. He agreed in theory to the five articles of Ignatius, but he
hated the monks so thoroughly for 'their abominable dissensions,
quarrels and contentions, both among themselves and with the
regular clergy' that he wished to suppress all but four of the orders,
and even those, he thought, might profitably be incorporated into
one. He would not agree to the foundation of a new order. It seemed
as if the Jesuits were to be stillborn.

Ignatius met this opposition in his usual way—by an appeal for
divine assistance, and by cunning diplomacy. He vowed three thousand Masses for a change of heart in Guidiccioni; nearly two years
later, Francis Xavier, on his way to India, was still running through
his quota of these Masses. Ignatius also enlisted the help of the Duke
of Ferrara and his brother Cardinal Ippolito d'Este, Cardinal

Ferreri, the senators of Parma, the Archbishop of Siena, and Constanza Farnese, the illegitimate daughter of the pope. Faced by this impressive artillery, Guidiccioni agreed to allow the order so long as the membership was limited to sixty. At last, on September 27, 1540, Pope Paul signed the Bull *Regimini militantis Ecclesiae* establishing the Society of Jesus. The Bull incorporated most of what Ignatius had set out in the five articles, but omitted the rules on asceticism and the prohibition on choir duties.

Through all the trials of 1539 and 1540 Ignatius acted as if confident of the final result. Indeed, from his conversion in 1521 onwards, he always acted as if opposition would collapse before him, and it always did. This particularly annoyed later critics who felt that here was a case of hubris going unpunished. But Ignatius always worked hard for his good luck, and marshalled his arguments and his patrons with ability. Even while the Church parties for and against the Jesuits deliberated, Ignatius was despatching men far and wide, directing them from Rome by letter (the start of a vast correspondence which includes some 6,800 of Ignatius's letters) 'in Portugal or in the Indies, in Spain, in Paris, in Ireland, in Naples, in Parma, in Placenza, in Brescia and in the March of Ancona'. Rodriguez and Xavier, on their way to Portugal in March 1540, left behind their votes for the general, even though the Bull of establishment had not yet been signed, and would not be signed for another six months. In September 1540, the original fathers were so scattered that the preliminary work on the constitutions was left to Ignatius and Codure, the only two available in Rome. After a delay of seven months, six original members met in Rome to elect the general. The votes of the two in Portugal were already at hand, Favre sent his from Germany and Bobadilla, mislaid in southern Italy, did not vote. The ballot papers were placed in a locked chest and taken out after three days of prayer. Eight of the votes declared for Ignatius, the ninth—Ignatius's own—read as follows:

> I give my vote for the superior in Our Lord to him who receives the most votes, except myself. I do this for good reasons, but if the company thinks otherwise, or that it is better and more for the glory of God for me to be particular, I am ready to be so.

Obviously Ignatius expected to be chosen, yet he insisted on being difficult. He demanded a second ballot, and the result was the same. He still wanted to refuse and insisted on putting the matter to his confessor. After three days the confessor advised him to accept. He

asked the confessor to consider for another three days, and then to
write out his decision and send it to the company. Finally, Ignatius
was prevailed on to accept.

This was a curious episode and not easily understood. Appointees
to the episcopacy were expected to be suitably humble, but Ignatius
was never one for graceful conventions. He thought his conduct
important, and gave this account of it at the time:

> Iñigo acted thus because he felt in his soul more will and desire to be
> governed than to govern. He felt that he was not strong enough to
> govern himself, so how could he rule others? Considering this and
> his many evil habits, past and present, his many sins, faults, and bodily
> miseries, he would declare until he had more light that he would never
> undertake such a task.

He was fifty years old and not in very good health, worn down by
privation, hard work and persistent stomach pains. Twice during
the years of his generalship he wished to resign. But more than this,
he alone knew what he had done in founding the order, and he alone
could guess at the future. He saw ahead a task that was daunting and
painful enough to deter any man. The life of the Society depended
on activity; rest and peace were both impossible and unthinkable.
The Society was constituted to take the dangerous missions, against
the Reformation and against the infidels, fighting the battles of God
on and on in a world which gradually came to deny that there were
any religious battles, and indeed wondered if there was a God. They
were a group of men bred by a particular occasion, by the collapse of
Christendom, and since most people either actively or passively
concurred with the collapse of Christendom, they set out to put
right what could not be remedied. For the good fight, they trained
themselves lean and hard, and carried no excess baggage and no
superfluous ideas. The consolations of art (one of Ignatius's hardest
struggles was to have the absence from choir duties written into the
constitution), the joys of contemplation, which the older orders had
encouraged and continued to encourage for the future, were not for
the Jesuits. And at the time they were right; for while popes such as
Leo X and Clement VII dabbled in the kind waters of art, which
erased all their cares, the Church rumbled on into the pit from which
it seemed there might be no escape. The Jesuits, more than anyone
else, helped to arrest that precipitate fall. But the dangers of the
sixteenth century, with all their peculiar circumstances, passed; and
the other orders that had been born of the occasion—the Theatines,

the Somaschi and the Barnabites—gradually and slowly declined, recognizing perhaps that they had done their work and allowing the older orders with longer experience—the Benedictines, the Cistercians, the Franciscans and the Dominicans—to bloom again, which they eventually did. Only the Jesuits refused to decline. Ignatius's great aim was not only to stop the disintegration of the Church, but also to recover the lost ground, and he saw that this was a work which went on to the end of the world. In the simplicity of his ardour he thought that his aim naturally coincided with the aim of the papacy, and so tied his order tight to the papacy with a special vow. In a way this guaranteed the existence of the Society. For as long as the papacy lasted and as long as the Society remained the servant of the pope, so the Society would continue. But Ignatius miscalculated. The papacy, an institution with a long and wily history and with plenty of worldly wisdom (a wisdom, alas, too often opposed to the 'heroic wisdom' of uncompromising men like Ignatius), knew there was a time to attack and a time to retrench. The Jesuits went on fighting; but, after a time, to their surprise they found they were fighting the Church and the papacy. Clement XIV suppressed the Society in 1773, and it remained suppressed for forty years. Although Ignatius could not have foreseen the dangers ahead, at least he knew the effort required of his Society. He was human enough to feel dismayed and incapable.

By 1541 the Society had a general and work to do throughout the world, but no constitution. After the election, the fathers had hurried back to the beleaguered outskirts of the Church and left the drafting of the constitution to Ignatius and Codure, agreeing beforehand to whatever they should decide. Codure died within a year, and Ignatius was so busy he did not begin writing until 1547. He finished the draft in 1550 and soon afterwards Nadal and Quadrio visited the various countries in which Jesuits were active to publish and explain the constitutions. Up to his death in 1556, Ignatius continued to make minor alterations and adjustments. In 1558 the first General Chapter of the Society confirmed what Ignatius had written and the constitutions became law.

Although Ignatius naturally benefited from the experience and recommendations of his wide-flung followers, the constitutions are as much his work and as personal to him as are the *Spiritual Exercises*. The *Exercises* foresee a certain kind of spiritual man; the constitutions provide an organisation for that man. The *Exercises* demand an active faith; the constitutions legislate for an active community. Ignatius recognized quite clearly that his Society was not for everyone and he was not accommodating to the unsuitable, even if they had the most pious and worthy motives for joining. The constitutions start with an 'Examen' which lets the candidate know exactly what he may expect. It begins:

> The object of this Society is not only to pursue the salvation and per-fection of our own souls, by God's grace, but also, by the same help, to seek zealously the salvation and perfection of our neighbour's soul.

The candidate then reads of the vows, the mode of life and the training. If the candidate survives this, he may yet be rejected for various reasons. Absolute bars to membership are heresy, serious crimes, such as homicide, membership of another order, marriage or servitude and mental deficiency. More important, there are a number of discretionary bars including bad habits, worldliness, in-constancy, questionable devotions causing illusions, lack of educa-tion or intelligence, obstinacy, debts, and age (either too old or too young). The constitutions themselves are divided into ten parts, moving rather haphazardly from the novitiate (Part 1) through education, rights and duties, conduct of missions, unity of the order, administration and the powers of the general, and finally an allocu-tion on how to preserve and increase the Society (Part 10).

With the great aim of the Society always in view—the work for a unified Christendom—the constitutions lay particular emphasis on the virtues of self-discipline and obedience. In a sense, the members of the Society possess only one right: to serve 'for the greater glory of God'. Their duty is to empty themselves of all that is merely personal and devote every action and every thought to the common end. A professed Jesuit voluntarily places himself under restrictions more severe than those of other orders. Besides the ordinary vows of the religious, he takes a fourth vow of obedience to the pope and a number of simple vows—to maintain the ideal poverty set out in the constitutions, not to look for office inside or outside the Society, and to refuse ecclesiastical appointments, such as a bishopric or the cardinalate, unless ordered to accept by the pope. A 'personality' is an ugly tumult on the surface of the waters; this must be stilled and the individual merged into the quiet depths of the unified order.

The doctors of the Church, and the founders of the monastic orders, thought obedience a very great virtue. For, as they saw the matter, the religious, making the vow of obedience, offers himself to God. St. Thomas, in the *Summa theologica*, says: 'The vow of obedience is the chief of the three religious vows. . . . Therefore, properly speaking, the virtue of obedience, whereby we condemn our own will for God's sake, is more praiseworthy than the other moral virtues, which contemn other goods for the sake of God.' Thomas à Kempis, Ignatius's favourite, says much the same in his more homely way: 'By obedience man becomes beloved of God, and on such friendly terms with Christ as to merit to be his brother.' The gentle Kempis stresses the glories of obedience; Bernard, an abbot of Monte Cassino who died in 1282, in a fierce passage which seems to anticipate Ignatius's thoughts, dwells on the sacrifices of obedience:

> As the sheep which is destined for the slaughter is fed, fattened and sheltered in order later to be killed, so the monk is also looked upon by others and must consider himself as fed in the refectory, served in the infirmary, and cared for in the cloister for no other purpose than to be God's host and victim, and to die under the sword of obedience.

And since a superior is vested with religious authority, obedience to God means obedience to superiors. 'The first principle of union among monks,' wrote St. Jerome, 'is to obey superiors and do whatever they command.' St. Basil speaks of the monk as a carpenter's tool in the hands of the superior, and Kempis says: 'He makes greater spiritual progress and becomes more acceptably pleasing to God who fulfils more quickly and readily that which the will of the superior declares should be done.'

But the thinking on obedience went through a subtle, and perhaps unnoticed transformation. The ideal is quite clear. St. Thomas, lucid as usual, wrote: 'For were one to suffer even martyrdom, or to give all one's goods to the poor, unless one directed these things the fulfilment of the divine will, which pertains directly to obedience, they would not be meritorious.' God must always be the object of obedience. However, the individual is both mulish and mutinous, and, as Kempis suggests, the person may best control himself and find the divine will by putting himself under the direction of a superior. Obedience to a superior is thus a great aid to selflessness and charity. 'Obedience is the only virtue,' wrote St. Gregory the Great, 'that implants other virtues in the soul, and preserves them.' And St. Augustine puts it even more strongly:

> By the precept he gave, God commended obedience, which is, in a sort, the mother and guardian of all the virtues in the reasonable creature, which was so created that submission is advantageous to it,

whereas the fulfilment of its own will in preference to the Creator's is destruction.

The spiritual and the psychological have become a little mixed. Obedience to God's will is a spiritual necessity; obedience to a superior, meritorious in itself as the superior stands in the place of Christ, is a psychological help to subdue self-will. In the earlier days of monasticism the slight confusion between these uses of obedience did not matter very much. The good superior had in mind always the spiritual advancement of his flock, and all his orders should tend to bring the individual closer to God. The first monastic orders existed primarily for the benefit of the individual monks, to exhort and lead them to save their souls. For this reason a monastery welcomed all the arts and all the trades, for a painter served God best through his paintings, a farmer through farming, a scholar through scholarship, and so on. The work which a monastery did for the Christian community was of secondary importance, and was in fact a sort of generous overflow of its other activities.

Then, in the sixteenth century, the new kind of religious order, of which the Society of Jesus is the best example, sprang up to deal with the problems of the age. Here for the first time in Western religious practice, the spiritual advancement of the individual member is not paramount; it exists equally in conjunction with another aim, 'to seek zealously the salvation and perfection of our neighbour's soul'—as Ignatius phrased it. And the unhappy history of Europe inevitably caused the Jesuits to concentrate on this other aim. No longer did the order exist only for the benefit of the individuals in it, rather the members were entirely at the service of the order; the individual still sought his salvation, but he did so by pursuing the just and holy aims of the Society. This mean a different interpretation of obedience. The superior, that intermediate between God and His subject, has suddenly grown very large; he has become less a guide and more a master.

Ignatius's writings on obedience are strongly worded but quite traditional. We should, he says, 'have God, our Creator and Lord, before our eyes in order that for His sake a man may give obedience to his fellow men', and 'look upon our superior, whoever he may be, as the representative of Christ'. In a rare excursion into imagery, he compares the obedient man to a staff in an old man's hand, and— repeating St. Francis—to a corpse in the hands of a dresser. He adds:

We must drop every occupation—leaving unfinished the letter we have begun—and band all our strength and purpose in the Lord, so that holy obedience is perfect in us in every respect, in execution, in will and in understanding; obedience in execution consists in doing what is ordered; obedience in will, willing the same thing as he who gives the order; obedience in understanding, in thinking as the superior thinks, and in believing what he ordains is rightly ordained. Otherwise obedience is imperfect.

Although there is nothing original here, the other provisions of the constitutions show the particular importance of Jesuit obedience. Ignatius had continually in mind the unity of the order—just as he worked always for the unity of Christendom—and to promote this he gave the general exceptional powers. The general alone held office for life. He had power to admit and dismiss, to nominate and remove all provincials and all rectors. He summoned general assemblies of the Society. Every three years every provincial had to submit a confidential report on the province. Ignatius did legislate that in certain matters the general must consult assistants, but they were to be helpers and advisers only and their advice did not bind the general. The general is subject only to the constitutions which may be altered only by a general congregation of the Society. Ignatius, a humane and generous man, naturally desired that the general be 'closely united to God and very familiar with the use of prayer', and also he should 'shine with the light of charity to all his neighbours'. Ignatius recognized that the best binding of his Society was love. But love is unenforceable while obedience is. The powers of the general applied without love look perilously like the absolute powers of a dictator. It is argued, and rightly so, that the followers of Ignatius have voluntarily taken the *Exercises* and then voluntarily embraced the restrictions of the constitutions, so there can be no question of compulsion or dictatorship. But obedience, as we have seen, has the double function of serving both God and the psyche. The rule of obedience seemed to hold rather different psychological attractions for the Jesuits than it did for members of earlier orders; and since the great aim of the Jesuits is 'the salvation and perfection of our neighbour's soul', the neighbour ought to consider the psychology of his relentless mentors. For society, even though fallen and wicked, still prefers to decide to whom it shall listen, even in spiritual matters.

The old monk welcomed obedience to keep his self-willed and erring human nature in order. He knew, as St. Peter Damian said, that 'sometimes no other burden is heavier for man than man himself. What tyrant is more cruel to man, what power harsher than man's own self-will?' The Jesuit Alfonso Rodriguez has this to say on the soothing effects of obedience:

One of the great consolations of monastic life is the assurance we have that in obeying we can commit no fault. The superior may commit a fault in commanding you to do this or that, but you are certain that you commit no fault so long as you obey, because God will only ask you if you have duly performed what orders you have received, and if you can give a clear account in that respect, you are absolved entirely.... The moment what you did was done obediently, God wipes it out of your account, and charges it to the superior.

Perhaps only by such a doctrine could the Society claim the absolute obedience which it required in order to meet its aims; but the denial of personal responsibility is uneasy and self-indulgent, and would have shocked St. Thomas. Aquinas wrote: 'Goodness of the will, proceeding from intention directed to an end, is not sufficient to make an exterior act good.' Yet the very great difficulty of the work which Ignatius had set the Society demanded special men under special discipline. The older orders could afford to accept most men of good-will, from the humblest intelligence to the most eccentric genius. Ignatius, in the eighth part of the constitutions, wants only carefully picked men; for 'a great multitude of persons whose faults have not been well subdued by self discipline, does not bear order, let alone union'. And once unity is achieved it is not to be endangered: 'Whoever is seen to be a cause of division among those who live together ... ought to be separated from that congregation like a pestilence which, if not remedied at once, will spread its contagion.' To illustrate Jesuit discipline, Polanco has a sad little story of a young, dying novice 'who set an example of great patience and obedience, and at the end he did something of great edification by asking the master of the novices for permission to die'.

In spite of all this stern writing, Ignatius himself had a flexible approach to obedience. In his years as general, he did not like advice on how to run the order, and savaged Laynez quite severely for tendering a little criticism. Yet he allowed his provincials and rectors a wide discretion in running their own affairs, merely sending them 'suggestions' which did not necessarily have to be obeyed, and often replying to their queries with a note saying, 'Do as you think best. Fit the rules to the place the best way you can,' and 'Cut your coat according to your cloth and your needs'. To some of his most devoted followers, for example Nadal and his industrious secretary Polanco, he was hard and unforgiving; but to a wayward son like Simon

Rodriguez in Portugal he was gentle and forgiving to a fault. To Simon he addressed the well-known *Letter on Obedience*.

Simon Rodriguez, one of the original fathers from Paris, had started for India with Xavier, but had stopped in Portugal at the wish of the king; and there he stayed, establishing a prosperous little empire which went its own way. Ignatius tried to lure Simon back to Rome to answer some dubious rumours, but the king would not permit him to go and, in spite of the rumours, Ignatius made Simon the Portuguese provincial in 1546. The province continued to flourish and the rumours continued to circulate, so that in 1551 Ignatius decided to remove Simon from Portugal. To do this, and also not to hurt Rodriguez, he divided the Spanish province into Castile and Aragon and ordered Simon to take Aragon. Simon was reluctant to go, but after much pressure and much mumbling he went, leaving the Portuguese province to Father Miron, an unimaginative disciplinarian who so stirred up the easy life of the province that the membership of the Society fell by a half. In the meantime Simon, from Spain, was sending out letters accusing Ignatius of coveting the riches of the Duke of Gandia, a recent recruit of the Society, and of denuding the Portuguese province of its best sons while sending in worthless foreigners. In spite of all this, Ignatius allowed him to return to Portugal for the sake of his health, even though no Jesuit house would have him. He stayed on the congenial estate of the Duke of Aveiro.

In 1553, Ignatius summoned Simon to Rome, threatening dismissal from the Society if he did not come. Six months later he arrived and was treated like a long lost brother, receiving the best room in the house and no recriminations. Perhaps seduced by these attentions, Simon demanded a trial. Predictably, four fathers found him extremely guilty and guessed that he had been led away by the devil. They imposed a just penance which Ignatius commuted into something much milder. To ease the blow to Simon's pride, Ignatius wrote to Portugal saying that Simon was thoroughly reformed—'from his conversation and company, I have every day more and more satisfaction'. The story did not end there. Simon began to brood again; Ignatius brought his old comrades Salmeron and Bobadilla from Naples and Ancona to reason with him. Simon appealed to the pope to be allowed to enter a hermitage near Lisbon, but Ignatius blocked this. Instead he offered Simon a summer holiday in Monreale 'which has the best air and the most beautiful position of all our houses'; indeed, he offered to let Simon go anywhere he pleased except to Portugal. But Simon continued to show a fretful temper and to be a nuisance, opening other people's letters and writing little poisonous ones of his own, until Ignatius died in 1556. Then unexpectedly Simon did reform, and for the next twenty years served the Society well in Italy, in Spain, and finally in his beloved Portugal.

If ever there was a 'pestilence' in the congregation, Simon Rodriguez was one, yet Ignatius allowed his contagion to spread despite the injuctions of the constitutions. Ignatius made the laws and could afford to bend them. Rodriguez was a friend and companion from the Paris days, and his treatment speaks well for Ignatius's heart. But it is doubtful if Ignatius would have allowed others to act with such latitude. The constitutions were strict and were supposed to be kept strictly, as the last words of the document show—'and finally let all set themselves to keep the constitutions, for which end it is necessary to know them: at least for each one to know those that relate to himself, and so they are to be read or heard read every month'.

The delicate point about the rule of the Jesuits is not that it is strict or oppressive, but that it illustrates a tendency of the age—the tendency deliberately to make individuals exist for the benefit of institutions. Whatever the drawbacks of the Middle Ages (and certainly they were brutal and horrific enough), men did not worry very much about to whom they belonged. One slipped at birth into a set place and, from lack of means and opportunity, rarely left it. In a fairly stable, agricultural society a man's loyalties were local and immediate; and when his vision did extend beyond the home or the farm he was generally possessed by some vague ideal such as Christendom, or the Holy Roman Empire. The simple theory of his institutions, both religious and temporal, was that they existed for his benefit—though they might not have worked like that in practice. And so long as he avoided the violence of his neighbours and accomplished his social tasks peacefully, he was left alone with his eccentricities and his prejudices. But that simple world broke down. There were no longer any set places and the individual wandered, awaiting re-organization. It came very soon. Paradoxically, the Renaissance with its great insistence on individuality, practically ensured that individuals should be rather less free than they were before. True, the Renaissance destroyed the old mental habits and prepared men to be Lutherans, Calvinists, or even agnostics and atheists, instead of slothful members of a corrupt universal Church.

But the old Christendom had asked for very little more than a formal assent to the ideal. The new institutions were not content with ideals, and realistically tried to tie their members down, body and soul. Perhaps the first step towards this end was taken by the nationalistic kings who taxed, dragooned and killed their subjects all for the glory of the country's name, usually with the enthusiastic support of the citizens. Where the temporal had led, the spiritual soon followed, and in the sixteenth century the forces of regulation proliferated. It was the age of the Roman Inquisition (covering the whole Church, unlike the limited jurisdiction of the Spanish Inquisition), the Index, the strictly defined orthodoxy of the Council of Trent, the age of Loyola, of Calvin in Geneva, of the Anabaptists in Münster, and of Henry VIII's state religion in England. It was an age of active institutions which seemed to lead a life of their own, using, condemning and discarding individuals according to principle. In other words, it was the birth of our modern world. And the Society of Jesus was the first successful example of the representative modern institution. It was a voluntary band of carefully selected men pursuing a corporate aim which transcended any individual desire. It had an apparently democratic structure, but the real power rested in the hands of one man, the general, who demanded from himself and from the members orthodoxy, conformity and obedience.

Chapter VIII

'WHAT ARE WE TO DO FOR GOD?'

IN THE fifteen years between his election as general and his death in 1556, Ignatius hardly left the Jesuit house in Rome. He became a prisoner to his own incredible industry, a story related fully—if tediously—by the equally hard-working Polanco in some four thousand pages of the *Monumenta Historica Societatis Jesu*, the official history of the Society. Before Ignatius's death, his men had landed in India, Japan, the Congo and Brazil; in his last months he turned his eyes to what Gonzales called 'Prester John's business' in Ethiopia, and addressed to that uncomprehending emperor a little book on 'The Primacy of the Roman Pontiff'. His Society began with ten men in a ruined Roman house; by 1556 the Society had a hundred houses and about a thousand members (Pope Paul III, in a Bull of 1543, had removed the limitation to sixty members) in eleven provinces, nine in Europe, one in India and one in Brazil. And over all this activity Ignatius presided personally, directing by letter great and small matters alike, from the founding of a college to the best way of preparing vegetables in the kitchen. By 1556, quite clearly the order was a success.

But the advance was not everywhere triumphal. North of the Alps progress was slow or non-existent. The broken politics of Germany allowed the Jesuits to gain some holds in the country, especially in southern Germany after the Council of Trent. From England and Ireland, the missioners returned perplexed and discomforted. In England the king's power made their success impossible, and in Ireland they met an alien chaos which was altogether too much for them. 'God be praised', said Salmeron, safe once more among the Latins, 'the time of our stay in Ireland was not without its share of the cross'. And he added, 'it was Lent and the right time for penance'. In the south, too, the Jesuits met opposition from the conservative and the jealous. Martinez Siliceo, the Primate of Spain, refused to allow anyone but a parish priest to give communion in his diocese, an ordinance directed mainly at the Jesuits. In

Salamanca the opposition was more serious and caused Ignatius some trouble, for it was led by Melchior Cano, the prize theologian of the Dominicans, and a voice much heard in the Church. He condemned the Jesuits as 'an order of loungers, whose members go to and fro about the streets like other people; they are given up to indolence, they take good care not to mortify the body, they procure for themselves permission to say their prayers out of the curtailed Roman breviary'. Cano saw them, along with 'hypocrisies' and 'Alumbrados', among the damned at the Last Judgment—they 'shall then be accursed and led down to hell'. It took letters from both the general of the Dominicans and the Pope to stem Cano's hot tirade. In Zaragoza, the Augustinians picketed the Jesuit college, carrying a cross draped in black and chanting the startling curses of the 109th psalm. Opposition might be expected in Spain, the most conservative and most independent Catholic country; but Jesuit affairs did not always run smoothly in Italy or France either. At Perugia the Franciscans disliked, as a daring innovation, the Jesuit practice of encouraging frequent communion among the laity, and they tried to introduce rules to stop this excess. In France where the contrary claims of the Gallican church and the Reformation caused much turmoil, things were even more difficult. The Bishop of Cambrai would not let the Jesuits preach or teach in his diocese for the forthright reason that by refusing to accept fees for their services they would soon bankrupt the other orders. Not even the approval of the pope could move the bishop who testily asked Father Bernard Olave, 'Why don't you go to the Germans, the Turks, the Indians, or even the English, to become martyrs for the faith if you are as good as you wish people to think?' Then answering his own question, the bishop declared that Jesuits were 'only hypocrites, vagabonds, seducers and floating scum'. The Jesuits retired before this onslaught, defeated. Paris, too, perhaps encouraged by Cano's opinion, found the Jesuits unorthodox and subversive. When Ignatius's application to open a college came before the Parlement, permission was denied. The theological faculty of the university, 'throwing', said Polanco, 'such poisoned darts as could hardly be believed by one not present at the hearing', found the Jesuits 'dangerous in matters of faith, disturbing to the peace of the Church, subversive of monastic religion, and greater in destruction than in edification'.

The Jesuits were different and revolutionary enough to make this dislike understandable. They offended the old orders, they offended local Church dignitaries whose horizons hardly ever extended as far as Rome and the pope; and, even more galling, the first Jesuits were incorruptible, pious and energetic. But some of the bad feeling was of their own making. Ignatius, who had the most exalted conception of the priesthood, always defended the right of young boys to enter the novitiate of the Society against the wishes of their parents. The problem was not new. Both St. Francis of Assisi and St. Thomas Aquinas had to battle their families when their vocations conflicted with family interests; and St. Thomas, who first went to the Dominicans at about the age of fifteen, was for a time locked up by his parents. But it seemed that the Jesuits, ever on the look-out for bright young lads, went in for a rather more systematic spiritual baby-snatching. This caused trouble, especially in aristocratic families whose plans for their aspiring sons rarely included a hard life in India, or a martyr's death in Brazil. Cases such as that of the fifteen-year-old Octavian Caesar delighted the enemies of the Society, with plot succeeding plot, and orders and anathemas airily winging their way between prelate and prelate. Carafa was for the parents, Ignatius tried to bundle the boy off to Spain. Finally the pope intervened on Ignatius's side only to find that the boy no longer wished to be a Jesuit, and, in fact, was saying all sorts of unpleasant things about the Society.

A more serious reason for dislike came from the Jesuits' attitude towards themselves and towards the rest of the Church. In their way, they were special and exclusive, and, encouraged by Ignatius, they tended to think themselves superior too. Ignatius would not agree to co-operation with other orders and to begin with this was a sound rule; for the other orders were all to some degree lax, and the Jesuits had an entirely new monastic method. Soon, however, this bred a mentality best expressed by the Jesuit habit of distinguishing 'ours' from the rest. On one occasion when a joint scheme was proposed, Ignatius refused 'lest a door might be opened for "ours" to mix in the affairs of that congregation'—though one feels the real fear is that the others might interfere in Jesuit business. Ignatius, according to Ribadeneira, did not like to hear accounts of piety and good deeds within other orders repeated inside Jesuit houses; he thought that enough examples were to be found within the Society. He also attempted at the Council of Trent to have the council endorse his Society, though he was dissuaded when a bishop pointed out that 'no religious order had ever before been approved by any general council of the Church'. Where Ignatius led, the other Jesuits followed. Polanco's official history has this to say about the Jesuits' special standing:

> It must be confessed that experience teaches that a very close friendship with priests who are not of the Society, even though in other respects they are good and spiritual men and actively help others, is not to be cultivated.

Later, the Jansenist de la Berthier, during the deadly controversy over Port-Royal, describes this Jesuit attitude less politely; they saw themselves, he wrote quoting from the Jesuit *Imago*, as 'a Society not of men but of Angels and the Spirits of Eagles, the Lights of Mankind, the Preceptors of all the world, the Reformers of Manners, who have banished vice and made virtue to flourish'.

So much of what Ignatius did is open to misinterpretation, and the very many later opponents of the Society have gladly put the worst construction on his actions. Far from being dishonest and secretive, Ignatius took no trouble at all to hide his dealings. He lived at a very bad time for the Church, in a difficult world where caution, subtlety and even deviousness were necessary to accomplish anything. The fact that he openly relates, or allows the Jesuit chronicler to record, his caution, subtlety, and occasional piece of deviousness, indicates his honesty. He never explained his motives because he never thought they needed explaining; he always acted '*ad majorem Dei gloriam*'—to the greater glory of God. The detailed instructions he gave to his spiritual sons seem now to be often cold, calculating, and to encourage insincerity. But Ignatius knew the realities of political life, and was aware that his Society could do little unless aided by those faithless men, the European princes. As active ministers among the uninterested or the hostile, the Jesuits needed the indulgence of princes and the good-will of the people. The instructions *Del modo de negociar y conversar in Domino* which Ignatius gave to Salmeron and Broet, bound for Ireland in 1541, are models of good sense:

> In dealing with everyone, especially equals or inferiors, according to their dignity or authority, speak little and reluctantly, listen long and willingly. Be brisk and courteous in farewell. In talking with those of rank or power, in order to win them to God's greater service, consider first their temperament and adapt yours to that. . . . In all conversation to win others and net them for the greater glory of God, let us follow the method of our enemy, the devil, in his dealings with a good man. . . . For he goes in by the good man's door to come out by his own, approving, not contradicting, habits, considering the soul and drawing it to good

and holy thoughts until little by little he bends things to his way, trapping the soul, under the guise of good, into some error of illusion. . . . So we, for our good purpose, may show sympathy and pass over things of a bad nature to win confidence and further our good plans. . . . In all dealing with others, specially when making peace or giving spiritual advice, it is necessary to be guarded, remembering that everything one says may or will become public. In business be free with time—that is to say, if you promise something for tomorrow, do it if possible today.

He continues with good practical advice on how to travel and how to help the poor, and concludes with a sound exhortation: 'Generally you will use all possible dexterity and prudence to avoid capture by the King's ministers.' Using the wiles of the devil—carefully studying the psychology of the listener—was a great help to the Jesuits abroad, where difficulties of language and culture made communication a problem. In spite of his simple terminology, Ignatius understood and used systematically the psychological knowledge of the Renaissance. Father Gaspard Berze, an engaging priest with a lurid secular past, whom Francis Xavier made superior in India in 1552, wrote to Ignatius describing how he won the confidence of the Indians:

I use all the tricks and stratagems that I learnt as a layman to see if I can now do God as much service as I did him disservice before. With those who laugh, I try to laugh; with those who sing, I sometimes sing; with those who make merry, I occasionally make merry; with those who weep, I try to weep.

This letter must have pleased Ignatius.

Inevitably, because of their aims and their methods, the Jesuits felt the temptation of political intrigue. Ignatius was well aware of this danger and strictly prohibited meddling in affairs of state. He wrote to a member in Corsica 'to attend to preaching the doctrines of the Christian life, and not to become involved in any way in affairs of state. Prudence and holy discretion demand this, and also it is expressly ordered in our Constitutions'. He once told Ribadeneira that he disapproved of some of the more enthusiastic members of the Society who 'thrust themselves into the work of government':

When similar things came to him he thought about the account he would have to give to Our Lord at the Last Judgment. It seemed to him that he would not be asked whether he had a plan to reform the whole world, but whether he has obeyed the laws of his society, hearing confessions, or preaching, or reading the scriptures, or governing the Society; in fact, helping souls like a poor monk.

But what Ignatius would not let himself recognize was that religion had become 'an affair of state', and any active religious group in Europe could not avoid playing politics. Very soon after Ignatius's death the rumours of Jesuit politicians caused such common scandal that even the Society took note of it. Father Manare criticized Riba-deneira's *Life of Ignatius* for using the phrase 'the Society ought to employ itself in *large things* which the Spanish translates as *great things*'. Manare goes on:

> I think it would be better to cut out both these phrases; because in every nation among all peoples we are falsely accused of interfering in great affairs which rightly belong to princes or states. Therefore, we must not give fuel for scandal.

In Ignatius's mind there appeared to be a strange gulf between his ideals and his practice. He attempted to fulfil the ideals of the Middle Ages using the techniques of the modern world. But there is always some sort of parity between technique and ideal—the technique of the modern world can only lead to the ideals of the modern world. Ignatius did not see that the transitional age to which he belonged had debased the value of religion in human affairs. The ultimate truths of religion may or may not have remained unshaken; but the churches, and the men who ran them, no longer permeated the European imagination. The ideal of Christendom in the Middle Ages had been a personal ideal, often divorced from political expediency so that Europe was led to act with outstanding foolish-ness, as at Nicopolis and the fall of Constantinople. Nationalism, the Renaissance and the Reformation had made religion the hand-maiden of princes, subject always to national expediency and politics. Eager to use the wiles of the devil for the work of good, Ignatius decided to fight on this ground. But to fight God's battles on the devil's ground is in itself a triumph for the devil; for victory there means possession not of the good, but only of the defeated bad. The Jesuits using the techniques of politics, could not help becoming politicians themselves.

The impression of Ignatius himself during the busy years of his generalship is one of perfect discipline. His self-control was a remarkable achievement, for in the fifteen years at the head of his order he was ill fifteen times, sometimes so seriously that he was forced to stay in bed for weeks at a time; yet the work of his expand-ing order was so diversified, so full of problems and so unremitting that it would have taxed the strength of the youngest and healthiest of men. Something of this varied activity can be seen from the second Bull of institution granted by Pope Julius III in 1550:

> The company exists to work entirely for the defence and propagation of the holy Catholic faith, and to help souls in Christian life and doctrine, by preaching and teaching the word of God, by giving spiritual exercises, teaching the faith to children and the uneducated, hearing confessions and giving the sacraments. It is also formed to reconcile quarrels, help prisoners in gaol and the sick in hospital, and all must be done freely without expecting any human wages or fees for this labour.

Much of what Ignatius did, quite apart from his religious work, was admirable and socially important. True, everything he did was done for the love of God, and in the hope of winning people to religion; but society generally benefited from his work. One of his first actions on coming to Rome was to press for a house for reformed prostitutes, providing most of the money for this endeavour out of Jesuit funds. And when the Casa de Santa Marta finally opened, Ignatius took upon himself the spiritual and practical guidance of the women, a job which won him little but laughs and calumny from the cynical Romans. He applied himself seriously as a peaceful arbitrator in the quarrels of the great. He persuaded the daughter of the Sicilian viceroy to marry the man her father had chosen (whether this was fair to the girl is another question). He even journeyed from Rome for the only time in fifteen years to reconcile Duke Colonna and his wife Juana of Aragon. Sometimes it even seemed as if his attempts at conciliation were at odds with his religious principles. When Bobadilla opposed the unhappy compromise of the Interim of Augsburg in 1548, Ignatius was angry at Bobadilla whose rashness had annoyed the Emperor Charles. Ignatius knew that by placating the great one might avoid destruction and bloodshed. He paid attention to the wishes of the great and tried to enroll them as patrons of his Society. But he worked far harder for the poor and for the sick. Every prospective Jesuit had to serve his time working as a menial in a hospital, and if he shirked or showed distaste Ignatius discarded him immediately. For the sick in his own house Ignatius became the most indulgent and thoughtful of fathers. The steward had to report to him twice a day the needs of the infirmary. At the beginning of Lent he had all members of the community examined by a doctor, and would not let a man undertake the Lenten fast unless the doctor agreed. He ordered special diets, and even delicacies, for the sick. He always kept an eye on his novices and if they seemed pale and out of sorts he ordered them to sleep longer and lightened their work. When Ribadeneira had been bled, Ignatius sent someone three times during the night to check and adjust the bandages; and when a person was seriously ill Ignatius usually called in sometime during the night. In 1554, his own health was so bad the doctor insisted he stop work for a time. He handed over the government of the order to Nadal, but he retained to himself the responsibility for the care of the sick. 'No mother,' said Ribadeneira, 'cared for her children as our blessed Father cared for his sons, especially those who were weak and sick.' His concern for health did not end with care for the sick; he knew the virtue of preventitive measures. He was keen on bodily recreation and light exercise. Once after an epidemic he wrote: 'If those in Modena had encouraged some bodily exercise, perhaps so many good young men would not have died.' In the kitchen he insisted that the food should be properly prepared and cooked. Though he himself lived almost exclusively on bread and water he ordered the minister of the house to visit the kitchen before meals and 'taste two or three times the food in each pot to see if it was well-cooked and appetizing'.

Without doubt Ignatius governed his Society usually with forethought and kindness. And most of his spiritual sons repaid him with their affection. But there was always something impersonal in his relations with other people. He loved not man, but God through man, and accordingly he disciplined his natural emotions. 'His dominion over himself', said Gonzales, 'is a thing to praise God for'. Perhaps it was; but to ordinary humans who live and die by their feelings for each other his calculations are chilly. He treated others according to what he thought they could be persuaded to do for God. Some of his best men he pressed unmercifully. Laynez, whom Ignatius chose as his successor and of whom he once said 'our Society is indebted to no one more than Master Laynez, not even excepting Francis Xavier', suffered continually in the last years from Ignatius's severity. Nadal, the trusted minister of the house in Rome to whom Ignatius handed over the government of the order when he was sick, was sometimes reduced to tears by harsh treatment. To Polanco, the secretary, 'for nine years his hands and feet', Ignatius 'hardly said a good word'. Yet the dull and pompous Bobadilla and the proud and disobedient Rodriguez were given every encouragement and their failings dismissed with leniency. His

intention always was to get the best work out of his subordinates.
Ribadeneira wrote:

> The love of our Father was not soft or remiss, but wide-awake and
> efficacious. . . . He helped each one to advance according to his strength
> and capacity. To those who were children in virtue he gave milk, but
> the more advanced received from him plain bread and that he gave to
> them roughly.

He may have succeeded, but there is something a little too politic
about the method. According to Gonzales:

> consideration always seems to precede his smile, as well as all his other
> displays of feeling. For example, he often shows an angry face when
> he feels no anger, or appears gay and loving towards someone for whom
> he has little affection.

The same careful rationality governed another of his less endearing
habits. He hardly ever gave disagreeable orders directly, but used a
subordinate who never told that the order came from Ignatius himself. Yet if anything pleasant had to be done, Ignatius made the
announcement or the order. He was capable, too, of secretly order-
ing a certain member to be treated harshly so that the man would
turn to him for consolation. This happened to the learned and sorely
tried Dr. Loarte who turned on the minister of the house saying,
'Father Ignatius is a fountain of oil and your Reverence is a fountain
of vinegar.'

Ignatius's early years show that he was not by nature a dispassion-
ate man, but rather quick and ardent. And every so often in his last
years his humanity peeps out beneath the austerity. Ribadeneira
has a story from his first association with Ignatius, when as a hotheaded fourteen-year-old page he sought the protection of Ignatius
who had only just arrived in Rome:

> I, a boy, admonished him, a holy man of fifty, because there were many
> mistakes in his speech, and many things to put right as he spoke a
> Spanish sort of Italian. 'Good', he replied, 'make a note of anything
> you think wrong, so that you can warn me.' I therefore observed him
> carefully and made notes of the foreign words he used, and of his
> mispronunciations, and of other faults, . . . but they were so many
> that I got tired of the task and told him so. 'Well, Pedro', he said, 'what
> *are* we to do for God?'

It is related that he delighted to have Benedetto Palmio sit near him
at dinner. Benedetto was fat and always hungry, and it gave Ignatius

'wonderful pleasure' to see someone enjoy his food so much. With one man alone he could not quite keep up the careful reserve. To Francis Xavier he wrote and signed himself, 'Entirely yours, without my being ever able to forget you, Ignatius'. But Francis was far away in India, and as they were never likely to meet again Ignatius could allow himself this small, human frailty.

The austerity and the discipline which Ignatius practised had been important elements in that old, ideal Christianity which Ignatius loved so much. The wish to die to oneself and to the world was very strong in the early Fathers and became one of the principles of monasticism. St. Augustine, the most forceful exponent of so much Christian doctrine, says: 'Man himself, consecrated in the name of God and vowed to God, is a sacrifice in so far as he dies to the world that he may live to God.' John Cassian, in a book addressed to monks, wrote: 'You must know that today you are dead to this world and its deeds and desires so that, as the Apostle says, you are crucified to this world and this world to you.' But the old monastic ideal meant not only a victory over the senses and the desires, but also an actual turning away and withdrawal from the world and its unfortunate operations. St. John Climacus made this quite clear. He begins, 'A monk is he who strictly controls his nature and un-ceasingly watches over his senses'; and later continues, 'Withdrawal from the world is voluntary hatred of vaunted material things and denial of nature for the attainment of what is above nature'. Ignatius deliberately refused to withdraw from the world. How was it possible to 'die to the world' and at the same time live in the world so as to bring it back to virtue? Ignatius evolved a very simple practical solution to this quandary. He would become as unworldly as disci-pline and self-control could make him, in the best monastic tradi-tion, but before this simple interior he erected a false front, a more gaudy affair, all smiles and deference and consideration to the world outside. It was a strange solution. Perhaps the exceptional powers of Ignatius were capable of accepting this odd psychological arrange-ment; whether it could be recommended for lesser men is uncertain. In later years a critical world thought that the Jesuit façade over-shadowed the simple interior. After all Ignatius had said 'a man who was little use in the world was less use in the Society'.

The problem of reconciling the ideal of religious austerity with a life in society was general in Europe after the Reformation, when religion became active and religious groups, whether they liked it or not, were drawn from their retreats to exist in the beastly world.

Whatever the difficulties of Ignatius's personal solution at least he recognized that life in the secular world, though often bad, was also often joyful; and since the joy in the world was encouraging it should not be blighted by a too gloomy religiosity. The tendency of all active religion after the Reformation was towards puritanical restrictions. Reformers, both Catholic and Protestant, thought that society would become virtuous if it practised the same disciplines as the religious. Ignatius wisely saw that such a plan was impossible, and not even desirable. The religious deliberately limited his humanity and his natural affections for a particular end. But the end was personal and not general. The Church had no right to expect the ordinary citizen, whose function was not that of the priest, to deaden affections and desires which were given by God. From the members of his Society Ignatius demanded an austere discipline that was almost as strict as Calvin's rule in Geneva; for these men were called to God and therefore lost to themselves. No one might leave a Jesuit house without permission. Letters in and out were scrutinized and censored. Every month a summary of faults noted in others was sent to the head of the house. Faults noted in the head of the house were sent to Ignatius in secrecy. Even recreation, which Ignatius encouraged, was strictly controlled. He allowed, at appointed hours only, 'strolling and pleasant talk', or a kind of crocquet, or a game he called *piastrelle*—'a game of round flat pieces of wood driven in long courses upon tables under certain regulations'. From society at large, he asked only Catholic orthodoxy and decent devotion.

Nevertheless, as Catholic reformers strictly trained by Ignatius, the Jesuits had a suspicious eye for popular amusements. In Spain particularly the Society battled with frivolity. Books of the type of *Amadis de Gaul* were considered serious moral hazards; on one ceremonial occasion some fifty romances were solemnly and publicly burnt. At Cordoba, a magistrate under the influence of the Jesuits won a remarkable victory—he had all bull-fights banned from the city. In another Spanish town the local Jesuits were disturbed by an exhibition of tightrope walking. 'Father Baptista sent to beg the magistrates in his name to order the acrobat to go away, and not to allow the people to see that sort of amusement; because it was as dangerous to the soul as to the body.' Jewellery, cosmetics and rich clothing were all suspect. In the kingdom of Naples where the women were traditionally highly decorated, the puzzled Jesuits, not wishing to offend local opinion, referred the question to Ignatius.

His reply is highly characteristic of the way in which he approached these worldly matters. 'If they do it as an aid to some evil action,' he wrote, 'it is a mortal sin and they cannot have absolution. If they do it because their husbands want them to, they may be given absolution. But try to impress them to persuade their husbands not to make them use that vanity.' That is very far from the spirit of Calvin, who had a seamstress, a mother and two bridesmaids arrested because they dressed a bride a little too prettily.

About Ignatius's piety there can be no doubt. He is claimed among the ranks of the mystics on the grounds of his illumination and his visions. He was frequently in tears and frequently rapt; 'his countenance shone', wrote Gonzales, 'so that I stood still in amazement'. Though he wrote very little about himself, a small spiritual diary covering about a year in his late fifties did survive his death. He was at this time drafting the constitutions, and his diary shows that when perplexed by a knotty problem he took to his knees and debated the matter extensively with God, nor did he commit himself until he had received some divine sign. His sanctity was so apparent to his contemporaries it led to many charming and unlikely stories such as this one which Laynez told Ribadeneira:

> Father Araoz [Ignatius's nephew] told Laynez for certain that the guardian spirit of Ignatius was not a mere angel, as other men have, but an archangel, so Laynez asked Ignatius if this were true. Ignatius answered nothing, but he blushed as if he were a maiden surprised by men.

But to Ignatius angels were as palpable as friends and far more intimate. He once told Gonzales that he wished to behave towards mankind as the angels behave towards us, supporting and guiding to the hereafter.

In his last years Ignatius was old, ill and tired. The year before his death he saw his old enemy, Carafa, elected Pope Paul IV. The news of this caused 'every bone in his body to shake'. The King of Spain and the pope were at war once more, and Rome, as so often in the past, was again full of soldiers, hate and intrigue. In July 1556, he fell sick but he did not fuss; the house had other invalids, Laynez in particular being dangerously ill. On July 30, in the evening, he called Polanco, telling him that death was near and asking him to fetch the pope's benediction. Polanco, who had urgent letters to write, consulted the doctors, and when he found that they were not seriously worried he decided to leave the journey until the morning. Polanco and Father Madrid sat with Ignatius and found him collected and able to talk business clearly. He ate with good appetite and the doctor recommended two boiled eggs in the morning. During the night he was restless, but lay quiet soon after midnight. At dawn he was awake and dying. Polanco rushed to the Vatican, someone hurried out for extreme unction, and while they were away Ignatius died, silent and alone.

Like others before him, he failed to establish the City of God. Europe remained fragmented, suspicious and angry. He handled kings and cardinals deftly, understood the backsliding and weakness of ordinary men, and helped the poor and the sick. He was the complete master of the psychology of the individual. But he did not understand the perversity and despair caused by economic and social conflict. In a thousand practical ways, with remedies, spiritual medicines, tricks and arrangements, he cajoled and persuaded and chivied society towards an end it no longer believed in. Christianity had always fought the State, and now the State had finally won and would impose its own terms. But in his unintellectual way he had grasped something great—the old ideal of Christendom; and the vision of this promised land possessed the higher regions of his mind entirely. At the same time, on a lower plane, his practical intelligence set aside all dreams and evolved the tightest and strictest of organizations. He bequeathed his Society an impossible ideal and a ferociously efficient technique. He was, in a sense, the perfect Machiavellian, or the perfect modern—a man whose dream of freedom and joy is made impossible by the restrictions and subterfuges imposed to attain it. The great ideals—Christendom, Freedom, Democracy— are as mistily far away as ever. The busy, active techniques remain to plague us to eternity.

PART THREE

THE DEFENCE AND PROPAGATION
OF THE HOLY CATHOLIC FAITH

Chapter IX

THE CHURCH MILITANT

THE DEATH of Ignatius in 1556 withdrew from his young Society its founder, prop and guide, and left the Jesuits in an inconvenient, even hazardous, position. Gian Pietro Carafa, the newly-elected Pope Paul IV, was known to dislike the order and his acidity increased with his age. The conservative Spanish Church suspected the Jesuit innovations. The Gallican French Church abhored the Jesuits' Roman connection and their special privileges. The Council of Trent, on whose deliberations the future of the Catholic Church, and the Jesuits, so largely depended, had temporarily floundered on the twin rocks of typhus and imperial displeasure. The Council, less the imperial party, retired to Bologna and did not return to Trent until death removed three of the greatest obstacles to its success—the Emperor Charles V, in 1558, the French King Henry II, in 1559, and Pope Paul IV, in the same year. The Jesuit constitutions, though completed by Ignatius and promulgated in his lifetime, had not yet been voted on by a general congregation and so did not carry the force of law. Altogether, in 1556, the Society of Jesus was well prepared to go seriously adrift.

The security of the whole Jesuit enterprise rested on the personality and authority of the general, and so the first hurried matter was to elect the new one. On Ignatius's death the house in Rome was almost empty. Nadal, whom Ignatius had appointed vicar-general during his illness, was away in Spain looking for alms and carefully placating the patrician Father Francis Borgia who ruled the Jesuit houses of the peninsula. Borgia, of the notorious family, the former Duke of Gandia, was a grandee of the highest water. In spite of a fat stomach and a jolly personality, he was a man very used to being first. In his secular days he had liked to take to horse and hunt down the bandits in his territory, and hang them on the spot as he caught them. The wise Nadal, though he had Ignatius's authority in his pocket, took care not to wave it in front of such a man. His days in Spain were thus difficult, and he could not get back to Rome to

149

claim the generalship which many thought was his due. In Rome, besides Laynez who was still very ill, the secretary Polanco could only gather together four professed fathers; and so taking this small group he organized a miniature election. These five men unanimously gave their votes to Diego Laynez, recently pronounced by the doctor to be off the danger list. Out of consideration for the invalid, Polanco refrained for three days from distressing him with the news of his appointment. Letters were immediately sent off to the various Jesuit provinces where they caused some surprise and disorder. Nadal, from Spain, commented in his diary on these events as follows:

> I thought that I was vicar and so did the other fathers here, the three provincials and the commissary. On their advice I wrote to the Portuguese fathers telling them to prepare for the journey to Rome. Father Francis [Borgia] said that he could not go, as the doctors were against it, and Araoz and Bustamante had the same story, only Estrada showed any desire to set out. A few days later we received notice from Father Polanco that Laynez had been made vicar. This news did not disturb me.

The dangers of the times perhaps justified Polanco's hasty action. Nadal himself thought so, and worked selflessly for the new general. But both the haste of the election and the mulish response from the Spanish provinces indicated some insecurity in the young order. Many members of the Society, though they had answered Ignatius's call, did not quite realize what they had let themselves in for. The personality of the founder impressed them more than the aims of the order. Nor had the Church, herself in the uncertain middle reaches of the suspended Council of Trent, stamped her final approval of the Jesuit way. Of Ignatius everyone approved; but the Society without him was another matter. The tendency, therefore, was to drift back to the form of devotion and religious practice that had been standard before the innovations of Ignatius. This happened especially in Spain, the most populous, the most old-fashioned and the most independent Jesuit territory. Father Araoz, the provincial of Castile, and Father Estrada, the provincial of Aragon—pious and difficult men—both gradually introduced into their provinces practices which would not have pleased Ignatius, practices that encouraged the meditation, contemplation and long hours of prayer of the older orders rather than the forceful activity of Ignatius. Pope Paul, another stern, moral, unhumorous man, also suspected the Ignatian method. Concerning the Jesuits, he had always hovered between ungracious acceptance and rage (he was a notoriously bad-tempered man). By 1558, the indignities he suffered from the King of Spain and the internal squabbles among the Jesuits—fanned by the expert trouble-maker Bobadilla—convinced Paul that the Society must be disciplined, and its rules brought into line with the sound older monastic usage. Laynez, recently confirmed as general by the congregation, and Salmeron were summoned in September 1558, to hear the pope's displeasure. As the two knelt before him, Paul rumbled on over their heads in a low, angry voice. He declared that Ignatius had ruled as a tyrant; in future the general should rule for three years and then be re-elected, if the pope agreed. Gathering steam, he next expressed himself on the subject of choir duties, shouting at the surprised Jesuits that their attitude encouraged heretics and he feared that some devil might arise from the order. The singing of choir was divinely ordained, he thundered, for the religious, and the Jesuits would henceforth adopt it. Nor would their studies excuse them. When the constitutions were printed later in the same year, Paul ordered his instructions to be printed with them. Fortunately, the old man died in the next year. Laynez secured an opinion from some eminent canonists that a verbal order of a pope (not incorporated in a Bull) did not bind after the death of that pope, and so the Jesuits felt free to ignore Paul's restrictions. 'The important thing,' as Polanco rightly said, 'was to please the pope;' but not a dead pope.

The movement in the Spanish provinces and the pressure from the Vatican both worked against Ignatius's declared purpose. The dissensions in the Society also, of course, destroyed Ignatius's ideal unity and caused cliques to form. And these cliques, following the enthusiasm of the age, tended to form into national groups. Again the Spaniards showed what could be done. Araoz claimed, with thorough-going prejudice, that the general milked Spain of both men and money for the benefit of less deserving provinces elsewhere. The distinctive character of Jesuit practice demanded unity, internationalism and activity, and the disruptive, nationalistic and contemplative trends within the Society must have worried Laynez very much. The problem was compounded. The future of the Jesuits—even whether they should continue to exist or not—could not be decided until the Catholic Church had made up her mind what course she was to follow. Laynez, the astutest and most intelligent of early Jesuits, had always seen this clearly. He had been a papal theologian at the early sessions of the Council of Trent and had

worked hard to swing the Church towards the disciplined activity
that the Jesuits advocated. The results of those first sessions were
encouraging for the Jesuits. Then the good work was interrupted.
Europe went to war, and Paul IV assumed the tiara. Would the
pope step aside from the new direction into old, familiar paths? All
this increased Laynez's apprehension. Although he entirely agreed
with Ignatius's intentions, he never managed Ignatius's serenity,
probably because he saw the dangers and the complexities far better
than his unintellectual master. Laynez's perplexities made him the
fiercest fighter for the Society. At Trent, in 1547, he ran foul of
Melchior Cano, the confirmed enemy of the Jesuits. 'Why do you,'
he asked the famous Dominican, 'take it upon yourself to condemn
what the Vicar of Christ has approved?' 'The dogs must bark,'
replied Cano, 'when the shepherd is away;' at which Laynez snapped,
'Yes, at the wolves, not at other dogs.' At this point politeness departed and Laynez fled from the room throwing back a word which
Cano blushed to think of, and could only refer to, in the future,
'hyperbolically, by aposiopesis'. Ten years later, when Cano came to
Rome to conduct his legal case against his fellow Dominican Soto,
Laynez made fun of Cano's wounded ambition: 'What a joke,' he
said, 'to find one tiny man up in arms against a whole religious order!'
Though Cano was a most dislikable man, what Laynez really battled
against was the Dominican's hostility to the Society. He fought very
strongly to make the Catholic atmosphere favourable towards the
Jesuits. He helped the Council of Trent, especially in the last
assembly from 1561 to 1563, outline the role of the Church in such
an uncompromising way that active orders, such as the Jesuits, were
guaranteed plenty of work. At the Colloquy of Poissy in 1561, when
it looked as if the temporizing Catherine de Medici would come to
an arrangement with Beza and the Calvinists, Laynez intervened in a
very lively fashion, calling his opponents *lupi, volpi, serpenti* and
assassini, and warning the queen-regent, as a temporal monarch, not
to meddle in spiritual affairs: 'the shoemaker should stick to his last'
was his unflattering image, and he went on:

> I have read, and I am convinced by experience, that it is very dangerous
> to treat with people who have severed themselves from the Church;
> for, as the Scriptures say: 'Who will pity an enchanter struck by a
> serpent, or any that come near wild beasts?'

He was fighting for Catholic orthodoxy; he was also fighting for
the continuing existence of his society.

And Laynez was right to attack compromise. For the various 'compromises' put forward between the Diet of Worms in 1521 and the Peace of Augsburg in 1555 were not real attempts to find religious solutions. Rather, they were part of European political diplomacy, concerned with limiting, preserving or extending the power of the princes and using religious differences for this end. At one time, in the hopeful days of humanist enthusiasm, it had seemed that good sense and tolerance might lead to a peaceful Church reform. Erasmus had thought this. There was nothing, he felt, that could not be put right by humour and elegant ratiocination. He regretted very much that Luther's violence had been answered by an equal violence on the other side. Charred corpses were a poor advertisement for Christian charity. 'In former days,' he wrote, 'a heretic was listened to with respect: he was acquitted if he gave satisfaction, convicted if he persisted. The severest punishment was not to be admitted to the communion of the Catholic Church. Now the charge of heresy is quite another thing.' He knew, too, that religious quarrels thrive on martyrs. After Henri Voes and Jan van Essen, the first two victims of Charles V's savage persecution in the Netherlands, were burnt in the Brussels market-place, in 1523, Erasmus commented 'that their deaths had made many Lutherans'. Erasmus's opinions recommended an ideal of humane and moderate behaviour. But he had misread the situation; it was far graver than he thought. He had not seen the extreme dogmatic division between the Catholics and the Lutherans, and he had not anticipated the guilefulness of the princes. Luther, on the other hand, a rugged peasant of tight and old-fashioned notions, would have nothing to do with compromise. He was the leader of a popular cause, a cause which he helped to inflame by his brilliant and resounding writings such as the *Liberty of the Christian* and *The Babylonian Captivity of the Church*. And his very popularity prevented him from being mild or accommodating. He demonstrated first the power of the press, and he was its first victim too. He could not moderate his opinions; yet he saw the violence that his opinions caused—among the Anabaptists at Münster for example—and this appalled him so much that he came to welcome the intervention of princes, as a regulator of religious passion.

But what could be expected, in the way of true religion, from the princes? The French kings Francis I and Henry II were at various times allied to the Turks. Carlo Carafa, nephew of Pope Paul IV, arranged Lutheran help for the pope against the Catholic King of Spain. The Lutheran Maurice of Saxony very eagerly assisted Charles V in the destruction of the Protestant League of Schmalkalden. The Lutheran Germans hailed the Catholic Henry II as 'the Protector of German liberty', and by the Treaty of Chambord in 1552 ceded to France the bishoprics of Metz, Toul and Verdun. These were the realities that made the idealism of Erasmus impossible and the moderate, intelligent compliance of Melanchthon and Bucer tragic. For at the end of all this dallying with the princes came the Peace of Augsburg, in 1555, with its curious formula *cuius regio, huius religio*—the king determines the religion of his subjects. Lutheranism, which had cried out for freedom of conscience, had come to this: the prince alone had freedom of conscience, the subject's duty was to obey and to support the State Church, set up and governed by the temporal powers. In the world of Christendom, in theory and often in fact, the subject had had recourse from the tyranny of the State to the disinterested other world of the Church. Now State and Church were joined together to govern the body and the spirit for the interests only of the State. The tendency of State and Church to come together for the discomfort of the subject was present not only in Lutheran countries, but also in Catholic countries, such as Spain. But only in the Protestant north did this tendency grow to a triumphant accomplishment. Part of the work of the Jesuits was to assert the rights of the Church and to keep the State in its place, in Catholic as in Protestant countries. For this reason Laynez thought there must be no compromise, and no truckling to princes.

No doubt it is sad that Erasmus's moderation could not prevail; and it is sad that we must judge religious men of the later sixteenth century, such as Laynez and Calvin, as much harder and less sympathetic than the earlier Christian humanists. But it took a while before the real issues and the real effects of the Reformation became apparent. Erasmus, with all his huge intelligence, did not quite understand. He was born too early. So too was Ignatius Loyola. He saw the disintegration of the Catholic Church; but, untheological as he was, he did not quite see the Protestant doctrinal position. Like Erasmus, he seemed to think that the Lutherans might be persuaded by sweet reasonableness and good examples. In the instructions he gave to Laynez, setting out for the Council of Trent in 1546, he said:

In preaching I would not touch at all on the differences between Protestants and Catholics, but simply exhort to good habits and devotion, stirring people up to know themselves truly and to acquire a greater knowledge and love of their Creator and Lord.

But Laynez, a younger man with a mind more attuned to the problems of Protestantism, saw that the Catholic position must be strengthened, not weakened, if the Catholic Church was to survive.

One natural result of the spirit of compromise, and the general desire to be reasonable in religious controversy, was that all over Europe men of learning rushed into print to debate the tricky question of justification. And often one was puzzled to know whether an opinion was strictly orthodox or slightly Lutheran. Erasmianism came to be generally suspect, yet Clement VII offered Erasmus the cardinal's red hat. Cardinal Pole, a pillar of the Catholic reform movement, was commended for leading Vittoria Colonna and the poet Flaminio out of the way of heresy, but his own teaching of justification was thought to be a little Lutheran. Seripando, the general of the Augustinians and one of the foremost theologians at Trent, found his own doctrine under much critical discussion at that Council. The canon lawyer Juan Arze claimed to find many heresies in the Breviary of his fellow Spaniard Cardinal Quiñónes, a work so popular that it was re-printed ten times in one year. The *Enchiridion* of Johann Gropper delighted such eminent churchmen as Contarini, Sadoleto and Giberti; but Johann Eck, the efficient, orthodox and unpleasant Catholic propagandist of the University of Ingolstadt, considered the work to be semi-Lutheran; the equally severe Pope Paul IV eventually made Gropper a cardinal.

Such uncertainty was not only worrying, but also dangerous. After the establishment of the Roman Inquisition in 1542 there were severe penalties for thinking incorrectly. The writings on both sides of the religious squabble became less polemical and more instructive. The outline of faith in Melanchthon's *Confessio Augustana*, on which a reunion with the Catholics might possibly have been based, gave way to Luther's Articles of Schmalkalden (1536) from which, Luther said, 'there must be no deviation, or yielding, though heaven and earth fall to pieces'. The Lutherans were the first to produce a popular catechism, the Catholics—slow to realize the power of the press to sway popular feelings—followed later. In 1542, the Sorbonne produced twenty-nine theses for the guidance of Catholic preachers; in 1544, the University of Louvain produced a much more comprehensive list of fifty-nine theses to which its professors had to subscribe. This tightening of the disciplinary screws was accompanied by a copious and happily inventive flow of invective. The

Lutherans suggested many interesting motives to explain Catholic intransigence: Fabri, they said, was against married priests because he was living off the fines collected from priests who had concubines. Cochlaeus, a man of very pure life, was rumoured to be seeing a bold hussy called 'kessen Anna'. The Catholics replied in kind. In the eighteenth century a whole dictionary of insults was compiled from the works of Cochlaeus. The diplomatic Cardinal Morone reproached the German champions for making their Catholicism merely hatred and abuse of Luther.

This was all evidence of hardening attitudes. But something more than spite and a vocabulary rich in expletives was required. Luther had given his followers a firm doctrinal base. Calvin, in the *Institution Chrétienne* of 1536, had done the same for his men. Only the Catholic Church had as yet no authoritative ruling on the disputed questions. And only a general council of the Church could do this. For a long time a council had been an absolute necessity; all men of good will had agreed to that. If it had come very soon after Luther's action in 1517, it might have prevented the Protestant Reformation; for at first the Germans clamoured loudly for a council. But the Church could not stir itself then; the popes, having been mauled by the conciliar movement in the Middle Ages, were afraid of councils; the enmity of France and Spain made an ecumenical council almost an impossibility. The Council of Trent, which did not meet until 1545—nearly thirty years after Luther's challenge— came too late to heal the Reformation. Its only purpose, then, was to reinvigorate the Catholic Church and to define strictly and clearly Catholic doctrine. And this it set out to do.

Discipline first? or dogma? Charles V thought the former; the Council preferred to tackle the latter. But to the general surprise by the time the Council ended, in December 1563, both had been more than adequately covered. The Council closed to relief and amazement. Paleotti, who saw it all, wrote: 'I myself saw many of the most solemn prelates weep for joy, and those who had the day before treated one another almost as strangers embrace with deep emotion.' They were confounded by their own virtuosity. And really, considering the hot antipathies of the times, the results were astounding. There were of course incidents. The Spaniards were noisy and insolent, the French theologically suspect, the Italians so numerous that they were accused of bringing the Holy Spirit in their baggage train. The Bishop of La Cava was clapped into gaol for tearing a handful of hair from a Greek prelate's beard. And over the whole proceedings loomed the ominous presences of the kings. Yet no council before had decided so many questions, defined so much doctrine, or initiated so much Church reform.

The puzzling points of difference with the Protestants were finally cleared up. Free will and good works were allowed to play their part in justification. The importance of the twin sources of Scripture and Tradition was affirmed against the Protestant reliance on Scripture only. Individual interpretations of the Bible were condemned, unless in line with the Church's authoritative teaching. The Council cast a stern eye over the entire Church hierarchy, and had something terse to say to each member. The pope was assured of his eminence, and reminded of his responsibilities. He is 'the universal Pastor ruling the universal Church' and 'nothing new in the Church can be done without consulting him'. But infallibility, tentatively put forward by the Jesuits who were the papal theologians, was rejected. Of the cardinals, the Council said, 'they should possess such outstanding virtue and govern their conduct in such a way so as to serve as models for the rest of mankind'. The bishops, the mainstay of the Catholic organization, were thoroughly reformed. The bishop was ordered to reside in his diocese, to visit all his churches at least once a year, to preach every Sunday and feast day, and to stay clear of politics and business. He was also reminded to deny himself the pleasure of raising a family. Naturally, it was some time before all these conditions were actually met. The Council also desired to make the priesthood more of a vocation and less of a vacation: 'Those who handle the Lord's vessels must be purified in order to serve as examples; those who are to be initiated into the sacred ministry must be trained in the practice of every virtue.' Taking the example of both the Jesuits and the Calvinists, the Church decided to set up seminaries for the education of priests, and every bishop was urged to start one in his diocese.

The results of the Council of Trent were very pleasing, and very important, to the Jesuits. The universality of the Church and the primacy of the pope had been stressed. The need for the Church to become active, preaching and teaching, was acknowledged. The Jesuits' place in the Catholic structure, as noteworthy preachers and the possessors of the finest educational system in Europe, was secured. The dark suspicions of Paul IV passed with his death in 1559. Under Pius IV and St. Pius V the Jesuits worked in the clear air of papal approval. With the direction of the Church made plain, and the need for missionary activity manifest, the movement among the Spanish Jesuits towards contemplation and the older forms of monasticism died away. Laynez, who had himself done much to influence the decisions of the Council, could at last assert the principles of the Society in all their force—unity, internationalism and activity.

Further, the psychological temper of the Church had become favourable to the Jesuits. The resolution of the problem of justification allowed for free will and choice, permitting a man to decide his own destiny. Justification was the crucial and obsessive doctrinal problem of the Reformation; and the decision, one way or the other, on this matter coloured the thinking, and therefore the morality, of both Protestants and Catholics. In the sessions of the Council, Laynez had fought hard for what became the Catholic doctrine, especially against Seripando, whose thought had a slight Lutheran tinge. For free will and choice were essential for the Jesuit mode of working. The whole *Exercises* of Ignatius had assumed that man had a choice which he could use freely. And all Jesuit activity in the world is concerned with rational choices. The Jesuit vision of the world of men is of a naughty, but sensible place which might be put right by hard work and persuasion. They did not see it as the absolute trap of Calvinist thought; and, being guided by a more shaded plan, they allowed themselves some latitude in dealing with it. Even the Jesuit liking for the doctrine of probabilism, for which they were much reviled later, is only a matter of choices. Choice gives a man dignity, but permits him some questionable practices.

Paolo Sarpi, the first historian of the Council of Trent, began his history with three questions:

> How did it happen that the Council which men longed for to restore the unity of the Church actually increased the division and embittered both sides so that reconciliation became impossible? How was it possible that the princes' plan to reform the clergy was frustrated, and that the bishops' attempt to regain their authority lost to the Pope ended in the loss of more authority, to which enslavement they contributed? Lastly, how was it that the Council feared and shunned by the Roman Curia as a threat to its power, in fact secured the Curia's supremacy—at least in the part of the Church that had remained faithful—so that it rooted itself even more strongly than before?

Sarpi was an entertaining, but very prejudiced Venetian; and he disliked the papacy. But, leaving aside his complaint, his conclusions were correct. The papacy, and the Curia, had been strengthened; the bishops had decreased their own power and increased the pope's;

the Church had resisted the princes' take-over plan; and, most important, the incompatibility of Catholicism with Protestantism had been affirmed very bluntly. The Church had put itself on a war footing—firm doctrine, centralized organization and an authoritative leader. The Calvinists were similarly constituted; an era of exceptional intolerance and bloodshed was inevitable.

The religious parties were no longer fighting primarily for unity, or the extirpation of heresy, or freedom of conscience, or whatever. They were now fighting for their lives. This was not yet acknowledged, and perhaps not yet recognized, for there was still much talk about unity. Michel de l'Hôpital, at the opening of the States-General of Orleans in 1560, after the death of Henry II, said very truly:

> It is folly to expect peace, quiet and friendship among persons of various denominations. No sentiment is so deeply rooted in the heart of man as the religious sentiment, and none separates one man more deeply from another.

And Laynez in the next year addressed an appeal for unity to the Protestant Prince de Condé:

> Excellency, it is easy to see the importance of finding a way of restoring union between the new Churches and the ancient Roman Church from which they have separated in our time. It is important not only for the temporal peace and quiet of the kingdom, but far more for the eternal peace of so many souls. There can be but one true Church, outside of which there is no hope of salvation.

The Calvinist agreed exactly with that last sentiment, and with equal idealism expected Laynez to abandon his idolatrous and foolish ways. And both sides were anxious to show their opponents the armed strength of their convictions. Yet l'Hôpital had also said

> The Christian religion is to suffer violence, not to create it, and those who wish to establish it with the help of arms, swords and pistols, act against what they profess. . . . They argue in vain that they take up arms for God's cause, because God's cause does not need to be defended by arms. . . . Our religion was neither started, nor maintained, nor preserved by armed force.

This was the crucial truth. The wars of religion mainly concerned power, and the right to exist, not Christianity. Unyielding dogmatism, rigid discipline and unmerciful brutality all grew from uncertainty, impotence and loss of prestige.

Since Catholics and Protestants were mutually threatened, each needed to evolve a technique for survival. The techniques decided on were in many ways very similar. The chief ingredients of the Catholic plan were devised by the Jesuits, those of the Protestant plan by Calvin. Both favoured activity. The corruption of the Church and the dissensions of the Reformation had in general made the population bored and suspicious of religion; if the people were to be brought back to virtue the denominations must go out and fetch them. Both believed in a well-prepared and strictly obedient ministry; both saw the need to educate the public. Both wished to exercise some control over public morality—the Calvinists absolutely, the Jesuits less completely. Both expressed a strongly idealistic Christianity. But there the similarities end. The Jesuits, guided by Ignatius's practicality and understanding of human motives, blended their idealism with a sound realism. Calvin made no concession to the secular world. By making the body of his Church the same as the body of his State, he tried to force his citizens to live up to the highest religious standards—standards which the ordinary citizen has no difficulty in repudiating. On the contrary, the Jesuits, who formed—in their own estimation and probably in fact—an élite within Catholic society, chose to infiltrate secular society and persuade rather than bully. This had been the preferred technique of Ignatius. However, Ignatius, who had not grasped very well the complexity of the contemporary secular world, might have been surprised at the amount of adaption and general shiftiness required to keep the Jesuits abreast of secular developments. Laynez had a clearer idea. *Destrezza*, dexterity, was a favourite word in his polity, and this insistence on dexterity led to the moral juggling act for which the Jesuits were later to become famous.

Yet at the same time the Jesuits without doubt maintained, among themselves, their high ideal. They resisted nationalism, they kept sound doctrine, and they were neither licentious nor slothful. The presence of the Society of Jesus perpetually reminded the Church of its aims and mission. Only in their dealings with the world did the Jesuits act ambiguously. More and more, the world decided its own values and modes of conduct without consulting the theologians or the Scriptures. If the Jesuits wished to remain active in the world, without being able to change the world, they must accommodate to the ways of the world. In the Jesuit mind, which was inclined to think that the furtherance of the Catholic faith rested largely on the efforts of the order, both the imperatives of the faith, and the security of the Society required an amicable arrangement with the public.

At some point, as must happen with all active groups surrounded by unfriendly or uninterested people, the Society of Jesus found that it must first aim at, and give most of its energy to, staying alive. And to stay alive in a secular world one must comply to, or control, that world. Where the Jesuits could control, as sometimes in the missions of India and Paraguay, they did so; where they could not, as in Europe, they complied. Yet their special strength, their integrity and cohesiveness, depended on the extent to which they realized Ignatius's ideal. Here, then, was a balance of beautiful ingenuity. The Society's virtuous ideal gave it a clear identity, and this was kept strong by rigid discipline and subjection of the individual will to the corporate aims. But the Society remained alive, and kept its power and influence, by accommodating itself to the secular world whose desires were, as usual, unedifying and self-seeking. Here, then, was a Society that revivified and helped sustain the Catholic Church, and at the same time, most paradoxically, provided the pattern of the modern active institution, concerned inevitably with self-preservation and aggrandisement, steely within and slippery without. Both aspects of the Jesuits must be kept in mind, in all their activities.

Chapter X

SCHOOLMASTERS

AMONG THE excitements and mental agitations of the Renaissance times, education, that poor child of the Church, became rather neglected. The brave new ideas and methods naturally demanded some recognition from the schools, but the harried Church could hardly maintain the perfunctory service it already gave, let alone take to its shaky heart a whole apparatus designed (or so it seemed to many churchmen) to undo the traditional claims of the Church. The humanists, and the exponents of the new learning, had of course very quickly found pupils eager to share the new enthusiasm. But the Italian humanist schoolmasters had developed no system which could be generally applied; and though their fame was high, their number of students was small. Even the Brethren of the Common Life, whose schools became the model for so much later educational practice, were tucked away in an obscure corner of Europe and had no ambition to expand.

The questions implanted by the Renaissance, and the increasing authority of the State, made it uncertain whether education could remain largely in the hands of the Church. Yet most obviously the Church had an interest, especially at this perilous moment, in keeping that traditional preserve. Wisdom, charity and self-interest all pointed to a thorough reform of schooling. This was the common experience, though few people were better placed than Ignatius to realize how much needed to be done. His own early schooling had been a disaster. His preparation in the rites of chivalry had taught him the virtues of killing and little else. And when, at the age of thirty, he had realized the need for sounder principles on which to base a life, he had discovered at first hand the amazing obstacles placed between the student and any useful knowledge. Manresa had taught him hardly anything except a little bad Latin. At Alcalá and Salamanca he had learnt to manipulate that bad Latin in a purely mechanical way according to a set of dusty scholastic rules. At Paris for seven hard years he slogged through a course on Rhetoric which left him with an appalling style, a course on Philosophy which failed to make a philosopher of him, and started a course on Theology which he did not bother to finish. Though he always retained his native good sense and clear judgment, fourteen years of schooling failed to make him a learned man. He did, however, see that the education he had been through was defective and troublesome, and, as usual, he formed some decisive notions about what might be done.

He did not at first intend that his little band of followers should become schoolmasters. That was a sedentary and time-consuming business, not suitable for an active, bustling set of preachers and missioners. Yet in this, as in so many other things, the needs of the time overtook Ignatius's intentions. Ignatius's conception of his new order made the members natural choices to rejuvenate a tired school, or start a new one where none had been before. For Ignatius insisted that his men be intelligent, and have some practical ability, and he insisted that they receive a thorough training. He sent out his men to defend the Catholic faith actively, and also 'to help their neighbours'. The combination of their quality and their aims soon caused others to see the value of Jesuits as instructors, even if Ignatius himself resisted this idea. But he soon gave way to the demands for the teaching services of the order. First Francis Xavier wrote from India that the College of Holy Faith, founded by a secular priest in Goa, had no staff: could the Jesuits oblige? Ignatius, who loved Xavier best of all his followers, permitted it. He saw, too, that the propagation of the faith in the East would suffer if the college collapsed. The interests of the Church and the Jesuits slid together. Within a few years of the foundation in 1540, the King of Portugal had secured some Jesuits for the University of Coimbra; the Duke of Bavaria had asked for Le Jay, Salmeron and Peter Canisius to teach at Ingolstadt; the Viceroy of Sicily wished the Society to look after colleges in Palermo and Messina; and the Duke of Gandia—who later entered the order himself and as Francis Borgia became the third general—wanted not one college, but a whole Jesuit university established on his territory.

Very soon Ignatius saw that these temptations to teach, which he had at first thought of as interruption to the real work, were in fact fortunate advantages for the Society. The Society needed somewhere to train its own young men, and the existing universities were nearly all to some degree unsatisfactory—either sunk into primitive ignorance, or tainted with false doctrine, or anti-clerical, or subject to frequent wars and disruptions. The earliest group of young recruits whom Ignatius had sent to Paris, the mother of European universities, in the spring of 1540, soon discovered to their cost what it was to be a Jesuit student in a foreign college. Jesuit training might be done more easily and more safely if the Society ran its own colleges in the older establishments, or even its own universities. Secondly, the awakened Catholic Church saw that the Protestants had made education a prime weapon in the battle for souls. Melanchthon had written wisely on *Reforming the Studies of Youth*, Sturm had started some excellent grammar schools in which the Protestant point of view was skilfully bolstered by the theories of the humanists, and Protestant universities sprang up at Marburg, Jena and elsewhere. The Society of Jesus, the most active element in the aroused Catholic Church, might be expected to reply. Both religious sides saw that minds caught young and carefully led according to the acceptable authorities were doubly secured against error—heretical or idolatrous as the case may be. Ignatius noted once that the safety of the faith would depend 'much less on preachers than on teachers'. The Jesuits, therefore, gradually came to provide a full schooling, from beginners to graduates. It was considered particularly daring, and burdensome, for a religious order to teach young boys, for, as Ribadeneira pointed out, 'boys are by nature giddy, restless, talkative and lazy creatures, so that even their parents cannot control them at home. Therefore our young men who teach them lead a very hard life, fritter away their strength and lose their health.' Nonetheless, in the altered circumstances of the Reformation, the Jesuits were willing to fatigue themselves in this way for the good of the faith. Most characteristically, in the Jesuit scheme of studies all questions were judged according to their effect on faith and doctrine.

In the fourth part of the constitutions Ignatius laid the foundations of Jesuit education, and his marvellous organizing powers devised something which, at the same time and in the same system, served the Society, the public and the Catholic faith. The schools were to cost the Society nothing—except time and manpower—and the pupil nothing. If a prince or a bishop required a Jesuit school he must pay for it. As the constitutions sternly said:

No obligations or conditions are to be admitted that would impair the integrity of our principle, which is—To give freely what we have received free.

And if a proffered foundation was considered insufficient to keep a college, the gift was declined. Sacchini, reporting the general congregation of 1565, which elected Borgia general, observed:

> the letters of several bishops and municipalities being read, in which foundations for five colleges were offered, they decided that not one of them should be admitted; and besides they gave the new general full authority to dissolve certain colleges already existing.

The Society, though always eager for a king's favour, sent an elegant refusal, by way of Father Campano, to King Stephen's request for more colleges in Poland. 'Apostolic men,' wrote Cardinal Allen to Father Parsons, 'should not only despise money; they should also have it.' The Jesuits demonstrated the force of this aphorism: by 1640 the order governed 372 colleges.

Ignatius's way of financing his colleges was a typical bold stroke. But the plan of studies which slowly developed between 1546 and the final form codified in the *Ratio Studiorum* by the general Aquaviva in 1599, proceeded much more cautiously. The humanist method, the Brethren of the Common Life and the Protestant schools all helped to form the *Ratio*; but the need to implant orthodoxy broods over the whole. For the time, the curriculum is wide, and even revolutionary. The *Ratio*, following and extending a rule of Laynez, decreed that the lowest schools must provide, at the minimum, instruction in Grammar, Rhetoric, Humanities, Languages and Moral Theology; and the higher establishment, or Jesuit university, must, besides these, teach Scholastic Theology, Scripture and Hebrew. In fact, the constitutions and the *Ratio* together see the Jesuit university as a worthy compendium of all knowledge, with professors of the Society teaching logic, philosophy, physics, mathematics and the particular sciences, strange tongues such as Arabic, Persian, Indian and Japanese as required; and with secular professors taking secular subjects, such as civil law and medicine. This range did not please the traditionalists, and as late as the 1580's Ribadeneira wrote to defend the Jesuit practice of teaching mathematics, modern languages and Greek to young boys. But the ideas incorporated in the *Ratio* had been fully tested, especially in the main Jesuit college, the Roman College founded on a gift of 4,532 gold ducats from Francis Borgia in 1550; and the Jesuit educated—clerics and civilians—showed a very superior learning. The excellence of the system was recognized by all who thought seriously about education in the late sixteenth and early seventeenth centuries. As with all Jesuit activities, the schools were as uniform and organized as discipline could make them. The haphazard wanderings of the schoolmaster's fancy were things of the past; the Jesuit master and the Jesuit pupil both knew where they stood. Ribadeneira wrote:

> In other places, one professor has many grades of scholar before him; he lectures at one and the same time scholars who are at the bottom, midway and at the top, and he can scarcely meet the demands of each. But, in the Society, we distinguish one rank of scholars from another, dividing them into their own classes and orders, and place separate professors over each.

And, as might be expected, the Jesuits actively stirred up the sleepy minds of their students:

> Many means are devised, and exercises employed to stimulate the minds of the young—assiduous disputations, various trials of talent, prizes offered for ability and industry.

That all this was new and wonderful is attested by the many Protestants who sent their children to Jesuit schools. 'As for the pedagogical part,' wrote that good Protestant Francis Bacon, 'the shortest rule would be, Consult the schools of the Jesuits; for nothing better has been put in practice.' And elsewhere, in the *Advancement of Learning*, he admits that the Jesuits 'partly in themselves, and partly by the emulation and provocation of their example, have much quickened and strengthened the state of learning'.

The Jesuit plan, neat and cunningly devised though it was, for a general system of education had one very great limitation. It intended primarily to train clerics—aspiring Jesuits—and the external students, those with no desire to become Jesuits or even priests, had to fit into the system as best they could. For no concessions, in the way of dispensations from strict religious attendance, were made for those not naturally devout. The fathers' keen eyes saw that the moral being was chastened and controlled. The regime, as Ribadeneira painted it, had all the typical severity of the Counter-Reformation:

> There are morning prayers to obtain grace from God not to fall into sin; night prayers and a diligent reflection on all the thoughts, words and actions of the day, to do away by contrition of heart with all the faults committed; the attentive and devout hearing of Mass every day; frequent and humble confessions of sin to a priest; . . . Besides, great pains are taken to root out the vices of boyhood, especially such as are somehow inborn and native to that age.

Both Catholic and Protestant schoolmasters concluded that youth is inherently vicious, and no sixteenth-century boy could expect much joy in his schooling. But much more questionable were the intellectual restrictions imposed by the Jesuit teachers. A class of Jesuit scholastics no doubt expected to take St. Thomas Aquinas as the standard for all theological and philosophical problems; but the external students were similarly restricted. Aquaviva ruled that all professors must adhere to St. Thomas. Respect for a Christian saint is understandable; but the pagan Aristotle was similarly elevated, even in the eighteenth century when his science had been laid deep in the grave. The seventeenth congregation of 1751 ordained that Aristotle was to be followed 'not only in Logic and Metaphysics, but also in Natural Philosophy [i.e. science], from which Aristotle's teaching as to the nature and composition of natural bodies must not be omitted'. 'The Congregation resolves to teach and defend the Aristotelian system in the physical instruction generally', and any rash teacher who 'either openly or under specious pretences, attempted to put other views in their place' was to be dismissed. Sometimes views somewhat newer than the two thousand-year-old ones of the Greek philosopher had to be mentioned, and these were sometimes unfortunately anti-Catholic and even non-Christian; in which case they may be mentioned, but 'the teacher of philosophy must do so without any words of praise, and if possible show that it is derived from some other source'. That was not very kind, and indeed hardly honest.

Very obviously, the whole system was designed to secure the Catholic faith; and everything considered to be of doubtful value to the Catholic cause, from non-Aristotelian philosophy to works of genius by immoral men, was excluded or slighted. One must be perpetually on the watch out, for, as the commission that drew up the *Ratio* sagely commented, 'whatever concerns us is public and, day after day, is before the eyes of all, even of those who are not well disposed towards us'. Therefore, as in all Jesuit matters, uniformity and discipline must come before speculation and experiment. In the bad old days, said the commission,

> when no common order or form was as yet prescribed, every one thought that he could hold what sentiments he liked, and teach them to others in the manner he himself preferred; so that sometimes the members of the Order disagreed as much among themselves as with others outside.

The *Ratio* of 1599 put a stop to this scandalous individualism, and instituted a standard instruction in standard thoughts.

If the Jesuit system weighed heavily on adventurous spirits, it did at least, as it was intended, produce exemplary and powerful priests and missionaries. In 1580, the Duke of Parma, embattled in the Netherlands, wrote to Philip II in Spain:

> Your Majesty desired me to build a citadel at Maestricht; I thought that a college of the Jesuits would be a fortress more likely to protect the inhabitants against the enemies of the Altar and the Throne. I have built it.

The German College, founded by Ignatius in Rome to help arrest the flow of Protestantism in its German homeland, sent out a bold stream of German secular priests trained to the exacting standards demanded by the Council of Trent. Within fifty years of Ignatius's death, students of the German College were installed in the bishoprics of Augsburg, Breslau, Olmütz, Passau, Salzburg, and Würzburg. From the colleges founded by Parsons in Spain and at St. Omer, English Jesuits went to meet Elizabeth's displeasure which several of them did not survive. The University of Coimbra, in Portugal, provided the breeding ground for the Jesuit missionaries to the Indies. In the East, the Jesuits had schools in Goa, on the Malabar coast, in Delhi and Agra, two schools in Japan and one in Macao. These schools, though reared and supported by Catholic orthodoxy and missionary zeal, were the first places in history where the ideas of the West could meet the unknown systems of the East, intermingle and, perhaps unintentionally, be modified by them.

Schoolmastering became part of the Jesuits' active ministry, and it is useless to complain that Jesuit teachers did not preserve a judicious impartiality between all schools of thought. They did not mean to. They tried to nourish not just the mind, but particularly the soul. And if Protestants sent their children to Jesuit schools, as they did, they knew that they were imperilling the child's Protestant soul for the sake of a good grounding. The Jesuit schools prospered and multiplied, in spite of the bad feeling that commonly existed between the Society and the local church or the State, because the Jesuits gave the best education. Yet the order was encouraged to overcome great difficulties not by a desire to teach. Faith, not professorial chairs, incites heroic actions. Nothing but a high idealism and a little fanaticism would have enabled the Jesuits to persevere and eventually triumph over the enmity their schools aroused in France generally, and in Paris especially.

In 1545, Guillaume du Prat, Bishop of Clermont and one of the

few French churchmen to attend the early sessions of the Council of
Trent, became quite possessed by the spirit of that council and
decided to enlighten his part of the Auvergne. He wished to re-
animate the ancient college at Billom, and establish at the Hôtel de
Clermont, his Parisian property, a hostel for students from his
diocese. The bishop in his enthusiasm forgot that he had neither
staff nor students. Therefore, his plan lagged until in 1546 he met at
Trent Claude Le Jay who spoke so well for his infant Society that
du Prat decided to place both ventures—Billom and the house at
Paris—into the Jesuits' hands. Both colleges were slow to start.
Pirates captured one of the two professors sent to organize Billom,
and the poor man died in captivity. Eventually, five days before
Ignatius's death, the college opened with seven Jesuit professors and
five hundred students. It was the first Jesuit school to cater for
external students only and was therefore the pattern for many later
schools.

The Collège de Clermont, intended for students from the Society
and the centre of Jesuit operations in France, had a more tempest-
uous history. Paschase Broet, one of the founding Jesuit fathers,
arrived to take over the small concern, in 1551, and immediately
faced French hostility and, worse, French bureaucracy, a very
dreadful impediment. He came bearing a full load of papal briefs,
bulls and apostolic whatnots, and even a permission from Henry II
won for him by the Cardinal of Lorraine—but all hopeless against
the privilege of the Parlement and the prejudice of the University
Theological Faculty. The Gallican Bishop of Paris, Eustache du
Bellay, an astringent relative of the witty poet, was also against the
Jesuits. Soon Broet was writing to Ignatius:

> I have been to present the king's new injunction and our bulls to
> Messieurs of the Parlement. Most of them, especially those of greatest
> influence, were exceedingly hostile. They told me that there were more
> than enough religious orders already . . . One man told me in a terrible
> temper that we were superstitious, proud, puffed-up, vainglorious
> people. I did not know how to answer him.

And a report of the Theological Faculty, in December 1554,
declared:

> This society, which has been endowed with so many and such various
> privileges, indults and liberties, especially in the administration of the
> sacraments, and in the office of preaching, lecturing and teaching,
> to the prejudice of bishops, or other religious orders, and even of

princes and temporal authorities, as well as to the detriment of universities, and the great grievance of people in general, appears to us to violate the honour of monasticism.

Battle was now well joined between the Society of Jesus, with its international ramifications subversive to decent local authority, and those Parisian interests who had made themselves cosy retreats, entrenched behind years of authority and malpractice. The situation was further greatly complicated by the precarious religious state of France, by the too-crafty policies of Catherine de Medici and by the clashes of ambition, principle and power between the Guise faction, the *politiques* and the Calvinists. Out of all this sad confusion came the wars of religion, in which the Jesuits were naturally involved on the Catholic side. The University of Paris and the Parlement, though bitter and prejudiced, were right to see that in the matter of the Collège de Clermont education was only a sub-issue. The real question was not whether a Jesuit college was to be allowed, but whether the Society itself was to be allowed; and this far graver question was fought with correspondingly greater passion. French logic saw clearly that the Jesuit educational work could not be separated from the general aims of the Society. So Broet, who seemed to have little conception of what was happening, wrote despairingly that every day the tribulations became heavier. 'The bishop is like a viper to us,' Cogordan, the procurator at Clermont, complained to Laynez, 'and he cannot bear the sight of me personally.'

In 1560, Bishop du Prat died, leaving a large estate to endow the Hôtel de Clermont. This generous act released a wave of avid litigation, and now Cogordan really had to run round trying to keep the money in Jesuit hands. He wrote to Laynez:

> The misery and weariness of the whole business have reached a limit. For two or three months now I have had to be at the Louvre at dawn and to hang about there all day, weighed down with my years and asthma and other ills. . . . Everybody wants the money bequeathed to us, and I have to fight not one, but five or six lawsuits. Day and night I must work drafting replies to these claimants.

In 1561, the vagaries of politics unexpectedly went the Jesuits' way. After the Colloquy of Poissy the French bishops were so annoyed by Theodore Beza's presence at the conference that they determined to legalize the Jesuits, though they hedged the decree with so many conditions that the Society had legality without any rights of action. In February 1562 the Collège de Clermont was formally instituted in

a fine new house bought with du Prat's legacy. It began a distinguished career with about a hundred students flocking to the distinguished lectures of Juan Maldonado, or Maldonatus as he is more
generally known. The future looked rosy. Then in 1565 a new rector
of the University revoked the privileges and forbade all lectures.
Again the grounds of the quarrel were not primarily academic, as
the University made quite clear:

> As the University, with the Gallican Church, ranks the Council above
> the Pope, it cannot receive any society or college which puts the Pope
> above the Council. Let the Jesuits, if they like, take themselves as
> Papal vassals to the unbelieving pagans whom they were founded to
> evangelize.

Events now became swift and confused. The Jesuits began a famous
but indecisive lawsuit before the Parlement. Later came more
energetic strife—pitched battles and student revolts. 'Again and
again,' wrote Father Manare, the new principal, 'the college under-
went a regular siege. Our windows were stoned and filthy rubbish
thrown into the house. Often we too were stoned when we ventured
out.' Protestant and Catholic champions were drawn into the fray—
the Prince de Condé and the Cardinal de Bourbon. And eventually
the college lived, changed its name to Louis le Grand, and took in
hand many young geniuses, such as Descartes, Corneille, Molière
and, most prickly of all, Voltaire.

The spread of Jesuit schools was achieved by faith and endurance,
usually against the odds. The history of the Collège de Clermont
shows the kind of civil and religious troubles the new schools
could expect to find. That the schools prospered and multiplied
indicates the importance the Society attached to education as part
of its ministry. And the Jesuits were surely right: the new schools
were good in themselves, and good for the order. Consequently, no
challenge was neglected. Southern Germany, where Lutheranism
and Catholicism met, was a rich forcing ground for Jesuit colleges.
The Society rushed into Pamiers, in the lands of the Calvinist Jeanne
d'Albret, and was thrown out equally quickly. Not dismayed, Father
Auger dashed on to Tournon, started a college, was captured by
Protestants, condemned to death, was romantically spirited away
and reappeared at Billom, still eager to teach. In the turmoil of the
wars of religion, colleges still opened at frequent intervals. In the
dark period of the mid 1570's there were some ten colleges operating
in France, from Verdun in the north to Toulouse in the south. At

the suppression of the Society in 1773 there were no less than ninety-two colleges in France. By then the Jesuits had become the teachers of the Catholic world; they possessed 728 universities, colleges and schools attended by nearly a quarter of a million pupils.

The Jesuit schools were brilliantly successful—successful for the Society, and for the students too. The order displayed its usual ability to divine psychological states and provided a firm regimen in which most boys could be reasonably happy. Some of the brightest stars of the system turned against the Society in later life; but one sometimes feels that what they particularly begrudged was that they were made happy in childhood by a Society which their maturity despised. Voltaire is the best example, for he delighted to combine inconsistency with honesty. In his mature years he disliked and ridiculed the Jesuits very much as fanatics and causers of dissensions and unhappiness. Yet he remembered them as fine, devoted masters:

> In the seven years I lived in the house of the Jesuits, what did I see among them? The most hard-working, frugal and regular life, all their hours divided between the care they spent on us and the exercises of their strict vows. I and thousands of others brought up by them attest this; not one will be found to contradict me.

All his life he kept his affection for his teacher, Father Porée. In 1746 he wrote to the then rector of Louis le Grand:

> Nothing will efface from my heart the memory of Père Porée, who is equally dear to all that studied under him. Never did man make study and virtue more amiable. The hours of his lessons were delicious hours to us. And I would have wished it the custom at Paris, as it used to be in Athens, that one of any age could listen to such lectures. I should often go to hear them. I have had the good fortune to be formed by more than one Jesuit of the character of Père Porée, and I know that he has successors worthy of him.

James Joyce, too, was another sad son of the Society, and wrote with uncertain meaning and Delphic gloom in *Finnegans Wake*, 'the soul-contracted son of the secret cell groped through life at the expense of the taxpayers, dejected into day and night with jesuit bark and bitter bite'. But he also wrote in the *Portrait of the Artist*, that fictionalized account of his own schooldays at Clongowes Wood and Belvedere:

> His masters, even when they had not attracted him, had seemed to him always intelligent and serious priests. . . . During all those years he had never heard from any of his masters a flippant word: it was they

who had taught him christian doctrine and urged him to live a good life and, when he had fallen into grievous sin, it was they who had led him back to grace.

The Jesuit plan of studies set down in the *Ratio Studiorum* may seem stern and over-organized. But the schooling of the time too often lacked any organization at all, and so nothing was taught; while the discipline, everywhere severe, was elsewhere so capriciously and wilfully applied that it amounted to brutality. Schooling was a desperate business. Godet quotes the goings-on at Montaigu, according to the account of a professor of Hebrew, in 1573. January 29, a 'poor' student drowned; June 2, another 'poor' goes mad. April 16, a 'rich' student jumps from a window; July 8, another 'rich' does the same. May 14, a porter beaten to death and another badly wounded. October 25, another assault leading to another death. Painful events such as these were greatly reduced in Jesuit schools by the solicitous eyes of the faculty. Ignatius had always tried to ensure that the young should not be pressed too hard; he even ruled that the office of corrector, whose job it was to give beatings, should be held by an employee from outside the Society who, not knowing the victims, would treat all equally. Unfortunately, correctors were hard to find and when the office devolved on senior boys the results were not as intended: the victim often turned on the corrector and corrected him. The Jesuit student was in the best position to make the best use of his studies. His day was cleared of distractions. He had a well-defined curriculum at clearly defined times. He was constantly exhorted to industry. His teachers, if not always exceptional, were at least well-trained, and practically always worthy moral men. His study books were sound, solid works without being exciting enough to upset him. He moved in an ordered way through a grave atmosphere. Nor was the enterprise dull: it was too immense to be that—a pioneer European undertaking. 'Tis a marvellous thing,' wrote Montaigne after visiting the Roman College, 'what a place this College holds in Christendom. I think there never was such another amongst us.' And of the famous teacher Maldonado, he noted with approval: 'Master Maldonatus asked me my views on Roman customs, especially in the matter of religion, and found that his opinions corresponded exactly with mine.' After so much dedication, application and enlightenment, the tribute of Lamartine to the Jesuits at Balley is not surprising:

It was a bitter and obstinate boy and I was softened and won over, so that I willingly put on a yoke which skilful teachers made light and

pleasant for me. . . . Our souls had found their wings and together
soared upwards towards the good and beautiful. . . . I there learned
what could be made of human beings, not by compulsion, but by
encouragement. . . . They began by making me happy—they would
soon have made me good.

Jesuit education aimed not to produce 'intellectuals', but moral,
informed men. Yet the Jesuits knew that young minds should
not only be filled with knowledge, but also extended actively and
captivated through the imagination. No one knew better than
Ignatius the force of sensual impressions. Displays which used the
students' talents and astounded the countryside were a popular and
original part of Jesuit method. The people could judge the superiority
of the Jesuit schools by their resplendence, and the Society's genius
for self-advertisement devised many rococo occasions. The opening
of the Gymnasium at Munich in 1576 was a typical bravura performance:

> The students, dressed in Roman costume, acted a play entitled *Con-
> stantine*, and after the conclusion of the performance forty of them,
> clad in steel armour, accompanied the Imperator on horseback through
> the town, as he rode in triumph through the streets in a Roman
> quadriga.

Plays, musical concerts, prize-givings and other ceremonies were all
carefully gilded and made glorious. And all this was done according
to the instructions of the *Ratio Studiorum*:

> These ceremonies must be conducted with exceptional solemnity,
> and with as large an attendance as possible of our own members and
> men of learning and high position from elsewhere. . . . On the day of
> the prize-giving, the names of the winners are to be publicly announced
> with all manner of pomp. . . . The prizes are then to be handed to the
> winners amid applause and the sound of music.

The form of display best liked by the Jesuits was the theatrical pro-
duction (one hardly dares to call the magnificent creatures produced
by the Jesuits mere plays—besides they nearly all had the minimum
of plot and the maximum of grandeur). For in the theatre moral
or pious instruction, ostentation and some creative work by the
students could be combined in the best possible way. Nonetheless,
the European stage owes much to the developments of the Jesuit
theatre, and stage management and property design owe even more.
    The end that the Jesuit theatre had in view was, of course, a
religious end, and what could be done and not done on the stage

was strictly regulated. Nothing should happen that was 'not serious and worthy of a Christian poet'. 'The subject of all tragedies and comedies,' the *Ratio* laid down, 'shall be sacred and pious. The plays are to be in Latin and are only seldom to be performed: a woman or a woman's dress must never appear on the stage.' Latin was insisted on as the international language of the Church and also, no doubt, to give the students practice in its use. The prohibition on women only indicates that the general puritanism of the Counter-Reformation had not yet worked out a sensible attitude towards women. But obviously a theatre as limited as this could not develop, except scenically, and if it was to serve the Jesuit purpose as religious propaganda it had to adapt to the theatre outside.

The usual strong Jesuit practicality enabled it to do this. In the foreign missions, where the drama was the Jesuits' best friend, the futility of serving Western dishes to uncomprehending palates was soon recognized, and Jesuit authors and actors learnt to change their ways. In countries like India and Japan where the native drama was well-developed, the Jesuit theatre adapted to the local modes, and as a result was very well received. In places with no dramatic tradition, simple moral stories understandable to local custom and prejudice were presented in the local dialect. These, too, were very successful and often highly polished. In Europe the changes came more slowly and more discreetly. In 1645, the Viennese house humoured the Emperor Ferdinand with a nationalistic piece called *Arma Austriaca*; and women—or at least women's dress—edged demurely on to the stage impersonating Esther, Mary Magdalene and other accredited biblical figures. Gradually clowns, thieves, beggars, lovers and lechers—the full theatrical troupe—came to the stage, and often in the vernacular language. Some Jesuit houses were in danger of forgetting the religious purpose of their drama, and allowing their theatre to develop according to the outside world. The general of the order did not permit this to pass without comment, and many curt notes went out from Rome. The triumph of the Jesuit theatre lay not in its own productions, but in the impetus it gave to others. Lope de Vega and Calderón both learnt from Jesuit plays, and Calderón, a great friend of the Society, acknowledged his debt nicely. In *The Great Prince of Fez* he makes the hero convert to Catholicism and enter the Jesuit order singing a hymn of praise to Ignatius.

Moreover, it is pleasant to recall all those splendid Jesuit entertainments enlivening and irradiating a world that was too often dark and too often destitute of amusement. It seems right that Louis XIV should, in his childhood, have enjoyed the plays at Clermont; it seems right that, in 1653, he should have taken the exiled Charles II of England to a special performance there, and one hopes that among the brightness and the tinsel, the groaning engines and dreadful effects, the angels and devils, the music and the dancing, the exiled king forgot for a moment the plight of his poor country sorely pressed under Puritan restraint.

The Jesuits took great care that their schooling should reflect the internationalism of the Society. For the greater good of the unity of Christendom, the masters avoided dwelling on national characteristics, both good and bad, and the *Ratio* ordained a uniform system equally applicable in Paraguay, India, Japan and throughout Europe from the bottom of Spain to Poland and Russia. The lessons were in Latin, a language drained of all emotional content but with strong ecclesiastical and imperial overtones. The students learnt from professors of many different nationalities. It must not be permitted, ruled the seventh general congregation:

> that in those towns where the Society has its own colleges and houses, the professors of theology, philosophy and humanity be chosen solely from that particular nationality, still less the superiors, for this is directly opposed to the customs of the Society.

These provisions naturally offended the zenophobic nationalism which nearly every European country of the time cultivated. One of the complaints by the University of Paris against the Collège de Clermont was that the rector was a Scot and the staff included too few Frenchmen. And Jesuit schools met similar troubles in other European lands. The open community of learning, which had been a glory of education in the high Middle Ages, now no longer befitted national dignity, nor was it politically desirable. The University of Paris in its great days had been made pre-eminent not only by the Frenchman, Abelard, but also by the Italian, Aquinas, and the German, Albertus Magnus; now it was prepared to receive only good Frenchmen. At Jesuit schools, the students had the chance to observe that strange animal, the foreigner, and measure him against the official propaganda. And since nationalities were treated equally under the Church, individuals, too were given an equal opportunity to prove worthy and respectful sons of the Church. Descartes, recommending the college of La Flèche which he attended, recounted the democratic and unstrained relations among the students:

Young people are there from all parts of France; there is a mingling of characters; their mutual intercourse has almost the same good results as if they were actually travelling; and, in fine, the equality which the Jesuits establish among all, by treating just in the same way those who are illustrious and those who are not so, is an extremely good invention.

When the Jesuit schools system worked well it provided a grounding scarcely rivalled anywhere else in Europe. But it did not always work well, and it had within it certain inherent blocks which made it rather difficult for the system to function as it should. The chief cause of the trouble was the old Jesuit schizophrenia—the conflict between a rigid, undeviating idealism and a pliant realism in the face of the facts. Also, the education attempted to do so much that the Jesuit schools never quite managed to get their priorities straight, and adopted an equivocal manner towards society and the students. How could the need for Catholic propaganda, the necessity to show the Jesuit flag, the desire to placate and influence local civil magistrates, the duty to teach strict orthodox doctrine and the wish to stir and fill young minds be adequately combined in the same school? Not surprisingly, the general Aquaviva, in his preamble to the *Ratio Studiorum*, suggested a cautious approach to both the public and the student. The good name of the Society required that local opinion should not be unnecessarily slighted:

If opinions, no matter whose they be, are found in a certain province or city to give offence to many Catholics, whether members of the Society or not, that is, persons not unqualified to judge, let no one teach them or defend them there, though the same doctrines may be taught elsewhere without offence.

And the same carefulness overflows into the teaching method:

Let no one defend any opinion which is judged by the generality of learned men to go against the received tenets of the philosophers and theologians, or the common consent of the theological schools.

Unhappily, most new ideas tend to go against 'the received tenets' of the past and a strict adherence to this instruction meant the mere handing on of undeveloped or out-of-date opinions. The new was decidedly suspect:

In questions which have already been treated by others, let no one follow new opinions, or, in matters which in any way pertain to religion, or are of some consequence, let no one introduce new questions, without consulting the Prefect of Studies or the Superior.

There is a lot of good sense in these injunctions, especially considering the difficulties the Jesuit schools contended with. But they are rules mainly designed for the preservation of the Society, and do not lead to a well-developed and inquisitive mind. Once again, a confusion of ends; were all young students to be treated like aspiring Jesuits? If so, this shying away from ideas was licensed by Ignatius himself. He had banned the works of Savonarola not because they were bad, but because they were controversial—'not that some of his books were without value, like the *Triumph of the Cross* and others, but because the author is a subject of controversy.' In fact, safety first:

> So the Society, inasmuch as there are so many good books free from all controversy, does not wish to use books of notorious authors.

But safety first is a bad principle for a teacher.

The Jesuit educational system bristled with so many unique features that problems were bound to arise in time. For example, the Society did its very best to keep tuition free for the student and to an extraordinary extent they succeeded. Jesuit colleges were small miracles of good-husbandry and providence. Frederick the Great of Prussia loved them because they saved the State the bother, and huge expense, of setting up its own system, and saved the subject the burden of finding tuition fees. The history of the college at Vannes, before and after the suppression in 1773, shows just what good value a Jesuit school was. In 1762, the Jesuit house with some twenty-two members, and supporting a college of about 1,200 students, lived on an income of 6,000 *livres* a year. After 1773, a faculty of ten secular professors in the same school cost 11,000 *livres* for their salaries alone. But schools are expensive operations, even for the frugal Jesuits, and funds were not always plentiful. A small loophole in the constitutions had allowed the possibility of tuition fees, 'the sons of noble or rich parents' might be accepted as paying students 'for good reasons'. This led to the foundation of several colleges exclusively for nobles, such as San Isidro in Madrid, and rather undermined the egalitarian character of Jesuit education. It seems that the Society was in some doubt about these noble schools. They were against the spirit of the Ignatian ideal, but they provided very necessary funds and allowed the Jesuits to keep an eye on the nobility—something which Ignatius had always carefully attended to. It may be a commentary on the progress of the Jesuits, or merely a commentary on economic life, that gradually more and more schools came to accept paying students.

The desirable was not always possible. Sometimes the Jesuits defeated themselves. The importance of Latin was clearly insisted on for a number of reasons which the *Ratio* sets out—'on account of the intercourse with different nationalities', to write books, to understand the Church Fathers and Church literature, and so on. In other words, Latin was studied purely for practical reasons, not for scholarly reasons or for the sake of elegant Latinity. However, Latin had gradually become of hardly any practical use at all. It lingered on in the universities as a good mental discipline, and in the Church as a sort of clerical jargon. But the 'different nationalities' no longer conversed in it, and the important books were no longer written in it; as for the study of Christian sources, Hebrew and Greek were now equally important. The Jesuits were left holding a useless practical tool, and as they did not have a scholar's approach, through lack of exercise, their Latin degenerated into something less than Ciceronian. Aquaviva admitted in 1586:

> It is a matter of universal complaint that humanistic studies have for the most part fallen into decay among our members, so that nothing is more difficult than to find a good grammarian, rhetorician or humanist. . . . The confessors, too, are in difficulty when they have to hear a confession in Latin, and they can scarcely understand the homilies of the Fathers and the lessons of the breviary.

Aquaviva thought that the *Ratio* would remedy this, but he was wrong for the educational approach was wrong. A century later, in 1680, the general Paul Oliva noted that Jesuit Latin was still usually appalling:

> Every effort must be made to raise the standard of the humanistic studies . . . The fault lies with the teachers, not only of the external students, but also those who instruct our own members of the novitiate. For they seem to take for Latin anything which differs from their own tongue and can be twisted into a semblance of Latin.

The Jesuits were burdened by a piece of their own mythology. Forwarding the international claims of the Church, they advanced Latin, the Church language, as the international language. But history had conspired against them and buried Latin. As practical men, the Jesuits knew the greater value of the various vernaculars, but the pretence had to be maintained though the pupils suffered as a result. Mariana, a troublesome child of the Society and a not very charitable witness, had this to say:

> There is no doubt that at this date [1625] there is less knowledge of

Latin in Spain than fifty years ago, and the main cause of this is that the Jesuits occupy themselves with these studies.

In education, as in other activities, the Jesuits judged all matters according to their usefulness to the Society. No one, whatever his opinions on the Jesuits, can accuse them of being disinterested. Ignatius had said that all things must be done *ad majorem Dei gloriam*, but that was pleasingly vague. Were all the acts of a fighting Catholic order in a hostile world quite for the glory of God? Was the glory of God quite synonymous with the glory of the Society? Puzzling questions. Safest to assume that God's glory demands a healthy and active Society of Jesus. With a recognition of self-interest that would have pleased Hobbes, the *Ratio*, in Rule 1 for the rector, outlined the true purpose of Jesuit education:

> Because the Society of Jesus undertakes the management of universities and schools in order that our own numbers may conveniently be instructed in knowledge and in all else that is profitable to the welfare of souls, and may be able to communicate to others what they have learnt, the first endeavour of the rector, after providing for religion and virtue, must be with the help of God to accomplish that end which the Society has proposed to itself in taking over the charge of gymnasia.

There is an impression, which is never quite dispelled, that the students in a Jesuit school were the innocent partners to a superior confidence trick. The roles were reversed. Are the teachers there for the benefit of the students? No, the students exist so that the member of the Society may practise instructing, and his power to 'communicate', before passing on to other business. Teaching was part of training, so general Caraffa, in 1646, ordered the Bohemian province to use as instructors in the lower schools 'all without distinction, and particularly those who detest this occupation'. This might be bad for the pupils, but it was a fine, bracing tonic for Jesuit character. 'Their work as teachers,' wrote the Jesuit Cornova, 'served as a school of morals for young Jesuits, since men never exercise more control over themselves than when they are compelled to control others.' Still, Cornova added very sensibly, 'even the advantage accruing to the Order did not exempt it from the obligation . . . to do the best in its power for the young people entrusted to its care'. Again, the Society felt the conflict of priorities, and resolved this to the benefit of the Society.

The view that education should be a 'leading out', as the word implies, is a recent notion, and generally irrelevant in any discussion of Counter-Reformation schooling. Neither Catholics nor Protestants had any doubts about what a child should learn, and both sides thought that the safety of the child's soul was in the hands of the schoolmaster. But the Jesuit schools existed to advance not just Catholicism, but more particularly the Society, and that was a very significant difference. It meant that the young external students (as opposed to the Jesuit novices) were embedded, like flies in amber, in a quasi-religious system which they had not assented to. This does not mean that they were unhappy: on the contrary, most felt secure in the quiet, watchful, well-ordered calm of the Jesuit establishment. But it meant that they were subjected to a monastic control, quite permissible among the voluntary candidates to the order, though a mental tyranny for the non-Jesuit. There is some evidence that the Society's liking for secret reports on the faults of one's fellows carried over into the school system. The original *Ratio* ordered that:

> Every teacher must have his own open and secret censors and a chief censor, through whom he may make inquiry as to the moral characters of the others.

The effect of such regulations may be imagined, though anyone who has been to an English Public School should not be surprised. Most of the distinguishing features of Dr. Arnold's peculiar brainchild were anticipated by the Jesuits. There is also some evidence that teachers exerted undue influence to persuade brilliant students to join the Society. One cannot entirely blame the Society; they wanted the best talents, and the material was there at hand. A system that extols a Jesuit vocation as the highest aim in life, particularly for the talented, encourages enticement. In private talk, says the *Ratio*, the lower grade teacher 'should insist on religious practices, but in such a way as not to appear to entice any into our Order'. If he found his little chats potentially fruitful, 'he should refer the boy to his confessor', who was of course also a Jesuit. Cornova admitted that, 'The Jesuits, as teachers of Rhetoric and Philosophy, made a special boast of promoting to the Society capable students.'

Every school is to some extent tyrannical; and every school tries to impress on its pupils the values, either social or religious, it happens to hold. But the Jesuit schools, scholastically, face a more serious charge. In attempting to create a mental atmosphere favourable to their kind of Catholic activity, they devised a plan of studies that was narrow, closed, incapable of development, and quite out of touch with what was happening in the secular state. It was, perhaps, inevitable. The Ignatian ideal was starry, but static. It could not develop because it had not yet been realized. And in the meantime the secular world was rushing on in its self-centred and nationalistic way, but also throwing off every so often bright flashes—literature in the national tongues, science that accounted neither Aristotle nor the traditional Christian cosmology, and philosophies that neither began nor ended with St. Thomas. To fight the world the Jesuits felt they had to oppose all its effects. The *Ratio* treated with national writers very cautiously:

> They must be carefully selected, and no author should be read or praised whose works the pupils cannot admire without risk to their morals or faith.

And characteristically, the Society worried about the effect of this risky stuff on the teachers. Jouvancy, a foremost seventeenth-century Jesuit educationalist, whilst having a soft spot for his beloved French, yet warned of the moral dangers in poetry:

> We must call to the attention a snare which is especially dangerous to young teachers, that of reading too much from works in their own language, poetry particularly. This not only wastes much time, but may also lead to spiritual destruction.

That the *Ratio Studiorum* managed to develop at all is a tribute to the Jesuit genius for adaptability. It was not meant to change. From the seventeenth to the late nineteenth century, Jesuit writers on education, like Jouvancy, Duhr, Pachtler and Hughes, all regarded it as something grandly immutable, brought down on tablets from a high pedagogical mountain. It married the difficult Ignatian ideal with the imperfect Counter-Reformation mentality— compounded of six parts prejudice and four parts obstinacy—and tried to make them permanent. This could not be, and the system collapsed very suddenly. Boyd Barrett, an ex-Jesuit, wrote of the early years of this century:

> Of the 24 Jesuit masters under whom I studied at Clongowes, only one had any knowledge of the *Ratio*. . . . As regards myself, although I acted, while a Jesuit, as Dean in one Jesuit college for a while, and as sub-Dean in another, I have never read the *Ratio*!

Adherence to the immutable often leads to many ironies. And one of the savagest ironies of Jesuit education is that it played wonderfully into the hands of the State. More than anything, it helped introduce the spirit of the bourgeoisie. This, according to the respected Father Daniélou, was the major Jesuit contribution to seventeenth-century European civilization. The Jesuit system impressed on young citizens the virtues of obedience, authority, quiet conformity and a reverence for duly stamped and acceptable thought; this was exactly what the State desired in its citizens. Of course, the Jesuits intended these virtues to be used for the benefit of the Catholic Church and the Society. But once the young student left the haven of the Jesuit school, as he must inevitably do (unless he joined the Society), it was the State that gave him his orders and directed his uninquisitive and obedient soul. And the general Jesuit policy of complying to State wishes wherever possible, made the work of the State easy. So valuable were the Jesuits to the State, that in the eighteenth century, during the troubled times which led to the suppression of the Society, their most fervent champions were the two greatest tyrants in Europe—Frederick the Great of Prussia and Catherine the Great of Russia, neither of them Catholics and both more atheist than anything else. Frederick, for all his many accomplishments, did not believe in freedom and despised human nature. But he was a realist with a clear judgment, and in his cynical way he saw that the Jesuits were producing good, disciplined Prussians, in schools that cost the State nothing. He wrote to Voltaire:

> Besides, there are reasons of economy for preferring such a body of men to mere seculars. The professor taken from the latter class will cost more, because his wants are greater. It is needless to remark that the property of the Jesuits would not be sufficient to remunerate their successors.

And in 1770, speaking of Clement XIV in another letter to Voltaire:

> For my own part, I have no reason to complain of him; he leaves me my dear Jesuits whom they are persecuting everywhere. I will save the precious seed, to give some of it, one day, to those who should wish to cultivate a plant so rare.

It is a sad thing for a Catholic order, which supported the universal claims of Christendom, to receive such a compliment from Frederick. The violence of Voltaire's opposition to the Society of his old schoolmasters is now understandable. He believed passionately in liberty and tolerance and curiosity, and he saw that the Jesuits in Europe—victims to the spirit of abstraction—produced none of these: out of their schools trotted useful little adjuncts to despotic aims.

Chapter XI

'THE FAITH WHICH DOES NOT DESPISE OR DESTROY THE MANNERS AND CUSTOMS OF ANY PEOPLE'

"WE LEFT Lisbon on April 7 last year, and I was seasick for two months. It was miserable off the coast of Guinea owing to the prolonged calms. We had forty days of them, and the weather was no help, but God in His great mercy brought us to an island where we now are.' So wrote Francis Xavier from Mozambique on January 1, 1542, a passenger on the carrack *Santiago* bound for Portuguese India. At the age of thirty-five he was setting out on a mission from which he never returned. In discomfort and sickness he began his great journey of unremitting pain and heroic trials which ended eleven years later on the small island of Sancian, in sight of the forbidden mainland of China, eight miles off but unreachable. It was, in its way, a typical Jesuit missionary journey.

Periods of mental agitation are nearly always periods of physical restlessness too. Increasing knowledge and increasing curiosity build up stores of energy and drive the feet onwards. After the tumult of the Renaissance, when Europe found its traditional way to the East blocked by a triumphant Islam, European men very naturally jumped into boats and attempted to sail round the obstacles. Though they found both a New World in the West, and islands beyond their old experience in the East, they carried with them their European muddle, in which the problems of religion played a conspicuous part. For so long Europe had been so pre-occupied by the great intimidating presence of Islam, which had thoroughly engaged most of Europe spiritually, intellectually and physically, that new lands were approached by the light of old conflicts. The Spaniard, Xavier, in his early letters from India, scattered the term 'Moor' indiscriminately over Arabs, Hindus and pagans, and seemed to approve that all should be treated as the Spaniards treated the Moors in Spain. Very few were averse to Christendom being extended by

DEVILS
ASSAULTING
IGNATIUS

FRANCIS
XAVIER
WRITES TO
IGNATIUS
FROM INDIA

THE INTERIOR OF THE GESÙ IN ROME: AN EXAMPLE OF
THE JESUIT BAROQUE STYLE

conquest; but unfortunately the discoveries were made by Portuguese and Spaniards in the name of the king, trade and national prosperity. In the name of Christ was tacked on too, according to tradition and because it had been assumed, for the want of any dissenting voice, that Christendom still existed. However, the merchant adventurers and the soldiers knew that they came first, and in their perverse pride even claimed the major credit for extending Christ's teaching. Bernal Diaz, in his *Historia de la Conquista de la Nueva España*, wrote of his companions, the formidable, merciless *conquistadores*:

> It is to be noted that, after God, it was we, the real conquerors, who discovered and conquered the Indians; and from the first we took away their idols, and taught them our holy doctrine and to us is due the reward and credit of it all, before any other people, even though they be churchmen.

And the Church, though it might have contested this attitude, had itself condoned it. In the fifteenth century the popes Nicholas V, Calixtus III and Alexander VI had intervened as umpires between Spain and Portugal so as they might divide the loot of the new discoveries between them, and not destroy themselves with fratricidal quarrels. The line drawn by Alexander VI, in May 1493, had finally delineated the two areas of robbery, and Alexander had chosen the occasion to add, rather as an afterthought, an injunction on the warlike entrepreneurs to:

> bring to Christian faith the people who inhabit these islands and the mainland . . . and to send . . . wise, upright, godfearing and virtuous men who will be capable of instructing the natives in good morals and in the Catholic faith.

How well men like Cortes, Pizarro and Albuquerque measured up to this standard is questionable. Most admitted very candidly their desire to denude the new land of its wealth in the shortest possible time; and others, such as Albuquerque, who believed in Christendom, practised a very terrible Christianity which had none of the New Testament in it. After the conquest of Goa in 1510, Albuquerque assured King Manuel of Portugal that 'our Lord did much for us', and added by way of illustration:

> I burnt the City and put all to the sword. For four consecutive days your soldiers slaughtered the Moors, not sparing a single one. They herded them into mosques and then set those buildings on fire. We reckoned that six thousand Moors had been slain. Sir, it was a great

deed, well fought and well finished, and the first time that vengeance has been taken in India for the treacheries and villanies perpetrated by the Moors against your Highness and your people.

This was evangelism of the old school, the sternest crusading spirit. Before Ormuz in 1507, the fearsome Portuguese general had sent an ultimatum to the defending forces, 'If you attempt to interfere with me in any way, I'll build the walls with Muslim bones. I will nail your ears to the door and erect the flagstaff on your skull.'

For some nine hundred years, from the time when Islam first began to expand, missions and war had gone together. Irreconcilable Islam and Christendom had guaranteed that. Albuquerque was only a type of representative Crusader, a stern, honest, just, and even pious, Christian, but a man who exterminated Moors as he would a plague of rats. The ways of the first Christian missioners, the men who had transformed pagan Europe, had been forgotten from lack of use. The crusading spirit was inextricably mixed with temporal aims, and Christianity could win no enduring spiritual triumphs so long as it was carried abroad in a soldier's knapsack or a merchant's purse. It had not always been so; mendicant friars in the Middle Ages had made some notable individual treks to China, Persia and northern India, and their message had been received politely and with some interest. The European priests advancing in India behind the skirts of the Portuguese forces found, on the southern coast, a community of Christians perhaps 100,000-strong, established peacefully and completely assimilated into the Indian scene. Unfortunately, these 'Christians of St. Thomas' were Nestorians, unacceptable to Roman orthodoxy, and therefore as likely to feel the strong European arm as the Hindu or the pagan. As Christianity had helped mould a mob of unruly barbarians into a European civilization, so the descendants of the barbarians, grown up into respectable nationals, recast Christianity; so long as Christian men approached other peoples according to the rules slowly worked out in the conflict with Islam, the spread of Christianity and the development of Christendom were hardly separable from military conquest and temporal ambition. The popes allowed the *Padroado* to operate— the placing of missionary activity under the 'patronage' of the princes—because that was the way in which the Crusades had been run. The princes, becoming increasingly nationalistic, tried to see to it that the sort of Christianity they promoted added to the wealth and glory of their nations. In time, the Church realized the dangers of the *Padroado*. In 1622, Gregory XV brought the conduct and care of missions under the control of the Congregation *Propaganda Fidei*. In doing this he acknowledged officially the death of the old ideal of Christendom, the spiritual and the temporal united to advance God's dominion. After 1622, *Propaganda* would try to establish a spiritual kingdom unencumbered by secular ties.

Francis Xavier, however, arrived in India well attached to Portugal. He was the personal representative of King John III, and he corresponded with the king directly. The finances for his mission came from Portugal. But he was also an Apostolic Nuncio, bearing the pope's authority. And, most of all, he was a follower of Ignatius Loyola, the man closest to Ignatius and the man, by temperament and talent, best able to interpret with generosity and genius how Ignatius's revolutionary plan for Catholic activity should be applied in the East. Ignatius, of course, felt very strongly the ideal of Christendom, and he was mediaeval enough to believe that the spiritual and the temporal could still work together for the good of Christendom. He was quite happy to send out his Jesuit missioners under the arrangements of the *Padroado*. But the Jesuit, even though incalculably distant in Japan and living on Portuguese money, still took his guidance from Rome and the general of the Society. In the far countries, happily freed from the complications of European politics, the Ignatian ideal 'to help one's neighbour' towards Christianity could flower and prosper. The internationalism of the Society saved it from taking sides in the greedy colonial rivalry of Spain and Portugal. The intelligence of the Jesuits enabled them to see that other continents presented quite a different case to Europe. However passionately the Jesuits might embroil themselves in the internal religious troubles in Europe, they could look dispassionately on other lands and other customs. For their time and their estate, they cleared themselves remarkably well of European prejudice. They thought that the non-Christian—pagan, Hindu or Buddhist—was not vicious or damned, but only in error, and that because he had not been taught; and this enabled the Jesuits, in general, to deal with alien peoples with dignity and respect. They were there to do the teaching. The problem was by what method, and that was gradually determined by experience.

Xavier landed at Goa on May 6, 1542, with a fairly representative set of misconceptions about non-Europeans and their religions, but with a keen desire to win converts. He immediately sought out the Bishop of Goa, and won the episcopal approval. 'The bishop,' wrote the Jesuit Teixeira, who knew Xavier, 'embraced him with great love, told him that he knew well who he was and his quality, and bade him use the Papal briefs in any way that the goodness of his heart might direct.' This was enough encouragement, and soon Xavier was out in the town. Teixeira pictured him thus:

> He went up and down the streets and squares with a bell in his hand, crying to the children and others to come to the instructions. The novelty of this, never seen before in Goa, brought a large crowd around him which he then led to the church. He began by singing the lessons which he had rhymed, and then made the children sing them so that they might become the better fixed in their memories.

It was a good beginning, showing energy and a love and care for the children; but this was not enough. Portuguese Goa, though sinful and disreputable, was not the mission field. And Xavier still had many disadvantages and mental follies to get rid of. He spoke only European tongues. At a later date it became part of the Xavier myth that he had the gift of languages. In fact he had only a small linguistic ability and never mastered more than a smattering of the various languages he met. But very early on he realized (unlike so many of the European priests in Goa) the importance of the native languages, and tried hard to learn them. In Japan nine years later, just before he died, though incredibly burdened with pastoral and administrative duties, he still struggled as a schoolchild with the mysteries of Japanese. A more serious deficiency than his lack of languages was his lack of understanding for any religion other than Christianity. In this he was a child of his times, and asserted the stubborn old absolute claims of the Christian West. 'God, the all-faithful,' he told a Moslem inquirer at Malindi, 'abided not with the infidels, and took no pleasure in their prayers.' He never lost his strong aversion to all non-Christian religious practice. From the Malabar coast he wrote to Ignatius describing the way in which he over-rode the native superstitions of a dying woman:

> All the invocations of the pagans are hateful to God because all their gods are devils. Accompanied by one of the native clerics I went to the house where the dying woman lay and began confidently to call upon the great name of Christ, nothing caring that I was in a strange land, but remembering only that the whole earth is the Lord's and all that dwell thereon.

And even in Japan, where he wondered at the high civilization of the country and tried to adapt himself to the ways of the people, he paid tribute to the culture but would have nothing to do with the religion.

If Xavier's theological knowledge was defective (Christian doctrine has never held that a person is damned for being a non-
Christian), at least his human heart was sound. He was drawn to the
poorest and most defenceless people under Portuguese domination.
In 1534, the Paravas of the southern tip of India, a gentle people
who lived mainly by pearl diving, had appealed to Goa for protection
against Moslem raiders. Protection had been granted, but only on
the condition that the Paravas become baptised. This they did, and
then found that they had merely changed tyrants. The Portuguese
oppressed and exploited them just as the Moslems had done.
Moreover, Goa failed to send priests to instruct these simple,
illiterate pearl-fishers in their new faith. Soon after Xavier arrived on
the Coromandel coast, at the end of 1542, he wrote to Ignatius of
this neglected people:

> No Portuguese live among the villagers because the country is so
> utterly sterile and poor. The Christians here were baptised eight years
> ago, but because they have had no priests to say Mass for them, or
> to teach them the creed, the Pater Noster, the Ave Maria and the
> commandments, they know nothing whatever of their religion except
> to say they are Christians.

They were the first people to benefit from Xavier's devotion. For
three years he hurried up and down among them, encouraging,
administrating, protecting. He preached to them, too, and tried to
instruct them in the faith, but it is doubtful if they understood
much, for his Tamil was rudimentary and he had very few helpers.
Perhaps his greatest service was to defend them against the Portuguese and the Hindus of the surrounding native kingdoms; Xavier
saw little difference between these two sets of brigands. To the King
of Portugal Xavier wrote bitterly of the rapacious Portuguese, and
warned the king, if he valued his soul, to govern his officials. From
Cochin, in 1545, he wrote to his old companion, Simon Rodriguez, in
Coimbra, savagely condemning Portuguese exploitation:

> Evil-doing is so much a matter of course that I see no remedy whatever
> for it. All go the same road of 'I plunder, thou plunderest', and it
> terrifies me to witness how many moods and tenses and participles
> of that miserable verb *rapio* those who come to India discover.

An old historian has Xavier saying to de Sousa, the Governor, 'If we
do not defend those who we baptise, we will have to preach Martyrdom along with Baptism, and we shall have to look for those with

enough courage to offer themselves to the Sacrifice as well as to the Sacrament.' To his suspicion of the Indian princes, Xavier added a rather characteristic contempt for the Brahmins:

> There is a class of men here called *bragmanes*. They are the mainstay of heathenism, and have charge of the temples devoted to the idols. They are the most perverse people in the world. . . . They do not know what it is to tell the truth but forever plot how to lie subtly and deceive their poor, ignorant followers. . . . They have little learning, but abundance of iniquity and malice. They regard me as a great nuisance as I keep on exposing their wickedness.

Xavier was forced by the nature of things to concentrate most on the physical needs and the safety of the Paravas. And here he showed for the first time an organizational ability worthy of his master and fellow-Basque, Ignatius. He began a work of communal reform in the pearl-fishing villages which was continued by his Jesuit successors, so that within fifty years the Paravas were distributed in sixteen strong villages, each one served by a resident Jesuit. As in the famous Jesuit mission in Paraguay in the next century, the Jesuits ruled sternly but justly. Laziness was discouraged and discipline was quite severe. Industry, devotion and solid moral worth were considered the important virtues. But the communities were noticeably peaceful and, apparently, well content. The missions, both to the Paravas and in Paraguay, have been criticized for not teaching the natives much beyond the simple tenets of the Christian faith. But with a naïve and illiterate people this alone was difficult enough, as the efforts of Xavier point out; after translating some simple prayers into Tamil, he would set out in his typical bold way to gather an audience:

> then, taking a bell, I went ringing it right through the town to collect as many children and adults as I could. Having gathered my audience, I held forth to them twice each day, until, at the end of the month, they had learned the prayers. I then arranged for the children to teach their fathers, mothers, sisters, brothers and neighbours the lessons they had acquired at my school. On Sundays I assemble all the people, men and women, young and old, and get them to repeat the prayers in their language. They take much pleasure in doing so, and come to the meetings gladly.

Xavier, the lean little Basque already going prematurely grey, tackling the Brahmins on their own ground and rounding up his parishioners like some clerical cowboy, gives the impression of superabundant energy and confidence. But it is well to recall the

loneliness and the difficulties of his mission. He remembered wistfully his comrades in Rome, the small band of first Jesuits with
whom he had been so happy in Paris and Italy. 'My recreation out
here, dearest Brothers,' he wrote, 'is to think of you constantly . . .
So I end by praying that as in His mercy He brought us together,
and then for His service separated us so far from one another, He
may again unite us in His holy glory.' And he asked for 'strength to
hold on my way among the heathens'. His experiences in India
taught him more about the failings of the Europeans than it did about
the nature of the Indians, and this was most valuable for it confirmed
his natural feeling that charity must lie at the heart of Christianity.
In his view the only justification for the Portuguese rule was that it
introduced Christianity and established peace and social justice.
He very soon saw that this was not the case, but he refused to con-
done the greed and self-interest which lay behind the Portuguese
protestations of devotion to the faith. Lisbon wanted the Paravas'
pearls, Xavier wanted their souls; he cared nothing for the pearls.
The insidious connection between colonial expansion and trade
exploitation must have surprised an idealist like Xavier. He protested
against it in the name of Christianity. From Manapad, near Cape
Comorin, he wrote to Rome:

> I have good reason to be troubled, as I am now so used to witnessing the
> aggressions, without power to intervene on the Christians' behalf, that
> the whole thing has become a permanent bruise on my soul, an over-
> whelming sorrow ever with me. I have already written to the vicars-
> general of Quilon and Cochin, telling them about the women whom the
> Portuguese snatched as slaves at Punnaikayal, that by the threat of
> major excommunication they may be able to learn the identity of the
> ravishers and their Christian victims. I took this step three days ago,
> immediately on receiving the headman's note.

The core of the Eastern missionary problem was in Europe, not in
the East. Xavier very sensibly realized that attitudes must change in
Europe before India could be put right. 'I have often felt strongly
moved,' he cried, 'to descend on the universities of Europe, especially Paris and its Sorbonne, and to cry aloud like a madman to those
who have more learning than good will to employ it usefully.' And
he knew what he was up against:

> But I fear that many university men [he went on] pursue their studies
> and conform to regulations only to gain dignities, benefices, bishoprics,
> which won, they say, it will be time enough to serve God.

It had not taken Xavier long to find the facts of European activity in the East; and having found them, he insisted, without compromise, that Christian charity must come before ambition, power and greed. This ideal, from which he never wavered, made Xavier one of the greatest ambassadors ever to come from Europe to the East. But he was a practical man too, as befitted a Jesuit, and knew that he had little chance of changing European ways from the distance of India. He could best serve Christianity by preparing an organization of missionary priests who breathed the spirit of the New Testament, and could resist the pressures of the secular powers. Obviously Xavier saw his newly-formed Society of Jesus, with its active idealism and its lack of temporal ties, as the best instrument for this task. He now constituted himself as a kind of advance-guard and frontrunner for the Society, not bound to any one mission, but breaking the ground from Goa to the Moluccas, from Celebes to Japan; those who came later would do the building.

It is arguable that Francis Xavier understood the physical needs of the East much better than he understood the East's mentality; and that he did more for the body than for the mind. Certainly he might be called a 'bigoted' Christian in the sense that he never recognized any good in any other religion. But that was a particular limitation from his European background which he had not managed to outgrow. To do so required time and study, and Xavier in his haste could spare neither. Later the slow, patient enquiry and assimilation of Jesuits like Valignano, Ricci, de Nobili and Beschi brought the systems of East and West closer together and able to regard each other more justly. Besides, to Xavier's quick look, Eastern religions often seemed oppressive or corrupt (what would a Hindu have thought of the religious wars of the Counter-Reformation?). He could not agree to the Indian caste system, seeing how miserably treated the lower castes were; and he noted that many of the Buddhist monasteries in Japan were idle and degenerate. The Jesuit Fernandez visited a Zen monastery at Hakata and discovered that 'the bonzes maintain many boys in their monastery with whom, according to public report, they commit unnatural sin'. Some of Xavier's methods seemed curious, too. Later missionaries, both Catholic and Protestant, were to question the use of mass baptisms. But Xavier, far from avoiding them, was eager to baptise all within reach. Anyone with a humble readiness to submit, no matter how illiterate and incomprehending, was accepted. In the poor, uneducated villages of the Paravas there was something to be said for his policy. Baptism brought the wretchedly oppressed Paravas under Xavier's tender care, and Christian charity was of far more use to these fishermen than the clearest exposition of Christian doctrine. That might be learnt later. Xavier also advocated the much more doubtful policy of bringing the Inquisition to India, not to watch over the Paravas, but to keep the faith of the Goan merchants pure. 'Many nominal Christians,' he wrote to King John, in 1545, 'dispersed widely through the various fortresses, openly live as Jews or Mohammedans, without any fear of God or shame before men.' India, where the Portuguese were established, was one matter. In Japan, where the Jesuits met a developed indigenous culture and a developed religion, the missionary problems were more complicated, and Xavier was still puzzling out this unique situation when he died at the early age of forty-six.

Xavier was not only a Christian idealist, he was also an incorrigible romantic, and at the first hint of a new land, no matter how startling the difficulties and how terrifying the prospects, he was off bearing the Christian banner. At San Thomé, near present-day Madras, where according to local tradition the Apostle Thomas died, shot in the side by an arrow from a bowman out hunting peacocks, Xavier heard in 1545 of strange heathens being converted in the furthest islands of the East Indies, the islands that bore the rarest delicacies of the spice trade. In a short time he was aboard a small ship sailing for Malacca, the Portuguese port won by Albuquerque in one of his familiar bloodbaths and governing the gate to the Far East. From there, though constantly harassed by pirates, the Portuguese commanded the essential narrow channel between Sumatra and Malaya.

Xavier spent about three months in Malacca, stirring up the lethargic Christian conscience. According to Father Valignano in 1574, Francis won all hearts. To the unruly garrison he said, 'You are soldiers, so there is no reason to live like monks,' and then he invited himself to join in their cards and dice. At the dinners given by merchants he would duck out and congratulate the cook, 'so that it came about not only the Portuguese but also their concubines and slaves learned to love the Father'. He acted as a marriage broker, and, as always, went out with his bell to collect the children for instruction. He produced such an impression that Dr. Cosmas Saraiva, in charge of the local hospital, thought that he had seen Xavier elevated into the air while saying Mass, but as a good man of science admitted that this might have been 'an hallucination brought on by my intense love and veneration for the Father as a saint'. But Xavier aimed at more distant lands, and on New Year's Day, 1546, he left for the Moluccas—Halmaheira and the tiny spice islands of Ternate, Tidore, Mutir, all nestling between the grotesque flailing arms of Celebes and the squat, humped shape of New Guinea. These little specks of land were the home of the clove and the nutmeg. Magellan's circumnavigating fleet had called in at Tidore, and after Magellan's death in the Philippines del Cano had taken the *Victoria*, the one remaining ship, back to Spain laden with twenty-six tons of cloves. He was then ennobled, and his arms showed two cinnamon sticks, three nutmegs and twelve cloves. Spain and Portugal valued the spice trade most highly, and the presence of contending merchants meant there was much Christian work for Xavier, and many poor natives to be protected from exploitation.

Xavier spent two years, 1546–8, in the spice islands, a wandering, unsettled time beset by hazards. The volcanic terrain was impossible, the jungle impenetrable, the animals fierce and the diseases unknown and malignant. Christians were harried by local head-hunters, Arab slave-raiders, Malay pirates and Moslem sultans. The usual Spanish and Portuguese jealousy undid whatever good the solitary priests had accomplished. The whole of Xavier's ministry, now that he had left the comparative safety of Portuguese India, was carried on against the continuous background of physical terror and almost unendurable hardship. He faced these steadfastly, with often only the slightest references in his many letters. 'What between storms and pirates,' he remarks of the journey from Malacca, 'I encountered many dangers on that voyage.'

> Our ship of 400 tons ran before a violent wind for more than a league, and during the whole of that time the rudder was scraping the ocean floor. . . . Then did I see tears flowing freely aboard.

But storms were nothing; he encountered one almost every time he put to sea. Much more disagreeable were the tribes and the topography:

> The people are a very barbarous lot and full of treachery, brownish-yellow in complexion. . . . There are islands whose folk eat the bodies of enemies killed in their tribal wars. When one of them dies from sickness his hands and heels are eaten, and considered a great delicacy. . . . There are abominable fleshly vices amongst them, such as you would find it hard to believe and such as I dare not put on paper. The islands . . . are full of great and dense forests. . . . So mountainous are they and difficult

to traverse that people climb them in time of war to be out of danger's way. . . . There are constant earthquakes out here and similar commotions under the sea. . . . For lack of anyone in these islands to whom one might preach of the torments of Hell, God permits Hell itself to open for the confusion of the infidels and their abominable vices.

Of a notorious tribe on Halmaheira, he wrote:

There is a heathen tribe called the *Tabaru* in these parts which makes a pastime of murder. I am told that when they can find nobody else to kill they slaughter their own sons or wives. They have also slaughtered many Christians.

The Portuguese historian Sousa, telling the story of the Jesuit Juan Beira in his *Oriente Conquistado*, pictures the appalling, flamboyant perils of the sixteenth-century missionary in these grim islands. Beira stayed nine years in the Moluccas, a time so terrible that 'it would be easier to count the hours of his death than the days of his life'. For almost a year he hid from Moslem persecution, living in the rain forests and sleeping in trees. He was twice betrayed, sold as a slave and tortured. He was compelled to watch the slavers dash the babies of captured Christians against the rocks. Twice he escaped and sought out his scattered Christian communities. His canoe was frequently overturned. He spent two days hanging to a plank of wood in a storm and was driven up on the shores of the head-hunting Tabaru. He dodged the natives and ate seaweed. After nine years his mind collapsed and he was returned to India, a gentle, inoffensive madman for whom men wept.

The Moluccas, the scene of European greed and of a tribal primitiveness almost beyond the European imagination, did not hold Xavier long. His questing spirit was drawn by the remote and obscurely-rumoured lands to the north where there was as yet no Western domination and rivalry. This was the 'Chipangu' of Marco Polo where, the fabulous and unreliable traveller had written, 'the people are white, civilized and well-favoured. They are Idolaters, and dependent on nobody. And I can tell you the quantity of gold they have is endless.' It looked an ideal catch for both Western trade and Western missionaries. And, as usual, the traders got there first. In 1542, some Portuguese merchants, driven perhaps by storms, had landed on the island of Tanegashima. Soon the news was known in Kyushu, the most southern part of Japan proper, and a mutual curiosity encouraged trade. Within two years the merchants from the China coast were rushing to Polo's land of gold and jewels.

The Japanese, in their turn, had never seen powder and guns before. The tales the merchants brought back, suitably fantastic, naturally kindled Xavier's visionary interest. Here would be a mighty conquest for God.

In 1546, a Japanese of Kagoshima, Anjiro by name, of decent family and some education, had taken refuge, a fugitive from justice, aboard the ship of the Portuguese Alvares. Anjiro was a youngish man who had failed to make a go of life. He had been foolish and reckless and had killed a man. He fled to a Buddhist monastery but found no peace. Full of remorse and dissatisfaction, one night he climbed aboard Alvares's ship, and there he stayed. Alvares found him pleasant and quick; in no time he had picked up a little Portuguese. And as they talked, this Japanese who was looking for something to live by heard of a good and holy man of the West, a certain Francis Xavier. He resolved to find him. At the end of 1546 he went the three thousand miles from Japan to Malacca. But the holy Westerner was not there, and Anjiro, after trying to receive baptism, turned back. The winds were against him driving his boat into shelter under the Chinese shore where he found some of the merchants he had known in Kagoshima. From the merchants he learnt that Xavier must by now have left Ternate for Malacca, so this man of much hope retraced the thousands of miles to seek a person he knew of only in a shadowy way through a few phrases of broken Portuguese. This time he found his man, and thus Xavier's future was decided. Francis wrote of the marvellous new possibilities:

> When I was in the city of Malacca, some Portuguese merchants of high standing brought me great news of certain very large islands recently discovered to the east, called the islands of Japan. . . . There came with the merchants a Japanese named Anjiro seeking for me. . . . He found me and was delighted as he had come with an eager desire to learn about our religion. . . . I asked him whether, if I went back with him to his country, the Japanese would become Christians, and he said they would not do so until they had first asked me many questions and seen how I answered and how much I knew. Above all, they would want to see if I lived in conformity with what I believed. If I did those two things . . . then, after knowing me for six months, the king, the nobility, and all other people of discretion would become Christians, for the Japanese, he said, are entirely guided by the law of reason.

Xavier was idealist enough to believe this statement which, if it had been true, would have been the most extraordinary event in human history, and could hardly wait to enlighten this well-disposed race.

Before he could do so he had to return to India and attend to some Jesuit and Portuguese business. And here he found much of his good work from three years before undone. Very vigorously he set the affairs of his own Society in order, grouping the numerous Jesuits now in the East and appointing superiors for each scattered mission. And he took up arms against the Portuguese rapacity once more. He wrote to King John in Portugal an outspoken letter demanding that even the Governor should be severely punished for allowing the oppression of the native Christian communities. As a Jesuit he believed in a central authority and felt that the Governor must bear the responsibility for all Portuguese acts in India; so in Japan, misled as to the politics of the land, he vainly sought the central and absolute authority of the emperor whose single command could clear the way for the Christian missionaries. With the business in India settled he was free to devote all his powers to the needs of Japan. And he faced problems which neither he nor any other European had encountered before.

On August 15, 1549, Xavier and Anjiro accompanied by two other Jesuits—Father de Torres and Brother Juan Fernandez—landed at Kagoshima, Anjiro's provincial hometown in southernmost Japan. And he found that the people, far from being super-rational, were quite fallibly human after all. To begin with the country was in a state of anarchy which surpassed even the troubles of Renaissance Italy. Valignano, appointed Jesuit Visitor to the Orient in 1574 and a man of great Japanese experience, wrote 'incessant war became and still is to this hour the lot of the country'. And Father Rodrigues, who spent the best part of his life in Japan, had an equally gloomy account of the period:

> The whole kingdom was full of robbers and highwaymen, and on the seas there were innumerable pirates . . . and thus it was impossible to travel through the realm save with the greatest trouble. Much of the land was not tilled and the parts which were cultivated were destroyed at sowing-time and plundered by neighbours and opposing factions, with men killing each other everywhere. And so the entire kingdom and all the nobles were left in the greatest poverty and wretchedness, and the sword was the only authority and law. . . . Thus everything was in complete confusion, with every man remaining in his house like a petty king and recognizing no superior as long as he could defend himself.

The *Dairi*, the emperor, had been kept a helpless puppet in the palace at Miyako by a succession of upstart adventurers, the *Shōguns*, who in their turn failed to control, and were disregarded by, the lesser lords. The Japanese refer to the hundred and fifty years before 1600 as 'The Era of the Country at War'.

Then there was the language. Tamil had been difficult, but this was far worse. Xavier began to take lessons from Anjiro. Writing to Ignatius about his slow progress he said that he had asked Anjiro why the Japanese did not write in the sensible European fashion, from left to right. 'Why do you not write in our way,' Anjiro answered, 'seeing that men's heads are above and their feet below and so it is natural for them to write up and down?' Altogether, Japanese rites and customs were so weirdly different, 'it looks as if they studied purposely to be unlike any other race on earth'. But after less than two months in Kagoshima, Xavier had taken the people to his heart. To the Jesuits in Goa he wrote:

> They are the best race yet discovered, and I think that among non-Christians their match will not easily be found. . . . They are a well-meaning people and very sociable and anxious to learn. They take pleasure in hearing of the things of God. . . . In my view, the ordinary lay people commit fewer sins and are more obedient to reason than those they call Bonzes and regard as their spiritual fathers. The Bonzes are addicted to unnatural vice, and readily admit it.

Full of good intentions and drawn towards the people, Xavier also realized that the missionary methods of India or the Moluccas would not work in Japan. The Christian truths must be presented in Japanese dress, and under the guidance of Anjiro, in the winter of 1549–50, the three Jesuits translated the Creed, the Ten Commandments and some prayers into Japanese. But Anjiro knew little about Buddhism and less about Christianity, so that the All-Powerful Christian God re-emerged in Japanese as a friendly local idol, the *Dainichi*. This helped to smooth the path ahead of Xavier, but created all sorts of problems for the future. It was the first example of the dangers in accommodation which were later to loom so large, and cause so much bitter argument, in the missions of the Jesuits Ricci, in China, and de Nobili, in India.

Xavier was never a man to keep still, and all the while he was studying Japanese language and manners he was at the same time exercising his little stock of words and attempting to preach. He would squat before the terrace of a Buddhist monastery and read from his notebook. The locals, even the bonzes, seemed to accept him with good humour—perhaps his Japanese was thoroughly incomprehensible. But his engaging personality won him a number of friends. The success of Xavier's two years in Japan is as much a tribute to Japanese tolerance and kindliness as it is to Francis's remarkable qualities. But Kagoshima was only an outpost. The local *daimyo*, feudal lord, was pleasantly amenable, but unimportant. Xavier, who had exaggerated hopes that one word from the emperor would open the whole country to Christianity, decided to go to Miyako, the modern Kyoto. Xavier always looked for the central power—that was perhaps a Jesuit characteristic. And one reason why his hopes turned soon to China was that the Chinese emperor might have the power that the *Dairi* lacked. But a central autocrat is equally powerful for good and bad, and he may ban as easily as he may allow. This the Christians found when the strong soldiers Hideyoshi and, after Hideyoshi's death, Ieyasu united the country. An edict expelled the missionaries in 1587 and a general persecution of Christians began in 1614. In fact, a state of anarchy is not an unhopeful state for missionaries. If they meet the enmity of one small lord they are likely to be compensated by the patronage of the opposition. Spiritual cures are also well received in desperate times. Xavier decided to leave Kagoshima. The *daimyo*, who had hoped that the Jesuits would attract trade, became a little less pleasant, and the bonzes were now hostile. He set out for the main island of Honshu.

'They saw us off with many tears,' wrote Francis as he left Anjiro and the small number of Christians in Kagoshima. And these tears were a suitable prelude to what lay ahead. First the Jesuit party went to Hirado where a Portuguese ship had put in, and there Father de Torres remained. In October 1550, Xavier and Juan Fernandez started for Yamaguchi and the far distant capital. It was a sad journey towards an inevitable failure, for there was no one at Miyako who could do anything for Christianity. Time alone could ripen the small seeds that Francis had so laboriously planted. But he was made impatient by his ideals, and wished to see this great country that he so highly admired shine immediately with Christian light. This wearisome journey with each step more painful than the last was only irradiated by Xavier's gaiety. They left in the winter, two men from the warm Iberian peninsula in thin tropical cottons. Fernandez later recalled the trip:

Neither the bitterness of the cold, nor the snow nor the dread of unknown and unpredictable people were able to hinder Father Francis from the pursuit of his designs in the service of God ... when striving over rough mountain tracks, we were overwhelmed by fierce snow storms and the icy winds. Our legs swelled under us and we collapsed where we stood. We were poor, badly clothed, obvious strangers. At some villages we were given a welcome frostier than the air, for the children ran after us shouting and throwing stones. . . .

In Yamaguchi, a large and prosperous city given over to secular pleasures, the Jesuits determined to upset hedonism and complacency. Every day, said Fernandez, they preached in the streets 'without licence or permission'. Fernandez, who spoke fair Japanese, condemned 'in a stentorian voice' the 'chief Japanese sins': their idolatory, their homosexuality, and their callous treatment of women. It was a wonder they were not struck down on the spot. But Xavier could not be muzzled. To one splendid and sneering lord he said sternly, 'however powerful you be, if you do not practise humility and bewail your sins, God will bring you low, yes, even as low as hell.' 'I'm sorry for that nobleman,' Francis, the friend of the poor, remarked to Fernandez as they left the house; 'the higher they rise, the less people of his class profit from the grace of God.'

Perhaps aware of the approaching end, Xavier in his conduct became almost extravagantly unpolitic. Just before setting out on the road to the Heavenly King in Miyako, Xavier had Fernandez read a little lecture on sodomy to the powerful *daimyo*, Yoshitaka, assuring him that 'men who practise such things are filthier creatures than swine and much below dogs'. On the way to Miyako he wore a jaunty 'Siamese hat' and trotted barefoot through the snow with a porter's load on his back. 'Never have I seen him so gay as on this occasion,' commented Fernandez, watching Francis skipping along behind the horsemen and throwing an apple up and down. And this joyous image is the best and most characteristic memory of Xavier in Japan. He had only a few more months in the country. At last recognizing the true state of the kingdom, he switched his hopes from the helpless emperor to Yoshitaka, the lord of Yamaguchi. From Mikayo he went back to Hirado and collected some Western gadgetry to present to the man he had upbraided for sodomy. He then came before the *daimyo* dressed in silks and resplendent with grandfather clock, a mirror, a music box, a musket with three barrels, a pair of spectacles, brocade, books, crystal vases, oil-paintings and port wine. Yoshitaka found all these much more acceptable than the lecture on his sexual habits.

The efforts of Xavier had secured for Christianity a small toehold in Japan, and now he was anxious to move on. The forbidden empire of China, to which the Japanese paid deference as Rome had to Greece, obviously beckoned, and Xavier was ready to attempt it. He sailed from Japan late in 1551, heading first for India, and on the way fell in with Diogo Pereira, a Portuguese merchant whose illicit trade with Canton from the island of Sancian had made him as expert as a Westerner could be on the mysterious country. Together they talked and planned how best to assault the guarded giant.

First, in India, Xavier attended to old friends and Jesuit affairs. Then he collected riches as presents (he remembered Yoshitaka), and arranged briefs and documents for Pereira and himself as emissaries to the Chinese emperor. His religious party numbered two other members from the Society and a Chinese lad to interpret. Unfortunately, this he could not do, for he had been away from his homeland so long that he had forgotten Chinese. Beginning on this ludicrous note, the expedition continued to go wrong. There was trouble and jealousy in Malacca and Pereira was left behind. Xavier arrived at Sancian in September 1552, and had to wait until a Chinese merchant could be bribed to slip him into Canton. Time passed, winter came on and still he could not find a passage; the Portuguese merchant ships set sail one by one to avoid the winter storms. It was very cold in November and Francis lived in a small hut built for storing goods. His last letter, addressed to India, moves between hope and resignation:

> As this voyage to China is difficult and full of peril, I know not whether it will succeed, but I still have good hopes.

For the future, China? Siam? God knows. 'For if it is the will of God I shall not die, though it is a long time since I felt so little inclined to live.' He fell ill, and was bled. On Monday, November 28, he lost his speech, recognized no one and ate nothing. On Thursday he suddenly revived and called upon the Blessed Trinity. For two days he endured, and died quietly at dawn on Saturday, December 3. He was forty-six and quite worn out.

About Francis Xavier's humanity and genius there is no doubt; about the value of his work there has been argument. He was a pioneer and is subject to the question mark that hangs over pioneering attempts. His success, or lack of success, cannot be judged merely by the number of his converts. Francis touched the European imagination and began to teach the provincial, contemptuous European mind to look on other cultures more sanely. His adventures were profoundly exciting. The idealism of the Society of Jesus could have had no better tonic than Xavier's rambling, repetitive but always surprising letters. A typical letter, written just before the journey to the Moluccas, set the European Jesuits in a whirl, so many scrambling to go east. Simon Rodriguez wrote from Coimbra to Rome: 'We must come to the rescue of Master Francis, as according to news reaching me he has converted countless numbers of infidels.' The rector of Coimbra found the minds of so many of his students fixed on India, he thought he might just as well transfer the whole college out there. 'I think it would not be unreasonable,' wrote Pierre Favre, Francis's friend from Parisian days, 'if our whole Society and each of its members were to dedicate themselves to the task of producing missionaries for India.'

Not every member did become a missionary to foreign lands. But the task of converting other religions and alien peoples to Christianity, a task so dear to Ignatius's heart, became a high priority for the Society. Carried on by the enthusiasm which Xavier kindled, the Jesuits became the most important, and revolutionary, Catholic missioners of the sixteenth and seventeenth centuries. And Xavier gave the Society more than enthusiasm; he left—practical man that he was—a sound organization as well. When he became provincial for India and all the lands to the east, he chose his lieutenants shrewdly with a good eye for the type of man he wanted. Particularly, he suspected Portuguese priests who might be tempted to put the good of Portugal, with her colonial ambitions, before the good of the poor Christian communities. He had had an unfortunate experience with Father Gomes, the rector of the Jesuit college in Goa, who at one time had cleared the college of all native students and would accept only good Portuguese. So, to avoid the complications of nationalism, Xavier had suggested to Ignatius that Germans and Flemings might be the best men for the East. The subordinates whom Xavier chose to rely on—the Netherlander Berze, the two Spaniards de Torres and Beira, and the Italian Lancilotto—were all men who understood his hopes and his methods. Those who failed to follow Xavier's example, who put Portugal before Christianity, he dismissed from the Society; the others he trusted to get on with the good work, and gave them only this typically cheerful advice:

> Avoid stiffness and surliness, for a gloomy face will deter many from approaching you and profiting by your counsel. So let your looks and words speak welcome to every comer, and if you have to admonish someone, do it with love and graciously. . . .

He left the Society an example, and gave it a direction.

To dismiss men from the Society was severe. But the idealism of the young Jesuit mission had to be nurtured most carefully if the Society was to avoid the corrupting pressures of the *Padroado* and the colonial rivalry of Portugal and Spain. Some of the jealousies and rivalries between the other missionaries—Franciscans and Dominicans—were sad to see, and caused largely by considerations of national prestige. 'One will say, "I'll do it";' Xavier wrote to the King of Portugal, 'another says, "No, leave it to me"; a third, "Since I'm not to do it, it gives me no pleasure to watch you trying". Again, some grumble, "I do all the work and another gets all the thanks and credit". So the time goes by with each striving for his own aims till there is no place left for the pursuit of the service of God.' Xavier rightly saw that nothing could be more disedifying in a missionary country than rivalry between Christians. Later, chiefly because of this, the Christian missions in Japan collapsed, with Jesuits arguing with mendicants and Protestants happily denouncing Catholics until the Japanese, understandably, banished the whole quarrelsome lot. Francis was very aware of the dangers of dissension. He warned Father Berze always to show himself as a very good friend of the Franciscans and Dominicans:

> Beware of any dissension, and above all, let no word ever escape in the pulpit which might shock or disedify the people. Let others say whatever their charity permits, it is your duty to be silent under criticism. . . . They and we are bent on one common course, which is the glory of God and the salvation of souls.

Good sense, practicality, organizing ability, kindliness—yes, Xavier possessed them all. But something else had happened during his incessant and painful travels, something of rare quality. He had penetrated just a little into oriental lives. He had not quite transcended the prejudices of his European environment, but he had seen enough to make him humble and curious. He had clearly dissociated his missionary work from the greed of trade and from the ambition of colonialism. He helped to make it possible for ideas to be exchanged. He had studied Tamil and Japanese, and though he was no great linguist himself he had encouraged younger and more fluent Jesuits to a mastery he never attained. Everything about the Japanese fascinated him, and he studied the race keenly not just because he wished to convert them, but because he wanted to know about this cultivated and sociable people. This attitude encouraged the rich observation, the sympathetic (and generally just) appreciation of Japanese ways which flowed copiously from Jesuit pens in the half century before 1600. Such men as Fathers Frois, Morejon, Rodrigues and Valignano commented on the history, the customs, the government and the art of the country. And though all was so strange to them, they are remarkably objective and remarkably accurate. 'They have but one language,' wrote Alessandro Valignano, 'and it is the best, the most elegant and the most copious tongue in the known world.' João Rodrigues—known to the Japanese as *Tçuzzu*, or Interpreter—delicately analyzed the beauties of Japanese painting 'fancied and conceived in the imagination rather than found in nature', noting its 'melancholy' and 'poignancy'. The mysteries of Japanese poetry were not hidden to Rodrigues and he describes and explains the technique of the *haikai, renga, uta* and *tanka*. It is said that Commodore Perry looked in vain for enlightening books before he rudely burst in upon the Japanese seclusion, in the mid-nineteenth century. A journey to the Jesuit archives would have been enough.

Xavier had suggested two ways of approaching missionary work. Among the Paravas the Society had established little Jesuit principalities where the fathers acted as legislators, administrators and protectors. Among the Japanese the Jesuits became students and scholars, accommodating as best they could the Christian teaching to the local civilization. In after years the Jesuits tried both methods elsewhere, and both produced their problems.

When the Jesuits established a paternal rule, they were usually forced to do so by the European colonists, whose rapacity threatened to destroy native life and society entirely. The Jesuit missions among the Paravas, and most particularly among the Guaranís of Paraguay, were saving operations trying to prevent annihilation such as that which later overtook the American Red Indians. The typical Spaniard in South America held the natives in such contempt that it became almost a duty to subject and exploit them; for they were, said the historian Oviedo y Valdés:

> naturally lazy and vicious, melancholic, cowardly, and a lying, unreliable people. . . . They are idolatrous, lecherous and commit sodomy. Their chief desire is to eat, drink, worship idols and do bestial obscenities.

The first task of the Church in the Americas must be to teach the Spanish and Portuguese Christians Christianity and support the rights of the Indians. Many of the early missionaries applied themselves to this business. The Dominican Montesinos, on Christmas Day, 1511, cried from the pulpit in Hispaniola, 'Tell me, by what right and justice do you keep these Indians in such cruel and horrible servitude?' And the saintly Bishop Las Casas, who spent from 1502 to 1547 in the New World, declared that:

> no nation exists, no matter how rude, uncultivated, barbarous, gross or brutalized its people may be, which may not be persuaded and brought to a good order of life, and made civilized, mild and amenable, provided the method that is proper and natural to men is used; namely love, gentleness and kindness.

But it was hard to show love and kindness when one's fellow-countrymen favoured indifference, cruelty and force. At Asunción in 1543, Nuñez Cabeza de Vaça, an exceptional and just Governor, noted what happened when he restored some abducted Indian girls to their families. 'With this,' he wrote, 'the natives were much pleased, but the Spaniards were angry and desperate, and for this cause they hated me.' It is not surprising that the Jesuits, when they came among the Guaranís in 1610, decided to isolate their poor Indians from the colonists.

Since 1550 there had been a small number of Jesuits in South America. The few in Chile, Bolivia and Paraguay, though they had conscientiously penetrated into the most desolated regions—the swamp lands of the Chaco and the mountains of Chiriguanás—had been less successful in moderating the Spanish tyranny. Father Valdivia, banished from Santiago for his uncolonial attitudes, returned to Spain and begged King Philip III to protect the Indians. In 1608, a royal letter patent appointed the Society of Jesus to convert and instruct the Indians in the province of Guayrá. Two years later two Jesuits from Asunción arrived on the banks of a tributary of the great river Paraná and founded the first Jesuit settlement among the Guaranís, the 'reduction' of Loreto. They had begun a great experiment, as much social and cultural as it was religious.

In the first few years the banks of the Paraná bloomed with villages bearing famous Jesuit names (naturally San Ignacio and San Francisco Xavier were among the first). Gradually the villages spread out of the jungle and on to the cattle-breeding country of the plains. At the heart of each settlement stood the church, grand and ornate, and often incredible where the baroque exuberance of the Jesuit style competed against the tangled foliage of the jungle. Round the church in orderly rows the long huts of the Indians stretched out; and beyond the settlements were the fields and pasturage. A ditch and fence bordered the village, as much to keep the Spaniards out as the Indians in. The community was mildly communistic, though ruled by the authority of the priest. The greatest problem was to get the Indians to work, for the Guaranís, an unwarlike people, had led idle lives in a land where nature scattered riches profusely. However, the godliness of hard work is a well-known article of Western religion and the Jesuits dragged the Indians into an ordered economy whether they liked it or not. But wisely, to mitigate the pains, the Jesuits made labour a stately communal business, preceded by processions and dancing, and accompanied by music. The industry of the reductions produced a wealth of goods. At the time of the Jesuit expulsion in 1767, the settlements possessed and tended well over a million head of cattle—cows, oxen, horses and sheep. They produced cotton and linen, hides, tobaccos, grain-stuff, honey, hard-woods (many of them rare and costly) and *yerba-maté*. Between themselves, the settlements bartered according to requirements; the rest they sold. The settlements had schools, though the education did not extend much beyond a little pious instruction. The Jesuits made useful studies of the Guaraní and related dialects. Art, and particularly music, was encouraged; church inventories included oboes, bassoons, chalumeaus, trumpets, lutes, harps, violins and violas. In the government of the settlements, Indians were appointed to subordinate positions of administration and discipline. The Jesuits raised a native militia under the *caciques*, or tribal chiefs. Originally the Spaniards had ordained that no Indian was to bear arms. But the settlements had suffered so severely from attacks by the 'Mamelukes', renegade Portuguese-Indians from Brazil, that eventually Father Montoya had petitioned for, and been granted, permission to arm his Indians. In 1678, the Jesuits had sent 3,000 armed Guaranís, paid for by the Society, to help the Spaniards repulse a Portuguese attack on the river Plate.

The civilized and orderly advantages which the Jesuits conferred on their converts were not won without pains. To the early fathers the wild desolation of much of the country was trial enough. Then at a very critical time, just when the first missions were showing a modest success, the continuous attacks of the Mamelukes on the then defenceless villages destroyed the settlements and drove the Indians back into the wilds, from where they could not be tempted to return. At this dangerous moment, Father Ruiz de Montoya arrived to convey his people to a safer land. In 1631, he planned an epic of the greatest heroism and faith. He proposed to lead some 12,000 Indians away from Guayrá, down the Paraná to the huge waterfall of El Salto de Guayrá. Then somewhere amid the rushing waters of the cataracts and whirlpools that lay for ninety miles below the fall, he would cross the river into unknown territory and re-establish his missions there. The forests were unexplored and almost impenetrable, the river was even more dangerous; the Mamelukes pressed from behind, the Spaniards had erected a fort below the cataracts to capture and enslave the migrating bands; the Indians were frightened and confused, burdened with families and possessions. Abandoning the churches of Guayrá, built with so much labour and pride, to the encroaching forest, Montoya successfully led his Indians to the new country, and stayed with them and supported them for thirty years. 'With my companions,' he wrote in his account of his herculean labours, 'I established thirteen reductions or townships in the wilds, and this I did with great anxiety, in hunger, nakedness and frequent peril of my life.'

The physical perils of the missions were bad, but it was the enmity of the colonists and the other religious orders that finally undid the Jesuits experiment. In 1643, Cardenas, the slightly demented Franciscan Bishop of Asunción, quarrelled with the Jesuits. The real cause of Cardenas's hatred is hard to find. For eight years he had played a strange game with the Governor and the town; at one time he excommunicated the Governor nearly every week. He was not a bad man—he kept the affection of the Indians—but whether propelled by ambition or insanity he managed to make chaos throughout upper Paraguay, and the politic Jesuits, who needed peace and quiet for their missions, refused to join his games. Consequently, Cardenas decided to expel the Society from Asunción, and brought forward a number of charges which, although never proved, have continued to sound through the succeeding ages. The bishop claimed that the Jesuits stopped the Indians from paying their annual taxes to the crown; that they kept back ecclesiastical tithes; that they had rich and secret mines in their possession. He said further that the Society had appropriated land that should have gone to colonists; that it had made itself a sovereign dictator; and lastly the bishop claimed to have secret orders from the king to expel the Society.

The accusations of 1644 were never substantiated. The Governor, Jacinto de Lara, searched in vain for the mines. When, in 1649, Cardenas did temporarily expel the Society from Asunción, the townsmen were disappointed to find no treasures in the Jesuit house and college. The *Audencia* at Charcas, the Spanish high court in South America, cleared the Society of the charges and permitted the Jesuits to return to Asunción. But the rumours had been set afoot, and the insidious damage done. The nature of the charges indicates what had really happened. All the accusations are about money, land and power. The Jesuits, concerned that the Indians should have a little Christian charity and justice, had set themselves against the territorial and economic piracy of the Spanish rule; they had to expect the consequences. Voltaire, who certainly did not love the Jesuits in Europe, wrote of their work in South America:

> When in 1768 the missions of Paraguay left the hands of the Jesuits, they had arrived at perhaps the highest degree of civilization to which it is possible to conduct a young people, and certainly at a far superior state than that which existed in the rest of the new hemisphere. The laws were respected there, morals were pure, a happy brotherhood united every heart, all the useful arts were in a flourishing state, and even some of the more agreeable sciences; plenty was universal.

And that seems to be the judgment of history.

The critics of Jesuit policy in South America (there are always critics of any Jesuit policy) say that the Society treated the Indians like children and prevented them from growing up. The fathers taught the Indians only a smattering of Christian doctrine and failed to prepare native candidates for the priesthood. And finally they kept the Indians in a lulled and sleepy security so that when the Jesuits were expelled the Indians were helpless before the outside world. In answer to that, all the evidence shows that the Indians were happy. To teach a 'young people' how to deal with the world would have meant teaching them the tricks, the lies, the greed and the power-hunger of the European conquerors. Then indeed they might have stood up to the world when the Jesuits went, instead of drifting back to the jungle and savagery. But would it have been worth it? The crime was committed by those who banished the Jesuits from the Indians, not by the Jesuits who protected the Indians from a brutal reality. There would have been a time to face that when the Indians became a little more sophisticated. As to the charge that the Jesuits held the full flower of Christianity from the Indians, the layman cannot answer that. Perhaps the question is whether the Jesuits should have been trying to convert such a simple, innocent people at all; and that was one question the Society of Jesus never asked. But they brought to the Guaranís—and to the Peruvian and Bolivian missions—a peaceful, happy and harmonious civilization, and surely that is enough for one country to give to another.

The problems of converting simple tribes were difficult enough;

but the problems awaiting those who ventured into the old and well-established cultures of India, Japan and China were far more perplexing. The most famous, and controversial, Jesuit missions were concerned with these countries; especially the long Jesuit attempt on China. Francis Xavier in Japan had hinted at a possible method; but the way of accommodation was not really laid down until Matteo Ricci began his suave operations at Chaoching in 1583.

The China that the Jesuits laid siege to was drifting through the last lethargic years of the Ming dynasty. The Wan-li emperor led a shadowy existence in the confines of the palace while around him a small army of eunuchs relieved him of the tedious burdens of political decision. The mass of scholar-administrators laboured at their protracted ritual of examination, making that bureaucratic dance an end in itself. Worldly-wise and slightly enervated, they favoured the mild materialism of the Sung school of neo-Confucianism. The country was quiet, uninquisitive and a little corrupt. In 1554, Peking, under pressure from Cantonese merchants, had opened Canton to a small amount of well-regulated trade with the West. In 1557 the Portuguese had boldly established themselves at Macao, actually on the Chinese mainland. Father Peres, the superior of the Jesuits at Macao, in 1565 had petitioned Canton for permission to enter China. After pointing out that he knew no Chinese, the officials politely returned him to Macao. And there the matter rested for a while. In the Society of Jesus there came to be two schools of thought on how to breach the Chinese defences. The impetuous school, true descendants of the crusaders, was all for force and frontal attack. Father Ribeira saw no hope of conversions 'unless one has recourse to force and unless they give way before the soldiers'. Father Valignano, however, a former doctor of civil law, advocated insinuation. 'The only possible way of penetrating,' he wrote to Rome in 1578, after four years in the East, 'will be utterly different from that which has been adopted up to now.' As he was the superior of all Jesuits in the East, as he spoke good sense and as he was merely following the hints of Francis Xavier, he won the day.

First, Valignano commanded Michele Ruggieri to learn 'to read, write and speak' Chinese. Then Ruggieri attended the Portuguese merchants on their trips to Canton and thoroughly captivated the Canton officials by his linguistic talents and his politeness. But poor Ruggieri was so harried by his Jesuit brethren in Macao, the spiritual storm-troopers, that Valignano had to make the tiny Chinese mission—only Ruggieri and the newly arrived Ricci—separate from

Macao. Valignano also decreed, in a decision of the greatest importance, that Chinese converts in Macao were not to be made into
eastern Portuguese, but to be allowed to remain Chinese who
happened also to be Christians. In 1583 Ruggieri obtained a permit
from the viceroy to buy a small plot of land in Chaoching and build
a house and church. Ruggieri left Macao for his minute Chinese
domain, taking with him the young Matteo Ricci. Ruggieri now
drops out of the picture and for the next twenty-seven years the
remarkable Ricci dominates the Christian campaign in China.

Ricci was not quite thirty-one when he landed at Chaoching but
he had already given evidence of a good intellect and, perhaps more
important, a temperate, just and kindly personality. At the time of
his arrival in the East, the Jesuits had not yet decided how to treat
the native Christians. The old, blind European view, which unhappily prevailed in Japan and India under men like Cabral, held
that native candidates to the priesthood might be taught Latin, but
not philosophy and theology. It was thought that these high studies
would make the natives proud, and cause them to despise the whites.
From Goa, Ricci wrote passionately against this silliness:

> But all of this could be said, and perhaps with more reason, of others
> who study in our schools, whether in India or Europe. Nevertheless, we
> do not on that account refuse them admittance to our schools. Much less
> should we do so in the circumstances here, since no matter how learned
> they are, native born Indians rarely receive due credit from whites. . . .
> Secondly, by this new policy we will encourage ignorance in the minis-
> ters of the Church, and in a land where learning is of much import-
> ance. . . . Thirdly, and it is this which disturbs me most, these people
> have been greatly humiliated in this land.

One can hardly imagine a more perceptive analysis of Christian
India, noting the colour-bar and the European jealousy and fright
of native attainments. His arguments were unanswerable even then.
But colonialism and the *Padroado* had firmly planted some sturdy,
ugly prejudices which not even a little Italian lucidity could clear
away. It is no historical accident that Valignano, Ruggieri and Ricci,
the prophets of good sense in the East, were all Italians and their
opponents were mainly Spaniards and Portuguese. The waves of
Spanish and French invasions in the last hundred years had taught
Italians to beware of empire builders. Ricci was the ideal man to
realize Valignano's hopes in China.

Ricci set to work to assimilate as completely as possible Chinese
language, customs and thought. This was slow work, but he was in

no hurry. He spent six years in Chaoching not only studying, but also by patience and example overcoming the Chinese hostility; for as a foreigner connected in some way with the brash Portuguese at Macao he was very suspect. He discovered, perhaps by accident, a fortunate way to raise his prestige. He discovered in conversation that the Chinese had a very deficient idea of geography and so he drew a world map which caused a great stir. It was, he wrote, 'printed time and time again and circulated throughout China, winning for us much credit'. The technique of putting Western knowledge to the service of the Chinese became a keystone of Jesuit method and worked very successfully. The Society gained such a reputation and was so useful that, in the next century, Jesuits under Adam Schall were invited to reform the Chinese calendar. Putting Western knowledge to work also had psychological advantages for the missioners. The Chinese prided themselves on the superiority of their scholars and thinkers, and only became abashed when they saw that Western knowledge was in some aspects in advance of their own.

Over a number of years, Ricci crept forward, illuminating his cautious advance with the scholar's lamp. His attainments were generally admired, especially his memory. The Chinese officials, whose lives were ruled by an unending succession of examinations, marvelled at a man who could memorize at once four hundred Chinese characters and repeat them forwards or backwards. Ricci, always obliging, tried to help his Chinese friends and composed a little book on Western memory techniques. Ricci's aim was to reach Peking, and he worked his way by easy stages towards the forbidden city. In 1589 he went with one companion to Shaochow. Six years later he tried to move to Nanking, but was turned away and fell back on Nanchang, where he stayed until 1598. During these years the road to Peking was particularly hard. In 1592, the aggressive Hideyoshi, having united all Japan, sent a large invasion against Korea. This eruption of hostile outsiders into Chinese territory greatly disturbed the fading Ming dynasty and made Peking and the emperor even more cut off from foreigners than they had been before. But Ricci went on quietly making friends, many of them important and influential men, and being helpful. There was a need for tact. Twice mobs attacked the mission in Shaochow and on the second occasion both the Jesuit priests were wounded. Up to this time the Jesuits had dressed as Buddhist monks. But as they had not acted as Buddhist monks the disguise had rather defeated itself. Now Ricci decided on a dress that was less objectionable and more obscuring; in 1594 Valignano gave permission to wear the silks and the head-dress of scholars which was both elegant and pleasing to the Jesuits' scholarly friends. Ricci, as he once admitted, would have changed his eyes and his nose, if he could, to help him become more Chinese.

Tact and charm helped; but Ricci, and the other Jesuits, impressed most through their publications. In China, with its high scholarly tradition, Ricci said, 'more can be done with books than with words [preaching].' And to prove his point he produced work after work on many different subjects from theology to science. In 1584 his *True Account of God* had been the first work on Christianity to appear in Chinese. There followed a little book on Friendship, the *Twenty-Five Sentences* on Christian morality, the *Ten Paradoxes*, a book of philosophical and theological conversation, scientific works on arithmetic and astronomy, and others. All were well received and much praised. The treatise on friendship was particularly successful, Ricci wrote,

> because the other things give us the reputation for ingenuity in making mechanical machines and instruments, but this book has established us as scholars of talent and virtue.

Ricci found that the ideals of the learned Chinese looked very much like the humanism of European Renaissance scholars; and as he was very much a Christian humanist himself—refined, intellectual and (it must be admitted) a bit separated from the stirring masses below —he made a profound impression. His fellow Jesuit, Vagnoni, reported from Nanking in 1605:

> Incredible is the reputation which the good Father Matteo Ricci enjoys among the Chinese, and the extent to which he is visited by important people, and esteemed throughout the whole empire of China . . . he captivates everyone by the graciousness and suavity of his manners, by his conversation and by the solid virtue which his life exhibits.

Since Ricci added patience and determination to these qualities, it was hardly likely that he could be kept from Peking for ever.

Ricci first arrived in Peking on September 7, 1598, and stayed only a month. The capital was still uneasy after the Japanese invasion; the emperor refused to see the foreigners. Additionally, the power struggle between the court eunuchs and the governing officials left nobody with any time for Jesuits. Ricci therefore withdrew in good order and improved the time on the way south with some geographical and linguistic studies. Ricci and Cattaneo calculated the longitude and latitude of the cities they passed through and measured the distance from one to another. Drifting towards Nanking on the Grand Canal, the two Jesuits and a Chinese friend turned to the knotty problem of the Chinese language, and passed the slow hours making 'a good vocabulary and drawing up orderly rules for the peculiarities of this language, with the aid of which it will henceforth be twice as easy to learn'. In February 1599, Ricci came to Nanking, the old southern capital, and in this beautiful city, which made a great impression on him, he continued his characteristic apostolate meeting and charming the influential men of the great city, and making some powerful allies for the future. In 1600, judging the times to be quieter, the censor granted the Jesuits another passport to Peking, and Ricci and two companions embarked on a silk-boat loaded with a cargo for the imperial court. It had taken him seventeen years to reach the emperor.

Of course, the emperor could not be approached immediately. First Ricci had to placate Ma-t'ang, chief among the eunuchs, who had found a crucifix and wanted to know what this naked man stretched painfully on a cross might mean. It looked cabalistic and suspicious. The Jesuits were, to begin with, confined, then lodged in the 'palace for foreigners', a rambling warren of a building where the many Asian merchants after the lucrative Chinese trade were kept together and politely watched. In January 1601, Ricci sent in his memorial and his gifts to the emperor. The gifts included some pious paintings and a breviary; a spinet, some glass prisms and two clocks. The gifts entered the palace, but no word came out. In May, at the intercession of friends, the Jesuits were released from the foreigners' quarters, though the emperor was still silent. Then amid consternation, one of the clocks stopped and the eunuchs in charge of it hurried to the Jesuits to demand what was wrong. They rewound it and sent it back. But the emperor, who was anxious for his precious clock, decreed that in future the Jesuits were to be allowed in the palace to service his clocks. Though Ricci never actually met the Wan-li emperor, he had been granted the right to visit the palace and was thus accepted. The Jesuits, wrote Ricci, became the beneficiaries of favourable rumours:

> From this there arose a report of the emperor's great benevolence towards the fathers, and it was said that he took great delight in talking to them, and thus a false report, not easily laid to rest, spread throughout China, that the emperor frequently spoke familiarly with the fathers, whereas important mandarins could not even see him.

For the nine years until his death in 1610, Ricci lived and worked in Peking. 'The mandarins of state all honoured this man,' says a Chinese history of the Ming dynasty, 'Ma-t'ou [Ricci] then remained peacefully and did not again depart.' His life ran along evenly enough but he was as busy as he had ever been. The character of his mission did not change; as the Jesuit superior in China he supervised his priests scattered over a good number of cities according to the methods he had established. His thoughtful methods did not lead to spectacular results; nor did he intend them to. Nonetheless, in 1608 he wrote that he thought there were 'already 2,000 Christians, among them many scholars.'

> We desired to build something solid, so that converts would answer to the name of Christian and, in these beginnings, spread the good odour of our faith. For this reason the number of baptized is not as great as might be wished.

To prepare the way for the missionary priests, he turned once more to the press and wrote the *Treatise on the True Idea of God*, which, he said, 'does not treat of all the mysteries of our holy faith', but touches on matters 'such as can be proved and understood by the light of natural reason'. He hoped that this work would be diffused throughout the empire, to be followed later by missionary groups. By a very bold measure Valignano, the Jesuit Visitor, attempted to solve the problem of finding funds for the large number of Jesuits in China (by 1590 there were 136). He won Church permission for the Society to invest in the profitable silk trade between Macao and Nagasaki. This step was questioned then, and has been frequently attacked since. But though a contract between a religious order and trade was an unfortunate precedent for the future, Ricci's efforts were at the time threatened by the capricious generosity of Spain and Portugal. The centralized Roman Propaganda did not take missions under its wing until 1622; in the meantime Valignano's provision allowed the Chinese mission to expand and prosper.

As this type of missionary work soon came under attack from Europe, it is well to recall the Chinese view of Ricci. In 1599, Wu Chung-ming, a judicious official in the Board of Civil Offices at Nanking who later rose to high position in the empire, wrote in a preface to Ricci's map of the world:

> This father is modest and asks for nothing; he finds his pleasure in practising virtue and honouring heaven. . . . Although his complicated mathematics on the relations of heaven and earth, moon and stars, are not easily understood, they seem to be well documented.

And Kuo Tzu-chang, Governor of Kweichow in the farthest reaches of China, wrote: 'Ricci has been so long in China that he is no longer a foreigner, but a Chinese.' When Ricci died in May 1610, the emperor granted a petition that Li Ma-t'ou, the Westerner turned Chinese, should be assigned a special plot for burial. Some years later, Wang Ying-ling, the Governor of Peking, caused a memorial tablet to be carved in his honour, and on it Wang listed twenty-two scholars and men of affairs with whom Ricci had been on close terms; and among the twenty-two names were the best and the highest men in the empire.

The accommodating way of Ricci and his brother Jesuits in China did not go unobserved by the other missionary orders. The Minorite Father Ibañez thought the Jesuits were 'posturing before the gentiles as men of wealth, power, authority and nobility'. He complained that the Society in the East used means 'directly contrary to those used by the Apostles, recommended by Christ our Lord and, except for the fathers of the Society, everywhere employed by those who evangelize the Kingdom of God'. The squabble was a complex one, involving missionary jealousies, clashes of nationality and clashes of method. In 1585, Pope Gregory XIII, fearing the results of Catholic dissension, had declared China an exclusive Jesuit preserve; the mendicants who regarded themselves as the traditional Christian missioners were upset. They also resented the Jesuits' lofty independence. Most of the mendicants operated out of the Philippines, under the Spanish aegis, and many of them did not seem to be clear where Spanish imperial conquest ended and where Christian missions began. There were, of course, many intelligent, dedicated and charitable mendicants in the East who spent their lives as generously as any Jesuit; but most of the friars stuck to the old, sturdy, uncompromising and unintelligent method, stumping the roads and preaching not only Christian salvation, but also Christian hell-fire and desolation. They claimed to be 'apostolic and humble' and certainly they were poor and austere; but a Chinese might have thought it barbarous pride for a torn and grimy man to brandish a crucifix at a crossroad and roar out to a cultivated people that they must mend their idolatrous ways or else. The question of methods was the bitterest hindrance between the Jesuits and the mendicants. In the past the Church had recommended accommodation. According to Bede, Pope Gregory the Great sent the following advice to St. Augustine of Canterbury:

Tell Augustine not to destroy the temples of the gods, but only the idols therein. . . . Let them eat and slaughter animals not to the devil but unto the glory of God. . . . Thus, if they are not deprived of such external joys, they will understand more easily the inner joys of faith.

Father Furtado, the Jesuit vice-provincial in China, when he had to answer the mendicants' charges in 1636 and 1639, rightly pointed out the practice of the Church in those days.

The controversy concerned two particulars: first, should Eastern Christians be allowed to follow local rites and customs as much as possible, or should they be forced to follow the strict practice of the West? Secondly, did the Jesuits slide over, or politicly ignore, any of the doctrinal teaching of the Church for fear of offending local opinion?

Under the first heading, the opponents of the Jesuits were merely dense and short-sighted Europeans. The questions debated included such matters as whether the Jesuits 'in baptizing women failed to apply saliva to their ears, salt to their mouths, and oil to their breast and head'. Furtado had a simple reply to this, pointing out that the Chinese thought it indecent 'to expose a woman's breast, to touch her hands and mouth'. Similarly, he asserted the folly of fasting in the Orient:

the Chinese live so close to the margin of subsistence, that in Europe itself Christians of long standing would be exempt from fasting if they lived in like circumstances.

Francis Xavier had already made remarks in 1550 about the frugality of Japanese meals. The complaints here were not really that the Jesuits had abandoned Christianity, but that they had abandoned European ways; and the rigid Catholic mentality induced by the Council of Trent could not accept that there was any Christianity other than European Christianity, legislated by European prelates and adapted to the Western way of life. This mentality particularly afflicted the clerical servants of Spain and Portugal, for Christianity became in their hands a colonial weapon making men subjects of the State rather than subjects of Christ. As the Church gradually disentangled its missions from secular patronage, so native rights became more and more recognized. In 1622, as has been said, Pope Gregory XV instituted the Congregation *Propaganda Fidei* responsible for all Catholic missions. In its early days *Propaganda* sent out many wise and humane directions, for example this one addressed to the vicars apostolic in 1659:

Do not regard it as your task, and do not bring any pressures to bear on

A DRAWING OF A JESUIT MISSIONARY IN CHINESE
DRESS, BY RUBENS

MATTEO RICCI IN CHINA

the peoples, to change their manners, customs and uses, unless they are evidently contrary to religion and sound morals. What could be more absurd than to transport France, Spain, Italy, or some other European country to China ? Do not introduce all that to them, but only the faith, which does not despise or destroy the manners and customs of any people, always supposing that they are not evil, but rather wishes to preserve them unharmed. . . . Do not draw invidious contrasts between the customs of the peoples and those of Europe; do your utmost to adapt yourselves to them.

The Jesuit method regarding rights and customs was temporarily vindicated.

The accusation that the Jesuits suppressed or twisted essential, but inconvenient, Christian truths is more difficult to resolve. Father Dunne, in his account of the Jesuits in China, argues strenuously and convincingly that they did not. But there were certain historical elements in Christianity which were impossible to hide, but unpalatable to relate. Quite understandably, the Eastern countries formed the impression that Christianity was a European white man's faith, and the Jesuits were driven to the edge of equivocation to counter this. Roberto de Nobili, who worked in southern India from 1606 till his death in 1656 adopted as fully as possible the life and manners of the Brahmins. He wore the saffron robe and called himself a *sannyāsi guru*. In Madura he had a great success. But in dissociating himself from the 'Parangi' (the hated 'Franks' or white men), in addressing only the Brahmin classes and in allowing his high-class converts to keep the *kudumi*—the tuft of hair—and the sacred thread, he took a strange view of Christianity. His converts were Christians who still adhered to the very unchristian Hindu caste system.

In China, too, there were some misunderstandings. One Chinese emperor was sympathetic to Christianity until he learnt that Chinese Christians owed some sort of allegiance to a pope in Rome. In his mind the Chinese owed allegiance to him alone. The Jesuits, as supporters of Roman orthodoxy, had to assert the papal supremacy; but knowing that their missions could not survive without the imperial approval, and working hard to secure it, they did not shout too loudly about the pope's role. Indeed, Roman orthodoxy gradually came to the opinion that Jesuit accommodation was a danger to the universal dominion that Rome ideally aimed at. The pope sent Charles de Tournon as special legate to report on the practices of the East. De Tournon, who knew nothing about the East, condemned all practice other than that used in Rome and Benedict XIV then banned all local rites, insisting on Roman rules and Roman customs. The Chinese were outraged, expelled the missionaries and generally dismissed Christianity from their minds.

Christianity failed in the East, and it failed because it could not be separated from European habits and temperament. In Japan the miserable wrangling between Jesuit and mendicant and, after the English and the Dutch in 1619 had resolved to make 'Spoile & Havock for all Portingalls & Spaniards', the open warfare between Catholic and Protestant so disgusted the ruler that he banished all Europeans and tortured and executed Catholics unmercifully. Hardly anywhere did Christianity make any spiritual gains. The Chinese experiment failed. The Jesuits at the court of Akbar and Jahangir were well treated but their religion was not taken very seriously. In South, Central and Northern America the missions, Jesuit and mendicant, opened up new lands and endured heroically, but they could not prevent their fellow Europeans from exploiting and destroying the natives. Christianity could not escape the tragedies attendant on Western expansion with its insularity, its greed and its destructive power. 'Western progress,' said Yen Fu looking at China in 1919, 'has culminated in four achievements: to be selfish, to kill others, to feel little integrity and less shame.' And the Indian poet Rabindranath Tagore has said, 'the West did not send its heart to conquer the man of the East, but only its machine.' Very sadly, Christianity entirely failed to humanize that machine.

The Jesuits came closer than anyone else to correcting the deficiencies of the West. Their missions were not always impeccable. There was often a haughtiness about the Jesuits, and a disregard for others, that must have been extremely trying. Juan de Palafox, in South America, complained that 'the terrible power in the universal Church, the great riches, and the extraordinary prestige of the Jesuits raised them above all dignities, laws, councils and apostolic constitutions'. Also the Jesuits were formally wedded to the ideal of Christendom, an ideal no more workable in the East than it was in the West. An Eastern prince, in a country with its own culture and its own religion, was as peremptory as any Western king in limiting the pope's dominion. The rigid enforcement of papal supremacy, as it was understood by the energetic supporters of Roman orthodoxy in the West, posed unsolvable problems in the East. The Eastern Christians might well have echoed the cry that John Donne, in his *Pseudo-Martyr*, raised in England at about this time:

To offer our liues for the defence of the Catholique faith, hath euer beene a religious custome; but to cal euery pretence of the Pope, Catholique faith, and to bleede to death for it, is a sicknesse and a medicine, which the Primitiue Church neuer vnderstood.

In former Christian ages Christianity followed conquest, or was imposed by a developed civilization on barbarians. That no longer happened in the sixteenth century. The conquests of the Europeans in the New World were not animated by Christian idealism. And the peoples encountered in the East had their own strong and self-sufficient civilizations. Missions in the future had to be based on knowledge, understanding and sympathy. The Jesuits were the first to realize this, and to try to put it into practice. They opened up the East to the West for the first time and showed it to be real, not the fantastic creation of Marco Polo. The Jesuits made China so solid and exciting that Leibniz hoped Chinese missionaries would come to Europe to expound their remarkable ideas and systems. Xavier's wanderings had caused a great stir. In North America, too, Jesuit activity caught the European imagination. The accounts sent by the French Jesuits, published in France as the 'Jesuit Relations', led to a lively interest in the new territories. But much more important was the great advance in knowledge which resulted from the Jesuit efforts. The journey of Bento de Goes, which lasted for four years, along the Moslem trade routes from Lahore to Suchow finally proved that the mythical Cathay and China were the same place. De Goes suffered so severely from his ordeal that he died in Suchow in 1607. More spectacular was the Jesuit contribution to Chinese science and astronomy under several notable men from Ricci to Adam Schall. Joseph Needham, a modern Western scientist, has called this contribution a peerless example of cultural relations at the highest level. The Jesuit services to Eastern languages were, if possible, even more valuable. Father Dunne relates that Ricci's little book on friendship reflected the Chinese taste so well that it was even re-published in serial form in a Chinese newspaper of 1914, three hundred and nineteen years after it was written. In India, Roberto de Nobili, master of Tamil, Telegu and Sanskrit, was—according to the great philologist Max Muller—'our first Sanskrit scholar'. And Giuseppi Beschi, who went to Madura in 1711, is recognized as the father of Tamil prose, a pioneer in Tamil fiction and the compiler of the first Tamil dictionary.

The best of the Jesuit missions had conducted international relations with dignity and intelligence and so had won both the love of the simple Guaranís and the respect of the cultivated Chinese. And this was the more remarkable because it was not the habit of Europeans at this time to treat other nations with kindness or with understanding. But the Jesuit hints were not taken up. Rome thought that the Jesuit method endangered not only orthodoxy, but also Roman rights and jurisdiction, and therefore condemned the Jesuit experiments. National rivalries, Western foreign policy and jealousies between the missionary orders then undid most of the Jesuits' laborious achievements, leaving only a nostalgia for what might have been and a memory of uprightness in a period of greed, cruelty and bad faith.

Chapter XII

ADAPTING TO THE SECULAR WORLD

THE ACTIVITIES of the Jesuits in distant lands are usually not difficult to follow. Freed from considerations which perplexed everyone in Europe, they allowed their idealism to expand and tilled the mission field charitably in Christ's, not Europe's, name. The judgments on these missions have a fair chance of being just. But to return to Europe is to re-enter the dark web of complexity. The era of the wars of religion reflects little credit on anybody, and the Jesuits, as the foremost Catholic propagandists, helped the blood to flow as freely as it did.

The problems of accommodation were not confined to the East. The questions as to whether God should be called *Dainichi* in Japan, or whether Ricci should wear the silks of the Chinese scholar, or whether de Nobili should permit Indian Christians to keep the *kudumi* and the sacred thread of the Brahmins, were not easily resolved; but a much more pressing matter for the Society of Jesus was how to 'accommodate' to a Europe which year by year seemed to wander further from the road that Ignatius had mapped. Accommodation in the East meant some slight readjustments to strict orthodoxy in both teaching and practice. In the West the Jesuits were not so much concerned with doctrinal matters but they tried to make the awkward, lumpy shapes of political and moral theory fit more easily into the Jesuit pattern.

The beginnings of the Society of Jesus had been distinctly unintellectual. St. Ignatius had had neither the time nor the inclination to put together systems; he had merely recommended St. Thomas Aquinas and passed on to more practical matters. And the early Jesuits, though a few of them—for example Laynez—were learned men, did not advance the causes of philosophy and theology very far. When the Society grew settled enough to allow the leisurely processes of philosophy, most of the Jesuit thinkers followed the direction of their founder and slipped easily into the Catholic neo-Scholasticism of the time. They produced works on St. Thomas and also on Aristotle, the master of St. Thomas known simply as 'The Philosopher'. Toletus and Fonseca commented on various works of Aristotle; Toletus, Vásquez and Gregory of Valencia, in the last decades of the sixteenth century, all produced commentaries on the *Summa theologica* of St. Thomas. Later Jesuits who followed this rather pedestrian road were Cardinal Lugo, Hurtado and Sylvester Maurus. Most of these Jesuit Thomists and Aristotelians were both Spanish and undistinguished. Though some non-Spaniards like Lessius and Fabri set out on independent courses, the bulk of this Jesuit neo-Scholasticism had little relevance to the developments in post-Renaissance thought. It was pious and earnest work, but unimportant.

In these matters the Society was perhaps at a disadvantage. The bent of the Society was towards practicality, and the insistence on works and preaching did not encourage the Jesuits to chase the abstractions of the Scholastics through a hundred dusty and wearying classifications. They were not members of a contemplative order and they had no traditions of scholarship, synthesis or exegesis behind them. It was only when their own interests were involved— when the Society could put a train of thought to use—that Jesuit thought took fire and produced quirky and controversial results.

The theological problems concerning justification and grace which had so convulsed the men of the Reformation were not completely still by the authoritative ruling of the Council of Trent. The questions were so arcane and clouded that new interpretations were always possible. A certain Michael Baius of the University of Louvain had undertaken to produce a complete defence of the Catholic position. But such were the difficulties of navigation in those theological waters, at the end of his journey he found he had arrived at Calvinistic predestination rather than Catholic free will. In 1567 the pope condemned seventy-three 'dangerous and heretical' propositions from Baius's work. About this time a young and brilliant Jesuit, Roberto Bellarmine, joined the faculty at Louvain, and he immediately set about his colleague Baius. The dispute was now well in its stride. Bellarmine began to formulate a theory of grace which, though difficult to grasp was certainly novel. In 1589, Luis Molina, a Jesuit theologian from the University of Evora in Portugal, published a large work called *Concordia liberi arbitrii cum gratiae donis* in which he presented the Jesuit ideas on grace as a development of the thought of St. Thomas. The quarrel had now passed beyond the local confines of Louvain and become general to the Catholic

Church. Jesuits like Bellarmine and Suárez expanded and modified
the 'Molinist' point of view while the Dominicans, who felt they had
a special duty to safeguard the ideas of the Dominican St. Thomas,
opposed the 'Molinism' of the Jesuits. The marvellous subtleties of
'efficacious' grace, 'sufficient' grace, 'congruous' grace and the
scientia media were debated with rich animosity. The Molinists
claimed that they were only securing the freedom of the human will
and accused the Dominicans of denying human freedom in all
except name. The followers of the Dominican Báñez retorted that
the Molinists subordinated the divine grace to the human will and
made man to some degree independent of God. As the points were
very obscure all felt free to join the fray; Cardinal de Castro wrote
to Clement VIII that 'all manner of persons, learned and unlearned'
had entered the dispute.

In 1598 Clement VIII considered that the scandal had gone on
for long enough and submitted the dispute to a Congregation *de
auxiliis*. Yet the affair dragged on. Trunk-loads of evidence were
examined, reports flowed thickly, some written by Clement himself. Pope Clement died and Paul V inherited the quarrel. A Bull of
condemnation was prepared against the Molinists; then the Jesuits
defended the papal cause so stoutly against the Venetian State that
Paul put that Bull aside. Finally, in 1607, the matter was closed with
neither side triumphant. The Dominicans were not to call the Jesuits
Pelagian heretics, and the Jesuits were not to call the Dominicans
Calvinists.

The aridities of this controversy, which we view so unsym-
pathetically now, were barely comprehensible at the time. The fight
between the Molinists and the Dominicans was, of course, partly a
matter of prestige. The Jesuits as pushing newcomers were still not
entirely at home in the Catholic family, and needed to assert themselves. In Spain they did their best to make the decision of 1607
appear a Jesuit victory. Placards proclaiming *Molina victor* were
paraded in the streets; the event was celebrated with bullfights and
fireworks. On the other hand, the Dominicans felt that they were
specially equipped to give the orthodox view of St. Thomas, and did
not like the Jesuit attempt to steal their theological possessions. In the
highly charged atmosphere of the Counter-Reformation everyone was
touchy. 'While the ancient philosophers always carried on their arguments in a peaceful way,' commented Voltaire with his usual bite,
'the disputes of the theologians are often bloody and always noisy.'

But the Molinist controversy represented something more than an anxious display of Catholic rivalries. It was only a moment in a long-drawn out conflict which started with St Augustine and Pelagius in the fifth century, which went on to encompass Luther, Calvin and the Reformation, which animated the parties for and against the Jansenists in the seventeenth century, and which still worries the existentialists of the twentieth century. Man is perpetually agitated by the extent of his freedom, and by the bonds of his slavery. Pelagius, a British monk, had exalted man's freedom, denying original sin and making man capable of leading a good life without divine grace. St Augustine had stressed man's constant need for divine grace. The Council of Ephesus decided for Augustine, and declared Pelagius's opinions heretical. But as the opposing views reflected the enduring perplexities of the human mind, the doubts were never settled. Luther and Calvin out-Augustined Augustine and made man's life rigidly determined. The Jesuits were naturally driven to the other side and adopted a position which appeared to some suspiciously Pelagian. Though the dispute was a theological one, it may be doubted whether the Jesuit interests were really theological. They were concerned with actions, and they wished to leave a man free to choose well and to master himself. The Molinists seem more like moral and natural philosophers than theologians, and their thought fitted in very well with the humanistic, Renaissance aspirations seen best in Hamlet's apostrophe on man. Ignatius had felt sure that the individual, with God's help, was certainly capable of saving himself through his own choices, and Molinism was an attempt to raise a philosophy to support this conviction. The Jesuits needed this backing, for as activists they hoped that Europe could be brought back to Catholic virtue by rational choices.

One of the criticisms against the Jesuits in the East was that they relied too much on human means and did not allow God's grace and inspiration a large enough part in the work of conversion. The same tendency can be seen in Europe. As practical men they tended to take theology out of religion and to concentrate on man in the world; and to this extent they were at one with those secular philosophers who increasingly felt that theological notions had no place in their deliberations. But the Jesuits were not primarily philosophers; they were persuaders. And because they were certain that men could make the choices they approved of, they tended to become manipulators and cunning arrangers rather than evangelists.

The practical spirit had some advantages. It at least accepted the world for what it was—unsatisfactory but real—and refused to approach it guided only by the astigmatic eyes of past ideals. There was a general tacit agreement among many Catholics, especially Jesuits, that Christendom was dead (though it might perhaps be re-animated), and that the church could not escape the new problems so unkindly presented by the secular states. As an example of the new realism, Molina was not content with the usual pious excuse that slavery was necessary to Christianize the Indians. He went down to the Lisbon docks and talked to the slave-traders who made it quite clear that they were interested in profit only. So when Molina wrote his *De iustitia* he unhesitatingly condemned slavery, except as a punishment for criminals. The very existence of new lands, and the presence of Europeans in them, was a new piece of reality which had to be taken account of. In a few places the mediaevals had spoken of the *ius gentium*, taking the idea from Roman law. In the age of discovery the subject suddenly became important. The Spanish Dominican, Francisco de Vitoria, reviewed the rights and obligations of states, and wrote the first important work on international law. In 1528 he said:

> International law has not only the force of a pact and agreement among men, but also the force of a law; for the world as a whole, being in a way one single state, has the power to create laws that are just and fitting for all persons, as are the rules of international law.

Vitoria was convinced that each country possessed its own sovereignty and its own dignity, and in his book *De Indis* he contended that the physical power of the Spaniards gave them no right to take over the Indians property; nor was Christianity a ground for declaring war on the heathens. There was still some remnant of Christendom in Vitoria's dream of a world-community, but he saw a civil community unified by law, not by Christianity. Francisco Suárez, the greatest Jesuit thinker and the second father (after Vitoria) of international law, was not quite so sanguine about international cooperation as his Dominican predecessor had been. He wrote more than half a century after Vitoria and by then his Society of Jesus had seen the lands and experienced the institutions of many peoples. Suárez was more aware of the differences, rather than the conformities, between countries. He did not think a world-state possible, but he believed in a 'law of nations' and thought that there was a certain natural unity underlying all mankind. In a noble passage from *De legibus* he expounds the interdependence of mankind:

> the human race, into howsoever many different peoples and kingdoms it

may be divided, always preserves a certain unity, not only as a species, but also a moral and political unity (as it were) enjoined by the natural precept of mutual love and mercy; a precept which applies to all, even to strangers of every nation.

Therefore, although a given sovereign state, commonwealth, or kingdom may constitute a perfect community in itself, consisting of its own members, nevertheless, each one of these states is also, in a certain sense, and viewed in relation to the human race, a member of that universal society; for these states when standing alone are never so self-sufficient that they do not require some mutual assistance, association, and intercourse, at times for their own greater welfare and advantage, but at other times because also of some moral necessity or need.

Those are prophetic words for the twentieth century. And Suárez drew notable conclusions from his fine principles. Although he admitted the right of Christian missionaries to carry on their work, like Vitoria he did not think differences in religion a just cause for war. He thought that neither strength nor sophistication gave a nation the right to meddle in the affairs of backward people. In his opinion, such intervention might possibly be allowed on humanitarian grounds, to stop some obvious tyranny, and he would no doubt have approved the Jesuit rule over the Guaranís in Paraguay. Finally, he hoped ultimately for some tribunal with jurisdiction to regulate international squabbles; until that time he feared there would be constant wars.

The relevance of Suárez's ideas to the modern world is obvious. And the degree to which the twentieth century has tried to follow his advice is equally obvious. The League of Nations and the United Nations are Suárez's children. Suárez's conception of the *ius gentium* was accepted by Hugo Grotius, and thus Catholic and Protestant thought came together. The old Christendom was no longer workable in Europe, and could not be applied in foreign lands. In its place, a new international ideal developed based on rational conduct, mutual respect and the rule of law. The recognition that Christianity could no longer be expected to bind mankind was a step towards realism: it also helped to take Europe further along the secular progress, and this increased the problems of the Jesuits.

It was not so difficult for a secluded and peaceful thinker to be bold and generous minded about lands well beyond the European shores. But to come home, and to re-adjust to conditions there, was much harder work, yet work which needed to be done. Two facts were quite clear: the pope was no longer an important temporal power and could no longer claim to direct the policy of princes; and secondly, the real power in Europe now lay with national monarchs who were becoming more and more absolute. The Jesuits, who had taken an oath of special loyalty to the pope, were forced to attend to his real position and to redefine his European role. The old pretensions of the Bull *Unam sanctam*, in which the papacy had asserted its spiritual and temporal pre-eminence, could no longer be taken seriously; yet the Church, still believing in the superiority of the spiritual over the temporal, could not allow the pope to become the servant of princes. Gradually the theory evolved that the pope, though not the king of the world, still possessed an indirect power over civil rulers. Again, the Jesuits were not the originators of this theory; but they developed it best, particularly in the works of Bellarmine and Suárez, and expounded it most forcefully. They expounded it so well that they managed to please neither Church nor State. The pope was not pleased to be told of his diminishing power, and promptly placed Bellarmine's treatise on the Index. Nor did a monarch like James I of England, who believed in the divine right of kings, wish to hear that the pope had even an indirect power over him; he had Suárez's *Defensio fidei catholicae* burned. Indeed, it seemed that the Jesuit theories could satisfy no one. The Parlement of Paris condemned Bellarmine's book because it undermined the independence of kings and attacked the Gallican liberties.

The re-examination of the relations between Church and State led to some new conclusions. If, from the point of view of the Church, the fading power of the pope needed a small boost, so too the burgeoning and dangerous power of the kings needed to be set down. And here again there were some old misconceptions to be cleared away. The myth of mediaeval polity, that Christians owed a temporal allegiance to the emperor, was dismissed. 'We assume,' wrote Suárez, 'that there are besides the emperor a number of temporal kings, like the kings of Spain, France and England, who are entirely independent of the emperor's jurisdiction.' The presence of national kings was disturbingly obvious, and Suárez, Bellarmine and Molina could see them as well as the next man. To allow the reality of kings was one thing; to describe the nature of their sovereignty was a more subtle matter. The civil ruler was not the vicar of the pope, but nor did he receive his sovereignty, as James I contended, directly from God. The power of political dominion, said Suárez, is derived ultimately from God; but between God and the government comes the community. Suárez, following St. Thomas, believed that a monarchy was the best form of government. But monarchy was not the only form of government. Government depended on the rational choice of the people.

Here, in the theories of Bellarmine and Suárez, were the beginnings of the idea of the social 'contract' which was to play such a large part, in many different guises, in the political theories of Hobbes, Locke, Althusius and Rousseau. The sovereignty of a state rests first with the people and is then, as it were, granted by them to the prince. As the Jesuits were in the active service of the Church, and asserted the Church's rights against the prince's, this theory was doubtless temperamentally attractive to the Society of Jesus. But, besides their wish to deflate the pride of kings, the Jesuits were following a well-marked path of political thought and also pointing out the very real dangers of absolutism. As early as the eleventh century a certain Manegold of Lautenbach had derived sovereignty from the people, and the finest minds of the Middle Ages, like John of Salisbury, St. Thomas Aquinas and Ockham, insisted that the ruler had a strict trust to fulfil towards the people, and if he abused this trust he may be deposed. In their political theory, as in so much else, the Jesuits were only following in the Scholastic tradition. Nonetheless, the rise of the royal power and the lessening authority of the Church did encourage the Jesuits to tilt at the kings, and to express some of their ideas rather indiscreetly.

In 1599, Juan Mariana published at Toledo a small work entitled *De rege et regis institutione*. It was a genial work addressed to the former Spanish Prince of the Asturias, now Philip III, in which the Jesuit theologian gives some sage advice on the difficulties and duties of kingship. Young princes were resigned and used to receiving these presumptuous missives from learned men. Mariana quickly gets down to his self-appointed task, and invites the prince to throw up his hands at the horrors of absolutism, and to work steadily to preserve constitutional rights. He has a little to say about the Church in Spain, but not much about the pope. He then moves on to a chapter called *De tyranno*, and this it was that caused all the trouble. There had been some judicious views on tyrants; two types were recognized—those who ruled legally but were oppressive, and those usurpers with no legal title. It was allowed, by Suárez for example, that the second type might be killed by an individual if there was no other remedy. In the past, the discussion had been pleasantly remote and abstract. Then, in the wars of religion, the point became urgent. Assassination became a political weapon. The Protestants needed justification for the murder of the Guises and the Cardinal of Lorraine; the Catholics had to explain the murder of Coligny and Henry III. Mariana, who was forthright and unwisely dealt with cases, said of Henry III:

> Henry III, King of France, lies there murdered by the hand of a monk, and the charm of the knife has been thrust into his entrails. This is an ugly but memorable spectacle calculated to teach princes that godless, hazardous enterprises do not remain unpunished.

Mariana sympathized strongly with the poor and much of his indignation against princes is on behalf of the poor. The new departure in Mariana's thoughts on tyranny is that he made no distinction between the types of tyrant, but wished them all destroyed:

> It is a glorious thing to exterminate the whole of this pestilential and pernicious race from the community of mankind. Limbs, too, are cut off when they are corrupt, that they may not infect the remainder of the body; and likewise this bestial cruelty in human shape must be separated from the State and cut off with the sword.

These rather bloodthirsty opinions perhaps do credit to Mariana's human concern for the oppressed (who had few enough champions). But his ferocious enthusiasm and lack of distinctions were potentially very dangerous. For example, Elizabeth of England and William the Silent of the Netherlands were both technically tyrants in Catholic eyes, and therefore, theoretically, both might be legitimately killed.

Mariana was not a typical Jesuit and his book was entirely individual and unique. His views were not the official teaching of the Society. But the Society of Jesus was strangely slow to condemn him. The book was, of course, passed by the censors of the Society before publication. Immediately it came out it caused a very fine scandal, yet only seven years later did Aquaviva, the general, issue a rather vague censure without mentioning Mariana by name. Later, the murder of Henry IV in 1610 caused the Sorbonne to have the book burned by the public executioner, and Aquaviva banned all teaching on tyrannicide in the French province. Not until 1614 was the ban extended to the other provinces, and Jesuits ordered, under pain of excommunication, to leave the subject alone.

Beginning with a sense of realism, the Jesuit thinkers of the Counter-Reformation noted the wide separation that had opened between Church and State. And since they did not like the nationalism of the States and their usurpation of Church prerogatives, they tended to stress the differences between Church and State, and thus widen the gap still further. The State was necessary and sovereign, but it was dangerous and liable to become evil, and not worthy of much reverence. The authority of the prince came from below—from the community—and so only indirectly from God; whereas the Church received its power directly from God and existed for the highest ends of man. But although the State was a grubby and lowly animal, the Jesuits had to admit grudgingly that it existed by its own right—it was, in its way, a *societas perfecta*. Having arrived at the same conclusion as the Protestants, the Jesuits had helped to put an end to Christendom and to open the way for the full secular society. It was not quite what they had intended.

However, the States were not to be allowed to go on their secular way unchecked. Some small remnants were preserved from the tattered ideal of Christendom. Since the State lacked in grace, the Church still claimed a right to advise and even, on certain grounds, to command. The theory of the indirect power of the pope permitted him to interfere not only when questions of faith and doctrine were in dispute, but also where the Church's privileges and prerogatives were threatened. The theory was, in its way, a licence to intrigue in politics and government. What the Church could no longer command by right, it could still perhaps arrange by influence and pressure. For both the Jesuits and the Calvinists felt that religion had a duty to compel society to be virtuous. This was loudly proclaimed on the Catholic side by Boucher and Louis d'Orléans, and equally loudly on the Protestant side by Knox, Calvin and Beza. And since neither side believed in tolerance, both believed that persecution was an acceptable instrument of state to secure uniformity of religion.

Caught between the fighting bigots of both parties, the poor country suffered. In France, the alliance between the Jesuits and the extreme Catholic party, the Holy League, benefited Spain more than anyone in France. Rather than see a Protestant dynasty arise in France, the Leaguers and the Jesuits were prepared to further the claims of orthodox Spain; yet this was something which neither the French nor anyone else outside Spain wished for. Because the Jesuits thought that political aims should serve religious ends, they were driven to support Spain's imperial designs. It did not matter that the Spanish government was cruel, bigoted and oppressive; it was at least orthodox.

The wish to make politics subservient to Church ends, besides wasting a great many human lives in the wars of religion, was insidious and demoralizing. The tendency of the Jesuits, while recognizing the independence of the State, was to take a very low view of the State. And believing that the Church had some supervisory rights over the State, the Jesuits often meddled in a rather cynical and Machiavellian way in politics. The teaching of certain Jesuits like Suárez and Mariana on the rights of the community against the prince, and on tyrannicide (though Suárez's ideas were liberal, just and far-sighted, and even intrepid Mariana was a great friend of the poor) encouraged some Jesuits to stir up disaffection against anyone they designated 'tyrant'. Father Parsons might have thought that Elizabeth of England was a tyrant, but very few of her subjects agreed with him; there is a good deal of justice in the claim of Elizabeth's ministers that they persecuted the Jesuits in England for their political meddling, not for their religion. The Jesuit contro- versial pamphlets of the late sixteenth and early seventeenth cen- turies, from such men as Parsons and Fitzherbert in England, and Bellarmine and Tanner for the pope against the Venetian state, indi- cate that the Jesuits were rather too embroiled in politics.

The Jesuits were always too fond of human means. They con- tended that the State must accept the tutelage of the Church, yet they seemed to feel free to fight the State with its own foul weapons of political cunning and subterfuge. To justify the confusion between religion and politics, the religious activists produced pieces of casuistry which led to a dangerous mentality. The problem was a puzzling one: the name of Machiavelli, who had said that religion hinders policy and good government, was anathema; so how were Machiavellian reasons of state to be reconciled with true religion? How could religious men be given a title to direct 'policy', and at the same time avoid the stigma of being called Machiavellians? The answer decided on was elegantly simple. Machiavelli was quite wrong: religion and policy are not antipathetic, on the contrary reasons of state are only good if they are directed by religion. 'Break not with the Church,' wrote Giovanni Botero, the secretary to St. Carlo Borromeo, 'for it will always seem impious and not likely to come to good effect.' Then, after all, 'policy' becomes prudence. Once again, the Jesuits were not the founders of this interesting piece of casuistry, but it supported their activities well and they quickly developed it. The English Jesuit, Thomas Fitzherbert, wrote in a book called *A Treatise Concerning Policy and Religion*:

> nothing can be truly political and good for the state which swerves from true religion; and lastly I will prove that only one (to wit, the Catholic religion) is truly political or fit for government of states.

Thus a suspicious piece of politicking may be redeemed by religious 'intention', for it then becomes Christian prudence:

> true wisdom and Christian charity concur how the prudence of the serpent is to be joined with the simplicity of the dove in so distrusting our enemies that we leave not to love them, and yet not loving them so that we trust them no further than may stand with our own safety.

Botero, says Meinecke, made reasons of state palatable to the princes of the Catholic Reformation. And the unfortunate conclusion to be drawn from the Jesuit glosses on Botero, as a modern American historian has commented, is that God becomes the master politician. Isaac Bargrave, an Anglican, was so disgusted by all this doubtful casuistry that he preached an acid sermon against the Jesuits in England which shows the inevitable results of marrying religion to politics:

> Hence it is that a good Christian is no more esteemed but a great Politician, the rule of state has banished the rule of charity. . . .

The Jesuits might produce political theories, but the Society officially discouraged active politics; the general Aquaviva warned members not to dabble in affairs of state. However, everything conspired to make the Jesuits politicians. Their theoreticians had provided a general philosophy which permitted the Church some direction over the State. As Catholic activists, they fought the Protestants according to the rules in force, and both Catholics and Protestants believed that politics was the business of religion. Henry Mason, in his *New Art of Lying* written against the Jesuits, thought there were two kinds of equivocation—the 'Jesuit' kind which was Catholic and bad, and the 'logical' kind which was Protestant and good. The ideas of both extreme religious parties were very similar. Both believed in the primacy of the Church, and both did much to make the primacy of the State certain. Intolerance, bloodletting and active intrigue made people hate religious direction of politics. The way of Henry IV, who put the peace of the kingdom before religion and introduced a little quiet and tolerance into troubled France, seemed to most people the right and admirable way. Moreover, Jesuit theorists like Suárez and Bellarmine, in allowing the State independent sovereignty, had given kings ground for claiming a dignity for the State equal to that of the Church. The Ignatian ideal of Christendom was brought low, and the men on the Catholic side who did the most industrious spade work were the Jesuits themselves.

Jesuit thought was not always consistent with the declared aims of the Society. The Jesuits were firm traditionalists and even their boldest strokes were developed from the ideas of the older Scholastics. Yet in so many cases the Jesuit ideas were thoroughly modern. They recognized the pope's limitations and they approved the separation of Church and State. Though they were not against kings, they condemned the king's divine right and affirmed the sovereignty of the community, thus paving the way for the very great changes in political theory which later engrossed thinkers from Hobbes to Rousseau. Perhaps their theories also foresaw the possibility of modern democratic government. All Jesuits were firm believers in religious unity, which of course meant to them a triumphant Catholicism. And most Jesuits seemed to think that persecution and coercion were permissible to achieve this. But Mariana, always a difficult case, suggests that a unified Protestant state enjoys the same rights as a unified Catholic state; and this was the germ of an idea which later became a tacit agreement. For the sake of unity the prince should accept the religion of the country. So Henry IV became a Catholic, and Elizabeth remained a Protestant. *Cuius regio, huius religio*, the formula decided on at Augsburg in 1555, was now reversed, and the people decided the religion of the king. It was a much more peaceful solution. At the same time, although the Jesuits acquiesced in the grandeur of the State, they did not give it a free hand. For Suárez in particular, individual states were part of a great human complex with an obscure, but real, unity. And partly what unifies them is their relationship to God. His great book is a work on laws, but his prime concern is justice rather than legality. To him laws should bind and secure mankind, not isolate, enrich and aggrandize Spain, France, England or even Europe. When Suárez died a famous Dominican said, with only a little exaggeration, 'The Church has today lost the greatest genius it has had since St. Thomas.'

There was much that was modern about the Jesuits, and much that was not. And sometimes they were hard pressed to know what to be. Not only the Jesuits, but the Catholic Church as a whole was afflicted with the pain of accommodation, and sometimes the Society was left a little breathless at the concessions won by ungodly men. Particularly, the conflict between Church teaching and economic practice caused the greatest difficulties. The relationship between religion and capitalism has exercised many eminent historians, from Max Weber to Professor Tawney. At one time there was thought to be something called the 'capitalist spirit' which arose about the time of the Reformation and advanced to majestic triumph hand-in-hand with Protestantism. However, there appear to have been capitalists in Catholic countries—in the Italian banking houses and in the Flemish and south German trading cities—well before the Reformation. Capitalism in Europe first grew, as did so many other novelties, in Italy; and aided by technical inventions, like bills of exchange and double entry book-keeping, was quite flourishing by the time of the Renaissance states. The Church had gone a little way to be kind to the speculative merchants; for example, the doctrine of the 'just price' still held, but the Church was no longer quite sure how to fix the just price. But even though some accommodation was made, the teaching of the Church was in general obdurate against maximization of profits. Partly the Church feared for the merchant's soul, and partly the Church thought that the speculative merchant grew rich at the expense of the community. Business was very nearly sinful; the Church still thought, with St. Jerome, that the merchant could hardly ever please God.

Soon after the founding of the Society, the Jesuits encountered the capitalist spirit in southern Germany. The mission in Augsburg, led by Peter Canisius, was in a very delicate position. Lutheranism must be stayed at all costs, but the Catholic merchants of Augsburg, led by the redoubtable Fugger family, were lions of capitalism, and so subject to the Church's displeasure. Canisius, who was a strong idealist and a fearless man, began in the boldest fashion. 'The whole world,' he informed his Augsburg congregation in 1560, 'is full of Matthews and publicans and usurers and those who grind the faces of the poor with various practices.' The matter for contention in Germany was the business contract known as the *contractus Germanicus*, subtly designed to get round the Church regulations against usury. To some it appeared highly usurious, to others it was good business. The question was whether to allow a 5 per cent return or not, and that this was no academic exercise can be seen from a letter written by Mark Fugger to his Jesuit confessor, Father Stotz:

> If the line of conduct which he [the bishop] laid down must be obeyed, then not only we Fuggers, but all Germany would be in beggary in three years. But neither the pope nor your company would mind that.

The problem was, as Mark Fugger saw it, that the Church could no longer control monetary policy, and also that some great Catholic princes shamelessly used the Church teaching for their benefit:

> It would be altogether good [Fugger went on] if you could bring it to the

stage that money was also given me without interest, for I owe approximately 1½ million Gulden for which I must pay 5, 8 even 10 per cent. Against this the King of Spain owes me 1 million and neither pays me interest nor returns the principal. What ought I to do now?

The Jesuits in the German and Austrian provinces were perplexed, and said so. They wrote to the general in Rome for guidance and he was perplexed too, for the Church position was shifting. In Austria, a long battle ensued between the provincial, Hoffaeus, who favoured the 5 per cent contract, and the English Jesuit Caspar Haywood, a relation of the poet John Donne, who was firmly against the contract. Eventually, in 1581, the question was put to a commission in Rome and it was decided that 5 per cent may be permitted on merchant enterprises, but not on pure loans. The Jesuits abided by this.

Calvinism, as Max Weber has shown, helped capitalism to flourish in England and North America. The Rockefellers, the Fords and the Carnegies were the dubious products of the Puritan ethic. In Catholic Europe the Church battled for a while, but as early as 1581 capitalism had won a partial victory. From then on capitalism was quite as widespread in Catholic Europe—except perhaps Spain where the spirit never seems to have become entrenched—as it was in Protestant lands. Once again, post-Reformation religion, on both sides, had smoothed the way for another secular victory. Whether either religion could have stopped the spread of capitalism is doubtful; changing social conditions and changing trade encouraged the inevitable. The Jesuits, with some misgiving, welcomed the merchant to the ranks of the virtuous. Tamburini wrote that the profit motive was perfectly respectable, and the more famous Lessius thought that English merchants might be allowed back to Antwerp because, although heretics, they were more likely to become Catholics than make the Flemings Protestant.

In one respect the Society tried to keep the old economic morality. The Jesuit houses were forbidden to trade. In the constitutions, the Rule for the Procurator read:

> He is to understand that everything with an appearance of secular trade in the cultivation of land, the disposal of farm produce in markets and similar matters is prohibited to members of our Society.

This was a wise rule, as a few later scandals made clear. In the early seventeenth century the Jesuit college in Seville went bankrupt through trading losses. The procurator, an enterprising lay-brother, had borrowed 450,000 ducats at interest and carried on a trade in linen, iron, saffron and cinnamon; he built houses and dealt in real estate; he was ready to attempt any business until he went bankrupt, when the books were conveniently lost. Nonetheless, under economic pressure, the Jesuits did engage in business, and as they were judicious men they did it rather well, which many held against them. The Society, as already mentioned, invested in the Nagasaki silk trade to support the Chinese missions, and in Paraguay some of the produce of the reductions was sold to the outside world.

On January 23, 1656, there appeared in the Paris streets a pamphlet which most found scandalously delightful. The august doctors of the Sorbonne had been meeting and agitating themselves over the question of the Jansenists; and since Rome, Cardinal Mazarin, the majority of the bishops, the king and the Jesuits were against Antoine Arnauld and his severe followers at Port-Royal, it seemed as if the Jansenists must be condemned and disbanded. Then came the pamphlet. It was in the form of a letter from a provincial, and it concerned the policy and the morals of the Jesuits. It was trenchant, amusing and unfair, and the police were unable to discover the author. Other letters appeared at intervals, the third being signed 'Louis de Montalte'. By mid-1657 eighteen had been published, then all the 'Provincial Letters' were brought together and put out in one volume. Louis de Montalte was, of course, Blaise Pascal. The dull and formidable Church quarrel over the Jansenists had been upset by the intervention of genius. And since the effects of genius are always incalculable, though Pascal failed to save the Jansenists, he dealt the Jesuits a blow from which they have not recovered to this day.

The *Provincial Letters* were very unfair. Pascal wrote as a satirist and controversialist and used all the tricks of the trade—the pruned quotations, the passages taken out of context, the qualifications left out. The attack was too inclusive and too rigid. Voltaire rightly complained that Pascal ascribed to the whole Society of Jesus the questionable sentiments of a few; Pascal, said Voltaire, seemed to think that the Jesuits were out to corrupt all mankind, but no society ever has had, or ever could have, such a design. Finally Voltaire pointed out that the contest was not only about religion and morals, but also it was a struggle for political power, and the Jansenists were quite as implicated in this as the Jesuits. However, Mazarin 'laughed heartily' over the Letters, and the damage was done. For who could resist the power of a work which, according to Voltaire again, in its first part had as much point as the finest comedies of Molière and in its last part as much sublimity as Bossuet? The Jesuits were foolish enough to reply, and their weak, inferior efforts sealed the popular vote against them. As d'Alembert later wrote:

> This masterpiece of pleasantry and eloquence diverted and moved the indignation of all Europe at their expense. In vain they replied, that the greatest part of the Theologians and Monks had taught, as well as they, the scandalous doctrine they were reproached with: their answers, ill-written and full of gall, were not read, while everybody knew the Provincial Letters by heart.

The question of the morality of the Jesuits is thoroughly bound up with the history of Port-Royal and the Jansenist controversy. And that conflict was such a French affair, so intimately connected with French history, character and politics, that an outsider would hardly dare to say he understands it. The enmity between the Jesuits and a certain section of the French clergy was traditional. The Gallican church, above all others, prided itself on its liberties and its independence from the supervision of the Holy See. France had won these rights by arms and intimidation from reluctant popes, and was not inclined to see them go. The Jesuits, above all others, asserted the rights of the pope against national churches (the view usually known as 'ultramontanism'): Jesuits and Gallicans were natural antagonists. Events were further complicated. As active Catholic reformers the Jesuits had spread throughout France and eagerly sought the public ear as confessors and directors of conscience. Ignatius had recommended this work highly and it was something that needed to be done. But as directors of conscience they were in a position to influence, and a suspicion arose that this influence might not be for the benefit of France. Did they allow their pastoral work to be ruled by their politics? In 1594, a certain Châtel, a student of the Jesuits, had attempted to kill Henry IV. Châtel was quartered and a Jesuit was hanged. The Society was expelled from France and the man who helped to secure this, and drew up the *plaidoyer* against the Society, was Antoine Arnauld, an ancestor of the founding family of Port-Royal. The fears which Châtel had aroused were intensified when the Jesuit Mariana published his views on tyrannicide in 1599. And certainly assassination was in the air; Henry IV, the opposer of intolerance, fell to Ravaillac's knife in 1610. The Jesuits could not be blamed for Ravaillac, but some contended that they had prepared the ground theoretically and morally for such acts. In 1618, the Jesuits were re-instated at their Collège de Clermont, but there remained in France a particular doubt concerning their opinions on Church and State, and a general doubt about the morality they taught. When the Arnauld family embraced Jansenism at Port-Royal the two sides of the contention crystallized: the Arnaulds and Jansenism against the Jesuits and Probabilism.

It has been rightly pointed out that there was no such thing as an official Jesuit morality. The doctrine known as 'probabilism' was invented by the Dominicans and preached, with varying ardour, by many within the Church. The ancient art of casuistry was universally used, by Catholics and Protestants alike. But Jesuits would naturally incline to a moral theory which suited their practice as confessors and directors of conscience, and which also supported their deepest conviction that the human will is free and able to make choices. Jansenism versus the Jesuits was just one more stage in the ever-recurring debate about grace—the attempt to reconcile man's sufficiency to act for himself and man's insufficiency to exist without God. The work of Bishop Jansen on which Port-Royal based its case was called *Augustinus*, and the Jansenists were yet another group of Augustine enthusiasts who tended towards Calvinistic opinions. The Jesuits had fought these opinions before Trent, at the Council of Trent and ever afterwards.

The best, and most admirable, expressions of Jansenism draw attention to the all-powerful nature of God and to the mystery and high wonder of religious experience. Man was supremely abased, and hardly worthy of anything except mortification for his sins and lack of grace. The Jansenists were drawn to those self-punishments which Ignatius had regarded so suspiciously; and though possessed by a sense of sin they made themselves virtuous by chastisement and faced the world haughtily. Bossuet, who saw the spiritual dangers, wrote that their 'severity puffs out presumption, fosters an arrogant sorrow for sin and a spirit of ostentatious singularity'. At its worst, Jansenism was a narrow, rancorous mentality which bound together an exclusive sect. Voltaire had this unflattering view of them:

> It would seem that there was no particular advantage in believing with Jansen that God makes impossible demands on humanity: this is neither a philosophic nor a comforting doctrine. But the secret satisfaction of belonging to some kind of party, the hatred of the Jesuits, the desire for notoriety, and the general mental unrest—all these factors soon resulted in the formation of a sect.

The quarrel had become a party matter and was fought with the

usual sectarian pettiness. Father Annat roundly declared the Jansenists to be heretical, and the followers of Port-Royal exclaimed in
horror when they learnt that Father Sesmaisons had permitted
the Marquise de Sablé to attend a ball after receiving communion.
The difference on communion was a typical point between them. The
Jesuits were great advocates of frequent communion, agreeing with
the opinion of Peter Canisius: 'Where, I ask you in all earnestness,
is to be found a more certain remedy for sickness of soul and a better
spur to holy living than in Holy Communion?' But the Jansenists'
exalted view placed communion almost beyond human aspiration.
The young Antoine Arnauld, the leader of Port-Royal, wrote a tract
called *Frequent Communion* in which he warned the faithful to avoid
the Jesuits with their easy absolutions and their hasty and profane
communions. There were other burrs to irritate delicate feelings.
Education had been almost a Jesuit monopoly; now the *petites écoles*
of Port-Royal seduced students away. Port-Royal taught in French,
not Latin, had a new system for Greek instruction and had a great
success in teaching mathematics. Clermont lost some of its aristocratic fame and the Jesuits were not pleased. A Jesuit confessor
refused the last sacrament to the Duc de Liancourt because he had a
connection with Port-Royal. The contention degenerated into the
bitterest wrangling with both sides mustering what political pressure
they could. 'Arnauld hated the Jesuits,' said Voltaire, 'even more
than he loved effective grace, and they hated him just as much.'
On the brilliant and youthful Antoine Arnauld, Voltaire had this
sober judgment:

> His own gifts and the times in which he lived turned him into a con-
> troversialist and party leader; but this is a form of ambition which kills
> all others. . . . A mind destined to enlighten humanity was wasted on the
> dissensions created by his determined obstinacy.

And on the whole tangled affair of Port-Royal, Voltaire said simply
that the Jesuits sought 'always to be important' and the Jansenists
wished 'always to intrigue'. Jansenism, which divided religious
France for more than half a century, failed. Louis XIV razed the
buildings of Port-Royal in 1710; the Bull of Clement XI, *Unigenitus*,
in 1713, described Quesnel, the then bearer of the Jansenist standard,
as 'a ravening wolf, a false prophet, a teacher of lies, a knave, a
hypocrite and a poisoner of souls'. The poisoner of souls was condemned and the matter rested. But fifty years before Pascal had made
some telling points against the Jesuits and they needed answering.

A large part of Pascal's case against the Jesuits was that they were cynically lenient in their moral judgments; for the sake of the advantage they gained over their penitents the Jesuit confessors were prepared to wink at offences and call grave sins right actions. The Jesuits had won some prestige as the most energetic and successful confessors. Ignatius had thought this work an important part of the Society's ministry and the Jesuits became very active in the confessional, the more so because few other priests seemed anxious to do this. As confessors, they inherited the moral perplexities of muddled humans, and in their confidence they thought they could resolve these problems, case by case. They paid dearly for this confidence. Ignatius had been a humane man and he had been convinced that the load of virtue should not be too heavy for the ordinary man to bear. He felt that man in his unreflective way usually made worthy choices for good reasons, and Ignatius put the most charitable construction on ordinary actions. He did not wish to make it easy for penitents, but he wanted to show that he was human and believed in the decency of man. To confessors, not all of them very perceptive, trying to apply this ideal, the doctrine of probabilism was very attractive. For this doctrine said that of two opinions it was not necessary to follow the more probable; the less probable may be adopted if it has good authority. This was first propounded by the Dominicans and taken over enthusiastically by the Jesuits Vásquez, Sánchez, Escobar and others.

Here was a fine instrument for the Jesuit confessor: it left the will of the penitent free to make a choice, and allowed the confessor to consider the penitent's intention. 'As the law was given to man and not to beasts,' wrote Busembaum, 'and, accordingly, must be fulfilled in human fashion, the fulfilment of every moral prescription, whether it be human or divine, must constitute a human act, and, consequently must be accomplished in freedom and with the will of the actor.' That was a very Jesuit statement, all for freedom and firmly against Augustinian determinism.

The Jesuits followed generous ideals, but unfortunately the spirit of legality soon elbowed the spirit of charity out of the confessional. The Jesuits were pre-eminently practical men, and the guides for practical men facing moral uncertainties were the moral case-books of the casuists. The Jesuits entered quickly into this field and produced for confessors a stream of those unreal and disembodied works, the books on 'cases of conscience'. Every possible variation of human behaviour was atomized and dissected and the answers given pat. This sort of moral theory, said Professor Möhler, a nineteenth-century Catholic theologian,

> split up everything into individual cases and, therefore, treated morality as mere casuistry; and as the infinite power of moral and religious inspiration was not sufficiently regarded, everything was gradually transformed into cunning calculation as to the manner of acting in individual cases, which often meant the best method of disguising our own egotism from ourselves.

Morality was treated as a 'law' which could be outflanked and even tricked just like any human law. 'Amphibology' (deliberate ambiguity) and mental reservations were permitted by the Jesuit casuists. Escobar, in the *Liber theologiae moralis*, gave this case:

> For instance, if Titius kills Caius in reasonable and blameless self-defence, he can deny having killed him before the judge, because what the judge means by his question is whether Titius has murdered Caius, and that Titius has not done.

The meanest intelligence knows after two seconds that the only right conduct in this case is for Titius to admit killing Caius, and then to plead self-defence. Escobar's solution is the miserable and deformed trickery of the legal mind. Poor Escobar led a most worthy and pious life, full of virtue; but he had a weak mind and his silliness was supported by the Jesuits so that he was savaged and ridiculed by Pascal, Molière, Boileau and La Fontaine. He has nothing to say to us today and, if we remember him, we do so with sympathy as one who was crushed beneath four men of genius.

The Jesuit confessor armed with his book on cases of conscience became too much a committee of ways and means deciding how the individual could avoid responsibility for his actions. The Jesuit casuists never taught that the end justifies the means, but sometimes they came perilously close. Escobar wrote, in his *Summula casuum conscientiae*, that 'Purity of intention may be justification for acts contrary to the moral code and human law'. The Church itself soon realized that there was a danger in this casuistry, that probabilism always tended to slide into laxism. Extreme works like the Jesuit Bauny's *Somme de péchés* and *Pratique du droit canonique* were placed on the Index. But even the combined condemnation of Pascal and Rome—enough to subdue the boldest—did not deter some Jesuits. After the *Provincial Letters* Father Pirot, in an *Apologie pour les casuistes*, tried to defend some of Pascal's more dubious cases. The wiser Jesuits also realized the damage which the Society was suffering. The French provincial, Father Renault, wrote to the general:

> Finally, your Paternity should enjoin on superiors and rectors to be assiduously vigilant that henceforth none of our men may write or say, whether privately or in public, anything savouring of the mildness of laxer discipline with which our enemies reproach us. And if superiors find that anyone has erred in this respect, they must not let him go unpunished.

Jesuit theologians like Camargo and Elizalde attacked probabilism. Elizalde, who held professorial chairs in Spain and Italy and who was a friend of the influential Jesuit Cardinal Pallavicini, in particular disliked the moral doctrine of his fellow-Jesuits Sánchez, Escobar, Moya and Tamburini. He wrote:

> I sought for Christ, but found Him not. I sought for the love of God and our neighbour, but found them not. I sought for the Gospel, but found it not. I sought for humility, but found it not. . . . The Gospel is simple and opposed to all equivocation; it knows only yea, yea; nay, nay. Modern morality is not simple but makes use of that equivocating probabilism, using yea and nay simultaneously, since its rule is the probability of mutually contradictory statements.

Tirso Gonzalez, who was thirteenth general of the Society from 1687 to 1705, tried hard to fight the morality so widely taught by his Society, but he was not very successful. The Jesuit Bonucci wrote an interesting letter suggesting that Gonzalez was driven mad by the intransigence of the members of the Society.

For there was a large section in the Jesuit order which was wedded to probabilism and refused to give it up. In 1706, long after Pascal's attack, Camargo wrote to Pope Clement XI about conditions in Spain:

> How many contradictions, dangers and difficulties I and all the others experienced who, in the direction of conscience, reject the common rule of probabilism so universally diffused throughout Spain, God alone knows, and it sounds incredible. Morals have grown so lax that in practice scarcely anything is regarded as not permitted.

And Camargo went on to wonder how it was that the Society continued to support this dangerous doctrine:

> I know not through what mysterious or, at any rate, terrible decree of God it has come about that this moral doctrine, which is so hateful to the Apostolic See and so contrary to Christian morality, has found such

favour among the Jesuits, that they still defend it, while elsewhere it is scarcely tolerated, and that not a few Jesuits believe themselves bound to defend it as one of the doctrines of the order.

Probabilism never was the official doctrine of the Society, and casuistry was used indiscriminately by other Catholics and by Protestants such as Ames, Perkins and Taylor in England. Yet the Jesuits clung to this morality most obstinately, and wrote on it most energetically. Why did they do it? The charitable explanation is that the Jesuits, as practical confessors, put the best interpretation on human weakness and were kind and tolerant to sinners; and perhaps something like this happened, for the ideals of Ignatius could not have been forgotten so soon. But when one remembers that the Jesuits were not kind and tolerant in other matters, that they allied themselves with the cruel bigots of the Holy League, that they supported the Spanish king's repressions in Spain and the Netherlands, and that Le Tellier, confessor to Louis XIV, himself drafted the revocation of the Edict of Nantes—Henry IV's measure of tolerance granted to the Protestants in 1598—and is said to have sung the *Nunc dimittis* in triumph when Louis signed the revocation in 1685, then one fears there might be some other explanation for the Jesuit approach to morality.

The motives look unhappily political. The Jesuits were the most popular confessors; they were also the most fashionable—kings, princes, and aristocrats came to them as penitents. They were in a most delicate position, and they used it to their best advantage—not to encourage immorality, but to secure the Society. From being the implaccable enemies of absolute kings, the Jesuits in France, in a strange and ironic turn-about, became the confessors and advisers to Louis XIV, the most absolute of all kings. And the morality which goes with affairs of state and with high personages must be lenient and accommodating. Father André, a Jesuit, complained:

> Every day I hear the casuists of our Order maintain that a king is not bound to abide by a treaty which he has only concluded to bring to an end a war that has turned out badly for him. I hold the opposite opinion. I stand almost alone among a crowd of persons who pretend to be religious. Neither law nor gospel is binding in matters of State—an abominable doctrine.

Cardinal Noris, while Consultor to the Inquisition, wrote to Cosimo III of Florence in 1692, explaining the opposition within the Society to the stricter morality of the general, Gonzalez:

> The doctrine of their General was dangerous to the efficacy of the

Society; for as they were confessors to so many great princes in Europe, so many princely prelates in Germany, and so many courtiers of high rank, they must not be so severe as their General desires, because if they wished to follow his teaching they would lose their posts as confessors at all courts.

Both the philosophy and the practice of the Jesuits made them liable to be drawn into politics further than a religious order should be. Moreover, the peculiar religious conditions of the Counter-Reformation, where religion was still struggling for some hold over the increasingly secular State, ensured that all active religious (and the Jesuits were nothing if not active) were to some extent politicians. The realists among all religious parties recognized the dominance of the State. Since religion could no longer command the State, it could best insinuate itself into the favour of princes by clothing 'reasons of state' (which princes were going to use whether morality said yes or no) in a proper moral dress. Thus certain Catholics and Protestants were keen to allow princes to do what they liked, and bless them for it. Morality obviously suffered. This bad situation was not put right until the realists came even closer to reality and allowed that Church and State were entirely separate; a statesman would answer for his conscience before God on judgment day, and religion had no right and no business to compel his politics one way or the other. The wise Jesuits Bellarmine and Suárez had already provided in theory for the separation of Church and State; but they had also spoken of an indirect power which religion held over princes. By this they probably meant a moral power. But in the conditions of the time, their fellow-Jesuits seemed to think this meant not just moral power, but also indirect political power, and acted accordingly. The best way to influence princes was to keep close to them and win their favour, and this the Jesuits did. They were, after all, only working for a version of Christendom.

The famous Abbé Bremond praises French religious thought highly, and he rightly comments on the many devout and profound spiritual works that came from Jesuit pens in the sixteenth and seventeenth centuries. But there was another and more sombre picture. The Jesuits, as the most widespread and most popular confessors, must take some blame for the temper of French society in the age of Louis XIV. That age was brilliant, witty, gay, civilized and glittering: genius abounded. But it was not notable for humanity, tolerance, kindness, justice and morality. It was also the age of the prig, the hypocrite and the tyrant. The easy bourgeois conscience triumphed. Man was enthroned, smug and self-sufficient. The Jesuits were the masters of a fashionable and a light religion. They failed, in general, to rise above the secular society around them; they shared its aspirations and faults and so helped that secular society on towards the end that awaited it—the French revolution. More than that, as directors of conscience (not just confessors) they were the active propagandists for this flawed age. Now, and perhaps for the first time, the priest in the confessional was the complete seer; armed with his exhaustive manuals he was the ultimate authority on everything from sexual relations to the cut of a dress. For the Society of Jesus, this was yet another means of self-preservation.

In all ages of religion there is a pull between strictness and laxity—in Catholic Europe of the seventeenth century, between Jansenism and the worst teaching of the Jesuits. One cannot say that the Jesuits were worse than the Jansenists; in fact they were probably better—more human anyway, and more charitable. But the tragedy was that the Jesuits won, and encouraged a bad moral age to be worse. This was seen by the Abbé de Rancé, the founder of the Trappist order, who attacked the 'Molinists' of the Jesuit order:

> The morality of most Molinists is so corrupt, their principles are so opposed to the sanctity of the Gospels and all the rules and exhortations which Jesus Christ has given us by His words and through His saints, that nothing is more painful to me than to see how my name is used to give authority to opinions which I detest with my whole heart.

The 'thundering abbot' rightly divined that the age was sick:

> What surprises as well as grieves me is that in regard to this matter the whole world is dumb, and that even those who regard themselves as zealous and pious, observe the deepest silence, as though anything in the Church were more important than to maintain purity of faith in the guidance of souls and the direction of morals.

De Rancé prescribed the severe, and even excessive, rules of the Trappist order, and the success of this remedy for the times can be seen in the number of people who left the cynical world to taste the strict observance and moral discipline of La Trappe.

Jesuit thinkers prepared a neat trap for the unwary members of their own Society. The theorists in the order approved the separa-tion between Church and State. And by continually stressing the lowly nature of the State, and its unworthiness, they encouraged the State to be as bad as possible. The secular attitude was this: since we are told we have no virtue, no one should be surprised if we act

without virtue. Secular society then brought this point of view to
the Jesuit fathers in the confessional, and the fathers on the whole
agreed with their penitents. Yes, they said, men are bad; but don't
fret. We have here some convenient casuistry which will allow you
to go on much as you are without pain to your conscience. The accommodating priest in the confessional helped to prevent the State rise
from the mire in which it happily sported. The Jesuit theorists
refused to bless the State, the Jesuit moralists refused to damn the
venal members of the State; between the two, the world grew in
selfishness and complacency.

Chapter XIII

CONFESSORS AND REVOLUTIONARIES

WORN OUT and bankrupt, the houses of Habsburg and Valois made peace at Cateau-Cambrésis on April 3, 1559. The Habsburg king, Philip II of Spain, was left in possession of the well-trampled body of Italy and both monarchs sat back to count their losses. 'I have already spent 1,200,000 ducats which I raised from Spain two or three months ago,' Philip had written before the signing of the peace, 'and I have need of another million in the coming months of March.' The Valois, Henry II of France, was equally impoverished, but hardly had time to assess the damage to his kingdom. After the treaty, during the feasting to mark the political marriages which failed to cement the dubious peace between the two houses, Henry was struck in a joust by the lance of the captain of the king's Scottish Guard, and died of the wound. France was left with a queen regent and four under-age sons of the king. Spain, under the 'phlegmatic and melancholy' Philip, had become the most potent force in Europe. Philip was no war-monger and he did not thirst for glory; he was conservative, meticulous and cautious. But he was a bigoted and fanatically orthodox Catholic, and behind him pressed the huge weight of Spain where so many shared the unlovely traits of their king. The rest of Europe took fright at this mass which threatened to devour the world. Spain began everywhere to meet agitated resistance.

Philip had no clear imperial ambitions and detested war. But he had a high notion of his duties as defender of Catholic orthodoxy, and was resolved to stamp out heresy. He took the stirrings of Protestantism in the Spanish Netherlands as an affront not only to Spain, but also to God, and he thus ensured that any opposition to Spanish power was also an opposition to the Spanish type of Catholicism. At the same time, Philip was the most gratifyingly orthodox Catholic monarch at the head of the most powerful and unified Catholic state; the beleaguered supporters of Catholic Christendom, threatened on all sides by Calvinists and Lutherans, thought their ideal would be satisfied—and Protestantism defeated—by a Spanish empire in Europe, ruled by a Spanish king. Policy and belief were now inextricably mixed, and the second half of the sixteenth century lurched into the wars of religion, choosing France for the first battle-ground.

The violent antipathies of the religious parties made sure that the wars would be bitter and horrible. Before the Reformation man's bestiality was quickly roused by religious quarrels, as in the French extermination of the Albigensian heretics between 1208 and 1235; after the Counter-Reformation man executed and tortured mainly for nationalistic and political reasons. But during the Counter-Reformation the old and the new incentives for murder reinforced each other, and the havoc was most terrible. The din of fanatical convictions thundered out from both sides. 'If we have power,' said Luther, 'we must not tolerate contrary doctrines in the State.' 'What is liberty of conscience?' asked Beza; 'A diabolical dogma.' The Anabaptist Münzer said, 'A man deprived of God has no right to live, for he is an obstacle to pious souls.' And the Anabaptists of Münster under Jan of Leyden, ruled with the sword of religion. They were, in their turn cut down by the sword of Lutheranism. Calvin had Michael Servetus executed at Geneva in 1553, and ever after believed in the persuasion of force. Zwingli declared that it was the Lord's command to 'Slay the wicked one in your midst', and even mild Philip Melanchthon would permit the State 'to employ the sword against the abettors of new doctrines'.

Among the Catholics similar black views prevailed. Mary of England, in her short and miserable reign, sent more than four hundred victims to the stake, as Foxe's *Book of Martyrs* loudly proclaimed. In Spain, particularly, the Inquisition sent burnt offerings to the god of intolerance. The Inquisitors Espiñoza and Guerrero took the sword to the moriscos—Moors forced to accept Christianity. The Grand Inquisitor Valdès by spies and agents sniffed out the Calvinists, the *Alumbrados* and the Erasmians. In 1559 and 1560 the great *autos-da-fe* almost cleared Spain of all except the most rigorous Catholic orthodoxy. And behind the Inquisition the grimly cold Philip II encouraged the flames from the Escorial, his penitential palace built in the shape of the grid on which St. Laurence suffered martyrdom. 'I would give a hundred lives and my kingdom rather than have heretics as subjects,' he once said. When he came to Spain he had sworn to the Grand Inquisitor, taking his oath on a naked blade, to uphold the faith and to help the work of the Holy Office;

no man kept his oath better. Isabella and Ferdinand had made the Inquisition an instrument of the monarchy: Philip made it almost his personal possession. The Venetian ambassador reported:

> It is fair to say that the real master of the Holy Office is the king. He personally appoints the Inquisitors. He uses this tribunal to control his subjects, and to chastise them with his characteristic secrecy and severity. The Inquisition and the Royal Council are always in step and constantly assist each other.

In 1556, when the Emperor Charles V had abdicated the Spanish crown in the great hall at Brussels, his son Philip had promised to guard the purity of the faith, and his ambition as a king was always guided by this promise. He had only one policy—a Catholic policy; and the religion that followed his policy was bleak and extreme because that was the Spanish faith.

The age was not genial. The Council of Trent in its hurry to control and repress unfortunate freedoms wanted to license even the imagination. The final session of the Council decreed that:

> all impurity be avoided, that images be not given suggestive charms; it forbids the erection anywhere, even in churches not subject to visitation by the Ordinary, of any unusual image unless first approved by the bishop.

In 1558, Pope Paul IV ordered that the nudes of the Sistine be covered and Pius V completed this chaste dressing. Pius also ejected from the Vatican the pagan sculpture so lovingly collected by the Renaissance popes. Paolo Veronese was summoned before the Inquisition who demanded to know why he had introduced certain low figures into the 'Last Supper'. Clement VIII and Carlo Borromeo wished to destroy all 'scandalous frescoes', and Bellarmine persuaded an artist friend never to paint a nude. The holy prudery of Innocent X had an infant Jesus by Guercino, new-born and naked, clothed in a shirt. The imagination now became apologetic, and something called 'Catholic art' was brought to the service of the Church. The new religious iconography celebrated all that the Protestants found most offensive—'The cult of Our Lady, the primacy of St. Peter, belief in the sacraments, in the efficacy of prayers for the dead and of good works, the veneration of images and relics— all these dogmas or ancient traditions were defended by art in alliance with the Church.' The new architecture reflected the aggressive confidence of the Church. The church of the Gesù at Rome, built for the Jesuits by Vignola in 1568, a famous confection of pinks and golds in marble, stucco and gilt, became the pattern for a new style which the Jesuits—adept propagandists—took with them all over the world.

Art, religion—everything was swallowed in the maw of policy. Even tolerance was drawn into the conflict of political attitudes. The awful antagonisms of the religious parties threatened to reduce Europe to anarchy; so many thought that a degree of religious toleration was the first step towards order. To restore order, the advocates of tolerance gave all their devotion to the State, and allowed some freedom of worship because they contended that religion could no longer bind society together. Differences of religion were permitted, not necessarily because of a belief in tolerance, but largely because religion was thought to be no longer terribly important. On the contrary, the State was all important and deserved the unserving loyalty that religion had previously claimed. The *politiques* in France, the advocates of mild religious toleration, wanted first of all orderly government and national prosperity. *Politiques* like l'Hôpital and Étienne Pasquier were Catholics, but they put France before religion and were against the extreme Catholic League, the followers of the Guise faction and the Jesuits. The *Apologia Catholica* of Du Bellay supported the claims of the Huguenot Henry of Navarre because he was the man best qualified to bring order to the State, and the *Brutum Fulmen* of Hotman condemned the excommunication of Henry by Sixtus V as a presumptuous interference in French affairs. The rights of the State had gradually usurped the rights of religion. In England, too, the same process went on. Elizabeth was a believer in tolerance so long as the rights of the State were not infringed. Barclay and James I, following the trend of Elizabeth's policy, produced against the divine right of religion the divine right of kings. But neither the *politiques* nor the English upholders of the State believed in tolerance for its own sake. Events after the Massacre of St. Bartholomew in 1572 made the *politiques* the natural supporters of Henry of Navarre and the opponents of the League and the Jesuits, and the *politiques* carried on the warfare in the old intolerant way. The attitude of men like Bodin and Pasquier was, persecute by all means, so long as the State doesn't suffer. And the attitude of Elizabeth and James in England was, let religion alone, so long as it does not offend the State. Elizabeth was anything but politically tolerant. The feudal Catholic 'Rising of the Earls', under Westmorland and Northumberland in 1570, was barbarically crushed and more than eight hundred executed in reprisals. The

queen's policy was equally horrible in Ireland. Whenever she felt
that religion pressed on the State she reacted violently. Catholics
and Puritans suffered alike. Hundreds of Jesuits and secular priests
were executed after Pius V excommunicated Elizabeth in 1570; and
Puritans such as Barrow, Penry and Greenwood were hanged as
seditionists. The State was sacrosanct and not to be criticized. John
Stubbs, a sturdy, loyal nationalist, wrote a pamphlet advising the
queen not to marry Alençon, and the queen ordered his right hand to
be chopped off for his temerity. He waved the bleeding stump from
the scaffold crying 'Long live the queen'. Tolerance, as history has
well demonstrated, is a virtue even more foreign to political feeling
than it is to religion. The universal politico-religious rancour in
Europe practically banished tolerance in this age. It lived in the
minds of only a few exceptional men. William the Silent perhaps was
one; another was Sebastian Castellion, driven from Geneva by
Calvin, who wrote:

> Having often sought to learn what a heretic is, I have discovered only
> that we consider as heretics all those who do not agree with our
> opinions.

And in another place he said, 'You do not prove your faith by burning heretics, but by dying for it.' Gentle Pierre Favre, one of the
Jesuit founding fathers, wished to treat the Lutherans in Germany
with kindness and respect. Guillaume Postel, an eccentric professor
of mathematics and languages, among other incredible notions
wished for a time of universal tolerance. Postel joined the Jesuits for
a short while, but he was not well suited to their discipline and he
left the order. His brother-Jesuits no doubt found his ideas on
tolerance as fantastic as the rest of his schemes, for most Jesuits
were very much men of an intolerant age.

The constitutions of the Society of Jesus are quite adamant that
Jesuits should not mix in politics and affairs of state:

> By virtue of sacred obedience, and under penalty of ineligibility for all
> offices and dignities, and loss of the right to elect and be elected, ours
> are forbidden to meddle with the public and worldly affairs of princes
> which concern the State, or to presume to be charged with things
> political. The superiors are strictly charged not to allow our members to
> interfere with such things in any way.

These prohibitions were repeated by the fifth general congregation
and in the *Monita generalia* of the order. Yet nothing is more certain
than that the Society did meddle, thoroughly and consistently, in

politics. It was inevitable that the Jesuits should do so. Luther's revolt had made religion an element in policy; and every action of the Reformation and the Counter-Reformation, whether made by princes or by churchmen, had confirmed the marriage between religion and affairs of state. Every active religious, Catholic or Protestant, was to some degree a politician. Perhaps this had not been apparent to Ignatius (he was wise, but his idealism often blinded him), and perhaps the early Jesuit leaders really did wish to avoid the troubles that go with politics. But once Laynez had made his stern intervention against the Calvinists at the Colloquy of Poissy in 1561, and so influenced the policy of the queen-regent Catherine de Medici, he must have known that the game was up. Besides its organization and aims, the Society had within it many inclinations and ambitions which drove the bulk of the members into the extreme Catholic camp. It was, to begin with, primarily a matter of Spain.

The Spanish Jesuit provinces had always been difficult. For a long time after Ignatius's death they refused to be satisfied, believing that the Society was first and foremost a Spanish order and that Spanish Jesuits deserved special consideration. Since the days of Isabella the Spanish church, while proud of its rigid orthodoxy and pretending due deference to Rome and the pope, had in fact looked first to the king and then to the Spanish churchmen, and had considered Rome hardly at all. The church in Spain was Spanish not Roman, and the Spanish Jesuits belonged to Spain not Rome. They were king's men and the abettors of all his Catholic designs. And the Spanish king's Catholic designs were not always the same as Rome's. After the battle of St. Quentin in 1557 Pope Paul IV had opposed the spread of Spanish power in Italy; the victorious Philip II—the 'Catholic king'—had sent Alba's terrible mercenaries to Rome to teach the Holy Father the true nature of Christendom. With the Spanish Jesuits so wedded to their country and their king, and so opposed to the administration of the general in Rome, they became the supporters of Philip's European aims, which were as much political as they were religious. From the example of Spain it is obvious that the Society had not completely avoided the fashions of nationalism. Something similar, though far less marked, seemed to have happened among the French Jesuits, and even among the English. It was not that the different provinces repudiated the universal Catholic ideal of the Society—far from it. But they seemed to say that their own countries presented special cases and they should be allowed to work as they thought best in their own lands. Jesuits like Matthieu in

France and Parsons in England intrigued in their own way in their own lands and were permitted to do so. Partly, the general in Rome allowed these arrangements because of the influence of the pope or the king of Spain. But to give way to these representations was itself a political act and against the constitutions of the Society. The Society had grown very large, especially in the generalate of Aquaviva who was elected in 1581 and governed for thirty-four years. Either he could not control the far-flung members of his empire and feared to bring them to order because of the scandal it would cause the Society. Or he deliberately winked at the activities of his Jesuit politicians in France and England, at the courts of Spain, Styria, Austria and Russia, thinking that their operations, though against the rules, were in the best interests of the Society.

The young Valois princes, the sons of Henry II, suffered from wretched health. Francis II, who came to the throne at the age of fifteen, died a year later, in 1560. He was succeeded by Charles IX, aged nine. In spite of his weak constitution he wished to be a mighty soldier and subjected himself to violent disciplines. He hunted in the saddle for fourteen hours at a stretch, and his hands, said the Venetian ambassador, 'were rough and calloused, and always full of scars and bruises'. In 1574 he died of consumption in his bed. He was followed by his brother, Henry III, who gave up the kingdom of Poland to rush back and claim France. He was a soldier who had defeated the Huguenots at Jarnac and Moncontour, and he had some brilliant qualities. But he surrounded himself with effete and perfumed men and squandered the time he should have spent in government playing with lapdogs. While the royal family hunted and played their delicate games, the great noble families—the Bourbon, Montmorency, Châtillon and Guise factions—enjoying feudal powers and large ambitions, fought for control of the kingdom. And the nobles were divided by religion.

Calvinism had bloomed marvellously in France. The missionaries from the Geneva Company of Pastors had poured into the country after 1555; by 1562 the Huguenots (as the French Calvinists were called) claimed 2,150 organized congregations. Much more important, the new religion had captured the French aristocracy. At the beginning of the civil war about one half of the nobility supported the Huguenots. At the head of the Protestant cause stood the noble house of Châtillon-Coligny, with Admiral de Coligny and Sieur d'Andelot particularly active, and the even more noble house of Bourbon, led by Louis de Bourbon, Prince de Condé. Against the

Protestants stood the house of Guise-Lorraine-Joinville, relentless agents of the Counter-Reformation and the organizers of the Catholic League. Francis, second Duke of Guise led the League, and he was succeeded by Henry, the third duke. Between the noble extremists came the *politiques* who gradually inclined towards the strong house of Bourbon, but not towards Calvinism. Into this play of forces, the Jesuits were naturally drawn—the missionaries from Rome to balance the missionaries from Geneva.

The war had begun in 1562 and was noted, like most religious wars, for its ferocity and lack of honour. The lawyer Pasquier, a *politique* and a reasonable man, noted:

> It would be impossible to recount the barbarous cruelties perpetrated by each of the opposing factions. Where the Huguenot is master he destroys all the images, demolishes the sepulchres and funeral monuments, carries off all sacred property. The Catholic, in retaliation, kills, murders, drowns all those whom he knows to belong to this sect, and gluts the rivers with their bodies.

'One man hanged was more frightening than a hundred in action,' wrote the Catholic general, Blaise de Monluc. 'It was possible,' he said in his *Commentaires*, 'to tell where I had passed, for the remains of those whom I had hanged could be seen suspended from the wayside trees.' He had the citizens of Terraube slaughtered to a man, and the bodies stuffed into a well, for harbouring heretics—'a very good riddance of very wicked fellows' was his final comment. The Protestant leaders were cast in the same merciless mould. Coligny called his fellow Huguenot, Baron des Adrets, 'a mad beast'. At Montbrison he forced the captured defenders to throw themselves from the walls on to his soldiers' pikes; and at Mornas he had men flung from windows, and those that clung to the bars had their fingers chopped off. Assassination and massacre both played their part. Francis of Guise was murdered outside Orleans in 1563. On the eve of St. Bartholomew in 1572 Henry of Guise squared the account, had Coligny killed and thrown into the courtyard where Guise spurned the body on the ground; this was the start for the famous massacre of the Huguenots which followed. This insane policy of political murder did not end until Henry III and Henry IV had both been killed by the assassin's knife. In general the Catholics had the better of the war, though the great estates in the south, the hereditary lands of the Huguenot nobles, were not overcome. Then from the ground irrigated by the blood of St. Bartholomew a new orientation sprang up. In 1572, Marguerite of Valois married Henry of Navarre, and as Henry III, immersed more and more beneath his mignons and his lapdogs, seemed unlikely to leave an heir, the crown would pass to Navarre of the Huguenot house of Bourbon. The bloody monstrosity of St. Bartholomew had hardened opinion against the Guise faction. Pope Gregory XIII—thinking it was a military engagement—had indeed welcomed it as worth 'fifty victories of Lepanto'; but the *politiques* came over to the side of Navarre, the party of legality. At the Peace of Monsieur, in 1576, Henry III granted liberty of worship to the Huguenots in all parts of France except Paris. The king made apology for St. Bartholomew, declaring it had happened 'against the will of the Crown'. The Catholics, under the Duke of Guise, looked to lose all that they had gained, and then to suffer under a Protestant king as well. It was too much and in desperation the Catholic League formed.

First the governor of Péronne called out for 'a holy and Christian union of all Catholics in defence of their heritage and the exercise of intelligence and co-operation among all the good, faithful and loyal subjects of the king, for the restoration of religion to the kingdom'. It was a standard invitation to sedition. Now, for the first time in these wars, even the monarch was to be opposed for favouring the Protestants. Article 4 of the Manifesto said:

If there is any obstacle, opposition or rebellion by anyone, or in the name of anybody, to what has been stated above, the associates of this union will be obliged to employ all of their goods and means, even to the sacrifice of their lives to pursue, chastise, and punish those who desire and make such obstacles.

Article 7 was an affirmation well known to fanatics before and since: 'Associates will be judged by their prompt obedience and service to the chief.' From Péronne the League spread. After the death of Anjou, the last of the male Valois, in 1584, the League grew in frustration and endeavour. A new organization known as the '*Sainte Ligue perpetuelle pour la conservation de la religion catholique*' was formed in Paris and headed by the Duke of Guise.

The affairs of France now passed from local to international importance. The very Catholicity of France was at stake and the pope, Philip II and the Jesuits showed a natural concern. Philip was further interested, for with Henry, the prospective king, he had a long outstanding quarrel over Navarre, to which Spain laid claim. The League opposed the lawful succession and asserted the duty to be a Catholic over the duty to be a Frenchman. The forerunners of Catholic activity, the Jesuits, moved in to work with the League, bolstered by the doctrine of the Jesuits Suárez and Bellarmine which, if loosely interpreted, allowed a king to be deposed for heresy. Philip alone stood to gain politically from the League. He was at one and the same time the paragon of orthodoxy, the political leader of Catholic Europe, and a man who had his eye on France. The inevitable connection between the League and Spain ensured that the League could not win; for no one in France, except extreme Catholics who were perhaps blind to the political import of their actions, wanted to be under Spain.

The League was quite democratic (why have the most violent tyrannies—the League, the French Revolution, the Russian Revolution—been democratic?), and drew its members from the shopkeepers, the merchants and the parish priests. From the sixteen political divisions of Paris a *Conseil des Seize* formed; and at the head of the Sixteen came the Duke of Guise, co-ordinating and arranging League affairs within France and beyond. The Leaguers met and conferred in the religious houses of Paris, particularly in the Jesuit houses. The Sixteen held their council sessions often in the Jesuit house near St. Paul's church. In 1584, there came to Paris as Spanish ambassador Mendoza, a wily man who had previously been to England and annoyed the Protestants there. 'I was sorry to see,' the English ambassador told the queen mother, 'the King of Spain had no more respect for the King and her than to send so bad a Spanish relic, retired out of England, to be here, to work as bad effects as he had done with us.' Mendoza advanced his master's plans cautiously, being careful not to be seen with Guise and the League. But he had the assiduous attention of the Jesuits as agents and messengers between himself and the League.

The official histories of the Society are silent on the Jesuit deeds for the League. The general Aquaviva was slightly scandalized by the actions of his men, but did little. Yet the Jesuit Claude Matthieu was an untiring worker, so much so that he earned the title 'the Courier of the League'. He was now in Switzerland, now in Italy, now in Madrid. In Italy he canvassed Pope Gregory XIII to support the League; in Madrid he helped to prepare the Treaty of Joinville in 1584 between Spain and the League. The next year he was back in Italy persuading Sixtus V to excommunicate Henry of Navarre. And now at last he seemed to have over-stepped the measure of priestly decorum; Aquaviva and the pope both resented his political interference. He was banished to the south of France, and then to Italy. But Matthieu was succeeded as provincial by another ardent Leaguer. Odon Pigenat was, if anything, even more influential than Matthieu. In 1589 he became a member of the governing Sixteen and, according to some unsympathetic witnesses, his voice was loud and furious. De Thou called him '*un ligueur furieux aussi fanatique qu'un corybante*', and Arnauld said he was 'the cruellest tiger in Paris'. The historians of the Society claim he had a moderating influence on events. The tie between Mendoza and the Jesuits was very close. Pigenat and the ambassador met at the Collège de Clermont or at the Jesuit professed house. Pasquier claims that every Sunday Mendoza, some of the Sixteen and the Jesuits of the *Confrérie du Chapelat* met at the Jesuit professed house in the Rue Saint-Antoine. The Jesuit preacher Jacques Commolet by his ceaseless tirade against the enemies of the League gained the title of the 'Orator of the Sixteen'. In 1589 he advocated that France should surrender to Philip II. The Jesuit professors at Clermont were also great supporters of the League, two rectors—Varades and Sanguenot—and the librarian Guignard making themselves useful. The Jesuit confessors throughout France, from the authority of the confessional as directors of conscience, were able to recommend the League as a sound Catholic enterprise. The English ambassador, Stafford, although a highly biased witness, told this story of Jesuit confessional activity in 1585:

> There occurred an event here yesterday which has made the king look about him and I think frightened him more than anything, though he dares not show it. A gentleman went to confession to a Jesuit, and after telling his faults, the Jesuit said he could give him no remission unless he promised to defend the League of the Duke of Guise 'to the last drop of his blood'. He told the king of it, who was greatly amazed and sent him and two others to other Jesuits, but all preached the same thing.

Again according to Stafford, Mendoza's own confessor in Paris was a Jesuit.

Not all Jesuits were Leaguers. One of the best known in France, Edmund Auger, rector of the college at Tournon and then confessor to King Henry III, was a bold critic of the League and its methods; and Lorenzo Maggio, Visitor to the French province, had much to say against the two provincials, Matthieu and Pigenat. The Jesuits who dabbled in the plots of the League were hotheaded or misguided and not the best examples of their order. But the superiors, who in a centralized and efficient order such as the Jesuits must have known what was happening especially as the Jesuit intervention was so blatant, did not prevent this activity in spite of the very strict injunctions against politics in the constitutions. Aquaviva, the general, was deprecating but unhelpful, perhaps because he was as puzzled as everyone else to know where religion ended and politics began. If only dubious questions could be pushed under the heading of 'conscience' and not 'policy' then the Jesuits may be allowed to play their part as directors of conscience. Unwittingly, Father Auger had shown how this could be done. The confessor to the king was entitled to review all matters, for everything concerning the State—policy, diplomacy, administration—affected the king's conscience. In the future, the Jesuits advanced into state affairs along two paths. Where the prince was Catholic he was likely to have a Jesuit confessor who, into the intimacy of the royal ear, suggested worthy Catholic policies. Where the state was heretical, or thoroughly against the Jesuits, the way was more difficult, and in these cases the Jesuit plans appeared more revolutionary than priestly. Such were the activities of Parsons in Elizabeth's England, and of Petre in the England of James II. Such, too, were the efforts of the Jesuits which helped to bring John IV of Braganza to the Portuguese throne in 1640. Even the Society could not deny its part in this revolution. The Jesuit Ravignan wrote:

> It was the only time, so far as I know, that the Religious of the Society took part in a political revolution that overthrew one throne in order to put another in its place.

The Society's approach to affairs of state only evolved slowly and was partly determined by the Jesuits' unfortunate experiences in the French wars of religion. For a while Guise and the League were triumphant. In 1588 Guise had Navarre excluded from the succession. Guise had grown so powerful that even the dilettante Henry III was afraid and forsook court pleasures long enough to arrange another expeditious assassination. Guise was killed in the king's presence trying to defend himself with a sweetbox he held in his hand: when Henry saw that Guise was truly dead, he cried out, 'Now I am the only king.' But not for long; in August 1589, Jacques Clément, a young Jacobin friar, having prepared himself spiritually, knifed the king and brought an end to the Valois line. There was great rejoicing in Paris and among the Catholics at Clément's deed. Some, like Mendoza, believed that God had inspired the act, and later Mariana wrote his indiscreet book praising the friar. And for a while it looked as if France, with a heretic as the heir to the throne, would fall into Spanish hands. The upholders of Catholicism descended like clerical vultures on French territory. Sixtus V sent his legate Cardinal Cajetan attended by the Jesuit Bellarmine. Philip was represented by the faithful Mendoza supported by the League. But the contending champions of orthodoxy could not agree and the war continued. Navarre slowly prospered. He clung to his rights of inheritance under the Salic law and as that Law was such a thoroughly French institution the French estates rallied to him. At the same time Navarre saw that the Catholic tradition in France was too strong to accept a heretic king, so he began to receive instruction in the faith. In 1593 he attended Mass at Saint-Denis and formally repudiated the Reformed religion. Then he entered Paris with the celebrated, but perhaps apocryphal, remark 'Paris is worth a Mass'. He was crowned at Chartres (since Rheims was still held by the League) in February 1594. He still met bitter opposition from the League terrorists in Paris. In 1593 a man broken on the wheel confessed that he was party to a Jesuit plan to kill Henry, and in the next year Châtel, the pupil of the Jesuits, struck but only cut the king's lip. For this the Jesuits were expelled from the kingdom. But the Catholic reactionaries, aided by Philip of Spain, could not hold out against the lawful king now converted to orthodoxy. The unworthy motives of the League were quite blown up by the *Satyre Ménippée* which ridiculed the Paris clergy, the Jesuits, the Guise family, the papal legate, Mendoza and Spain. Pope Clement VIII, advised by some enlightened Roman Jesuits and bullied by his own confessor St. Philip Neri, who threatened to refuse the pope absolution, at last recognized Henry IV's legitimate title. In 1598, Henry signed the Edict of Nantes, which granted the Protestants some freedom of worship, and with this statesmanlike and peaceful gesture the triumph of Henry was complete. But the old intolerance would not die; when Clement VIII heard of the Edict, he exclaimed 'This crucifies me'.

The expulsion of the Jesuits after 1594 gave the Society a jolt. The conduct of many members in France had been bad and indefensible. More than that, the Jesuit-supported League had failed and the order was thrown out. Father Guignard had been hanged for his part in the Châtel affair, the reputation of the Society with the Parlement and with the French government was at its lowest. Yet it was unthinkable that the Jesuits, the spearhead of Catholicism, should be kept out of a Catholic country. The way back to France was through the favour of the king.

The king was greatly offended by the Jesuits. They had made attempts on his life and they had disturbed his peace. He was too wise to think them responsible for the League, but he knew they had worked hard in that cause and he believed they benefited Rome or Spain, not France. He also abhorred their views on regicide. All the same he was a little afraid of them and, as a master tactician, wanted them on his side. He wrote to James I of England, who also had Jesuit trouble:

> The principal reason which prevents me from treating the Jesuits with the utmost rigour is that they are a corporate Order, and one so powerful today in Christendom, being composed of men of judgment and learning . . . so that, in persecuting them or driving them to despair of remaining in my kingdom, I should band against myself many superstitious spirits and displease a great number of Catholics, giving them a pretext to rise against me and bring about fresh troubles in my said kingdom.

He continued to outline his fears and reflected how he might circumvent the danger:

> I have likewise considered that, by leaving the said Jesuits some hope of being recalled and reinstated in my kingdom, I should create a diversion and prevent them from giving themselves entirely over to the ambitious will of the King of Spain, in respect of which I learn I have not miscalculated. . . . This is why I am minded to make provision by wise ordinance, which being strictly observed, they shall not be able, should they desire it, to serve the said King of Spain or even the Pope to my prejudice.

The Society was eager to be recalled; the king was tentatively agreeable to receiving them. The smoothing of the path to the king's confidence was entrusted to the remarkable Father Pierre Coton. At Fontainebleau, in May 1603, the two men met for the first time, and the frank, good-hearted king 'begot in Père Coton's heart a tender affection for the person of this great monarch, such as one has for a friend rather than a master'. The two got on famously; although Coton did not become the king's confessor until 1608, his influence worked from the beginning. It was agreed that the Society might return, but under certain conditions. Most important, each Jesuit must take a vow of fidelity to the king once a year. Coton managed to change this to a vow of fidelity taken only once, and on these grounds

Henry IV, on September 1, 1603, signed the Edict of Rouen permitting the return of the Jesuits.

The vow of the Edict of Rouen was a revolutionary act for a Jesuit. It was the first time the Jesuits had taken a vow to a temporal power and thus recognized the claims of the State above the claims of Christendom. The pope and general Aquaviva were understandably upset. But Coton knew that he had taken the only realistic way. He knew that the Society must either fight the State, or work with it. The experiences of the fighting Jesuit Leaguers were fresh in his mind. If the king were Catholic—as Henry happily was—then all Catholics must support him. That appeared to be common-sense; also there was enough in Jesuit political theory, in the works of Suárez and Bellarmine, to justify this conclusion. In a dignified letter to Aquaviva, Coton, after shuddering at the general's displeasure and protesting his loyalty and obedience to the Society, yet goes on:

> Your Paternity thinks that the affair might have been handled otherwise and have fallen out differently. Such is not the belief of those acquainted with this Court, the disposition of the King's Council, and the character of the Prince.

In that he only spoke the truth.

The precedent was established. Henry and Coton cemented the mutual interest between Jesuit and French king which lasted for over a century. Nor was Coton's influence anything but good. As a priest he was both devout and kind, and in the short two years in which he served the king as confessor, before Henry's assassination in 1610, he managed to moderate the king's unbridled sexual appetite. 'If he did not succeed in preventing all the evil he might have wished,' remarked Louis de la Rivière, 'at least he prevented there being more.' He was, of course, in the manner of Jesuit confessors to princes, more than a mere confessor. If he did not become the close political adviser that later confessors were to Louis XIV, it was because his own interests were more religious than secular: as a youth he had been brought up to detest the excesses of the Catholic League. If not a politician, he was at least a diplomatist. While Ubaldini was nuncio Coton was official representative of the Holy See. He was tutor to the dauphin, and attended to the delicate matter of the marriage of the royal children. In a thousand little ways he was useful, and while subjecting himself to the royal will he imperceptibly inclined the royal mind towards the Jesuit way of doing things. When Henry was killed in 1610, his heart was taken in procession to the Jesuit college of La Flèche. Coton lived another sixteen years, cautiously placating Louis XIII and Richelieu and guarding the Society of Jesus against Gallican suspicions. In March 1626, Pierre Coton died, and Paris mourned him for he had been close to the heart of the great King Henry IV. 'Without exaggeration,' said Father Garasse, 'two-thirds of Paris visited the body of the holy man.'

Father Coton had succeeded. The Society was re-instated in France and had the king's confidence. Jesuits followed one after another as confessors of the French kings. But this very success caused its own little problems. In the early days, knowing that confessors to the great occupy equivocal positions, the Society had been against any Jesuit holding such a post. In 1565, the second general congregation 'decided not to appoint any of our people either to a sovereign or any other lord of Church or State', except for 'the very short period of one or two months'. In the next forty years the involvements of the Jesuits in various courts of Europe—in Madrid, Paris, Graz and elsewhere—led to a slight revision of official attitudes. Whether the general liked it or not, the Jesuits were at the heart of European affairs; it was time to invest their activities with a small amount of legality. In 1602, Aquaviva drew up some instructions for royal confessors:

> If the Society can no longer escape such an office because, for various reasons, the greater glory of God seems to require it, then care should be taken as to the choice of suitable persons, and the manner in which they carry out their duties, so that the sovereign should derive benefit, and the Society sustain no injury thereby.

At the same time, remembering the Ignatian prohibition on politics, the confessor is to persuade himself that 'affairs of state' are all 'matters of conscience' to a sovereign:

> The sovereign should listen with equanimity and patience to whatever his father confessor should think fit to suggest to him daily according to the voice of his conscience. For as a prominent person and a sovereign is concerned, it is fitting that the priest should be allowed to suggest what he considers good for the greater service of God and the sovereign, and not only in regard to such things as he might know from the prince as a penitent, but also in regard to those things he might hear elsewhere.

That was pleasantly Machiavellian and seemed to save the appearances. For conscience had a marvellously wide application. Caussin, confessor to Louis XIII, wrote to general Vitelleschi:

If he dissuaded the king from an alliance with the Turks, it would not be interfering with politics; for the question whether an alliance with the Turks should be permitted was not a political one, but a matter of conscience.

And so it was, too: it depended on one's point of view.

The Jesuits in the Catholic courts of Europe espoused a bewildering multitude of views, most of them faintly political and some of them downright intriguing. Father Blyssem, the Austrian provincial, was very busy in the Styrian court. 'Before Christmas I was summoned to Graz by the Archduke Charles,' he wrote to the general in 1580, 'and had various discussions with him regarding his person, and the general position of things.' Blyssem's prescription for saving Catholicism in the archduchy included manning the arsenal and artillery with Catholics, stocking the forts, appointing Catholic officials, making treaties with Catholic princes, expelling Reformed preachers and banning heretical sermons. All very sound steps, but hardly apolitical. But as Father Haller, the rector of the Jesuit college at Graz, wrote to Aquaviva in 1598, the cause of Catholicism needed the intervention of the Society. Disputes between Bavaria and Austria endangered true religion, so Haller concludes 'it would be well worth the Society's while to try with greater zeal than before' to reconcile the quarrel, especially as the 'influence of the Society of Jesus on princes and their councillors is well known'. In the following years, the Jesuits Viller, Becan and Lamormaini worked for this fortunate conclusion. Father Lamormaini, confessor to the Emperor Ferdinand II, took an energetic part in all the policies of the Thirty Years' War. In 1626 the nuncio at Vienna wrote to Cardinal Barberini:

> It is certain that the Jesuits, through the favour of the emperor which cannot be overestimated, have attained to overwhelming power. . . . They have the upper hand over everything, even over the most prominent ministers of state, and domineer over them if they do not carry out their will. . . . Their influence has always been considerable, but it has reached its zenith since Father Lamormaini has been confessor to the emperor.

In 1629, Lamormaini, among others, advised the Edict of Restitution which deprived Protestants of their property, just as later in France the Jesuit Le Tellier worked for the revocation of the Edict of Nantes which deprived Protestants of their right of worship. When Wallenstein, the great imperial general, wanted to sue for peace with Gustavus Adolphus, Lamormaini opposed him and pressed for his dismissal. 'There are three Ls,' said Gustavus Adolphus, 'I should like to see hanged: the Jesuit Lamormaini, the Jesuit Laymann, and the Jesuit Laurentius Forer.' Coming from the most predatory Protestant in Europe, that was a kind of testimonial for Catholics.

No doubt the drift of Jesuit policy generally was to attempt the completion of the work of the Counter-Reformation, to bring all Europe back into the fold of Roman orthodoxy; and to this extent the Jesuit hold on royal consciences was pleasing to the general of the Society and to Rome (though Pope Clement VIII, for one, grumbled about the Jesuits political power). The task of restoring Christendom was undeniably political work in the sixteenth and seventeenth centuries, and the Jesuits did it well. As a measure of their success, famous observers like Saint-Simon and Leibniz testify to their influence. 'Sire', wrote Fénelon to Louis XIV concerning Father La Chaise, 'you have turned a member of an Order into a Minister of State.' The loyal Jesuit Cordara noted in his sad *Memoirs*, written after the suppression of the Society in 1773:

> Nearly all kings and sovereigns of Europe had only Jesuits as directors of their consciences, so that the whole of Europe appeared to be governed by Jesuits only.

The way in which the absolute king, Louis XIV, in his old age gradually abandoned Gallicanism and bent his stupendous ego under the Roman yoke was a triump of Jesuit sympathy and perseverance. And the Jesuits in Austria and Bavaria did most to keep those lands from Protestantism. But which was more admirable— and of more enduring value—there, the self-sacrificing and devoted pastoral work of the early Jesuits Favre, Goudanus and Canisius? or the bold and apparently successful politics of the later Jesuits like Becan, Forer and Lamormaini? Was it a real triumph of religion to link the future of Christendom with the squalid, temporal ambitions of Louis XIV, Philip IV and V of Spain, Ferdinand of Austria and Maximilian of Bavaria? Sadly, the Society did not heed the prophetic warning conveyed by Father Mengin to general Mercurian in a letter of 1579:

> The other day a father wrote to me that a man of great distinction had said to him: 'Your people would do well, and it would be much to the Society's credit, if they kept within their limits.'

Out of their work as court confessors the Jesuits gained influence, prestige, reputation. And they worked hard for their success; it was no easy job to check royal appetites. But the influence at court was bought dearly; this work was divisive, and slowly destructive of the Ignatian ideal. The descent into politics may perhaps have been impossible to avoid. There is enough in Ignatius's own conduct, in his conciliatory approach to princes, to suggest that he too would have wandered down that barren way, drugged by the gases of the all-pervading political atmosphere. But he could not have agreed to the factionalism, and contrary aims within the Society, that attendance at court bred. A court confessor, no matter how well he forwarded Roman ideals, was in a sense a hostage of the king, and his interests were connected with the king's. Father Bermudez, confessor at Madrid, was the creature of Philip IV; and Coton and Henry, Le Tellier and Louis, Lamormaini and Ferdinand, Contzen and Maximilian were all so tightly bound that when princes fell out, their grieving confessors (though brothers in the same order) fell out too. That was not all. For the sake of the prince, the Jesuits at court resisted the common opinion of the Society and even the authority of the general. The dilemma had arisen in Father Coton's time, and that upright man, with some qualms of mind, had chosen to agree with Henry IV and not Aquaviva. Doubtless he chose the sensible way, but it was an ominous sign. Coton faced the problem again. In the next reign, that of Louis XIII, the Parlement sought to break the growing power of its old enemies the Jesuits. The Italian Santarelli had written a book putting forward in a rather blunt manner the thesis of the indirect power of the pope over princes. This Jesuit work appeared among the Jesuits in Paris, and now the Parlement thought they had the Society, for these were sentiments that no Frenchman would tolerate. The book had received the *imprimatur* of the Society and merely echoed the well-established doctrine of the unimpeachable Jesuit authorities, Suárez and Bellarmine; yet Coton had to assert that theories of the Society were not the doctrine of the French Jesuits, and whatever Rome thought French Jesuits were entitled to think differently. Again Coton saved the day, but the international integrity of the order was slightly eroded.

The general of the Society allowed this to happen. What motives the general had one may only speculate, for Aquaviva had a supple personality not easy to grasp. Partly he realized the value of the confessors to the spread of Catholicism. He drew up a set of instructions for royal confessors according to which the confessors were to ask their penitents many curious questions about ministers and judges, about income and expenditure, about the work of the Inquisition, and about the royal attitude to the pope. Information was potential power, and the Society was determined to have it. Also, the presence of confessors at court helped the self-perservation of the Society. The kings ruled in Europe. Nationalism was triumphant and no supranational political force could stand against it. The Jesuits had learnt, in the wars of religion, what action against the legitimate prince could lead to. The Society, to remain active in the van of the Catholic ministry, needed—absolutely required—the good-will of princes. The Society considered its own interests. Saint-Simon, that vivid but fanciful guide through the thickets of the Sun King's court, thought the unattractive Le Tellier a typical example of Jesuit self-interest. If met in a forest, he would inspire terror, said Saint-Simon, and remarked that Le Tellier had 'dedicated his body and soul to the Order', and 'knew no other nourishment than its deepest secrets, and no other God but the Society'. Maréchal told Saint-Simon a malicious little story of how the confessor La Chaise (an admirable priest) had advised Louis XIV to pick another Jesuit after La Chaise's death, or else the Society might work against the king: 'he besought the king not to drive the Society of Jesus to extremities, for it was easy to play him a nasty trick.' The favour of princes was angled for so nimbly and wholeheartedly that, unawares, factionalism crept into the order. While gaining influence the Society forgot something of its high internationalism. The spirit of opposition developed within the Society (the inevitable result of politics), and the old integrity was lost so that soon the probabilists in the Society could defend their dubious morality against the authority of general Gonzalez himself. It was a retrograde move.

Ignatius had been a diplomat. He had soothed imperious tempers and opened the way for calm and discussion. In the years after the Reformation, the papacy needed such men. The old papal bombardment of anathema and excommunication did not harry and lay waste the opponents as it used to. The Church was forced to bargain with the princes, and for this purpose needed a corps of discreet men. The Jesuits were admirably suited. They were trained, grave and resourceful, and devoted to Roman ways. Among the papal ambassadors of the Counter-Reformation (the popes used many besides Jesuits) was the Jesuit Antonio Possevino. In the last decades of the sixteenth century Possevino accompanied Catholic business from one end of Europe to another. He was at Venice, trying to mollify the Republic's dislike for the papacy. He was at Vienna and Graz trying to make the emperor forget the Habsburg dynastic ambitions and instead take up the defence of Catholicism against the Protestants and the Turks. In the late seventies he followed his fellow-Jesuit, Stanilaus Warsewicz, to Sweden, attempting to bring the kingdom of John III back to the true faith. He arrived in 'costly headgear with a black silk veil, more like a courtier or the ambassador of a prince than the member of an Order'. While the Polish Catholic, Catherine Jagellon, was the king's consort Catholicism advanced; but when she died, and a Lutheran became queen, Possevino packed his courtier's trunk and passed to more fruitful fields. In 1580, he went as papal arbitrator to make peace in the wars between Poland and Russia. And in the Russian court at Staritsa he met Ivan the Terrible, a man as strange to Europe as any Eastern potentate and twice as fearsome. The tactful negotiator and the maniac Tsar seem to have got on well, in spite of their irreconcilable differences. Possevino tried to ween the Russians from Greek Orthodoxy, and Ivan had humoured the Jesuit who was arranging a prudent treaty with the Catholic Poles. Then, when the work was done, Possevino was sent away loaded with gifts and well-turned compliments. Possevino returned to King Stephen Bathory in Poland and encouraged Peter Skarga, another Jesuit who was doing exemplary pastoral work. Then, in 1583, Possevino, who had impressed Stephen very much in the Russian negotiations, journeyed to Transylvania, the Bathory hereditary lands, sowing Jesuit schools, colleges and missions in his trail.

Possevino was careful, patient and expert. As a go-between for princes he was extraordinarily skilful, and his negotiations were as successful as man could make them. But in the larger cause of Christendom his diplomacy achieved very little. Sweden remained heretical, Russia remained schismatic and the emperor remained devoted to Habsburg interests. In many Catholic countries the Jesuit missions had an anxious time. In countries where the king and the people, for whatever reason, had taken to some non-Catholic form of religion, the Jesuits faced a very difficult problem. The Society had undertaken to serve in the lands of the infidel and of all those who hated the pope; it was unthinkable that the Jesuits would shirk their Catholic duty. The ideal way in which to do their work was clear. They would go to the heretical lands to debate, preach and convert, teaching and doing acts of charity. But in many Protestant lands the Church had become part of the State, and to deny the authenticity of the Reformed religion was to question the jurisdiction and legality of the State. Monarchs did not take this kindly and made strenuous efforts to keep the Jesuits out. If Jesuits were caught, they were treated as enemies of the State, imprisoned, tortured and executed. In Catholic countries the Jesuits relied on the favour of the king. In Protestant countries, with king and government against them, what were the Jesuits to do? In answering this question, even the highest wisdom might have made mistakes. But the political and revolutionary course which some unwise members of the Society adopted in England and Scotland was spectacularly wrong and gained the Jesuits and the Church nothing except hatred and persecution.

Rome was slow to turn its attention to the British Isles. The lands were far off, wet and uncomfortable, and few continentals understood the ways of the islanders. Ignatius had sent two fathers to Scotland and Ireland on a short journey of discomfort and puzzlement. Father Ribadeneira had visited England in Mary's reign. There had been two or three Jesuits in England during the 1560's, and in 1562 Pius IV had sent the Jesuits Goudanus and Crichton on an embassy to Mary Stuart in Scotland. Their reception was sobering. Crichton wrote in a memoir of the mission:

> Almost from the first day the heretical ministers knew about it and clamoured from their pulpits that the Papal Antichrist had dispatched an ambassador to corrupt the queen with his bribes and to destroy the Gospel. Wherefore, let all true gospellers search for, capture and slaughter that enemy of Christ and His Gospel. It would be, they said, a noble sacrifice to God to wash their hands in his blood.

The murderous threats of John Knox and his intolerant crew in Scotland were serious enough. But any Catholic missionary to the British Isles also had to overcome two historical obstacles. First, the memory of the execution of Anglicans in Mary Tudor's reign, which won her the name of Bloody Mary, lived on. Secondly, the Catholic cause had become mixed with the personal destiny of Mary, Queen of Scots, and this did Catholicism no good. Mary Stuart is a tragic and romantic figure, and she suffered in Elizabeth's cruel and vindictive hands. But Mary was a foolish woman who allowed herself to become entangled with assassins and who had unfortunate connections by birth with the Duke of Guise and the extreme Catholic party in France. In this luckless woman, Protestants thought they saw

combined the cynical immorality of Roman religion and the desperate political intrigue of the French Catholic League. The presence
of Mary Stuart as the local Catholic champion, and the centre of
Cardinal Allen's and Father Parsons' hopes, set Catholicism at an
immediate disadvantage.

The plight of Catholics in the first twelve years of Elizabeth's
reign was not too severe. There were fines for recusants who refused
to defer to the state religion. Elizabeth demanded only lip service
to the legal forms and did not enquire very closely into her subjects'
real opinions. Secular priests and Jesuits, when caught, were imprisoned, but treated well enough. Father Thomas Woodhouse, a
Jesuit and the first priest to be executed by Elizabeth, was taken in
1561 and shut up in the Fleet prison for twelve years. To begin with
he lived a gentlemanly life: 'his keeper allowed him to make secret
excursions to his friends by day, and gave him the freedom of the
prison.' He could say Mass in his cell and was permitted to preach
to his fellow prisoners. Then, in February 1570, Pope Pius V excommunicated the queen and released her Catholic subjects from their
allegiance. Elizabeth's ministers interpreted this as a political threat
to English independence, and they were to some extent right. Taking
the advantage of the pope's action, Ridolfi, the agent of Mary Stuart,
Philip II, the widower of Mary Tudor, and the high Spanish clergy
met in 1571 to discuss various action against Elizabeth, including,
possibly, assassination. Elizabeth tightened the provisions against
Catholics, and in June 1573 Woodhouse was executed for treason.
Now events moved into fore-ordained sadness. Philip of Spain, the
inveterate opportunist ready to snap up in the name of orthodoxy
any heretical country, had his eye on England. England, small,
unsteady and poor, feared the Spanish designs. The English seminaries and colleges, in which the banished English Catholic priests
were trained, were in northern France and Spanish Flanders, built
on the land and founded on the money provided by the Duke of
Guise and the King of Spain. The English government was well
aware of this connection and saw the English priests as the instruments of Spanish policy. They were persecuted accordingly. And the
Catholic Church hastened her priests to death by permitting the
views and the methods of William Allen, later cardinal, and the
Jesuit Robert Parsons to prevail. Allen and Parsons were the best
known and loudest Catholic opponents to Elizabeth's England, and
both openly and actively sided with Spain.

William Allen set the trend for the Catholic policy in England;

the men who followed his prescriptions most carefully were the Jesuits. In the years after the Bull of excommunication the outlook for Catholicism in England seemed more and more gloomy. In 1580, at the insistence of Allen, the Church consented to send the Jesuits, the most experienced of her missioners, in a sustained spiritual assault on England and Scotland. On June 12, Fathers Robert Parsons and Edmund Campion landed at Dover, and Parsons at once struck an incongruous note. Campion pictured him thus:

> He was dressed like a soldier—such a peacock, such a swaggerer, that a man must have a very sharp eye to catch a glimpse of any holiness and modesty shrouded beneath such a garb, such a look, such a strut!

The keen eyes of historians have peered at Parsons and most of them have been able to discern nothing holy or modest in Parsons generally. In July 1580, the two Jesuits met the Catholic clergy at Southwark and took an oath that their purpose in England was 'apostolic' and unconcerned with matters of state. The instructions which the Jesuits brought from Rome prohibited them from speaking against the queen except perhaps to those 'whose fidelity has been long and steadfast', and then only with the greatest caution and restraint. Campion, in his famous 'Ten Reasons' addressed to the 'right honourable Lords of the Privy Council', asserted that he took no part in politics:

> I never had mind, and am strictly forbidden by our Fathers that sent me, to deal in any respects with matters of State or policy of this realm, and those things which appertain not to my vocation, and from which I do gladly restrain and sequester my thoughts.

But the Jesuits were in touch with a group of lay Catholics led by young George Gilbert, and these men, from some of the best known Catholic families, were often rash and impetuous and liable to plot. They also formed an association, blessed by Pope Gregory XIII, which the government found particularly hateful. The minister Cecil wished to keep all secret associations in his own hands. In July 1581, Campion was captured. He was tortured and interrogated. Campion, a good and even a great man, had come to England with the truly apostolic desire to succour the Catholic faith; at the same time he wished to remain a loyal Englishman—'your queen is my queen', he cried on the scaffold. But his simple intention had been rendered impossible by the actions of the great men in Rome and Westminster. All that he did was construed as treason. He was allowed no

defence and like Thomas More before him refused to join his
accusers in the little charade of the court:

> Edmund Campion being demanded whether he would acknowledge the
> publishing of these things before recited, by Sanders, Bristow and Allen,
> to be wicked in the whole, or in any part; and whether he doth at this
> present acknowledge her Majesty to be a true and lawful Queen, or a
> pretended Queen, and deprived, and in possession of her Crown only
> *de facto*: he answered to the first that he meddleth neither to nor fro,
> and will not further answer, but requireth that they may answer. To the
> second he saith, that this question dependeth on the fact of Pius Quintus,
> whereof he is not to judge, and therefore refuseth further to answer.

He was condemned and executed.

Campion was a man of honourable intentions who tried to avoid
the political perils of his task. Parsons did not. He was always a
schemer and used whatever means he could to advance the cause. In
1582, when Parsons was trying to drum up military aid for Lennox
in Scotland, he was asked how he knew Catholic military requirements. He answered that 'he knew all this from what many of them
had declared when he treated them for their conscience'. It is a bitter
irony of history that Campion should have been taken and executed
and that Parsons should escape and through his polemics make the
English air even more deadly for Catholics. Parsons escaped from
England after Campion was arrested and did not return; but for
many years, together with Allen, he was a tireless agitator against the
English government. In 1582, Parsons, Allen, Crichton and Matthieu, the old stalwart of the Catholic League, got together with
Guise and Mendoza to assist Lennox in Scotland. Two years later
Crichton, on his way to Scotland, was captured by the English. He
tried to destroy his instructions, but they were recovered. Father
Knox later published them in his *Records of the English Catholics*:

> Lastelie and especially to depose her Matie [Elizabeth] and set up the
> Scottish Queen, which indeede is the scope and white whereto all this
> practise dothe level.

After the execution of Mary Stuart, Allen and Parsons were ardent
supporters of Philip's claim to the English throne. In a joint memorandum they wrote:

> his Catholic majesty, besides the cause of the Catholic religion and the
> injuries which he has received from England, has in the vengeance due
> for the blood of the queen of Scotland, which she herself commended
> to him, a most just ground and necessary cause for going to war, and,

therefore, if he seizes upon the kingdom in so just and praiseworthy a war, the title of conquest will be legitimate.

Parsons pressed in Rome for Allen to be made a cardinal and so did Philip II, so wedded were Parsons and Allen to Spanish policy. When Sixtus V raised Allen to the cardinal's purple, he wrote to Philip: 'This morning I have held a consistory and made Allen cardinal to satisfy your majesty.'

The intrigue, the Catholic pressure and the English counter-measures gradually drove Philip to attempt the great invasion of 1588. In 1581 a special English parliament had met 'to find a remedy for the poison of the Jesuits'. An Act of March 18 made it treason to be reconciled to Roman Catholicism, or to be absolved by a priest. In 1583, Tassis, the Spanish agent, informed King Philip that Parsons had a new plan for invading England. From 1585 to 1587 Rome and Spain advanced the plans for the Armada. Olivares, the Spanish ambassador in Rome, called Parsons a man of 'great fertility of resources and very good discretion'. On the eve of the Armada, Allen signed a document possibly drawn up by Parsons. This 'Admonition to the Nobility and People of England and Ireland, concerning the present wars, made for the execution of his holiness's sentence, by the Catholic king of Spain' invited the people to rise up against Elizabeth the 'incestuous bastard, begotten and born in sin, of an infamous courtesan'. The English people looked at the Spanish alternative and decided to stay with their bastard queen whom they admired greatly. Even after the Armada failed, Parsons still advocated invasions, and as a true revolutionary he knew that an invasion could not succeed without the support of an underground Catholic resistance in England. How much Parsons' fellow-Jesuits did to foster this resistance is an obscure question, but Parsons' own forthright opinions are clear. He wrote to Juan de Idiaquez, the Spanish Secretary of State and War:

> To think to get the upper hand in England without having a party within the realm is a great illusion, and to think to have this party without forming it and keeping it together is a great illusion.

Fine sentiments in a guerilla, but less appropriate to a priest. In 1592, in reply to some rude words from Elizabeth, he composed a *Responsio ad edictum Elizabethae* declaring that the pope's right to depose kings was an article of faith. And in the *Conference about the next Succession* of 1594 he supported the people's right to alter the succession on religious grounds, and he put forward the Spanish

Infanta, a very distant descendant of John of Gaunt, as the best candidate for the English throne on Elizabeth's death. This work was
highly offensive to the English. Dr. Gifford declared it the most
pestilent ever made, and Parliament made it high treason to possess
a copy. The papal nuncio in Flanders wrote that Parsons 'could not
have done anything more disgusting to the pope'.

Father Oliver Manare said that his fellow-Jesuit, Parsons, was
subject to 'inveterate prejudice' and 'easily deceived'. How far the
other Jesuits in England followed the precepts of Parsons is not
clear. The evidence used against the Society by the English government was supplied by paid spies and informers, and these are not the
most trustworthy witnesses. Yet, in commenting on affairs in the
British Isles, the papal agent in Brussels wrote to Cardinal Aldo-
brandini in 1596:

> The Jesuits consider as one of their established axioms confirmed by the
> authority of Father Parsons, that the Catholic religion can only be
> restored by force of arms. . . . They believe that only the arms of Spain
> may be used to bring about this event. They, no matter whether from
> Rome or elsewhere, come to these parts with this idea, which has been
> firmly impressed upon them by their Superiors.

There were some notorious scandals in which Jesuits were involved,
for example Father Crichton's journey to aid Lennox in 1584. Most
spectacular, however, was the supposed Jesuit connection with the
Gunpowder Plot of 1605, for which Father Henry Garnet, the Jesuit
superior in England, was executed. The Jesuits Greenway and Garnet came to hear of the plot through the confession of Catesby, one
of the conspirators. The Jesuits were bound by their priestly office
to respect the confidences of the confessional, and so Catesby could
not be denounced. Garnet, a quiet and rather weak man, was shocked
and afraid. Moreover, the Church had by now turned against the
conspiracies and violence that Rome in the days of Pius V had advocated, and Garnet had a letter from the general of the Society
charging him to prevent plots. Garnet showed Catesby this letter,
but did very little else. This was enough to convict Garnet, and to
blacken the Jesuits horribly in English eyes.

The Society was no more popular with the English Catholic secular priests than it was with the English government. Between the two
there was jealousy and feuding. A memorandum drawn up by the
seculars in 1601 made the Jesuits the cause of all the Catholic tribulations. 'If they had not sought by false persuasions and ungodly

arguments to have allured the hearts of all Catholics from their allegiance,' said this document, then the State would have borne with the Catholics and spared them the racks and tortures. In 1602, in *The Jesuits' Catechisme*, the seculars continued to belabour their fellow priests:

> To receive Jesuits into a Kingdom, is to receive in a vermin, which at length will knaw out the heart of a State both spiritual and temporal. They work underhand the ruin of the countries where they dwell, and the murder of whatsoever Kings and Princes it pleaseth them.

In the government prison for Catholics at Wisbech there were unseemly quarrels about rights and jurisdiction. The seculars, fatigued and crushed by years of persecution, leaned towards some accommodation with the English government; they resented the Jesuit activity which added burdens and dangers to their lives. They produced, too, the now familiar argument that the Society deliberately stirred up social and political ferment to maintain its position and influence in the Church. In 1598, the Jesuit Father Tichborne feared that a policy of toleration would not suit the Society. It would lead, he said, 'to the disfurnishing of the seminaries, the disanimating of men to come and others to return, the expulsion of the Society'. Father Preston claimed that neither the Holy See, nor the Jesuit superiors in Rome wished Elizabeth to be lenient. According to Preston, an English Jesuit in Rome, Father Fitzherbert, had written to advise the pope 'that it was not good and profitable to the Catholic cause that any liberty or toleration should be granted by the State of England'. His idea was that a church thrives on persecution: the persecuted secular priests in England were less enthusiastic.

The struggle for power between the seculars and the Jesuits in Catholic England burst out into the rich acrimony of the Archpriest controversy. In the last years of the sixteenth century Rome decided to cure the English dissensions by appointing a superior for all the priests in England. George Blackwell, to be known as the Archpriest, was chosen and sent to England with instructions to govern with the advice of Garnet, the Jesuit provincial. The seculars objected and sent two delegates to Rome. Parsons had these two pent up in the English College, put on trial and then banished. The seculars were more than ever resentful; in November 1600, thirty-three of them signed an appeal against Blackwell's tyranny, and against Jesuit dominance and interference in politics. The seculars were weak, demoralized and lacking in heroism. Their appeal had little effect against the Jesuits' iron resolution. The Society kept its influence in English Catholic affairs; in the reign of James II the king very unwisely made Father Petre a member of the Privy Council. Sunderland suggested to Pope Innocent XI that he might make the 'resolute and undertaking' Petre a cardinal. The pope refused and ordered the general of the Society to rebuke Petre for ambition. The common people hated Petre thoroughly and made up many damaging rumours about him. One of the least credible was that he had introduced an alien baby into the queen's bed so as to give James an heir and insure the Catholic succession. The baby was said to have been conveyed in a warming-pan. The favours which James granted Petre seriously harmed the king's cause. James admitted in his *Memoirs* that he 'was so bewitched by my lord Sunderland and Father Petre as to let himself be prevailed upon to doe so indiscreete a thing'.

Once more, the attitude of the general of the Society towards the Jesuit goings-on in England was enigmatic. Father Parsons, an unabashed troublemaker, prospered in the Society. In 1597 he was appointed rector of the English College in Rome and remained there until his death in 1610. Parsons was a man of great abilities, efficient, energetic and eloquent. 'His dexterity in writing and acting,' wrote Cardinal Allen, 'surpasses all belief.' His powers as a writer were acknowledged by Jonathan Swift. He also had the protection of Philip of Spain and of at least one pope: Gregory XIII used him as an ambassador. But Parsons' machinations in Rome and Madrid were so obviously political that Aquaviva must have used some ingenious sophistry to reconcile his conscience. And too many English Jesuits, taking their cue from Parsons and Allen or encouraged by ambitious or foolish Catholic laymen, tried to make English Catholicism an underground resistance movement against the state. The general did indeed condemn some of these antics; but he did very little to prevent them. Elizabeth's state was in many ways tyrannical and the Jesuit fathers endured and suffered torture and execution with the greatest bravery. But religion could not defeat tyranny with the tryant's own weapons of subterfuge, plot and violence. The Society of Jesus demeaned the apostolic calling by playing the State's game, a game that it could never win.

The activities of the Jesuits in the Protestant countries of the Counter-Reformation leave a lasting impression of revolutionary politics. Of all Catholic groups, the Jesuits drew the finest and most variegated haul of abusive Protestant literature; they would hardly have done this if their purpose had been to expound doctrinal points only. For men were now animated to cut each other's throats more by politics than by dogma. Politics and the pursuit of power had become the enduring European pre-occupations. The Jesuits were hated because men saw them as the political jackals to the ravening Spanish lion: Ignatius was that Spanish statist, the great politician. Both John Donne, in *Ignatius, his Conclave*, and Phineas Fletcher, in the *Apollyonists*, caste Ignatius in the council sessions of Hell. Here is Fletcher's account of Ignatius's diabolical plans for the Gunpowder Plot:

> That blessed Isle, so often curst in vaine,
> Triumphing in our losse and idle spight,
> Of force shall shortly stoop to Rome and Spayne:
> I'le take a way ne're knowne to man or spright.
> To kill a King is stale, and I disdaine:
> That fits a Secular, not a Jesuite.
> Kings, Nobles, Clergy, Commons high and low,
> The Flowre of England in one houre I'le mow,
> And head all th' Isle in one unseen, unfenced blow.

The connection in the English popular mind between the Jesuits and Spain failed to die. When James I thought to make a diplomatic marriage between his son and the Spanish Infanta, Thomas Middleton, voicing true bourgeois hatred for the old enemy, pilloried the twin bogies—Spain and the Jesuits—in his ingenious play, *The Game at Chesse*, in which the wicked Iberian black pieces on the chessboard are overcome and checkmated by the virtuous English white pieces. Naturally, Ignatius makes an appearance in the Prologue boasting of the Society's presumptuous ambition to govern the world and to cover 'the earth's face and make dark the land, like the Egyptian grasshoppers'. When the play went on at the Globe in 1624 it ran for a record nine days, and outraged the Spanish ambassador.

Perhaps the Society of Jesus could not have avoided the fall into politics. They were activists devoted to the Roman cause, which they took to be the cause of Christendom. Since the Church no longer had the means to compel, it was forced to persuade; and since princes no longer listened to moral arguments, some Jesuits tried to use other reasons. The Jesuit ideas on the relation between Church and State were important, and some of them were borne out later. England, the country which had reacted so violently against Parsons' argument of 1594, that the people could alter the succession on religious grounds, in 1688 did exactly as Parsons had advocated. In the Glorious Revolution the Catholic James II was set aside and the crown of the Protestant country was given to the Protestants William and Mary. The principle which had established Henry IV as a Catholic king of France also established William as a Protestant king of England. This principle was a matter of statecraft, and had little to do with the religious emotion. The sad and ironic shock to the Jesuits was that a Protestant state could, in spite of all the Jesuit efforts, choose a Protestant king quite as easily as a Catholic state could set up a Catholic king.

The Jesuits have been presented by their imaginative opponents as powerful Machiavellians operating kings and princes like marionettes. But their voices in the councils of Europe, though they often seemed loud at the time, were futile and hopeless. Whatever the Society may have done by its preaching and teaching for the spiritual condition of Europe, it did not for one moment divert the policies of the kings from their narrow, secular, nationalistic courses. The Jesuit fiddlings with political method seem like desperate and tragic attempts to gain importance and power, not for cynical or evil reasons, but to make the ideals of the Society appear still substantial and possible, and to make the presence of the Society appear indispensable to the success of the Roman cause. The Society sought to anchor itself through the favour of kings, and to gain this Jesuits sometimes became mean lackeys to bad men with monstrous policies. But the Jesuits needed their princes more than the princes needed the Society; when kings turned against the Society, as the later Bourbons did, then the Jesuits were doomed, for they had nothing to fall back on and little popular support to sustain them. The Jesuits chose to live with kings and so were nearly destroyed by kings. The efforts of the Bourbons, and the jealousy of rivals who coveted the Jesuit privileges and influence, secured the suppression of the Society in 1773. Also, the Society was so much a handmaiden to royal authority that when kings themselves went out of fashion the Society was hard hit. After the Society was restored in 1814 it found that Europe was much more republican and democratic than it had been forty years before. Republicans and democrats suspected the Society's royalist past and its authoritarian and autocratic constitution. In the nineteenth century, the Society kept its influence in the Church, for the Church was autocratic too; but in the outside world it suffered an eclipse. The Society of Jesus was at its most imperious, if not at its best, in the age of the absolute kings.

Chapter XIV

REALISM AND THE COMMUNITY OF MAN

THE TREATY of Westphalia, at the end of the Thirty Years' War in 1648, brought to a close the era of the wars of religion. Religion, which had once claimed superiority over the State, and then asserted at least a right to judge the State, was now agreed by ministers to be nothing more than a hindrance to sound policy, and therefore should not be allowed to press on reasons of state any longer. The ministers of Europe—both Catholic and Protestant—found it difficult enough to direct the policies of their masters, even when those policies were animated only by such respected considerations as national pride, territorial claims, greed and dynastic ambitions. When policies were muddled by religious sentiment, as they were from the time of Luther until 1648, it became almost impossible to preserve that dexterous balance of power which all wise ministers appreciated. What, for example, might Cardinal Richelieu have achieved if he could have scrapped his conscience, forgotten the claims of Catholicism, and devoted himself entirely, instead of mainly, to the good of France? True, he allied himself with the Protestant Gustavus Adolphus against the Catholic Habsburgs; but the thoroughly bad Habsburg ambitions might have been checked more successfully if Richelieu had not, in the name of Catholicism, drawn back from his Protestant ally. In 1648, the European powers agreed that such trifles would bedevil state affairs no more. Religion was declared to be subject to the internal policy of the State, and nobody else's business. Article 5 of the treaty, marking the complete triumph of the State over religion in Catholic and Protestant countries alike, stated that 'together with the right of territory and sovereignty, the governments would enjoy that of reforming the Church'. Christendom was pronounced officially dead. The political 'realists' had won.

Some distressed voices were raised against this conclusion. The papal nuncio, Chigi, protested in the pope's name and refused to attend the signing of the treaty. The Jesuit Wangnereck, writing under the name of Ernestus de Eusebiis, violently attacked this complicity to subjugate religion. In November 1648, Pope Innocent X drafted the resounding Bull *Zelus domus meae*, declaring the treaty to be 'perpetually null, worthless, invalid, iniquitous, condemned, frivolous and without authority'. But the Swedish and German troops were still in Rome, and the prudent pope did not dare to publish the Bull until they departed in 1650. Even then no one stirred. Indeed, by this time the popes were hardly noticed at all. It is said that when Innocent died five years later his body lay in a gardener's hut for three days before someone remembered to bury him.

For the Society of Jesus the Treaty of Westphalia was a particular disaster. The princes had declared that religion was a private matter for each state to decide free from outside interference, and without the support of the princes the Jesuits' active work for the Counter-Reformation could not continue. When they agreed to the provisions of the Council of Trent nearly a century before, the Catholic kings of Europe had allowed that Christendom was at least still possible; they had granted a licence for the work of the Counter-Reformation. The papacy, the Capuchins, but most of all the Jesuits, had accepted the hint gratefully and become busy. In the next eighty years European life, infinitely complicated by religious contention, grew more chaotic and more dangerous. In 1648, the unhappy princes, who enjoyed neither peace, security nor leisure during the wars of religion, withdrew the licence. They admitted that State policy only felt at home with the comfortable motives of aggrandizement and national interest, and could not handle the supranational and overriding claims of religion. They no longer subscribed to the ideals of Trent, and halted the Counter-Reformation. But the Jesuits, born at the time of the Council, had given their youthful energy to Trent and had grown up as the agents of the Counter-Reformation. Their characteristic way of doing things was determined by the eighty years of the wars of religion. They had become specialists in a particular kind of Catholic activity. Now that their peculiar skills were no longer required in Europe, what were they to do? The order never quite found the answer to this question. In the next 125 years the Society suffered a long, slow decline until the suppression in 1773. They tried to continue their activities in the old way, but the world, even the Catholic world, was not friendly any more. Governments grew impatient at the aggressive and faintly intriguing methods of the Jesuits. Why bring up all that old-fashioned stuff? Europe seemed to say; the relation between Church and State had been worked out satisfactorily in favour of the State long ago. Why annoy with that ridiculous din about the supremacy of the pope? Why act as if a universal Catholic order could still be imposed over all Europe? And really the Jesuits had no answer except that this is what they had always believed, and this was the way in which they had always acted. The members of the Society became demoralized by the lack of sympathy for their cause. Quarrels broke out within, such as that between the probabilists and the general, Gonzalez; yet at the same time the Jesuits clung tenaciously to their influential positions at court where they naturally met the enmity of the ambitious, the unscrupulous and the anti-clerical: for the Jesuits were priests and did try to trim the luxuriant immoralities of the court. Cardinal de Bernis declared that if the Jesuit, Father de Sacy, had granted absolution to Madame de Pompadour the Society might not have been suppressed in France. Governments thought that the Society had become both an anachronism and a nuisance. Once more they demonstrated the power of the State over the Church, and caused the pope to suppress the Society. In the brief, *Dominus ac Redemptor*, on July 21, 1773, Pope Clement XIV pronounced the European judgment on the Jesuits:

We have recognized that the Society of Jesus was no longer in the position to produce those rich fruits and remarkable advantages for the sake of which it was instituted, approved by so many popes, and accorded so many splendid privileges; it appears, moreover, quite impossible to maintain a true and lasting peace within the Church as long as this order exists.

This, too, was the voice of realism. In the secular state, given over to temporal ambitions, there was no place for a religious order at the king's court and in the councils of government. In the future, apostolic work would have to begin with people, not governments.

Religion bowing before the State was the triumph of realism, a recognition of the trend which had begun with the collapse of the feudal system and the rise of the monarchal power in England and France, and ended with nationalism enthroned. All the new men, all the advanced thinking of the humanists and the Renaissance supported the kings' growing powers and their nationalistic aims; for those powers were the vital forces of society and were continually nourished and encouraged by the economic and intellectual liberties introduced by capitalism and humanism. By the time of the Renaissance the princes were the dominating political figures in Europe; no

reformation of State or Church could be done without their permission. Reformers of all kinds were thus the natural allies of princes.
The Renaissance and the Reformation, says Henri Pirenne, wisest
of mediaeval historians, shared in 'this conspiracy of all the great
social forces on behalf of the sovereign power'. And of the Reformation he continues, 'Whether the princes protected it or fought
against it, they none the less profited by it.'

To the bright, reforming minds, with their realistic eyes firmly
on the political power of the princes, Christendom was a pleasant
myth, but dead and unpracticable. To act as if it existed led to the
extravagant conduct of the Byzantines at Constantinople, or of
Duke Philip at the Oath of the Pheasant. Even the champions of
Christendom realized that their old ideal was served by an impracti-
cal and rarefied mentality which could not hope to contend with the
contemporary problems in Europe. Ignatius and the Jesuits rightly
saw that if the Church was to assert its old claims with any hope of
persuading, it must come to grips with the political realism which
surrounded it. And this meant coming to terms with the princes.
Unhappily, Ignatius miscalculated. He had hoped that Catholic
kings would be Catholics first and kings afterwards, and would
subordinate the national order of their countries to the international
order of Christendom. Ignatius was wrong; such a course would
have meant a slight loss of sovereignty, and no prince would tolerate
this. Monarchs, to a man, were kings first and religious men after.
The sad, but inevitable, result of the Jesuit temporising with princes
was that religion became the slave of the State, for governments to
set up and tear down as they wished. By the strangest of ironies
Ignatius, as much as anyone, helped to send the Church reeling
down this road to captivity by the State.

Once the Church became involved with the policy of princes, and
religion became a 'reason of state', it was not long before the Church
felt the rage of nationalism which held the rest of Europe in its grip.
No prince in Europe, whatever well-bred compliments he paid to
religion, put the claims of Christianity above the claims of the State.
The Valois kings of France supported the Gallican liberties against
interference from Rome; the Bourbon successors to the Valois
strengthened the absolute rights of the king, and waged war in the
name of France against Catholic and Protestant alike. The kings of
Spain theoretically acknowledged the supremacy of the pope, but
disregarded and bullied the pope whenever it suited them. The heavy
Spanish rule in Italy, the pope's land, snuffed out what remained

of the Italian Renaissance civilization. Even when the Spanish power began to decline in the seventeenth century, Philip IV brooded in Madrid over his plans for an empire twenty times greater than that of Rome. His cousin in Vienna, the Emperor Ferdinand II, wished to see the Holy Roman Empire established in all its old glory. But he was not moved by Christian feeling. He wanted to strengthen the power of the Habsburgs and weaken the power of France; if he could breath life into the old office of Holy Roman Emperor, that was a good weapon to use against France. The Christianity of the Catholic kings was the thinnest veneer covering the most profound self—interest and national ambition. The real nature of their aims was shown by their attitudes towards the Turks. For more than two hundred years after the fall of Constantinople, in 1453, the Turks still threatened the eastern borders of Christian Europe. But no alliance of the powerful European kingdoms, in spite of papal pleas, ever met to repulse them. Only the degeneracy of the Turkish empire prevented the Sultan from penetrating further into Europe and enslaving more Christian people. The Catholic kings of Europe valued the Turks very much as a check on each other's power, and were very careful never to send too strong a force against them. The French king, Francis I, had shown the way when he sought Turkish help against Charles V, and France had maintained her Turkish alliance against the Habsburgs in the next century. Louis XIV, the Most Christian King, respected the hundred-year-old alliance between the Turks and France. In 1687, the papal nuncio wrote accusingly to Louis:

> If your Majesty, having rid your own country of heresy, were to be favourably disposed towards the barbarian and the infidel, the whole of Christendom would stand amazed. You cannot do this without serious injury to your glory and, which is more important, without grave detriment to your conscience, of which you will one day have to give the most strict account to God.

Conscience and God could wait: in the meantime the Turks were wonderfully effective for limiting the Habsburgs. The Habsburgs, too, made subtle use of the Turkish menace. The defeat and death of young Louis II of Hungary, at Mohacz, fighting against Soliman II in 1526, gave the Habsburgs the crowns of Hungary and Bohemia. After that the minority groups of the Habsburg empire, the Czechs and the Hungarians, were usefully employed keeping the Turks at bay, and so had little time to rebel against the hated house of Austria.

Amidst all this gross self-interest, which religion was powerless to control, the Church became a little infected with the spirit of the age. The pope lost much of his international prestige, and settled down to be the leader of a small Italian monarchy. The last non-Italian pope was Adrian VI, an austere Dutchman who died in 1523; after that the exclusively Italian popes could hardly claim to speak for all of Europe. Several popes ventured a few timid steps into the tangles of policy, but despaired of ever finding a way through. Attempts to intervene between Catholics and Protestants were often disastrous: the excommunication of Elizabeth by Pius V in 1570 was in fact a death warrant for numerous English priests. Attempts to arbitrate between the factious Catholic princes were not successful. Only when the popes refrained from action and incitement, and instead spoke out clearly for morality and justice, did they seem worthy of their great office. Pope Paul V told James I of England that his theory of the divine right of kings was presumptuous nonsense; Gregory XV founded the Congregation of Propaganda, and so took the conduct of the foreign missions out of the venal hands of Spain and Portugal; and Innocent XI was brave enough to remind Louis XIV of his Christian duty. But as few people consulted the popes they were left with too much time to wonder at their declining influence, and to seek what satisfaction they could in Rome. In their uncertainty, some of them returned to the bad old habits of the Renaissance popes. One of the effects of nationalism in Europe was an anxious preoccupation with succession, for national fortunes depended so much on the prince. France suffered terribly trying to decide whether Henry of Navarre should be king or not. Elizabeth's last years were made miserable by the problems which her lack of heirs created; she died with her face to the wall, silent and bitter that James of the house of Stuart should inherit the throne of England. The papacy, too, showed its Italian national consciousness, and took up the old Italian pastime of nepotism. From 1623 to 1667, the successive popes Urban VIII, Innocent X and Alexander VII promoted their family interests with a zeal worthy of that old Renaissance rogue, Pope Sixtus IV. Worst of all was Maffeo Barberini, Urban VIII, who waged war for his family over the Duchy of Castro, and of whom it was said in Rome, 'What the barbarians did not do, the Barberini have done.' Innocent X, of the Pamfili family, under the blandishments of his sister-in-law, made her son a cardinal, and when that young man decided he would rather be married than be a prince of the Church the pope elevated another relation, aged seventeen, to the vacant office. Alexander VII surrounded himself with a homely little clan of Chigis. Though these favoured relatives could not be promised the papal tiara, at least they were enrolled in the College of Cardinals and guaranteed a share in the fruits of the Church. Security and narrow interests came before the universal Church and its good.

The Jesuits of the seventeenth century shared the faults and the uncertainties of the contemporary Church. As the light of Christendom dimmed and then went out, and as the Society's own practical mission was frustrated by the attitude of the European powers, the Jesuits fell back into the insularity and selfishness that surrounded them. Nationalism had always threatened the Society. From the earliest days, the Spanish province had shown a proper Spanish disdain for all the other provinces and wondered why the general of the Society had rooted himself in fickle and mutable Rome, so far from righteous Spanish orthodoxy. The Society grew larger and more unwieldly, and the hopes for the success of the Counter-Reformation, to which the Jesuits were devoted, dwindled. At the same time the Jesuits at the princes' courts breathed in the nationalism of their masters, and were tempted to discover Christ's business in their masters' policies. The Jesuits in Madrid followed Philip, those in Paris followed Louis, and those in Vienna followed Ferdinand. The general in Rome was unsure which of these tarnished Catholic champions was the least evil; he failed to control the contrary tugs of his outriders in the courts.

In the seventeenth century, the Society seemed to have lost the clear direction which Ignatius had given to the first fathers. Europe had conspired to make the active Jesuit method of the Counter-Reformation almost unworkable; religious ideals were gradually losing force. In the face of this catastrophe, the Jesuits asserted even more loudly the uncompromising claims of Catholicism, and this at a time when religious Europe was relaxing slightly, and when the princes, through their very indifference to religion, were preparing for a little religious tolerance in the future. In 1606, when Maximilian of Bavaria decided to force Catholicism on the Protestant city of Donauworth, the Jesuits were installed as soon as the soldiers left. The Jesuit Lamormaini aided and advised Ferdinand II when he signed the infamous Edict of Restitution, in 1629, which deprived Protestants of property that they had held for seventy-five years, and which allowed Reformed groups to be driven from the country. The Jesuit Pazmany, Archbishop of Gran, was the loudest advocate of the policy of violence and terrorism which the Catholics used against the Protestants in Bohemia and Hungary between 1620 and 1632. While the work of the Counter-Reformation was still possible, there may have been some justification for the Jesuits' stern refusal to compromise; the Protestants were equally refractory, and the earlier, compromising efforts of Catherine de Medici, the queen-regent in France, had been completely useless. But after 1648, when it was clear that the Counter-Reformation could not succeed, the Jesuits still pressed for the grimmest measures against the Protestants. Most Jesuits in France—though there were exceptions like Father Raimbourg—were on the side of that movement of prejudice, greed and intolerance which led to the revocation of the Edict of Nantes in 1685. The concessions to the Huguenots which the enlightened Henry IV had made at Nantes in 1598 had never worked very well. The Huguenots felt uneasy in their privileges; the Catholics thought that the Huguenots formed a state within a state, which good Catholics should not tolerate. Eventually such powerful voices as Bossuet's, and such intimate voices as Madame de Maintenon's, persuaded Louis XIV to harry the Huguenots with all the subtle resources of the State. They were bound to the letter of the law. Anything that the Edict had not mentioned was forbidden them. The Edict had said nothing about Huguenot marriage parties, so they were forbidden; the Edict was silent about Huguenot judges, lawyers, doctors, etc., so all professions were closed. Mixed marriages were forbidden, the children of these unions were declared illegitimate, taken away by the State and brought up as Catholics. These measures were applauded in books like the *Édit de Nantes éxécuté selon les intentions de Henri le Grand*, by the Jesuit Meynier. Then the State moved from restrictions to intimidation. Special troops, called *Dragonnades*, were billeted with Huguenots with instructions to apply their military talents to the Catholic cause. They raped, tortured, stole and converted at the gun-point. At last the Jesuit confessor of the king, Le Tellier, himself prepared the draft of the revocation, and Louis signed. The Huguenots were driven from the land while France rejoiced. Racine and La Fontaine approved; Madame de Sévigné called it 'the greatest and finest thing that has ever happened'. Bossuet paid the event mellifluous compliments from the pulpit. Saint-Simon was not so sure, and Queen Christina of Sweden rudely pronounced what has since become the judgment of history. France, she said, was 'a sick man who cuts off his arms and his legs'.

The French persecuted the Huguenots for a number of reasons, most of them odious, but very few of them to do with religion: Madame de Maintenon wrote to her brother, 'Protestant estates are going cheap; now is the time to buy them.' But one must presume that the Jesuit opposition to the Huguenots was entirely based on religious principle, and this at a time when the papacy, in the person of Innocent XI, was advocating reasonableness and understanding. The Jesuit attitude showed the uncertainty of the Society, and its wish to retain its importance at all costs now that its mission in Europe was partly frustrated. Voltaire once noted that the Society wished 'always to be important'. Ignatius had bequeathed his Society a bold image and a strong sense of identity, and in the after years the Jesuits were remarkably efficient at winning special privileges and considerations for themselves from both the Church and the princes. The papacy granted the Jesuits several relaxations from the rules that bound other orders, and even from the rules that bound clergymen generally. Also, and equally strangely, the papacy permitted the internal affairs of the Society to be placed beyond outside investigation, and even beyond papal inspection. Urban VIII ruled that the Bull *Cruciata*, whereby a member of a religious order could make his confession to a priest outside the order, did not apply to the Jesuits. Further, a member of the Society had no right of appeal to any outside ecclesiastical authority. A member could be chased, apprehended and imprisoned at the Society's discretion, and judges, civil and ecclesiastical, were forbidden to interfere under pain of excommunication. Jesuit rights were given an extraordinary precedence. The Compendium of Privileges for the Society said that 'as long as there was doubt in the understanding of the privileges of the Society, doctors of law and judges were always bound to interpret them in favour of the Society'. And again, 'No letters or Apostolic privileges granted to individuals, colleges, chapters, universities or convents were to prejudice those granted to the Society'. No wonder Bishop Palafox, during his controversial struggle with the Jesuits in South America, complained that the Society was raised 'above all dignities, laws, councils and apostolic constitutions'.

In the early days of the Jesuits, when the Church had singled out the Society to do an extraordinary task, it was perhaps right that it should have extraordinary privileges. But when that task could no longer be done, the Jesuits held on to their privileges with a conviction which showed more a sense of self-preservation than a sense of humble submission before the will of the universal Church. Nor was the Society slowed down by the special vow of obedience which every Jesuit took to the pope. The vow was subject to an interesting interpretation. Popes who were for the Society were naturally supported joyously and wholeheartedly. But those who were critical of the Jesuit constitution, for example Paul IV and V, and Innocent X, received a stubborn and mulish response. The best tactic was to wait until the unsympathetic pope died, and then persuade the next one to restore the old privileges; in other words, the constitution of the Society must be granted the benefit of the doubt even against the wishes of the pope. The integrity of the order must be supported even against the pope.

So long as the aims of the Society of Jesus were the same as the aims of the Church, the Jesuits, with their integrity and their discipline, were in a matchless position to serve the cause of the Catholic faith. But when those aims diverged, as they did, it was seen that the Society was merely superbly organized to perpetuate its own myth and to secure its own position. No doubt, when taxed, the Jesuits argued that they supported the true aims of Catholicism, and that the Church, not the Jesuits, had fallen from the high ideal. The besetting sin of such monolithic and self-contained organizations as the Society is pride. We see it today in America, where a notable member of General Motors (an institution whose corporate thinking shows remarkable affinities with the Jesuits) can argue that what is good for General Motors is good for America. The pride of the Society is best indicated by the *Imago primi saeculi*, an official compilation by the Belgian province to mark the first centenary of the Society in 1640. This 'Picture of the First Century' ran to a thousand pages, luxuriously printed and lovingly illustrated, and has made Jesuits of later ages blush with shame and annoyance. For it appears from the *Imago* that the Society is something really gloriously special, more divine than human: the work is divided into six books of fulsome praise. Concerning the birth of the order, the *Imago* says:

> It is evident that the Society of Jesus is distinguished as to time only from the community of the Apostles. It is not a new order, but only a renewal of that first religious community whose one and only founder was Jesus.

In the third book, on the work of the Society, the ingenuous *Imago* presents the Jesuits as the most unlikely paragons:

> Equipped with wisdom, virtue, intelligence, sagacity and industry, they distinguish truth from falsehood; they examine, perceive and understand everything, nor do they occupy the lowest place in the arena of

art and science. All that is flourishing in the humanities, all the intricacies of philosophy, all the hidden things in Nature, all the difficulties
in mathematics, all the mysteries of the Godhead shining in darkness
would be proclaimed by their works, which fill great libraries, though I
were to pass over them in silence.

This modest appraisal continues for another seventy-four folio
pages. The fourth book proves quite conclusively that the tribulations of the Society are unmerited wrongs inflicted by wicked and
venomous men. The fifth book is a catalogue of Jesuit honours; the
fifth chapter even shyly reveals the miracles of the Jesuits. Pane-
gyrics follow, including the following from a bishop:

O sacred Society, formerly not sufficiently known or appreciated by me,
you excel the pastoral staff, mitres, cardinal's purple, sceptres, empires
and crowns!

It takes 147 pages to extol the honours of the Society. A century
later, in 1759, it was reported in Austria that the Society was quietly
buying up, at exorbitant prices, the remaining copies of this embarrassing and damning book. But according to good testimony, the
Imago was a sadly accurate reflection of Jesuit pride. Cordara, a
loyal and respected Jesuit and generally recognized in the Church
as a sound historian, mourned the suppression of his Society in
1773, but in his *Memoirs* he thought he saw the justice of God in
that act:

Our churches were splendid and their adornment expensive. The festi-
vals of the saints were celebrated with pomp and splendour. But was it
solely for the sake of religion, or rather to show off our power? . . . I
have often wondered why it was with us that any transgression against
chastity was so severely punished, whereas our Superiors were so mild
and indulgent towards other transgressions of a more grievous nature,
such as backbitings, slanders and revilings. And I believe that it was not
because the former were worse and more displeasing to God, but
because, if they had become known, they might have obscured the power
and glory of the Society. The sin of pride is secret.

And concerning the haughty and exclusive spirit of the Society,
Cordara continues:

With this same spirit the youths are inspired during their studies, as
no authors are praised except Jesuits, no books are prescribed but such
as are written by Jesuits, no examples of virtue quoted but such as are
represented by Jesuits, so that these poor youths are easily convinced
that the Society of Jesus excels all other Orders in learning and holiness.

And some weakminded persons even believe that everything praiseworthy done in the world was done under the auspices of our Society.
This opinion, adopted in youth, the majority do not abandon in later
life, and I know some old men who continue to live in this delusion.
And I confess that I myself was thus deluded for a long time.

Let those sorrowful words of the sensible and moderate historian
be the memorial to a hundred years of Jesuit history. They show a
corporate spirit we recognize all too clearly today. Professor Galbraith, in a recent book on *The New Industrial State*, has some pun-
gent passages on what he calls 'the mature corporation'; and in those
corporations Professor Galbraith finds a rigorously disciplined body
of men pursuing a corporate aim which transcends any individual
ambition. The members are endlessly bombarded with a subtle propaganda which encourages them to think the company thoughts, to
act in the company way. As far as possible, the corporation tries to
insure that the aims of the government coincide with its own aims,
and when they do not a careful, discreet, political and industrial
pressure is brought to bear on the errant government. The corporation is efficient and ruthless in a quiet and undemonstrative way, for
its aims can be best realized thus. It continues to grow, and makes
its loyal and long-serving members happy with pensions and decent
silverware to mark twenty-five years close association. Do we find
the institution of the Jesuits behind all those baleful conglomerates
of initials that punctuate our modern life—G.M., I.T. & T., I.B.M.,
I.C.I., A.E.I., B.P. and many others? Were the Jesuits the first to
hit upon the philosophy of the 'mature corporation', managing the
spiritual 'market' to their best advantage, and giving Europe a
remarkable foretaste of modern methods? That such an institution
should have anything to do with the Christian spirit is puzzling;
but history is full of puzzles. The Jesuits, in their fresh years,
rendered the Church, and so the life of Europe, a unique service,
and they were only able to do this because of their philosophy and
their special constitution.

The Jesuits, more than any others, helped to introduce the sense
of realism into the Church. Ignatius himself had prepared them to
do this. His whole life was an essay in practicality, and his constant
injunctions taught his followers to make their way towards the ideal
they desired through the world they found round them. The base
world should indeed be transmuted by religion into the pure gold
of Christendom, but religion had to work with the world as it
existed. The opening of Ignatius's *Exercises* said quite clearly that

'the other things on the face of the earth were created for man's sake, and to help him fulfilling the end for which he was created. Hence it follows that man should make use of creatures so far as they do help him towards his end, and should withdraw from them so far as they are a hindrance to him in regard to that end'. When Ignatius governed the Jesuits he liked to say that 'a man who was no use in the world was of no use to the Society'. The sense of realism is not by itself a perfectly admirable quality. Applied without the softening and ennobling influence of a touch of idealism it leads only to the pursuit of power in a world governed by self-love alone. Europe in the Counter-Reformation finally banished the voice of religion from international councils, and after 1648 the 'realistic' policies of the European powers quickly led to the hypocritical, ruthless and savage world of polity that the twentieth century knows so well. But at the time of the Renaissance and the Reformation the realism of the humanists and the reformers was the strongest and freshest spring of vitality in the life of Europe, and if the Church had not drunk that effervescent water it might have been overborne by the new forces and have collapsed completely. Many good churchmen and many devout laymen realized this well enough in the late Middle Ages. The popes, too, were not entirely blind; even the spectacularly immoral careers of Alexander VI and Julius II were attempts to apply a realism of a kind to Church affairs. But it was hard to discover how to inject the body of the Church itself with the sense of realism, and so bring it out from beneath the dead hand of impossible ideals and patterns of thought which the secular world no longer followed.

The Jesuits took this task upon themselves. Other orders such as the Theatines, the Barnabites and the Capuchins played their part; but the Jesuits had the most rigorous training, the most cohesive discipline and the most settled and incisive philosophy. Ignatius had anticipated the needs of the Church. When the Council of Trent reached its successful conclusion some twenty years after the founding of the Jesuits, the Church was ready to put her new troops to work. The Jesuits advanced into the world armed with sound learning, probity, energy and conviction, and pulling behind them to plant wherever they went a modern and revolutionary educational system. Just how startling their results were can be seen from the hatred with which they were received by the anti-clerical and the Protestants. Works against the Society, for example the *Monita secreta* and the *Stupenda Jesuitica*, are monuments of vindictive spleen. But even more astonishing than their effect on the outside world, the Jesuits, partly by example and partly by practice, helped to transform the interior life of the Church. The temporal and the spiritual were moving apart, and religion was less and less able to influence the secular world; not even the Jesuits could prevent the separation from widening; their attempt to re-establish Christendom failed completely. But the Church reconstituted its own interior life, and discovered sufficient stores of vitality to be able to face the antagonism of the secular world. The Church was no doubt defeated in the world, but her own spiritual ideals were undiminished, and the sense that she served the highest ends of man grew as the secular world became more ugly. Yet in the bad and sad time before the Reformation the Church seemed likely to disintegrate, not because of the opposition without, but because of the deadness within. Fixing her eye on a misty ideal born of a muddled past, the Church had remained immovable and decaying while the world crept by and away, threatening to abandon the Church as an encumbrance and an embarrassment.

Realism was not enough. The mediaeval polity, with its erroneous assumptions about the nature of Church and State, had to be changed to suit the altered world; but if the Church had abandoned its old idealism completely, that would have been an assent that secular selfishness and pursuit of power was the correct way of the world. The Catholic Church was defeated by worldly power, but it never surrendered to the world. Protestantism tended to do just that. In their realistic way, Protestants placed their faith under the patronage of the prince and became members of State churches that were individualistic and local. Catholicism bowed inevitably to the political power of the State, but kept its doctrine and its morality free from interference by princes, governments or any lay assembly. Ignatius Loyola was one of those rare people who blended extreme idealism easily and naturally with extreme practicality. He taught his Society the realistic approach, but he also left it an uncompromising ideal. Doubtless the practical difficulties of reconciling these contrary pulls caused many of the problems which the Society suffered in the seventeenth century. The Jesuit methods perhaps became too realistic; they were persecuted more for their practice than for their ideals. They tried to play the princes' game of power politics, much to the annoyance of princes and governments. Among these troubles, however, the wistful universalism that Ignatius and the Catholic Church preached still made up a characteristic part of the Jesuit mentality. But it was an universalism tempered by close observation and experience. Believing in Christendom, the Jesuits still believed in the community of man; they echoed Cicero's words that 'we are born to justice, and right is based, not upon man's opinion, but upon nature. This is immediately plain once you have a clear conception of Man's fellowship and union with his fellow-men'. And they took their principles with them to the foreign missions, treating foreign peoples generally with dignity, restraint and respect. They were the first, and perhaps the only, large group of Europeans, scattered throughout the world, who ever did this. At the same time, their realism saved them from the fallacy of universalists which treats all men as the same. The design the Jesuits worked out for Paraguay was very different to that devised for China, or India; yet all were appropriate. Whether these plans were capable of making foreign peoples into good Catholics is a question for the theologians to answer. Christendom was possibly as impracticable in the East as in the West. But acting in the spirit of Christendom, the Jesuits became the finest ambassadors that Western culture has ever sent to alien people. The Jesuit mission was an image and an example from which the West refused to profit.

Christendom did not work. Although the Jesuits saw this, they refused to abandon the hope of unity and universality. While Europe was gathering itself into little groups behind narrow, sectarian views, and the papacy was turning itself into an Italian family business, the Society, though afflicted with recurrent bouts of nationalism, held on to its international composition and outlook. In its first hundred years, the Society took its generals from Spain, Italy, Flanders and Germany. Several distinguished fathers, notably Laynez, were of Jewish descent. Once a man had entered the order, he might go for many years, sometimes a lifetime, without seeing his native land again. And this was at a time when men felt their nationality was the best part of them.

Even when Christendom had to be decently buried and forgotten, the Jesuit thinkers gave their devotion to other forms of universality. Francisco Suárez envisaged a commonwealth of men held together by international law which recognized the rights and the sovereignty of all peoples. Though Suárez was a clergyman, his commonwealth was frankly secular, and therefore realistic and relevant to the world outside the Church; it is towards Suárez's vision of unity that the secular world of the United Nations still gropes rather hopelessly today.

The need for Jesuit realism passed. During the Counter-Reformation the Jesuits taught the Church a sense of the present. The occasion was important and urgent, and the Jesuits met it superbly. They led the reform of the Catholic Church; they helped, by theory and practice, to adjust the ballast of Europe so that the ships of State and Religion, both very weatherbeaten, could get back on even keels. To do this, they were forced, as sensible men, to stress the very obvious separation between Church and State. This encouraged the formation of modern political theory, but made their own kind of active ministry at first uncomfortable and then impossible. Unhappily, the Society refused to recognize this and retire gracefully from their labours which had become more political than apostolic. The Bull *Regimini militantis Ecclesiae* had established the Jesuits, and as true soldiers of the Church Militant they fought on with military stubbornness. In time the Society began to show some of the less fortunate attributes of the military mind—narrow, rigid and doctrinaire. The Jesuits became proud, the great temptation of soldiers, and they tended to equate the interests of the universal Church with their own interests. The Church had enough of them and for various reasons, both honourable and dishonourable, temporarily suppressed the Society from 1773 to 1814.

The Jesuits failed in their European task. Realism has its limits and leads to unexpected results. The idealism of the Society, more hidden but ever-present, has been ultimately more fruitful. The very presence of the Society in the Catholic family was a constant reminder to the Church of its universal ideal. The international composition of the Society and its unified world view quietly reprimanded the nationalism of the papacy, the insularity of states and the subservience of Protestantism to secular control. Reinhold Niebuhr, the Protestant philosopher, has recently commented on religious attitudes to the racial issue in America, the great pain of our time. He approves the Catholic and Jewish faiths. But the witness of Protestantism to desegregation, he says, 'too often was sadly lacking'. He notes that southern Protestantism was 'congregational in character and polity', and was 'dominated by the mores and viewpoint of its congregation'. 'Thus neither the congregation, usually under the aegis of a White Citizens' Council, nor the traditional emphasis on individual conversion could root out social evil of long standing.' To see steadily beyond the limitations of one's land and culture takes long practice. Fine ideals are not enough; all faiths have fine ideals. Ideals must be constantly expressed and constantly lived with before they become effective. If the Catholic Church is able now, from time to time, to speak in the universal voice of conscience and justice, it is to some extent because the Society of Jesus has always fostered the supranational mission of the Church, and has refused to see in the policies of secular states much beyond selfishness, deceit and greed. The Catholic Church which closed down the Jesuit missions through jealousy and incomprehension has now rather tardily learnt to treat all races and all cultures justly and with respect: the Church had made amends to St. Ignatius.

A SELECT BIBLIOGRAPHY

General Works:

Cambridge Mediaeval History
Cambridge Modern History
DANIEL-ROPS, HENRI. *History of the Church of Christ:* v. 4 'The
Protestant Reformation'; v. 5 'The Catholic Reformation'; v. 6
'The Church in the Seventeenth Century'
Monumenta Historica Societatis Jesu
PASTOR, LUDWIG VON. *History of the Popes from the Close of the
Middle Ages*

Part I:

COULTON, G. G. *Mediaeval Panorama*
GIBBON, EDWARD. *Decline and Fall of the Roman Empire*
HEARNSHAW, F. J. C. (Editor). *The Social and Political Ideas of some
Great Mediaeval Thinkers*
HUIZINGA, J. *The Waning of the Middle Ages*
LA BROCQUIÈRE, BERTRANDON DE. *Travels to Palestine*
LA MARCHE, OLIVIER DE. *Mémoires*
LEWIS, C. S. *The Discarded Image*
PIRENNE, H. *Economic and Social History of Mediaeval Europe*
— *History of Europe*
RANKE, L. *History of the Popes of Rome*
RUNCIMAN, S. *The Fall of Constantinople, 1453*

Part II:

BRODERICK, J. *The Origin of the Jesuits*
GODET, MARCEL. *La Congrégation de Montaigu, 1490–1580*
HARVEY, ROBERT. *Ignatius Loyola*
HOLLIS, CHRISTOPHER. *Saint Ignatius*
HUIZINGA, J. *Erasmus of Rotterdam*
HYMA, ALBERT. *The Christian Renaissance*
IGNATIUS LOYOLA. *Letters* (trans. W. J. Young)

IGNATIUS LOYOLA. *Spiritual Exercises* (ed. J. Rickaby)
— *The Testament of Ignatius Loyola* (trans. E. M. Rix)
MERRIMAN, R. B. *Rise of the Spanish Empire*
RIBADENEIRA, PEDRO. *Vida de Ignacio de Loyola*
SEDGWICK, H. D. *Ignatius Loyola*
VAN DYKE, P. *Ignatius Loyola*

Part III:

BELLESSORT, A. *St. François Xavier*
BRODRICK, J. *St. Francis Xavier*
— *The Economic Morals of the Jesuits*
— *The Progress of the Jesuits*
CAMPBELL, T. *The Jesuits*
COPLESTON, F. *History of Philosophy*: v. 3 'Ockham to Suarez'
CRÉTINEAU-JOLY, M. J. *Histoire de la Compagnie de Jésus*
CRONIN, V. *Wise Men from the West*
DUNNE, G. H. *Generation of Giants*
FARRELL, A. P. *The Jesuit Code of Liberal Education*
FIGGIS, J. N. *Studies of Political Thought, 1414–1625*
FOUQUERAY, HENRI. *Histoire de la Compagnie de Jésus en France, 1528–1762*
FÜLÖP-MILLER, R. *The Power and Secret of the Jesuits*
GRAHAM, R. B. C. *A Vanished Arcadia*
HUGHES, T. *Loyola and the Jesuit Code of Education*
JEDIN, HUBERT. *A History of the Council of Trent*
LECLER, J. *Toleration and the Reformation*
NEILL, STEPHEN. *Christian Missions*
SAMUELSSON, KURT. *Religion and Economic Action*
STARK, W. *The Sociology of Religion*
TACCHI-VENTURI, P. *Storia della Compagnia di Gesù in Italia*

ACKNOWLEDGMENTS

I would like to thank Mr R. Browne, librarian at the Jesuit house in Farm Street, for help in finding books and illustrations. I also thank my friend Maurice Cochrane for photographing a number of the illustrations. The quotation from Joyce's *Portrait of the Artist as a Young Man* is by permission of the Executors of the James Joyce Estate.

M.F.

INDEX

297